# RESEARCH IN PERSONNEL AND HUMAN RESOURCES MANAGEMENT

# RESEARCH IN PERSONNEL AND HUMAN RESOURCES MANAGEMENT

Series Editors: Hui Liao, Joseph J. Martocchio and Aparna Joshi

Recent Volumes:

RESEARCH IN PERSONNEL AND HUMAN RESOURCES
MANAGEMENT   VOLUME 30

# RESEARCH IN PERSONNEL AND HUMAN RESOURCES MANAGEMENT

EDITED BY

## APARNA JOSHI
*University of Illinois, USA*

## HUI LIAO
*University of Maryland, USA*

## JOSEPH J. MARTOCCHIO
*University of Ilinois, USA*

United Kingdom – North America – Japan
India – Malaysia – China

Emerald Group Publishing Limited
Howard House, Wagon Lane, Bingley BD16 1WA, UK

First edition 2011

Copyright © 2011 Emerald Group Publishing Limited

**Reprints and permission service**
Contact: booksandseries@emeraldinsight.com

**British Library Cataloguing in Publication Data**
A catalogue record for this book is available from the British Library

ISBN: 978-0-85724-553-3
ISSN: 0742-7301 (Series)

Emerald Group Publishing
Limited, Howard House,
Environmental Management
System has been certified by
ISOQAR to ISO 14001:2004
standards

Awarded in recognition of
Emerald's production
department's adherence to
quality systems and processes
when preparing scholarly
journals for print

INVESTOR IN PEOPLE

# CONTENTS

# LIST OF CONTRIBUTORS

| | |
|---|---|
| *Matt Bloom* | Mendoza College of Business, University of Notre Dame, Notre Dame, IN, USA |
| *Joyce E. Bono* | Carlson School of Management, University of Minnesota, Minneapolis, MN, USA |
| *Prithviraj Chattopadhyay* | Department of Management, Hong Kong University of Science and Technology, Clear Water Bay, Hong Kong, China |
| *Amy E. Colbert* | Tippie College of Business, University of Iowa, Iowa City, IA, USA |
| *Cristina Cruz* | IE Business School, C/Maria de Molina, Madrid, Spain |
| *Michelle K. Duffy* | Carlson School of Management, University of Minnesota, Minneapolis, MN, USA |
| *Niclas L. Erhardt* | Maine Business School, University of Maine, Orono, ME, USA |
| *Shainaz Firfiray* | IE Business School, C/María de Molina, Madrid, Spain |
| *Timothy M. Gardner* | Owen Graduate School of Management, Vanderbilt University, Nashville, TN, USA |
| *Elizabeth George* | Department of Management, Hong Kong University of Science and Technology, Clear Water Bay, Hong Kong, China |

*Theresa M. Glomb*              Carlson School of Management,
                                University of Minnesota, Minneapolis,
                                MN, USA

*Luis R. Gomez-Meija*           Department of Management, Mays
                                Business School, Texas A&M
                                University, College Station, TX, USA

*Luis L. Martins*               McCombs School of Business,
                                University of Texas at Austin, Austin,
                                TX, USA

*Carlos Martin-Rios*            Department of Management, Carlos III
                                University of Madrid, Getafe, Madrid,
                                Spain

*Carmen Kaman Ng*               Department of Management,
                                Hong Kong University of Science
                                and Technology, Clear Water Bay,
                                Hong Kong, China

*Marieke C. Schilpzand*         College of Management, Georgia
                                Institute of Technology, Atlanta,
                                GA, USA

*Tao Yang*                      Carlson School of Management,
                                University of Minnesota, Minneapolis,
                                MN, USA

# GLOBAL VIRTUAL TEAMS: KEY DEVELOPMENTS, RESEARCH GAPS, AND FUTURE DIRECTIONS

Luis L. Martins and Marieke C. Schilpzand

## ABSTRACT

*Global virtual teams (GVTs) – composed of members in two or more countries who work together primarily using information and communication technologies – are increasingly prevalent in organizations today. There has been a burgeoning of research on this relatively new organizational unit, spanning various academic disciplines. In this chapter, we review and discuss the major developments in this area of research. Based on our review, we identify areas in need of future research, suggest research directions that have the potential to enhance theory development, and provide practical guidelines on managing and working in GVTs.*

Global virtual teams (GVTs) – composed of individuals in two or more countries who communicate primarily using information and communication technologies – are increasing in prevalence and importance in organizations. Estimates of the use of GVTs indicate that over the last two decades there has been a tremendous increase in the number of large

Research in Personnel and Human Resources Management, Volume 30, 1–72
ISSN: 0742-7301/doi:10.1108/S0742-7301(2011)0000030003

organizations using GVTs in some part of their operations (Carmel & Agarwal, 2001). For example, Eastman Kodak used a GVT consisting of members from 14 countries to launch its photo CD system (Snow, Snell, Davison, & Hambrick, 1996), Air Products & Chemicals, Inc. used GVTs to transfer the company's global technology (Massey, Montoya-Weiss, Hung, & Ramesh, 2001b), and Shell Services International used GVTs for strategic decision making (Qureshi & Zigurs, 2001). Indeed, the GVT is shaping up to be a very important organizational unit that is typically charged with critical organizational tasks such as innovation, new product development, and implementation of global initiatives (Kerber & Buono, 2004; Maznevski & Chudoba, 2000).

There are several reasons for the increased prominence of GVTs. They give companies access to a worldwide talent pool (Alexander, 2000), thereby enabling the selection of the most qualified individuals for a team. They can be used to shorten product-to-market cycles through 24-h productivity (Solomon, 1998). They are useful in facilitating "cross-pollination between cultures as well as business units and thereby adding depth of knowledge and experience" (Solomon, 1998, p. 13). Additionally, the greater diversity typical in GVTs enables them to produce "better insight and idea generation than teams in traditional settings where team members tend to share similar cultural heritage and work history" (DeSanctis, Wright, & Jiang, 2001, p. 81). Also, GVTs enable the leveraging of dispersed organizational resources without transferring them to a central location, thereby realizing significant cost savings (McDonough, Kahn, & Barczak, 2001).

The academic literature on GVTs has grown in tandem with their prominence in organizations, and there is now a sizeable body of work on the topic. This growing literature spans a variety of disciplines such as management, international business, information systems, communication, cross-cultural psychology, sociology, and operations management. Perhaps due to its relative infancy and its distribution across multiple disciplines, the literature on GVTs appears to lack coherence. It also demonstrates numerous research gaps and areas in which additional research is needed to resolve inconsistencies in findings, both of which present exciting opportunities for future research.

In this chapter, we first define GVTs and then provide a review of the literature on GVTs, using the Input → Mediator → Output → Input (IMOI) model of teams (Ilgen, Hollenbeck, Johnson, & Jundt, 2005) as the organizing framework. We then assess how the literature has addressed the three component concepts in GVTs: "global," "virtual," and "teams." Throughout the chapter, we point out areas of consistency and inconsistency in findings, and highlight directions for future research. Our intent is to provide a comprehensive overview of research on GVTs and to highlight the major themes within the literature. We focused on studies that examined GVTs specifically rather than on those that examined virtual teams in general; comprehensive reviews of research on virtual teams in general are provided by Hertel, Geister, and Konradt (2005), Kirkman, Gibson, and Kim (in press), Martins, Gilson, and Maynard (2004), Powell, Piccoli, and Ives (2004), and Stanko and Gibson (2009). This chapter is aimed at providing researchers with a snapshot of where we stand in research on GVTs and at providing elements of a roadmap for future research in the area. It also seeks to provide organizations and their members with an overview of what is known about the functioning of GVTs, in an attempt to help them better constitute, manage, and work in GVTs.

## DEFINING GLOBAL VIRTUAL TEAMS

Perhaps not surprising, given the rapid proliferation of research on GVTs, they have been labeled and conceptualized in various ways. Among the labels used for a GVT are: dispersed multinational team (James & Ward, 2001), geographically distributed team (Hinds & Mortensen, 2005), multi-national group (Hambrick, Davidson, Snell, & Snow, 1998), transnational team (Haas, 2006; Shapiro, Furst, Spreitzer, & Von Glinow, 2002), virtual global team (Solomon, 1998), virtual intercultural team (Uber Grosse, 2002), global team (McDonough et al., 2001), and multicultural global virtual team (Mockaitis, Rose, & Zettinig, 2009). Of course, researchers have also used the label global virtual team (e.g., Jarvenpaa & Leidner, 1999; Maznevski & Chudoba, 2000), which appears to be the most prevalent in the literature, and is the one we will use here.

Most authors agree that a GVT crosses some boundary between nations, and that GVT members use technology to communicate. Beyond this basic agreement, there is a great deal of disagreement, primarily around which boundaries should be included in the definition and how much technology mediation is necessary to consider a team a GVT. The disagreement essentially arises from an attempt to use categorical distinctions to capture what is inherently a continuous phenomenon. Therefore, we propose that GVTs vary in their extent of globalness, virtualness, and teamness, thus making a team more or less of a GVT depending on its location in a three-dimensional space defined by the three continua. Each dimension in this definition is affected by a variety of factors.

Teams vary in their extent of teamness based on the degree to which team members have to work interdependently on the team task and have mutual accountability for goal completion, and the extent to which the team is identifiable to outsiders as a unit (Katzenbach & Smith, 1993). Also, within the virtual teams literature, the extent of virtualness has been proposed to be a continuous construct, in contrast to the prior focus in the literature on a dichotomous distinction between face-to-face (FtF) and virtual teams (e.g., Bell & Kozlowski, 2002; Griffith & Neale, 2001; Griffith, Sawyer, & Neale, 2003; Martins et al., 2004). This literature suggests that the extent of a team's virtualness, or "virtuality" as it has also been labeled (e.g., Chudoba, Wynn, Lu, & Watson-Manheim, 2005; Kirkman & Mathieu, 2005), depends on "the extent to which team members use virtual tools to coordinate and execute team processes, the amount of informational value provided by such tools, and the synchronicity of team member virtual interaction" (Kirkman & Mathieu, 2005, p. 702). We propose that, similar to the other two components of GVTs, the "global" component must also be conceptualized as a continuous construct. We also propose that a virtual team's extent of globalness is defined by the degree to which it spans multiple national boundaries, differing cultural value systems, multiple languages, and different time zones.

Therefore, we define a GVT as a group of individuals located in two or more countries, working on an interdependent task, using information and communication technology as a primary means of interaction. This is a minimal definition of GVTs. As discussed in the preceding text, GVTs can be further distinguished based on the number and variety of cultural, linguistic, and time zone boundaries that are represented in the team, the extent to which they use information and communication technologies to interact, and the extent to which they function as a true team. Consistent with our thinking here, Chudoba et al. (2005) combined the three dimensions of GVTs into a single definition of team virtuality, which they measured using a virtuality index that aggregates responses to 18 questionnaire items assessing six discontinuities: (1) geography, (2) time zone, (3) culture, (4) work practices, (5) organization, and (6) technology.

# A REVIEW OF RESEARCH ON GLOBAL VIRTUAL TEAMS

The literature on GVTs spans a wide range of subject areas, is voluminous, and is growing rapidly. Our intent here is to provide a comprehensive overview and assessment of the major developments and findings in the literature. We organize our discussion using the IMOI framework proposed by Ilgen and colleagues (2005) as a model of team functioning. *Inputs* are the initial conditions and resources of a team such as team design, leadership, reward structure, technology, and the national culture of team members. *Mediators* are typically divided into team processes and emergent states. Team process factors are those variables that explain "how" teams do their work, such as communication, coordination, and conflict resolution. Team emergent states are "constructs that characterize properties of the team that are typically dynamic in nature and vary as a function of team context, inputs, processes, and outcomes" and can be cognitive, motivational, or affective in nature (Marks, Mathieu, & Zaccaro, 2001, p. 357). Finally, *outputs* represent the end results of a team's work, such as task performance and member satisfaction. The IMOI model states that team outputs often become inputs into the future work of a team, thus highlighting feedback processes in team functioning. In the following text, we discuss the findings of the literature on GVTs within each of the components of the IMOI model.

## GVT Inputs

The primary GVT inputs that researchers have focused on can be classified into three levels of analysis: individual, team, and organizational. Examples of individual-level inputs are GVT members' national culture, knowledge of technology, and experience with working in virtual teams, GVTs, or multicultural teams. Team-level inputs include GVT design, leadership, and technology. Organizational-level inputs include staffing, reward structures, training, and organizational culture.

### Individual-Level Inputs
The major individual-level input that gets at the core of what makes a virtual team global is members' national culture. Culture is "the collective programming of the human mind that distinguishes the members of one human group from another" (Hofstede, 1980, p. 25). Even though cultural differences within GVTs may stem from national, ethnic, organizational, or functional differences (Kayworth & Leidner, 2000; Massey, Hung, Montoya-Weiss, & Ramesh, 2001a), the primary aspect of culture that has been addressed in research on GVT inputs is members' national culture. Classifying member national culture is tricky because the variable can exist at multiple levels in a GVT – individual, group, organizational, and

national. Although national culture was originally discussed as a country-level construct (Hofstede, 1980), since individuals do not always adhere to the dominant cultural values of their respective country, researchers have also operationalized it at the individual level in the form of individual cultural value orientations (e.g., Triandis & Gelfand, 1998). In this review, we categorize this variable as an individual-level input, treating individuals with their own cultural orientations as inputs into the team, while recognizing that team-level diversity in these individual cultural orientations is a team-level input. Rather than split up the discussion of GVT members' cultural value orientations across the two input categories, we combine the two in the following discussion to maintain continuity and coherence.

The basic argument made for why GVT members' national cultures matter to GVT functioning is that team members tend to have their own assumptions, expectations, beliefs, and perspectives based on their respective cultural orientations. These are argued to influence behavior within GVTs, and their variety is expected to complicate communication, decision making, and ultimately task completion (e.g., Kayworth & Leidner, 2000). Although this argument appears rather straightforward, it has not been validated consistently across studies.

A significant number of studies examining national culture differences in GVTs have found that they create challenges due to various factors related to the globalness of GVTs. For example, most of the GVTs in a study by Kayworth and Leidner (2000) stated that cultural differences greatly impeded their effective functioning. The most pronounced cultural issue these teams experienced was a language barrier, but difficulties related to the members' variation in their sense of urgency and approach to time were also important. DeSanctis and colleagues (2001) also found that time-related information was important for the GVTs they studied, where time was mentioned in 44% of the teams' discussion board postings. In addition, Saunders, Van Slyke, and Vogel (2004, p. 19) argued that GVT members may differ by type of time visions (e.g., clock, event, timeless, or harmonic), which are "different perceptions of time across sets of time dimensions" that have their roots in ethnic or national culture. They propose that differences in time visions will have an effect on team tasks and processes such as scheduling and deadlines, team rhythm – a repeating, synchronized cycle of activities, – and in measuring team performance. These processes in turn (i.e., deadlines, rhythms, and performance measures) are argued to influence GVT success.

Reinig and Mejias (2004) found that GVT member national culture affected communication behaviors in the team; in particular, US (individualistic) teams expressed more criticism in their comments than did Hong Kong (collectivistic) teams. In an experimental study, Zhang, Lowry, Zhou, and Fu (2007) investigated the effects of national culture on majority influence in US–Hong Kong GVTs. They found that the extent of majority influence on minorities was more pronounced when the minorities were collectivistic rather than individualistic, in that minorities from Hong Kong reached consensus with the majority faster than did minorities from the United States. Additionally, Dekker, Rutte, and Van den Berg (2008) found that GVT member national culture determines which behaviors are considered crucial for satisfaction and performance in GVTs.

Massey and colleagues (2001a) examined the effects of differences on three dimensions of national culture on communication styles and perceptions of the fit between GVT task and technology. The three cultural dimensions are individualism–collectivism, which refers to the inclination to identify with the self or the collective (Hofstede, 1980); uncertainty avoidance, which denotes the degree to which individuals feel threatened by uncertainty and ambiguity (Hofstede, 1980); and communication contextuality, which is the "amount of extra information needed to make decisions versus 'just the facts'" (Massey et al., 2001a, p. 208). Based on exploratory interviews with members from culturally diverse and culturally homogeneous GVTs, they found that, even though the GVTs had access to the same communication technology, communication in culturally diverse GVTs was perceived as more problematic and time consuming, and the final products were less successful than in culturally homogeneous GVTs. Therefore, they concluded that cultural diversity is a determining factor in GVT functioning. In a follow-up experiment, they found that differences in cultural orientations (i.e., individualism, uncertainty avoidance, and contextuality) influenced members' communication behaviors, which in turn affected their perceptions and preferences for task–technology fit. Zolin, Hinds, Fruchter, and Levitt (2004) found that cultural diversity was significantly negatively associated with perceived trustworthiness of fellow GVT members, while McDonough et al. (2001) found that culturally diverse GVTs faced more behavioral challenges (e.g., trust, interpersonal relationships, and effective communication) than did culturally homogenous teams.

Despite a large amount of research suggesting that members' national culture differences matter to GVT functioning, some researchers have found that, at least under certain conditions, they may not. For example, in their analysis of several case studies, Qureshi and Zigurs (2001) point out that culture may not be the large impediment that some researchers argue it to be. They suggest that staying task focused is easier in a virtual context than in a traditional context, and therefore, culture should not play a significant role, allowing GVTs to fully capitalize on their cultural diversity. McDonough and colleagues (2001) found that, compared to colocated teams, GVTs and non-global virtual teams both encountered greater project management challenges (e.g., budgeting and scheduling). Based on this finding, the authors suggested that "the deterioration in communication rather than cultural or language barriers leads to greater difficulty in managing project management challenges" in GVTs (p. 116). Paul, Seetharaman, Samarah, and Mykytyn (2004) found only marginal support for the proposed negative relationship between GVT national cultural heterogeneity and the teams' collaborative conflict management style. Finally, Jarvenpaa and Leidner (1999) found no significant difference in perceived trust for individuals from individualistic or collectivistic cultures at either the midpoint or the end of their study.

Overall, the findings discussed in the preceding text suggest that although it may make intuitive sense that heterogeneity in national cultures affects interactions in GVTs negatively, it is not always the case, and the virtualness of a GVT may often pose greater challenges than its globalness. This is a very interesting inconsistency in findings on GVTs and one that suggests that rather than deterministically assuming that GVTs will encounter challenges in their functioning due to differences in national cultures, researchers must more seriously take into account variables related to virtualness and teamness, which are factors over which team managers may sometimes have more direct control and influence than they have over the globalness of GVTs.

Although GVT members' national culture is the most salient individual-level team input studied to date, there are others that have also received research attention, such as knowledge, skills, and abilities (KSAs), and demographic differences. For example, Kayworth and Leidner (2000) noted that the success of GVTs may be impacted by their members' level of expertise and experience with communication technologies. Pauleen and Yoong (2001) also reached a similar conclusion based on their observation of relationship problems in several GVTs, stemming from lags in response times due to time zone differences or technology infrastructure issues, which were especially pronounced when members had little experience with working in a virtual context. Martins and Shalley (in press) found that whereas differences in nationality and age had negative effects on team creativity, differences in race and sex did not have any significant effects.

*Team-Level Inputs*

Researchers have examined several team-level inputs, including team size, structure, design, leadership, management, facilitation, and technology. In a study of 18 GVTs consisting of 4–18 members, Bradner, Mark, and Hertel (2005) found that GVT size was a determining factor in the teams' behaviors, attitudes, and choice of communication technology. Members of smaller GVTs had higher levels of participation, rapport, commitment, and satisfaction, and had greater knowledge of team goals and of their fellow team members in terms of their roles, expertise, communication style, and personal situation. Smaller GVTs also reported lower levels of coordination precision such as through published detailed meeting agendas. Finally, smaller teams indicated a preference for synchronous collaboration technology, whereas larger teams were more likely to adopt asynchronous collaboration tools.

Prasad and Akhilesh (2002) proposed a conceptual framework of GVT design that maximizes fit between a team's structure and its strategic objectives, work characteristics, and situational constraints. They argued several relationships relating these variables to four dimensions of GVT structure: degree of virtualness, team processes (e.g., control and coordination), alternate informal socialization mechanisms, and attitudinal factors (e.g., team norms), and suggested that the structure of GVTs needs to be carefully managed since the four structural dimensions have a direct impact on GVT performance. Along similar lines, Workman (2004) found that GVTs whose structural characteristics reflected higher process orientation, greater job centeredness, more parochial orientation, tighter control, and higher pragmatism demonstrated higher performance (in terms of percent budget variance, percent schedule variance, and human-induced errors).

In an experimental study of the structure of student GVTs in which geographical location was treated as a dimension of diversity, Polzer, Crisp, Jarvenpaa, and Kim (2006) found that GVTs developed faultlines based on location, especially when the individuals in the location-based subgroups were of the same nationality. In a quasi-experimental study using six-member student GVTs with members from the United States and Canada assigned to teams in various configurations (with 6-0; 5-1; 4-2; and 3-3 splits across two locations), O'Leary and Mortensen (2010) found that teams with subgroups (4-2 and 3-3) reported less identification with the team, lower transactive memory, higher conflict, and greater coordination problems than colocated teams (6-0) and teams with isolates (5-1). Also, within imbalanced groups (4-2), members of the smaller subgroup had less identification and lower transactive memory than did members of the larger subgroup (O'Leary & Mortensen, 2010).

Designing GVTs has been found to involve a complex set of decisions. Based on case studies of three GVTs, Gluesing and colleagues (2003) identified several GVT design conditions that were beneficial for team development: (1) a task that is well defined, strategic, critical, urgent, and meaningful, (2) clear process guidelines, (3) cross-cultural skills, (4) respected and competent team members who have command over resources, and (5) diffusion instead of clustering of members across locations. They also found several conditions in the initial team start-up environment that can help GVTs mature effectively: (1) a facilitator trained in GVT processes such as cross-cultural communication and team building, (2) use of storytelling to transfer implicit knowledge, (3) a strong team identity, (4) taking time to develop fundamentals such as business knowledge and virtual collaboration basics, and (5) FtF time early in the team's life.

Not surprisingly, GVT leadership has received a significant amount of research attention. Researchers have argued that GVT leadership is very different from leadership of traditional teams due to reduced social presence (Short, Williams, & Christie, 1976), a "lack of task visibility and structural boundaries" (Harvey, Novicevic, & Garrison, 2004, p. 280), and diminished control and reward power (Kayworth & Leidner, 2000). It has been argued that these constraints mean that GVT leaders have access to only a limited set of tools to manage teamwork issues, thereby making leadership in GVTs inherently simpler than in FtF teams (Kayworth & Leidner, 2001). Supporting this argument are observations that GVT work is often characterized by self-management, shared leadership, or rotational leadership (e.g., Harvey et al., 2004; Rutkowski, Vogel, van Genuchten, Bemelmans, & Favier, 2002).

Several researchers have sought to identify the set of qualities that make for effective leaders in a GVT context. In a field study of 41 GVTs in a global Fortune 500 firm in the hardware and software industries, Joshi, Lazarova, and Liao (2009) found that GVT members' perceptions of their team leader's inspirational leadership were positively related to their trust in and commitment to other team members, and that these positive effects were stronger for more dispersed GVTs. GVT members' commitment to and trust in each other, aggregated to the team level, predicted team performance. In a qualitative study, Kayworth and Leidner (2000) identified several characteristics of effective GVT leaders: the ability to set clear goals and give continuous performance feedback, the ability to develop a cohesive team, a high degree of understanding and empathy for team members, and a high level of cultural sensitivity. In a subsequent study, Kayworth and Leidner (2001) found that GVT leaders who were perceived as effective by their team members engaged in high levels of both relational (consideration) and task management (initiating structure) aspects of leadership, suggesting that effective GVT leaders display higher levels of behavioral complexity than those who are considered less effective. As in their previous study, they found that the teams with the most effective leaders scored the highest on project quality.

In a case study, Pauleen (2003b) highlighted the importance of proactive communication by team leaders, and found that "effective virtual team leaders demonstrate a general capability to deal with paradox and contradiction by performing multiple leadership roles simultaneously, and specifically to demonstrate empathy while asserting flexible, collegial authority" (p. 160). Using a case study of a global training and development team, Kerber and Buono (2004) concluded that to elicit high GVT effectiveness, a GVT leader should provide a task that is challenging and personally relevant, develop the team's identity, goals, and work processes through consultation with the team, define a clear performance management process, establish and maintain constant communication, and demonstrate a high level of commitment.

From interviews with 18 GVT leaders, Dubé and Paré (2001) concluded that a successful GVT leader should manage cultural, language, communication, and IT proficiency differences among team members, while overcoming technology difficulties to "create an electronic workplace that supports the specific and changing needs of the team" (p. 73). Majchrzak, Malhotra, Stamps, and Lipnack (2004) found that in addition to constantly communicating and managing the technology, it was also important for GVT leaders to establish a common national and technical language, combine work process and climate differences, actively elicit input from all members to take advantage of the team's diversity, and have an upfront discussion of GVT time commitments.

Based on a study of 10 student GVTs comprised of members from the Netherlands and Hong Kong, Vogel et al. (2001) proposed several best practices in managing GVTs: (1) provide timely responses and follow-up, (2) ask for progress updates to avoid inactivity, (3) be supportive rather than directive, (4) balance proactive and reactive support, (5) develop a common frame of reference, (6) use the right technologies to avoid technical problems, (7) provide opportunities for synchronous communication, and (8) alternate FtF with virtual interactions. Monalisa et al. (2008) investigated eight GVTs via case study methodology and concluded that the leadership behaviors most critical for GVT success are: scheduling frequent meetings with offsite members, responding to emails from offsite members in a timely manner, clarifying and repeating ideas and instructions often, developing a central repository for work files, and clearly defining roles, responsibilities, and expectations.

Team facilitation has emerged as an important aspect of managing GVTs. O'Hara-Devereaux and Johansen (1994, p. 121) defined facilitation as "the art of helping people navigate the processes that lead to agreed-upon objectives in a way that encourages universal participation and productivity." Pauleen and Yoong (2001) discussed how GVT facilitators can use technologies to build relationships among team members. They suggest that facilitators should use a greater level of relationship building as the number of boundaries (cultural, language, organizational, departmental, functional, time, and distance) between GVT members increases. Additionally, Monalisa and colleagues (2008) remind managers to remember to assess whether GVTs are appropriate for the task at hand and to realize that the management of GVTs may take on a different form than that of traditional FtF teams.

Although the team-level inputs discussed in the preceding text are increasingly the focus of research on GVTs, technology is the team-level input that has received by far the lion's share of attention in the literature. GVTs vary in the types of technology they use, and the role of technology in GVTs has been studied extensively. Researchers have used several terms to describe the technologies that GVTs use to communicate: advanced information and communication technologies or ACTs (Evaristo, 2003), information and communication technologies or ICTs (Pauleen, 2003a, 2003b), computer-mediated communications or CMCs (Walther, 1997), and computer-supported cooperative work or CSCW (Huysman et al., 2003). Qureshi and Zigurs (2001), in a study of GVTs from several corporate environments, found that GVTs use a broad array of collaborative technologies also called "groupware applications" (Davison & de Vreede, 2001, p. 69) including email, shared calendaring systems, chat rooms, videoconferencing, audioconferencing, e-meetings systems, knowledge repositories, document management systems, and video whiteboards. "Groupware has been widely promoted as a technology that can facilitate the global integration of geographically distributed teams and organizations by overcoming time-space barriers to communication and hence promoting knowledge sharing" (Kelly & Jones, 2001, p. 77). Even though more sophisticated groupware technologies exist, not all studies support their proclaimed benefits and use. For example, despite the availability of a wide range of technologies, Huysman and colleagues (2003) found that video-conferencing and email were the technologies most often used by the GVTs, and Jang, Steinfield, and Pfaff (2002) found that teams preferred email as their main means of communicating virtually.

The most common distinction made in describing the technologies supporting GVT functioning is between synchronous and asynchronous technologies. Technologies such as the telephone, audioconferencing and videoconferencing, instant chat, and text messaging are synchronous, whereas email, voice mail, fax, shared drives, and web bulletin boards are asynchronous. Thus, "in synchronous teams, the communication takes place in real time, whereas in asynchronous teams, members perform their tasks at different times, at their own pace, and according to their own time limitations" (Paul et al., 2004, p. 303). Since members of many GVTs are from different nations, the likelihood that they live in the same time zone, and therefore, have overlapping work hours, is reduced. When work-hour overlap is very low (e.g., between the United States and India), it becomes increasingly necessary for GVTs to communicate via asynchronous rather than synchronous collaborative technologies (Harvey et al., 2004).

Because each communication technology has its advantages and disadvantages, the choice of GVT communication medium has been found to depend on a variety of factors such as message complexity (Maznevski & Chudoba, 2000), GVT task (Dubé & Paré, 2001), the culture of GVT members (Massey et al., 2001a), the type of communication needs (Kayworth & Leidner, 2000), team size (Bradner et al., 2005) or simply convenience, accessibility, or cost (Pauleen, 2003a).

*Technology and Type of Message.* Daft and Lengel (1984) proposed a model of managerial information processing that suggests that the more complicated the message, the richer should be the communication medium used to convey it. They defined information richness as the potential information-carrying capacity of a medium, which is based on four factors: feedback speed, channel type (e.g., audio, video), type of communication (personal or impersonal), and language variety (e.g., numeric, body, natural). However, Carlson and Zmud (1999) argued that media richness may be a *perception* instead of an objective quality, because whether a technology provides a rich interaction is ultimately in the eye of the beholder, based on factors such as experience with the technology. Successful interaction takes place when there is an appropriate fit between the complexity of the message and the communication medium. However, when there is a mismatch between the richness of the medium and the complexity of the message (oversimplification or overcomplication), the outcome is ineffective information processing (Daft & Lengel, 1984). Media richness theory was supported in an in-depth study of three GVTs by Maznevski and Chudoba (2000) who found that in effective interactions there was an appropriate match between communication medium and the decision process and message complexity. More specifically, when the level of decision process and message complexity increased, so did the richness of the communication technology in effective GVTs. They did not find such a relationship in the ineffective GVT.

*Technology and Task.*   Qureshi and Zigurs (2001) found that knowledge sharing and structured or detailed tasks are especially well suited to a virtual context. Based on a typology of task complexity by Bell and Kozlowski (2002), Riopelle et al. (2003) suggest that higher task complexity increases the need for synchronous, tightly coupled interaction, and therefore, requires technologies that allow real-time team collaboration. In a longitudinal study of six GVTs, they found that when the teams' task environment changed, they altered their choice and use of communication technologies to match the team's new situation. Therefore, they suggest that in addition to matching the technology medium to task complexity, managers must also incorporate the team's contextual constraints (i.e., the local technology infrastructure of the members' nations and organizations, the GVT's cultural and language diversity, discrepancies in access to information, the extent of time zone differences, team size, and the level of technology reliability) into their decisions regarding technologies usage (Riopelle et al., 2003). Similarly, Cheng and Beaumont (2004) reported that the GVTs in their sample adopted different technologies for different tasks; they used synchronous tools for decision making and asynchronous communication technology for more complementary tasks such as evaluating members' contributions or distributing project deliverables.

Majchrzak and colleagues (2004) found from survey and interview data that email alone was insufficient as a means for team communication because one-on-one email interactions led to feelings of isolation and distrust, whereas copying all team members on email messages created an insurmountable email backlog. In addition, the participants in their study found email to lack functionality in terms of search and storage capabilities. The GVTs they studied preferred conference calls for generating solutions and reconciling conflicting viewpoints, but for updates and reports the teams relied heavily on virtual work spaces where members posted their ideas and work for review by others. Finally, they found that almost half of the GVTs used instant messaging technology, but mainly for social interaction.

*Technology and Culture.* In an experimental study with 30 graduate student teams, Massey and colleagues (2001a) addressed the idea that differences in cultural orientation affect perceptions of fit between the GVT decision-making task and the Lotus Notes© technology. They found that subjects from individualistic, low context, and low uncertainty avoidance cultures (e.g., United States) did not perceive a good task–technology fit since they preferred decision making via interaction and debate, which are better enabled by synchronous and rich communication media. In contrast, participants from collectivistic, high context, and high uncertainty avoidance cultures (e.g., some Asian countries) reported a better fit between the task and the asynchronous nature of the Lotus Notes© software since they tend to prefer indirect communication and conflict avoidance, which, coupled with the fact that the text-based software gave them the ability to better express themselves in English, suggests that members of such cultures may prefer leaner, asynchronous communication media for decision making. Based on interviews with GVT members, Shachaf (2008) also found that a team's cultural diversity influenced the usefulness of information and communication technologies; she found that email, teleconferencing, e-meetings, and team chat rooms were more effective for those GVTs with higher cultural diversity.

In a study using 24 global learning teams, DeSanctis and colleagues (2001) found that asynchronous tools were considered more critical than synchronous technologies for coordination in teams with larger cultural and geographic distances among its members. They suggest that this is because asynchronous media give culturally diverse members the time to process and respond to postings of other members. In particular, the preferred technologies of the global learning teams were in order of high to low preference: discussion boards, email, audioconferencing, chat rooms, file transfer, fax, and instant messaging. This is consistent with Overholt's (2002) finding that in GVTs, asynchronous media were more effective than FtF interactions when working with international members, since they preferred to give feedback via text-based technology rather than during conference calls or in-person meetings, simply because their written English was better than their spoken English. In addition, Uber Grosse (2002) also found that asynchronous technology such as email helps GVT members with language difficulties because it alleviates the pressure to respond "on the spot," thus allowing for time to reflect on contributions and providing a safe environment where questions can be asked without losing face.

*Other Factors Affecting Technology Use.* Pauleen and Yoong (2001) identified several conditions influencing technology selection and use in their study of seven GVTs: (1) project complexity and time frame, (2) distance among team members, (3) culture, (4) security issues, (5) budget, (6) availability and compatibility of the technology, (7) knowledge management systems, and (8) training. Furthermore, Uber Grosse (2002) noted that the nature of the audience (e.g., level of formality and familiarity) could also influence the selection of communication technology. Rutkowski, Saunders, Vogel, & van Genuchten (2007) found that GVT members with a higher mean score of focus immersion (i.e., engagement, attention, and task focus) favored asynchronous technologies, whereas synchronous technologies were reported as more useful by members with a higher level of temporal dissociation (i.e., losing track of time, multitasking, and time distortion).

Authors have also found that synchronous communication media have their specific advantages within GVTs. For example, Rutkowski et al. (2002) found that especially in the early life stages of GVTs, a short period of synchronous work was often more effective than longer periods of asynchronous work. They emphasized that synchronous media are also important for social interactions and for the delivery of timely feedback. The idea that both synchronous and asynchronous technologies are important for GVTs also received support in a study by Huysman and colleagues (2003) who found that of the communication channels available to the GVTs, all teams in their sample used email and videoconferencing much more frequently than other channels. Additionally, Shachaf (2008) concluded from her interviews with 41 GVT members that GVTs should have access to a suite of communication technologies so that teams can choose different media channels to fit their specific needs at different times. Similarly, in their ethnographic study, Cheng and Beaumont (2004) reported that for teams to perform well, they should have a wide choice of both synchronous and asynchronous communication technologies at their disposal. These authors also concluded that familiarity and previous experience with communication technologies influenced future adoption choices.

GVT technology choice has also been found to be affected by team size (Bradner et al., 2005) where larger teams were more likely to use asynchronous communication tools such as central repositories, calendars, and meeting facilitation software to help with team coordination and logistics, whereas smaller teams preferred synchronous communication technologies such as telephone conferencing, chat, and virtual meetings to facilitate their collaboration.

Even though the preceding discussion suggest that the type of technologies used affects team outcomes such as consensus and decision-making quality, several researchers argue that the effects of technology choice on outcomes do not depend on the technologies themselves as much as they do on how GVT members actually use them (DeSanctis & Poole, 1994; Qureshi & Zigurs, 2001). DeSanctis and Poole (1994) proposed an approach based on Adaptive Structuration Theory, which suggests that the technology and the teams' interaction with the technology work together to influence team outcomes and organizational change. Some support for this idea has been provided by Huysman and colleagues (2003, p. 430) who found that "group technologies have a reinforcement effect on group dynamics rather than a deterministic one," and by Rockett, Valor, Miller, and Naude (1998) who concluded that in GVTs that had appropriate team design factors in place such as superordinate goals, mutual accountability, and appropriate team norms, technology helped rather than hurt project success and team member satisfaction.

The type of technology used by a GVT has also been linked to team processes and outcomes. The effectiveness of building relationships in GVTs was found to be significantly impacted by the selection and use of the teams' communication media (Pauleen & Yoong, 2001). Comparing multicultural teams in a group decision support system (GDSS) environment to those in an FtF environment, Daily and Teich (2001) found that teams using GDSS reported lower *perceived* contribution levels (rating of others and by others), but yielded higher *objective* contribution levels (number of nonredundant, realistic ideas) than in the FtF environment. Further, in an experiment using 12 GVTs, Kayworth and Leidner (2000) discovered that richer communication technologies such as web pages and instant messaging gave teams an advantage in managing their project, exchanging information, and making decisions. In addition, teams that used richer technologies in addition to email were also more satisfied, while suffering less information loss than those teams that utilized only email as their means of communication.

Two studies (Chudoba et al., 2005; Lu, Watson-Manheim, Chudoba, & Wynn, 2006) investigated the effects of three aspects of virtualness: team distribution (i.e., teams consisting of members who work across time zones, in different countries, and via communication technology), workplace mobility (i.e., teams with members who work outside the regular office context), and variety of practices (i.e., teams with a variety of cultures and work processes) on team processes and outcomes. They found that team distribution was not significantly related to participation, trust, communication, coordination, commitment, and quality and timeliness of team deliverables. However, they did find that team distribution was positively related to the perception of fair work distribution. The mobility aspect of virtualness negatively affected communication and performance. Variety in practices negatively influenced team participation, work coordination, communication, trust, timely completion of projects, and team performance. Their findings suggest that rather than member dispersion, variety of practices is the more problematic aspect of team virtualness within GVTs.

Zhang and colleagues (2007) investigated the effects of technology on majority influence. They found that majority influence was stronger in culturally diverse FtF teams than in GVTs that communicated both FtF and via technology, or in completely virtual GVTs. They argued that because technology removes nonverbal cues, majority members may have less influence over minority members in more virtual GVTs. Information technology has also been researched as a moderator of effects within GVTs. For example, Shachaf (2008) discovered in an exploratory study that communication technologies enhanced the positive aspects of cultural diversity, while eliminating or lessening the negative consequences of cultural diversity on team decision making, communication, and performance.

*Organizational-Level Inputs*
The GVT inputs that have received the least attention in the literature are organizational inputs. The ones that have been studied include staffing, training, organizational culture, and organizational structure. Harvey and colleagues (2004) argued that the staffing of a GVT is just as important as the management of a GVT. They suggested that staffing teams for global virtual work is difficult because it is often unclear what cognitive skills are necessary, how to adequately assess these skills, and how to generate the right mix of cognitively diverse members for successful GVT work. They propose that, in addition to considering diversity on traditional characteristics such as education and language proficiencies, GVT staffers should pay attention to diversity on several other cognitive characteristics: (1) type of IQ, categorized as analytical intelligence, practical intelligence, and creative intelligence; (2) learning styles; (3) thinking styles; (4) experience with GVT work; (5) level of functional expertise; and (6) ability to adjust to new

environments. Furthermore, they suggest that since GVT staffing is complicated, managers should look critically at the need to create a GVT in the first place. After the need for a GVT is established, its task, its operating environment, size, and performance metrics need to be determined before staffing is begun.

Given that processes and dynamics in GVTs vary significantly from those in an FtF environment, it has been argued that GVT members require unique competencies (Pauleen & Yoong, 2001). Most authors stress the importance of cross-cultural training to ensure that GVTs are equipped to take advantage of their cultural differences (e.g., James & Ward, 2001; Kayworth & Leidner, 2000). Dubé and Paré (2001, p. 71) argue that "such training should address issues that might affect team performance such as normal working hours, expected behaviors, expected levels of performance and involvement, how decisions are made, how work will be reviewed and approved, and how to resolve conflicts." Anawati and Craig (2006) found that team members who received team training incorporating cultural issues in a virtual team context were more mindful of their culturally diverse GVT members, in terms of adjusting their written and spoken communication and considering religion-related factors in scheduling meetings and dead-lines, than were members without any training or those who received virtual team training without the cultural dimensions. Kayworth and Leidner (2000) observed that GVT members also require training on cultural differences regarding communication style.

In addition to enhancing intercultural awareness, some researchers also suggest that GVT members should receive training on a wide range of communication technologies (e.g., Dubé & Paré, 2001; Kayworth & Leidner, 2000; Uber Grosse, 2002), team building (Rockett et al., 1998), dealing with ambiguity (Pauleen & Yoong, 2001), collaboration and facilitation (Paul et al., 2004), trust development (Evaristo, 2003), task/topical material as well as member background (Rutkowski et al., 2002), and creative problem solving (Chen, Liou, Wang, Fan, & Chi, 2007).

Research indicates that training and development should be an ongoing effort throughout the project life cycle (James & Ward, 2001; Pauleen & Yoong, 2001). However, research also suggests that team building through training may not be as successful in a virtual environment as in an FtF context (Jarvenpaa, Knoll, & Leidner, 1998; Rockett et al., 1998). Additionally, there is evidence that colocation may not always be superior to dispersion in facilitating team interactions. In a 5-month case study, Bjørn and Ngwenyama (2009) found that a lack of shared meaning regarding background knowledge and assumptions was more salient in a

FtF than in a virtual environment, leading to communication problems during team interactions.

An organization's culture is an interesting input condition into GVTs, given that the very definition of organizational culture may be affected by the extent of globalness and virtualness of an organization. Pauleen and Yoong (2001) found that difference in organizational culture was the major determinant of the complexity of GVT dynamics. In a study of MBA students from schools in three countries, Rockett and colleagues (1998) observed major differences in behavior with regard to delegation, consensus building, information seeking, and autonomy due to differences in the participants' school cultures.

Finally, the effect of an organization's global hierarchical structure on GVTs in the organization is demonstrated well in a study by David, Chand, Newell, and Resende-Santos (2008). In a 3-year ethnographic study, they discovered that the organization they studied unintentionally undermined collaboration between onshore and offshore sites by developing a global hierarchical structure, where US onshore sites were at the core, Irish sites at the semi-periphery, and Indian sites at the periphery. This hierarchical structure originated from the company's top-down strategic decision-making approach, which created power differences between sites thereby compromising the development of trust. The authors suggest that global relationship management can be used to overcome dysfunctional core versus periphery dynamics "to establish a 'flat', integrated and collaborative workforce" (p. 53).

*GVT Inputs: Summary and Future Research*
The preceding discussion of GVT inputs indicates that individual, team, and organizational input factors all play critical roles in the successful functioning of GVTs. Of the literature on GVT inputs, a very large amount has focused on types of information technologies and their uses. However, it is still unclear what factors play a role in the selection and use of GVT technologies (Kayworth & Leidner, 2000). More complex research models using mediation and/or moderation effects are needed to uncover the circumstances under which various technologies facilitate or impede GVT functioning and performance.

The research on demographic characteristics in GVTs as individual-level inputs has focused primarily on cultural differences, such as on differences in individualism–collectivism, communication contextuality, and uncertainty avoidance (Massey et al., 2001a; Reinig & Mejias, 2004; Zhang et al., 2007). Although DeSanctis and colleagues (2001) and Saunders and colleagues (2004) theorize on the effects of cultural differences in time visions, this type of diversity has not been empirically investigated. Additional research is needed on other dimensions of differences within GVTs such as other demographic characteristics like age and ethnicity.

Given that GVTs are typically very diverse, it is somewhat surprising that besides cultural value orientations, individual differences have not been researched much in a GVT context (Martins et al., 2004). One exception is a study by Rutkowski and colleagues (2007) who examined two dimensions of the individual difference variable cognitive absorption, which is defined as a state of deep involvement: focus immersion (i.e., extent of engagement, attention, and task focus) and temporal dissociation (i.e., extent of losing track of time, multitasking, and time distortion). In a study of 13 GVTs consisting of 7–10 members from the Netherlands, Hong Kong, and the United States, they found that cognitive absorption influenced interpersonal conflict, technology preferences, and performance. There are clearly tremendous research opportunities for future research on how individual difference variables, such as Big Five personality traits and cognitive styles, affect individual- and group-level experiences in GVTs.

Researchers have found that a person's capability to understand and empathize with different cultures is an important skill that individuals working with people from different cultures should possess. Some researchers term this intercultural sensitivity (e.g., Bennett, 1986), whereas others (e.g., Earley & Gardner, 2005) have named it cultural intelligence. Since this capability has been argued to have a profound influence on team dynamics (Earley & Gardner, 2005), it would be worthwhile to investigate its effects in future research on GVTs. Few studies have focused on other KSAs that individual members contribute to the GVT. There is some indication in the reviewed literature that skills and familiarity with communication technology and/or teamwork may have a facilitating effect on team performance (Kayworth & Leidner, 2000; Pauleen & Yoong, 2001). In addition, some authors have suggested other specific KSAs that may assist in better team performance and can be learned through training, such as team building skills (Rockett et al., 1998) and flexibility (Pauleen & Yoong, 2001). However, the relationships between individual member KSAs and GVT processes and outcomes have not yet been specifically examined.

Related areas ripe for examination are the value and content of GVT training. The literature has pointed to the idea that training of GVT members is a critical success factor. At the same time, there is some indication that training may not be as effective when delivered via virtual means. For example, Jarvenpaa and colleagues (1998) found that team building exercises did not have a direct effect on trust in GVTs, and Rockett and colleagues (1998) found that team building may be more effective FtF. Therefore, several questions remain: What exactly is the value of training for GVTs in terms of enhancing team processes, emergent states, and outcomes? What should be the content of this training? How, when, and where should this training take place?

A related avenue for future research on GVT inputs is human resource management for GVTs, such as staffing, evaluation, rewards, and career planning. Harvey and colleagues (2004) proposed a model of managerial approaches and a set of member characteristics that may increase the successful staffing and management of GVTs, both of which should be tested empirically. Additionally, they raise several other questions that need to be addressed. For example, how should GVT member contributions be measured, evaluated, and rewarded? How should organizations design their appraisal and reward structure to match the complex nature of GVT tasks? Also, today's high-performance employees have increasingly high expectations that often include global career aspirations. Therefore, a major HRM challenge will be to develop appropriate career planning for GVT members, an area in need of future research (Harvey et al., 2004).

Lastly, few studies touch on the organizational and environmental context in which GVTs operate, and the team's external context is an important input that promises to provide excellent opportunities for future research on GVTs (Joshi & Roh, 2009). For example, the effects of organizational culture on the functioning of GVTs within the organization are not yet clear. GVT field research tends to examine individuals from the same organization working across borders and thus organizational differences have not been given much research attention. The most likely reason is because it is assumed that GVT members from the same organization adhere to the same shared values, symbols, language, and organizational norms due to their organizational membership. However, this may not always be the case as in reality subsidiaries or even functional units of the same organization can have very distinct cultures. This similarity assumption could create an illusion of shared meaning, which may add a layer of complexity to GVT functioning as the assumption of shared understanding can lead to miscommunications, misunderstandings, and feelings of animosity as members do not understand why things are not being done/understood as they intended. The lack of shared meanings may lead to less cohesiveness, dysfunctional team interactions, and lower performance in the long run. Besides organizational culture, other contextual variables that would be interesting to examine are organizational size, structure, strategy, physical environment, and environmental stress levels.

How these variables relate to the dynamics within a GVT, to technology use, and to GVT performance should be examined in future research.

## *GVT Mediators: Processes and Emergent States*

Researchers have examined a wide range of GVT mediators, which include processes and emergent states. Team processes are "members' interdependent acts that convert inputs to outcomes through cognitive, verbal, and behavioral activities directed toward organizing task work to achieve collective goals" (Marks et al., 2001, p. 357). In contrast, emergent states are constructs that describe cognitive, motivational, and affective states of teams that emerge in the course of the functioning of teams (Marks et al., 2001). The processes that have been focused on most in the literature on GVTs include conflict and its management, communication and collaboration, relationship building, feedback, group development, learning and knowledge transfer, and influence and politics. The emergent states receiving the most attention are trust, cohesion, and team identity. Each of these processes and emergent states in GVTs is discussed in the following text.

### *Conflict and Conflict Management*
GVTs are by definition diverse in membership as they tend to span multiple organizations, nationalities, cultures, functions, or departments. This diversity is expected to foster conflict among team members (Paul et al., 2004). However, national diversity itself has not been consistently found to be related to conflict in a GVT (Hinds & Mortensen, 2005; Mortensen & Hinds, 2001), suggesting that factors associated with nationality differences, such as cultural differences, may be more likely to generate conflict. Staples and Zhao (2006), in a study of student teams working on a short-term task, found that virtual teams diverse in a combination of cultural values, language, and nationality experienced greater conflict than did homogeneous teams. Similarly, in a case study of three student GVTs, Kankanhalli, Tan, and Wei (2007) found that higher team cultural diversity led to greater task and relationship conflict. Finally, Paul, Samarah, Seetharaman, and Mykytyn (2005) found that cultural value orientations influenced collaborative conflict management style, where more collectivistic teams demonstrated higher levels of collaborative conflict management than did more individualistic teams.

There is also evidence that the communication technology used may itself be a source of conflict in a virtual context. In a field study of 43 teams, Hinds and Mortensen (2005) found higher task and interpersonal conflict among distributed teams than among collocated teams. The positive relationship between team distribution and *interpersonal* conflict was weakened when teams had a strong shared identity or spontaneous communication (unplanned, informal communication), whereas the positive relationship between team distribution and *task* conflict practically disappeared when teams had a shared context or spontaneous communication. Also, Rutkowski and colleagues (2007) found that among virtual teams, one dimension of cognitive absorption (i.e., state of deep involvement) with virtual teaming technologies – temporal dissociation – was significantly related to increased interpersonal conflict, whereas the other dimension of cognitive absorption – focus immersion – was unrelated to conflict. In addition to their main effects, the two aspects of cognitive absorption together influenced levels of interpersonal conflict.

Conflict in GVTs could also stem from the team's workflow patterns. For instance, in a study that used social network theory to examine a GVT of 30 HR managers distributed across six countries in a MNC, Joshi, Labianca, and Caligiuri (2002) found that rather than conflict being the result of power differences between headquarters and subsidiaries as is typically assumed in the literature, the conflict within the GVT was better explained by the pattern of workflows. They found that in instances where "negative affective networks overlap with the workflow and communication networks, conflict can have the maximum negative effect on team functioning" (Joshi et al., 2002, p. 282).

In addition to conflict itself, the conflict management style used in a team has also been found to affect GVT processes and outcomes. In an experimental study of teams with US and Indian participants, Paul and colleagues (2004) found that a collaborative conflict management style had a positive effect on self-reported decision-making satisfaction, decision-making quality, and participation, but not on group agreement. However, their hypothesis that heterogeneous GVTs would have lower levels of collaborative conflict management style than nationally homogeneous groups received only marginal support. In another study of MBA student teams, Paul and colleagues (2005) found that collaborative conflict management in a GVT had a positive influence on team performance, especially for more culturally diverse teams. Montoya-Weiss, Massey, and Song (2001) found that successful GVTs used either a collaborative or competitive style to manage conflict among GVT members rather than avoidance, accommodation, or compromising conflict management styles. Since they found a positive effect of competitive style but a negative effect of compromising style on performance, the authors suggest that existing theories of conflict may not completely hold up when used in a virtual environment. In addition to elaborating on the effects of the conflict style used, the literature also provides some guidance on the role of technology choice in conflict resolution. For example, Rutkowski and colleagues (2002) suggest that GVTs experiencing conflict should use videoconferencing in the process of resolving the conflict.

*Communication and Collaboration*
Communication involves the transfer of meaning from a sender to a receiver. In a study of six GVTs comprised of US and Dutch students, Huysman and colleagues (2003) found that despite similar start-up conditions, each team developed a specific communication pattern based on their choice and use of communication technologies. Once established, these communication routines were difficult to change, a phenomenon that the authors labeled "media stickiness."

In contrast to some other areas of research on GVTs, there appears to be consensus about several aspects of communication in GVTs. First, many authors have emphasized the need for GVTs to set ground rules and develop routines about when, how, and how often to communicate to improve knowledge sharing and ultimately team performance (e.g., DeSanctis et al., 2001; James & Ward, 2001; Kayworth & Leidner, 2000; Massey et al., 2001b; Munkvold & Zigurs, 2007). However, James and Ward (2001) caution that these ground rules and patterns must be subject to revision when the project or team environment changes. Second, most research is in agreement that an initial or periodic FtF meetings are critical for GVTs as they enhance communication (Kayworth & Leidner, 2000; Pauleen, 2003a), team momentum (Rutkowski et al., 2002), performance, and trust formation (Pauleen, 2003a; Uber Grosse, 2002). When FtF meetings are not possible, videoconferencing may lessen the communication difficulties stemming from a lack of physical proximity (Dubé & Paré, 2001; Pauleen & Yoong, 2001; Rutkowski et al., 2002). In contrast to the majority opinion, Bjørn and Ngwenyama (2009) observed that FtF interactions may actually hurt team functioning as they make members' differences more salient. Third, researchers generally agree that continuous communication is a key to successful GVTs (e.g., Kayworth & Leidner, 2000; Majchrzak et al., 2004; Pauleen, 2003a; Rutkowski et al., 2002; Uber Grosse, 2002).

In a study involving a single organization with multiple offices worldwide, Anawati and Craig (2006) discovered that most members of a GVT changed the way they communicated with other GVT members and that they adapted their *verbal* communication more often than their *written* communication. The most common ways in which individuals altered their communication were speaking more slowly, avoiding slang and jargon, keeping words and sentences short and simple, using confirmation and repetition, changing language or accents, and keeping to the point. The authors found a significant correlation between communication adaptation behavior and team member tenure so that GVT members who were part of a GVT for less than 3 months were least prone to change their communication, those who had a team tenure of 3–6 months were most likely to alter their methods, and those of longer tenure used a medium amount of communication adaptation behavior, possibly because by that time the members have become accustomed to each other's communication styles (Anawati & Craig, 2006).

Maznevski and Chudoba (2000) found that effective GVT communications are ordered in a repeating temporal rhythm of interaction incidents, where longer, high-intensity FtF interactions were alternated with shorter, less intense virtual interactions. They also found that successful teams used only a limited number of interaction configurations, suggesting that the range of communication media used may not be as important as their appropriateness for the task. Also, researchers have found that it is not necessarily the amount or the frequency of communication that is related to higher performance, but more so the depth and focus of the communication (DeSanctis et al., 2001). Uber Grosse (2002) provides some general guidelines for effective communication in GVTs: communicate frequently and clearly, listen actively, use the appropriate technologies, build relationships and trust, employ cultural sensitivity, check for understanding, and ask for clarification.

Not only is *structured* communication essential for the effective functioning of GVTs, Hinds and Mortensen (2005) argue that spontaneous communication is similarly important as it was found to increase both team identity and shared context, which in turn reduced the amount of conflict in distributed teams. Examining two different types of communication, criticalness (pointing out mistakes or faults) and flaming (unwelcome verbal attacks that may include insults, personal attacks, and offensive language), Reinig and Mejias (2004) discovered that anonymity and culture had a significant effect on the number of critical comments, but not the number of flame comments. Specifically, anonymous teams generated more critical comments than identified teams and US teams (which were assumed to be individualistic) expressed a greater number of critical comments than did teams from Hong Kong (which were assumed to be collectivistic).

Dekker and colleagues (2008) found that critical incidents within GVTs could be grouped into 14 categories of interaction behaviors that are critical for team performance and satisfaction: media use, handling diversity, interaction volume, in-role behavior, structuring of meetings, reliable interactions, active participation, including team members, communication regarding task progress, extra-role behavior, sharing by the leader, attendance, social–emotional communication, and respectfulness. Among these categories, the importance that team members gave to different categories varied across cultures, suggesting that the particular behaviors viewed as vital for GVT performance are culture specific.

In addition to examining facilitators of effective communication in GVTs, researchers have also examined some barriers. Rutkowski and colleagues (2002) proposed that these barriers can be represented via an "onion skin" model, where the layers (barriers) on the outside of the "onion" need to be cleared before a GVT can move to overcome subsequent layers of barriers. The barriers from the outside inward represent issues related to: motivation, lack of preparation on members' backgrounds, technology, communication habits, level of structure imposition, process differences, cultural diversity, variety of work practices, and lack of agreement on project deliverables and content. McDonough and colleagues (2001) also found that team diversity in national culture background is a barrier to effective communication. Additionally, Cramton and Webber (2005) found that greater geographic dispersion was associated with less effective communication and coordination. Geographic dispersion has also been found to reduce cooperation within GVTs, by increasing the propensity for higher status group members to dominate the group (Metiu, 2006). Also, Levina and Vaast (2008), using a case study, found that status differences based around national and organizational boundaries negatively affected collaboration within GVTs.

Panteli and Davison (2005) examined the role of subgroup formation on GVT communication patterns. In a sample of eight GVTs, they found that colocation and organizational homogeneity facilitated subgroup formation but that subgroup emergence did not have the same effect on team processes in all teams. Teams with high-impact subgroups had a more task-oriented communication style without many social team interactions, which made the development of cohesion and collaboration more complicated. Teams with medium- or low-impact subgroups engaged in more frequent social communications to build familiarity and shared understanding and thus were able to collaborate more effectively.

*Relationship Building*
There is an emerging consensus on the importance of social interaction among GVT members and its impact on GVT processes, emergent states, and outcomes. Getting to know one's GVT peers through social interaction is vitally important because it leads to subsequent communication and collaboration effectiveness (Kayworth & Leidner, 2000; Panteli & Davison, 2005), and to the formation of cohesion, trust, and a common team identity (Jarvenpaa et al., 1998; Panteli & Davison, 2005; Rockett et al., 1998). Maznevski and Chudoba (2000) found that GVTs were more effective when the building of relationships was actively attended to. Based on case studies, Pauleen and Yoong (2001) found that the facilitators of more successful teams focused on relationship building throughout the team's life. In a subsequent study, Pauleen (2003a) found that in high-stress negotiation situations, virtual work is more effective when relationship building has been done FtF.

Given the large amount of research indicating that relationship building is a key success factor in GVTs, it is important to understand how GVTs can foster effective relationships among its members. Among the major determinants of effective relationship building appears to be the number of boundaries the GVT crosses. For example, McDonough and colleagues (2001) found that crossing both cultural and distance barriers made the development of effective interpersonal relationships more challenging in GVTs than in culturally homogenous virtual teams or in FtF teams. Pauleen and Yoong (2001) proposed that when GVTs span more boundaries, they need a proportionately greater extent of relationship building, and should therefore, use richer communication media. Consistent with this suggestion, Maznevski and Chudoba (2000) found that as the level and number of boundaries they crossed increased, effective GVTs spent more time and effort on boundary-spanning activities such as relationship building.

*Feedback*
A significant drawback of the physical separation of GVT members is the challenge that it creates for team feedback processes. For example, Thompson (2000, p. 236) observed that "greater distance tends to block the corrective feedback loops provided by casual encounters" that are typical in FtF teams. Researchers have also observed that though it is more difficult to provide in GVTs, timely feedback is extremely important (e.g., Rutkowski et al., 2002).

*Group Development and Temporal Patterning*

Group development refers to "the patterns of change, growth, or progression of a team to a more mature state as team members interact across multiple contexts to achieve a task over time" (Gluesing et al., 2003, p. 356). Researchers have found that initial conditions at the launch of a GVT affect its subsequent development and outcomes. For example, Munkvold and Zigurs (2007) recommend that in their initial interactions, GVT members should familiarize each other with all team members' background experiences and competencies, define roles/responsibilities, establish guidelines for frequency of communication as well as for communication media to be used, and agree upon intermediate and longer-term milestones and goals.

Not only do GVTs need to be mindful of their start-up conditions to ensure successful team development, they should also pay close attention to team processes during the team's existence. Gluesing and colleagues (2003) argued that a GVT's successful development depends on the ongoing management of positive integration processes throughout the team's life. They propose that the following key integration processes can facilitate GVT development: (1) frequent communication via appropriate media, (2) periodic FtF interactions, (3) establishment of specific language processes to avoid misunderstandings, (4) when necessary, aligning members' perspectives on the team task and work practices, (5) fostering an open line of communication links with individuals outside the team, (6) engaging in frequent task evaluation, and (7) paying attention to disintegrative forces such as unresolved conflict.

Temporal patterning is defined as a set of "rhythms by which teams synchronize or coordinate their activities" (Massey, Montoya-Weiss, & Hung, 2003, p. 132). Similar to Gersick's (1988) observations in FtF teams whose behavioral patterns were set very early in the teams' lives, several studies on GVTs (e.g., Huysman et al., 2003; Jarvenpaa & Leidner, 1999; Rockett et al., 1998) have also found that the behavior patterns that continue throughout the lifecycles of GVTs are generated in their initial communications. A representative example comes from a study by Rockett and colleagues (1998) in which the US members of a GVT failed to attend the crucial first meeting with their European counterparts due to a snowstorm; their absence during this initial meeting established the US members as outsiders in the eyes of their fellow team members, a stigma that the US members were unable to overcome during the team's life.

In contrast to research on traditional teams which finds that teams go through a midpoint transition during which they change their previously established behavioral patterns (Gersick, 1988), researchers have not observed a similar pattern in GVTs. For example, Jarvenpaa and Leidner (1999) found that only 1 GVT out of the 12 cases they examined demonstrated a clear midpoint transition as evidenced by a radical change of communication practices. Similarly, Huysman and colleagues (2003) reported that only one of six GVTs they studied experienced a transition, which involved the unlearning of a stable communication style as a consequence of an approaching deadline. However, this transition did not take place at the midpoint but instead it occurred close to the end of the project. Additionally, Massey and colleagues (2003) found that of the 35 GVTs they studied, the behavior of only 2 teams supported the punctuated equilibrium model. In a study that did produce evidence of a consistent temporal pattern, Maznevski and Chudoba (2000) found that the rhythm of GVTs was very different from that of traditional teams. In their study, the temporal rhythm of GVTs mimicked a "heartbeat," which consisted of several high-intensity FtF meetings altered with longer periods of shorter, less intense virtual interactions. More importantly, they found that GVTs with this sequence of interaction episodes were more successful. Montoya-Weiss and colleagues (2001) provided further evidence of the importance of temporal influences in their study of graduate student GVTs. Specifically, they found that a temporal coordination mechanism, which they define as "a process structure imposed to intervene and direct the pattern, timing, and content of communication in a group" (p. 1252) (e.g., a deadline, setting time limits on tasks), moderated the relationships between five conflict management strategies and performance. In particular, the existence of a temporal coordination mechanism significantly weakened the negative effect of avoidance and compromise behavior on performance, but it did not moderate the relationships between accommodation, competition, or collaboration behavior and performance. Using a similar sample, Massey and colleagues (2003, p. 150) concluded that "temporal coordination mechanisms can influence temporal workflow patterns and GVT interactions, which, in turn, can lead to differential levels of performance."

*Learning, Knowledge, and Team Cognition*
Given that access to the best knowledge and expertise regardless of its location is one of the driving forces behind the use of GVTs, learning and knowledge transfer in GVTs have received considerable research attention. Using seven case studies, Qureshi and Zigurs (2001) found that virtual collaboration technologies give rise to effective knowledge sharing via the creation and maintenance of knowledge networks, such as virtual

communities where individuals, groups, and even organizations have access to each other's resources and recorded information. Huysman and colleagues (2003) observed that over the course of the teams' life, GVT members continued to gain project-related knowledge but ceased to learn about how to use the communication technology after their initial meetings. From a quasi-experiment with South African and US students, Cogburn, Zhang, and Khothule (2002) found that students perceived that working FtF supported their overall learning to a greater extent than working in GVTs and that the South African students rated their experience with GVTs as a learning community as more satisfying and more valuable than did the US students.

Using a combination of case study and survey methodologies, Malhotra and Majchrzak (2004) studied knowledge creation and sharing in 55 GVTs. Successful teams developed explicit communication and knowledge sharing norms such as frequent and decentralized communication. The authors propose four behaviors that enable knowledge sharing and promote knowledge creation in GVTs: make available knowledge within the team accessible, make it clear that knowledge sharing is invaluable, instill a motivation to share knowledge, and ensure integration of this knowledge.

In a study of 96 GVTs, Haas (2006) found that internal knowledge in the teams was increased by both cosmopolitan members (those with extensive global experience) and locals (individuals with experience in one country), and that the cosmopolitan members additionally provided access to knowledge from outside the team. However, in a study of 13 student teams, Cramton (2001) identified several factors that make it difficult for GVTs to develop mutual knowledge, such as difficulties in communicating contextual information, differences in information salience, variation in speed with which information can be accessed, uneven information distribution, and interpretation of nonresponses. These factors were also found to be barriers to trust formation in a study of a large GVT (Henttonen & Blomqvist, 2005).

Baba, Gluesing, Ratner, and Wagner (2004) examined knowledge sharing and cognitive convergence among members of a GVT over a 14-month period. They found that shared cognition improves GVT performance only in situations where teams experience both an increase in cognitive convergence and a decline in divergent knowledge at the same time. The authors found that cognitive convergence was influenced by knowledge sharing, parallel learning processes stemming from shared experiences, discovery of hidden knowledge via knowledge brokering mechanisms such as third party intervention, and alignment of team members' self-interests.

In a two-team case study, Bjørn and Ngwenyama (2009) also investigated shared cognition in GVTs. They found that shared meaning necessitates translucence of communication at three levels: (1) lifeworld (e.g., beliefs, values, and assumptions), (2) organization (e.g., policies, norms), and (3) work practices (e.g., work language). Without translucence, sense making failures at these three levels resulted in communication breakdowns that hurt GVT performance.

In addition to the aspects of knowledge in GVTs discussed in the preceding text, the process of knowledge transfer has also received significant research attention. A series of studies by Sarker and colleagues (Sarker, 2005; Sarker, Sarker, Nicholson, & Joshi, 2005) examined the "4C Framework" (capability, credibility, communication, and culture) of knowledge transfer proposed by Sarker et al. (2003, 2005). Studying 12 GVTs comprised of members from the United States and Norway, Sarker and colleagues (2005) discovered that of the four C's, communication, credibility, and culture, but not capability, have an impact on the extent of knowledge transfer in GVTs. Specifically, they found that members from a more collectivistic culture (Norway), who communicated frequently and were credible (i.e., trustworthy and high performers), were viewed as greater knowledge transferors. Member capability was not a determining factor in the extent of knowledge transfer; the authors suggest that this may be due to the fact that highly capable members are not able to convey their ideas to less capable members in terms they understand. In a second study using US–Thai GVTs, Sarker (2005) found similar results to the US–Norwegian sample, in that communication, credibility, and culture, but not capability, influenced the extent of knowledge transfer in the GVTs. However, in contrast to the earlier findings, this study found that members from the individualistic US culture were perceived as greater knowledge transferors. Sarker (2005) suggests that language may have been a barrier to knowledge transfer for the Thai (collectivist) students.

Oshri, van Fenema, and Kotlarsky (2008) examined the role of transactive memory systems (TMS, which refers to a team-level understanding of who knows what in a team) in knowledge transfer between members of two GVTs. They found that TMS supported the transfer of knowledge between GVT members, but that GVTs experienced problems in building a TMS, due to differences in work practices, skills, and local context between the onsite and offsite locations. The difficulties in developing a TMS caused by these differences were minimized by organizational mechanisms such as standardization of work methodologies and work lingo, frequent tele-conferences, periodic FtF meetings, and rotation of team members. In a study of 38 student GVTs, Yoo and Kanawattanachai (2001) found that a greater amount of communication enabled GVTs to develop a TMS and subsequently a "collective mind." Over time, these team cognition variables had an increasingly positive impact on team performance, whereas the positive effect of team communication on team performance, which was strong early in the teams' life cycle, diminished. In another article on student GVTs, Kanawattanachai and Yoo (2007) examined the development of TMS over time in GVTs as well as its effects on performance. They found that early in the life of the GVTs, task-oriented communication facilitated TMS formation and performance. However, the positive effects of task-oriented communication diminished over time and in its place task–knowledge coordination became more important to team performance. They also found that of the three components of TMS they studied – expertise location, cognition-based trust, and task–knowledge coordination – the former two remained stable after initial formation, but the last one changed over the lifetime of the team.

Two studies investigated the effects of awareness, defined as "knowledge about the current status and actions of the various components in a collaborative system" (Jang, 2009, p. 400), in GVTs. Jang and colleagues (2002) examined the use of a groupware application designed to increase awareness in GVTs, and found that higher levels of awareness positively affected satisfaction with team interaction and information exchange. However, more detailed awareness is not always beneficial for team interaction; instead awareness seems to have a reinforcing effect, where well-functioning teams benefit from and badly functioning teams are hurt by team awareness. In a later study, Jang (2009) found that task interdependence and communication frequency were positively related to awareness and that awareness mediated the relationship between task interdependence and trust.

*Influence and Politics*
In an exploratory study based on interviews of 21 GVT members, Elron and Vigoda-Gadot (2006) found that influence tactics and political processes are more subdued in GVTs than in collocated teams, pointing to a major benefit of GVT dynamics. The authors also found that organizational culture has a direct effect on influence and politics within the GVT. Further, they propose that the relationship between GVT cultural diversity and the use of influence and political processes is mediated by member familiarity, whereas the relationship between GVT communication technology and influence and

political processes is mediated by task orientation and centrality of the GVT as a part of the members' organizational identity.

*Trust*
Trust at the team level is defined by Cummings & Bromiley (1996, p. 303) as "a common belief among a group of individuals that another individual or group makes good faith efforts to behave in accordance with any commitments, is honest in whatever negotiations preceded such commitments, and does not take excessive advantage of another even when the opportunity is available." Trust is important in any type of team because it enhances communication and collaboration (Newell, David, & Chand, 2007), but it may be even more critical in GVTs (Jarvenpaa et al., 1998; Gibson & Manuel, 2003). In fact, O'Hara-Devereaux and Johansen (1994, pp. 243–244) referred to trust as "the glue of the global workspace," while recognizing that "technology doesn't do much to create relationships." Trust is often best developed via FtF exchanges. However, since GVTs mostly communicate via information and communication technologies, the members may never meet FtF, and therefore, trust development may be problematic (Paul et al., 2004). Even worse, the physical distance between team members may lead to psychological distance (Snow et al., 1996), thereby further complicating trust formation. In addition, since trust is a psychological state that tends to emerge after numerous interactions over a considerable period of time, GVTs are often placed at a disadvantage because GVT membership is often dynamic (Paul et al., 2004).

Consistent with these arguments, McDonough and colleagues (2001) found that developing and maintaining trust is more difficult in GVTs than in virtual teams in general or in FtF teams. A case study by Newell et al. (2007) also showed that trust is difficult to develop in a GVT. Even though the organization they examined put forth tremendous effort and resources (such as diffusing organizational norms to all worksites, standardizing technology, delivering cross-cultural training, and allocating funds for FtF meetings) to aid their GVTs, it was not enough to generate high trust among GVT members. In fact, cross-cultural training made cultural differences more salient, fostering an "Us versus Them" (p. 158) attitude that reduced trust. However, FtF meetings helped ease feelings of mistrust.

Several studies have focused on the determinants of trust development in GVTs (e.g., Jarvenpaa et al., 1998; Jarvenpaa & Leidner, 1998, 1999). In their study of the antecedents of trust in GVTs, Jarvenpaa and colleagues (1998) found that team building exercises influenced beliefs about other members' integrity, ability, and benevolence, which all subsequently predicted levels of team trust. They discovered that the antecedents of trust changed over the course of the life of a GVT; in particular, perceptions of integrity and ability as well as propensity to trust were major determinants of trust early on, whereas integrity and benevolence perceptions and trust propensity were key antecedents of trust later during a teams' life. Also, they found that successful GVTs developed "swift" trust (depersonalized, action-based trust between people who have not previously worked together) right at the outset, which spurred an action orientation among their members, which then reciprocally strengthened the level of team trust. Vieira da Cunha and Pina e Cunha (2001) found that the emergence of swift trust fosters improvisation, in that GVTs that developed swift trust had an increased level of successful improvisation compared to GVTs that experienced either low or high trust in general. In their study, the main antecedents of trust were teamwork experience, institutional reputation, and a superordinate goal.

Once trust is formed, whether it is swift trust or trust in general, it seems important to maintain it throughout the team's life cycle. In a study of 36 MBA student GVTs engaged in an 8-week business simulation game, Kanawattanachai and Yoo (2002) found that despite starting with the same levels of trust at the launch of the assignment, the more effective GVTs were better able to sustain trust during the life of the team. However, maintaining trust may not be easy in a virtual environment. Piccoli and Ives (2003) suggest that behavioral control mechanisms (e.g., specification of tasks, rules, and work processes) successfully used in FtF contexts may have a negative impact on trust in virtual contexts such as GVTs because they make members' psychological contract breach, such as failing to meet obligations or reciprocate other members' contributions, more obvious and significant, thereby reducing trust.

Surprisingly, Jarvenpaa and Leidner (1999) found that trust was not related to culture or international experience at the midpoint nor at the end of their study. However, they did find that GVTs experiencing high trust were better at resolving problems and conflict. As compared to low-trust teams, they found that high-trust teams were characterized by frequent social exchanges, an optimistic and enthusiastic dialog, explicit communication about task requirements to minimize task uncertainty, high initiative, predictable communication patterns, timely and detailed feedback, effective rotational leadership, and a transition from an initial procedural orientation to a task orientation. DeSanctis and colleagues (2001) suggested that the discussion of positive feelings and emotions online promotes trust in GVTs.

Based on case study analysis, Baskerville and Nandhakumar (2007) distinguished between personal trust and abstract trust in GVTs, with the former being based on the relationship between individuals and the latter being based on expertise and organizational norms. They found that FtF interactions among GVT members increased personal trust, and that sustaining that trust required periodic FtF interactions. Additionally, abstract trust functioned similarly to personal trust, in that they both fostered effectiveness in GVTs.

In a study of seven GVTs, Jang (2009) found that perceived task interdependence and awareness (of what other teammates are doing or working on) had positive impacts on trust. However, media usage, defined as communication frequency and level of groupware usage, was not associated with team trust. Examining the determinants of trust in a 3-week study of 59 student GVTs, Mockaitis and colleagues (2009) found that teams' mean level of collectivism and task interdependence were positively related to trust, whereas both relationship and task conflict had a negative effect on trust. Surprisingly, they did not find team cultural diversity to be significantly related to perceptions of trust. In contrast, Zolin and colleagues (2004) found that cultural diversity *was* significantly negatively associated with perceived trustworthiness, an effect that became stronger over time.

Zolin and colleagues (2004) also suggest that traditional models of trust should be adapted to account for the global and distributed nature of GVTs. In their study of 108 student dyads from 12 GVTs, they found that follow-through on commitments was the main driver of trust, whereas in traditional contexts, individual performance is an important antecedent. The authors suggest that the reason for this difference may be that project deliverables are more difficult to evaluate in a virtual context. Also, they found that early impressions of trustworthiness positively influenced levels of perceived follow-through on commitments, and that levels of perceived trustworthiness, follow-through, and trust changed little over the course of the 3-month GVT project.

In contrast to the findings of Zolin and colleagues (2004), in a study of a 23-member GVT, Henttonen and Blomqvist (2005) found that the antecedents of trust in a virtual team context were essentially the same as those in an FtF team context. They note that, since team members treated the virtual work environment just as they would FtF teamwork, the GVTs were unable to take advantage of the benefits of virtual work.

Most researchers appear to assume that more trust is better for team processes and outcomes. However, Jarvenpaa, Shaw, and Staples (2004) did not find a significant relationship between trust and task performance, indicating that high levels of trust do not necessarily translate into better GVT performance. They also found that trust had different effects on team outcomes, such as cohesiveness, satisfaction, and perceived project quality, depending on GVT contextual variables such as structure and time. Specifically, they discovered that the impact of trust depended on the structure of the situation, where trust had the strongest positive effect under conditions of weak structure (i.e., high uncertainty and ambiguity) and the weakest influence in strongly structured situations. Also, although trust related directly to team cohesiveness early in the life of a GVT, in later stages it moderated the relationship between communication levels and team cohesiveness, satisfaction, and perceived project quality.

*Cohesiveness*
Cohesiveness is a multidimensional construct that refers to the extent to which team members are interpersonally attracted to each other, have task commitment and group pride, and are motivated to stay in the group (Hamner & Organ, 1978; Mullen & Copper, 1994), and has been linked to important positive processes and outcomes in FtF teams, such as higher group performance (e.g., Gully, Devine, & Whitney, 1995) and increased satisfaction (e.g., Dobbins & Zaccaro, 1986). Cohesion should be equally or more important in a GVT setting. However, there has been very little research on the antecedents or outcomes of cohesion in GVTs. Jarvenpaa and colleagues (1998) found that constructs related to cohesion – a positive team spirit and collective commitment – can increase communication effectiveness in GVTs. Further, in a study of 50 GVTs, Knoll (2000) found that the level of immediacy in a virtual context positively influenced cohesiveness; however, this effect was moderated by the pattern of communication among GVT members, where GVTs with members who communicated equally and in a consistent pattern had higher levels of cohesion.

*Team Identity*
Individuals categorize themselves and the people around them into in-groups and out-groups, based on their perceived similarity to themselves (Tajfel, 1981). A common team identity creates a sense of oneness among team members, in which the team members are classified as the in-group defined by the boundary of the team. Researchers have examined the development, antecedents, and consequences of a common team identity in GVTs. For example, DeSanctis and colleagues (2001) found that higher performing GVTs cultivated a positive group identity online. In contrast,

Rockett and colleagues (1998) found that the GVT members in their study failed to build a team identity because of differences in perceived project goals; they stress the importance of an underlying superordinate goal for developing a strong team identity.

O'Leary and Mortensen (2010) found that GVT configuration affects member identification with the GVT; specifically, they found identification to be lower in teams that had subgroups based in different locations. Shapiro et al. (2002) proposed that creating a salient team identity is more challenging in GVTs because of "the many local demands and related identities facing employees" (p. 457). They propose a model where the main GVT characteristics – national/cultural diversity, electronically mediated communications, and lack of FtF exchanges – have indirect effects on team identity salience via reduced socio-emotional understanding, face visibility, frequency of timely assistance, and feedback.

Walther (1997), in an experimental study of 10 student teams comprised of US and UK members, investigated the effects of individual identity and group identity. He found that long-term group members with a salient group identity received the greatest amount of affection during communication from their partners, were rated highest in social and physical attractiveness, and displayed the greatest degree of academic effort, whereas short-term group members with a salient group identity received the least amount of affection, were appraised as being least socially and physically attractive, and showed the smallest amount of study effort. Compared to those with a salient *team* identity, short-term and long-term members with a salient *individual* identity reported moderate amounts of affection, were perceived as moderate in social and physical attractiveness, and showed a moderate level of academic effort. These findings suggest that focusing on team identity in long-term GVTs is beneficial, that the influence of time on the development of positive relationships in GVTs is hindered when team members have a salient individual identity, and that a salient group identity is not a sufficient condition for perceptions of social attraction or affective communication (Walther, 1997). Walther, Slovacek, and Tidwell (2001) found in a study of 8 GVTs composed of 24 students that although seeing a photograph of one's teammate enhanced affection and social attractiveness in newly formed GVTs without a history of interactions, it had the opposite effect in longer-term, experienced GVTs.

*Other Emergent States*
In addition to trust, cohesion, and team identity, researchers have also examined other emergent states in GVTs, such as psychological safety, team

potency, and team efficacy. Gibson and Gibbs (2006) found that psychological safety moderated the negative effect of national diversity on team innovation, such that the effect was less negative when psychological safety was higher. In a study of 52 student GVTs, Fuller, Hardin, and Davison (2007) found that team potency and collective computer efficacy positively impacted virtual team efficacy, which in turn positively affected team performance. In a similar study, Hardin, Fuller, and Davison (2007) replicated findings of a mediating effect of virtual team efficacy on the relationship between team potency and team outcomes. They also found that culture influences group self-efficacy and virtual team efficacy, such that members of an individualistic culture (United States) reported higher levels of both types of self-efficacy than members of a collectivistic culture (Hong Kong). However, members of both cultures possessed lower levels of self-efficacy regarding virtual teamwork than regarding FtF teamwork. Interestingly, when the referent of efficacy was the collective rather than the self, individuals from the collectivist cultures reported a higher increase in both computer efficacy and virtual team efficacy than did individuals from the individualistic culture.

*GVT Processes: Summary and Future Research*
The discussion in the preceding text illustrates the wide range of team processes and emergent states that have been studied in the context of GVTs. Team processes are vital because GVTs are more prone to process losses than are colocated teams are (Shapiro et al., 2002), and as such, more research is needed on processes within GVTs, and in particular, on how they interact with inputs and with other processes and emergent states to affect outcomes.

The processes that have received the most research attention are communication and collaboration. The research findings suggest that ground rules for communication and behavioral patterns are important for GVT success (e.g., James & Ward, 2001; Kayworth & Leidner, 2000). These rules and patterns tend to emerge at an early stage in the team's life, frequently during the first couple of meetings. After these routines are developed they become ingrained in team processes and are very difficult to change (Huysman et al., 2003). Therefore, it is important to ensure that GVTs develop appropriate rules and patterns that will generate positive team outcomes (Munkvold & Zigurs, 2007). The research questions this raises are: How do GVT members identify and chose among different process options? What can organizations and team leaders do to assist and support GVTs in selecting the right communication routines? And do these routines vary depending on the GVT task, member or organizational cultures, and/or technologies?

Very few of the studies of group development and temporal patterning in GVTs have reported a clear midpoint transition (e.g., Huysman et al., 2003; Jarvenpaa & Leidner, 1999; Massey et al., 2003) as has been found in traditional colocated teams (Gersick, 1988). It is possible that part of the reason for not finding a consistent midpoint transition is that GVTs reduce the ability of team members to take accurate stock of their progress toward a goal. On the other hand, it could be that a midpoint is less meaningful in GVTs because of lower intensity of interactions in the early part of the team's life, compared to those in traditional teams. Another possibility is that a midpoint transition may be challenging for GVTs, with dispersed members of different cultures and in different time zones. These GVT characteristics may make it difficult to coordinate a shift in task focus and adopt new work practices in the middle of a project when the team has reached a steady and acceptable rhythm in its work processes. These and other possibilities should be explored in future research.

The topic of GVT management has been given some attention, but there is still some debate about what constitutes good GVT management (Vieira da Cunha & Pina e Cunha, 2001). As pointed out in the preceding text, there are very few empirical studies that examine this phenomenon, and this is an important area for future research, with direct practical implications. Most of the research offering management implications does so after drawing conclusions in hindsight by comparing the successful teams to the unsuccessful ones in their samples. Little research actually defines or manipulates different management strategies up front. We believe that the time is ripe for more systematic approaches to studying GVT management. Also, since a dynamic environment is a characteristic of GVTs, researchers should investigate the management of changes within GVTs. How do team managers deal with member turnover and organizational, technological, and structural changes that impact the team? What does successful change management within GVTs entail?

Among the processes that could benefit from further study are influence, power, politics, and leader–member exchange (LMX) in GVTs. There is some indication that influence and political strategies are not as prevalent in a virtual environment (Elron & Vigoda-Gadot, 2006), however, it is not apparent how GVT members and leaders/facilitators use political behavior or power to achieve positive processes, emergent states, and outcomes. Also, how do culture and communication technologies shape the way that influence, power, and politics are used and perceived in a GVT context?

As suggested by Kayworth and Leidner (2000): How do GVT members try to favorably shape others' perceptions in a virtual environment? And what are the types and nature of communications that GVT members use to show themselves in a more positive light?

Additional processes in need of future research are decision making and information sharing in GVTs. It is not clear from the literature if GVTs have an advantage or disadvantage when it comes to sharing information and transferring knowledge. There is evidence that knowledge transfer to achieve shared knowledge and TMS is more difficult in GVTs (e.g., Bjørn & Ngwenyama, 2009; Oshri et al., 2008). If information sharing in GVTs is constrained, how can these barriers be overcome? What is the best way to transfer tacit knowledge via technology? How do the acquisition, sharing, and integration of knowledge take place in GVTs? Does the amount, process, or quality of knowledge transfer vary, based on the type of GVT, the culture of the GVT members, the technologies used, or the life cycle stage of the GVT? Finally, "how is knowledge best transferred from one globally dispersed virtual team to another?" (Jarvenpaa & Leidner, 1999, p. 813). These issues should be addressed by future research. Furthermore, if there is less information sharing among GVT members, then the probability of group decision-making pitfalls such as the common knowledge problem or hidden profile effects may be greater than in colocated FtF teams.

In contrast, some researchers (e.g.,Townsend, DeMarie, & Hendrickson 1998; Qureshi & Zigurs, 2001) have suggested that collaborative technology in teams may promote member knowledge sharing and participation in decision making, which would suggest that the virtualness of a GVT could enhance information sharing and decision making. The mechanisms through which the communication and collaboration technologies used by GVTs facilitate information and knowledge sharing need to be examined further in future research. Also, the impact of different communication technologies on decision-making process and quality should be examined.

GVT tasks often are international in nature and "strategically important and highly complex" (Maznevski & Chudoba, 2000, p. 473). Because of their complexity, such tasks require varying skills and expertise in different stages of the GVT project's life. Therefore, GVT membership can be dynamic as experts are brought in as needed at various points in the life of a GVT (Carmel, 1999; Gibson & Gibbs, 2006; Harvey et al., 2004). When GVTs are faced with changing membership, new team members need to be brought up to speed as quickly as possible to reach their full potential before being assigned to new teams. For this reason, it is important to understand how GVTs can effectively and quickly socialize their new members.

Harvey et al. (2004) suggest that individualized socialization programs for new GVT members may be in order, an approach that may substantially deviate from most traditional organizational socialization strategies. Without in-person contact, how do team members get socialized and how can organizations design a successful socialization program for new entrants into GVTs? Also, how are norms developed and maintained in a GVT? These are interesting questions that can illuminate the social dynamics of GVTs.

*GVT Emergent States: Summary and Future Research*
Although GVT emergent states in general have not been studied as much as GVT processes, trust is an exception. The findings suggest that trust is more difficult to achieve in GVTs than in virtual teams or colocated teams (e.g., McDonough et al., 2001; Newell et al., 2007; Paul et al., 2004), but that GVTs can develop swift trust which has a positive influence on decision processes (e.g., Jarvenpaa et al., 1998) and improvisation (Vieira da Cunha & Pina e Cunha, 2001). Also, the formation of a common team identity has positive effects on performance (DeSanctis et al., 2001), and in the long-term, on communication, affection, ratings of attractiveness, and academic effort (Walther, 1997).

Many authors agree that a shared team identity leads to positive GVT processes and outcomes (DeSanctis et al., 2001; Shapiro et al., 2002). The challenge, however, is understanding how to build cohesion and a strong team identity in a global virtual environment, across distance and differences, and this is an issue that should be looked at in more depth in future research. In addition, researchers should also examine team member identification in GVTs. Identification has been proposed to be "a 'critical glue' in virtual environments" (Ashforth, Harrison, & Corley, 2008, p. 326; Wiesenfeld, Raghuram, & Garud, 1999, p. 777; Fiol & O'Connor, 2005; Pratt, 2001). Yet the antecedents, form, and consequences of identification have not been the focus of research on GVTs. Given its potential importance, research on identification in GVTs promises to generate interesting theoretical insights as well as practical guidelines for managing GVTs.

Collective cognition, team mental models, and TMS have been examined extensively in research on traditional teams (e.g., Moreland, 1999; Smith-Jentsch, Campbell, Milanovich, & Reynolds, 2001), but surprisingly little research has examined these concepts in the context of GVTs, save for some notable exceptions (e.g., Kanawattanachai & Yoo, 2007; O'Leary & Mortensen, 2010; Oshri et al., 2008). A team mental model is an emergent cognitive state that represents team members' organized understanding of their task environment (e.g., Klimoski & Mohammed, 1994). Mental models are important because they are associated with increased performance and better team processes (Marks, Zaccaro, & Mathieu, 2000; Mathieu, Heffner, Goodwin, Salas, & Cannon-Bowers, 2000). They may be particularly useful to GVTs given the challenges of working across differences and distance, and for the same reason, they are likely more difficult to develop. Future research on GVTs would do well to further investigate these important team emergent cognitive states.

In contrast to conventional global teams, which have the advantage of FtF interactions, GVTs generally lack a shared collaborative culture (Harvey et al., 2004). This brings up the question: How does culture manifest itself in GVTs? Some have argued (e.g., Earley & Gibson, 2002, p. 44) that nonvirtual multinational teams create hybrid cultures – "an emergent and simplified set of rules and actions, work capability expectations, and member perceptions that individuals within a team develop, share, and enact after interactions." These authors propose that in a multinational context, the creation of a team culture is critical because teams with strong team cultures are most effective. Do hybrid cultures emerge in GVTs and how can they achieve and successfully maintain this culture so that it yields positive team outcomes such as higher performance and satisfaction? Also, is creating a strong GVT culture even a worthwhile undertaking given the fact that GVTs have a frequently changing composition and often are not permanent?

Interestingly, most of the research on GVT mediators has focused on what may be called active aspects of a GVT, such as conflict management, communication, trust development, and building of shared identity. However, given the geographic dispersion and low media richness confronting GVTs, it might be insightful to examine more passive aspects of GVT functioning such as ignoring members who do not make themselves salient in virtual interactions, not engaging others in the team, and letting issues remain unresolved. We propose the notion of *GVT dormancy*, which captures various aspects of passivity in GVTs due to geographic dispersion and technology intermediation, as an area for future research on GVTs.

## GVT Outputs

Team outputs or outcomes are the end results of a team's work. The two main outcome factors examined within the GVT literature are performance/ effectiveness and satisfaction, however, other outcomes have also received some research attention.

*Performance/Effectiveness*

As with the research on teams in general, the team outcome that has been researched the most within GVTs is team performance/effectiveness, which is the extent to which the team meets standards of quantity, quality, and timeliness of task outputs that the team was assembled to achieve. Overall, although there is evidence that greater globalness and/or virtualness may reduce team performance, there are several direct and contingent influences accounting for variance in GVT performance. We first discuss the influence of input factors on GVT performance and then discuss the impacts of team processes and emergent states.

Cramton and Webber (2005) found that greater geographical dispersion of a GVT is associated with lower team performance. Similarly, McDonough and colleagues (2001) found that the mean performance level of FtF teams in their sample was statistically greater than that of virtual teams, which in turn was statistically greater than that of GVTs.

The preceding studies suggest that being dispersed has harmful effects on GVT performance. In contrast, in a study of 1,269 Intel employees, Chudoba and colleagues (2005) did not find that to be the case. Defining team virtualness as being composed of team distribution, workplace mobility, and variety of work practices, they found that the team distribution component (i.e., teams consisting of members who work across time zones, different countries, and via communication technology) itself was not significantly related to perceived team performance in terms of trust, communication, coordination, commitment, quality, and timeliness of team deliverables. They speculate that this may be because the advantages and disadvantages of team distribution may have influenced team performance equally, yielding a null result, or because team members had developed skills and/or communication patterns to overcome barriers related to working with distributed members. However, they found that variety of practices (i.e., teams with variety of cultural and work processes) significantly negatively influenced team performance as did team mobility (i.e., teams with members that work outside the regular office context), though the latter was marginally significant. Finally, work practice predictability and social interaction had significant positive effects on team performance.

From a case study of one GVT, James and Ward (2001) identified the following success factors for GVT performance: shared leadership and shared responsibility among team members, development of effective work patterns, appropriate training throughout the teams' development, and active management of the changing project scope. In a study of nine

US–Taiwan GVTs, Chen and colleagues (2007) found that group decision outcomes were enhanced when training was given on creative problem solving as well as on the collaborative software used by the team.

Massey and colleagues (2001a) deduced from their case studies that the degree of diversity in national culture in a GVT affected perceptions of team performance, such that culturally diverse GVTs were perceived to have lower performance than culturally homogenous teams. However, an exploratory study by Shachaf (2008) found that cultural diversity had a positive influence on team effectiveness by enhancing decision making via the leveraging of diverse skills and knowledge. Additionally, Haas (2006) found that a mix of cosmopolitan and local members increased GVT performance.

In a study of 55 student dyads from the United States and Turkey, Swigger, Alpaslan, Brazile, and Monticino (2004) reported that a dyad's cultural make up measured by the Cultural Perspectives Questionnaire (CPQ, Maznevski, 1994) was significantly related to dyad performance (programming accuracy, efficiency, completeness, and style). In particular, they found that certain combinations of cultural attributes between the members resulted in higher (e.g., when at least one member scored high on the "harmony" dimension) or lower performance (e.g., when both members scored high on the "hierarchical" and/or low on the "future oriented" dimension). Rutkowski et al. (2007) found that teams' average score on the cognitive absorption dimension of focus immersion was significantly positively related to team performance, whereas the other cognitive absorption dimension – temporal dissociation – was not related to GVT performance.

Maznevski and Chudoba (2000) compared the effectiveness of three GVTs that differed on three structural characteristics: task, composition, and team tenure. They found that within interaction incidents, GVT effectiveness was determined by a fit between the decision process required, the complexity of the message, and the selected form of interaction (the medium and the interaction incident's duration), such that as the level of decision process and thus message complexity increased, there was a commensurate need to increase the richness of the communication technology and the duration of the interaction.

Several processes have been found to impact GVT effectiveness. McDonough and colleagues (2001) demonstrated that the extent to which the teams in their study faced behavioral challenges (e.g., trust, communication, and interpersonal relationships) was not significantly related to performance; however, project management challenges (e.g., scheduling and budgeting) did have a significant negative effect on performance.

Forester, Thoms, and Pinto (2007) investigated goal setting in 12 GVTs of a single company and found that setting goals and committing to these goals had implications for perceptions of GVT performance. In particular, they found that quality of goal setting and goal commitment were related to perceived project success, whereas only goal commitment was related to members' satisfaction with the project. Using a sample of 24 student software development teams, Edwards and Shridhar's (2005) analyses at the individual level indicated that trust, but not project structure, was positively related to project quality in GVTs.

Paul and colleagues (2004, 2005) found that a collaborative conflict management style has a positive influence on GVT performance, which was measured as satisfaction with the decision-making process, perceived decision quality, perceived participation, and group agreement. Montoya-Weiss and colleagues (2001) empirically demonstrated that an avoidance or compromising conflict-handling style had a significant negative effect, a competition and collaboration style had a significant positive effect, and an accommodation style had no effect on GVT performance. They also showed that a temporal coordination mechanism moderated two of the aforementioned relationships by weakening the negative relationships between avoidance and compromise conflict management behaviors and team performance.

Massey and colleagues (2003) found that the successful development of temporal coordination mechanisms generated interaction behavior patterns that resulted in greater GVT performance, which was defined as the quality (comprised of range, depth, and organization) of the team rationale used to support the team decision. Similarly, DeSanctis and colleagues (2001) found that depth and focus of communication, but not its frequency, was related to higher performance in GVTs. They also found that sharing personal information to build a positive team identity and developing routines for collaboration were associated with higher GVT performance. Similarly, Saphiere (1996) found that more social communication, effective discussion of issues, and effective bridging of cultural differences resulted in greater GVT effectiveness.

Knowledge sharing is important for GVTs in that it increases shared cognition among team members, thereby improving GVT performance (Baba et al., 2004). This is in line with findings by Yoo and Kanawattanachai (2001) that the amount of communication was positively related to GVT task performance early on, but that the team cognitive constructs of TMS and subsequently collective mind positively influenced performance later in the teams' life. Interestingly, Panteli and Davison (2005) did not find a negative effect of subgroup formation on team performance, suggesting that subgroup formation does not always harm GVTs performance. Kanawattanachai and Yoo (2002) found that the formation of cognition-based swift trust, but not of affect-based swift trust, was positively related to GVT performance. Finally, Fuller et al. (2007) found that virtual team efficacy positively affected both objective and subjective team performance.

*Satisfaction*
In a quasi-experimental study of GVTs and FtF teams consisting of graduate students from two US and South African universities, Cogburn and colleagues (2002) found that group mode (GVT or FtF) and leadership style (relationship- or task-focused) did not have a significant effect on student satisfaction. However, geographic location and the presence of a faculty member did. Specifically, South African students reported greater levels of satisfaction than the US students, and students in both countries were more satisfied when a faculty member was physically present than when the faculty member resided in a remote location. Bradner and colleagues (2005) found that members of smaller GVTs were more satisfied and committed than members of larger GVTs. Also, an exploratory study of 24 GVTs by Edwards and Sridhar (2005) indicated that higher levels of trust and project structure increased members' learning effectiveness and satisfaction with the virtual project experience.

*Creativity and Innovation*
Although cultural and national diversity has the potential to enhance creativity and innovation in GVTs, these outcomes have received hardly any research attention thus far. A notable exception is a study by Gibson and Gibbs (2006) of 70 GVTs composed of 443 employees from 18 countries, which found that national diversity and geographic dispersion in a GVT had negative effects on team innovation, but that the effects were less negative among GVTs that had established a more psychologically safe team environment. Another exception is a study by Martins and Shalley (in press) using two-person short-term graduate student teams working on human resource management tasks. They found that national differences had a strong negative effect on team creativity, which was attenuated when there was greater equality of experience between team members in using virtual working technologies, but was not reduced by process factors such as equality of participation and establishment of rapport between team members.

*Improvisation*
In an in-depth study of a global new product development team, Vieira da Cunha and Pina e Cunha (2001) investigated team improvisation and identified three guiding principles for achieving greater improvisation, based on paradoxes that exist in GVTs: plan to adapt and change, balance structure and freedom, and use pressure and urgency to foster creativity. The first principle is based on their finding that when a GVT defined a plan as "a resource to be adapted at will, rather than a prescription to be carried out" (p. 341), improvisation was successful. The second principle is based on their finding that independence goes hand in hand with control such that the most successful improvisations happened when a well-defined, time-bound goal existed in combination with a culture of experimentation. The third principle is based on their finding that the most creative improvisations in the GVT took place during high-intensity (in terms of significance, complexity, and urgency) events, that is, the GVT needed some pressure to foster creativity, but too little or too much pressure resulted in lower levels of improvisation.

*GVT Outputs: Summary and Future Research*
As is evident from the discussion in the preceding text, most of the research on GVT outcomes has focused on GVT performance, with a few studies focusing on other outcomes such as satisfaction and creativity. A wide range of factors has been found to affect GVT performance, including conflict management style (Montoya-Weiss et al., 2001; Paul et al., 2004), project management challenges (McDonough et al., 2001), depth of communication (DeSanctis et al., 2001), goal setting (Forester et al., 2007), cultural diversity (e.g., Massey et al., 2001a), geographical distance (Cramton & Webber, 2005), trust (Edwards & Sridhar, 2005), virtual team efficacy (Fuller et al., 2007), team virtualness (Chudoba et al., 2005), team cognition (Yoo & Kanawattanachai, 2001), and temporal patterns (Maznevski & Chudoba, 2000). Although the dominance of team performance as an outcome variable is understandable, future research could expand the set of GVT outcomes studied to focus on other team outcomes.

For example, little research has been conducted on the attitudinal outcomes of GVTs such as team satisfaction, commitment, and viability. This may be related to the often temporary status of GVTs where members transfer to different teams after the task is completed, and therefore. satisfaction and team viability may not be considered to be important. It could also be a consequence of the preponderance of use of student teams in the literature on GVTs; these teams are usually constituted for one task and team members are unlikely to work together again. A related team outcome that has not yet been widely studied in a GVT context is commitment. Commitment "reflects an individual's feeling of identification with and attachment to the group's or organization's goals or tasks" (Bettenhausen, 1991, p. 364). What factors affect a GVT member's commitment to the team, and how can these factors be manipulated to generate high team commitment among GVT members? Do commitment and the ways it develops within GVTs vary across cultures?

In terms of the content of team outputs, there is growing research interest in examining GVT creativity and innovation. This focus coincides well with the increased importance paid to innovation and creativity by companies, as well as with the fact that one goal of using GVTs is to increase innovation and creativity by utilizing diverse perspectives represented by members from various locations of the organization and the globe. Working across nationalities using virtual communication media on creative tasks is challenging (Martins & Shalley, in press), but prior research on diversity suggests that if effective working relationships are established, a GVT should be able to leverage its cognitive variety to enhance its innovation and creativity. Training in creative problem solving may be beneficial to the creativity of GVTs (Chen et al., 2007); other factors that researchers have found to affect creativity in traditional teams should also be examined in GVTs in future research. Related to innovation and creativity, future research should also examine knowledge creation as a GVT outcome (Prasad and Akhilesh, 2002).

## *GVT Outputs → Inputs*

The final link in the cyclical IMOI model of teams presented by Ilgen and colleagues (2005) is made up of the effects of team outputs or outcomes on future team inputs. On this topic, the literature on GVTs is practically silent. For example, it is not known how prior experiences in global virtual teaming affect individuals' abilities and motivations as members of subsequent GVTs. Also, although the practitioner literature has sought to develop and implement best practices (ostensibly based on prior experience), researchers have not systematically examined how GVT outcomes are factored into the design and management of future GVTs within organizations. When individuals have experience working in GVTs they may be better equipped with KSAs such as cultural sensitivity and awareness of the opportunities and pitfalls of working virtually, which may enhance their performance in their next GVT assignment. However, if and under what circumstances such KSAs are developed and transferred to subsequent GVT assignments remains an empirical question.

Several other interesting avenues exist for conducting research on feedback effects of GVT outputs on inputs. For example, as GVTs become more global (i.e., increased variety in represented countries, cultures, languages, and time zones) it becomes increasingly important for GVT members to develop the right mindset about working in GVTs. The literature on international business suggests that people vary in the mentality they hold about working with people from different countries and cultures. For example, Bartlett and Ghoshal (1989) discussed different mentalities accompanying different stages of the internationalization of multinational corporations (international, multinational, global, and transnational mentalities), whereas Perlmutter (1969) proposed three mindsets in managing a multinational enterprise (ethnocentric, polycentric, and geocentric). These same mentalities could relate to team members' mindsets about global teamwork. Essentially, as GVTs develop and members get more exposure to working in GVTs, they may take on different mentalities related to their global work, which has implications for GVT processes and outcomes.

At one end of the spectrum, an international mentality basically views the GVT members belonging to the domestic home office as the dominant party; in this case, instructions and decisions are transferred from the domestic members to foreign members. This is similar to an ethnocentric approach that treats everything from the home office's domestic culture as superior, and shows lower regard for ideas, values, and input of members of foreign cultures. On the opposite side lies a transnational or geocentric orientation in which GVT members integrate all the resources at their disposal regardless of country, culture, or position within the team, thereby capitalizing on their diversity (Estienne, 1997). This global mindset is marked by a high appreciation for diverse perspectives of foreign members and by the ability to adapt to working with different cultures (Levy, Beechler, Taylor, & Boyacigiller, 2007). The development of a global mindset by GVT members, through their experience with working on GVTs, should enhance the enabling conditions and reduce barriers to GVT effectiveness. Similarly, working on GVTs should provide members with greater familiarity with virtual working technologies (Harvey et al., 2004), which could enhance their ability to perform well in future assignments in nationally diverse virtual teams (Martins & Shalley, in press). Also, experience in working in GVTs should increase team efficacy in future

GVT assignments, which research suggests should result in higher team performance (Fuller et al., 2007).

# GLOBALNESS, VIRTUALNESS, AND TEAMNESS IN GVT RESEARCH

Our review of the literature on GVTs indicates that a tremendous amount of progress has been made in advancing our understanding of the opportunities and challenges presented by GVTs. As happens in most literatures, some aspects of GVTs have received greater research attention than others. Over time, the GVT literature has progressed from simple designs and questions to more complex models of GVT functioning and outcomes. In this section, we discuss how the literature has addressed the three components of our definition of GVTs – globalness, virtualness, and teamness. In addition to assessing existing research in this regard, we also point out avenues for future research within each component.

## *Globalness*

Globalness has been treated variously within the literature on GVTs, with very little convergence on what exactly "global" means. In our definition of GVTs in the preceding text, we proposed that GVTs lie on a continuum of globalness such that a team can be described as more or less global. The level of globalness depends on several factors, such as the number and variety of countries, cultures and cultural value orientations, languages, and geographic locations represented in the team. There is considerable variance in how these aspects of globalness have been treated in the GVT literature. For example, there is extensive research on nationality differences and cultural differences in GVTs (discussed in the subsection Individual-Level Inputs), but not very much research on language differences and variation in geographic location. However, even within the aspects of globalness that have been studied extensively, there remain several opportunities for additional research as well as for improvements in operationalizations of and theorizing on the dimensions.

### *Countries*
In terms of the extent of globalization, teams can be characterized along a continuum ranging from purely domestic (one country), to cross-national or

international (two or more countries), to multinational (three or more countries). Although there is little debate about the continuum itself, pinpointing where along the continuum a team becomes "global" has turned out to be tricky. For example, some authors use the term GVT but use participants from only two nationalities (e.g., Huysman et al., 2003; Massey et al., 2003), whereas others have used members from three or more countries (e.g., Mockaitis et al., 2009; Rutkowski et al. (2007).

Furthermore, what the argument about the number of countries needed to consider a team global does not take into account adequately is that a team with members from three countries with similar cultures and in close proximity may face less of a globalness challenge than a team with members from two countries that are geographically far apart and have very different cultures. The GVT literature has done a good job of capturing the challenges of globalness in the samples that have been used to test hypotheses, in that a large number of the studies have used GVTs that span long distances and very different cultures (e.g., United States and India). Among the studies that have reported the nationalities of GVT members in their samples, the modal number of countries represented in the GVTs studied has been two, with a sizeable number of studies using three-country GVTs. A few studies (e.g., Mockaitis et al., 2009) have used GVTs with more than three countries represented.

The number of countries represented in a GVT certainly affects its extent of globalness, but so does the variety of countries. Thus far, researchers have equated country differences to differences in culture or input factor costs, such as labor costs. However, countries differ on many different dimensions, such as political, regulatory, and socioeconomic characteristics, and these characteristics should be taken into account in theorizing on how variety of countries in a GVT affects team functioning and outcomes.

*Cultures and Cultural Value Orientations*
Research suggests that although there is variance in cultural values across countries, individual members within a country can also vary significantly on cultural values and may not represent their country's dominant cultural value set (Hofstede, 1980). However, there has been a tendency within the empirical literature on GVTs to equate nationality with cultural orientation, by making implicit or explicit assumptions that individuals from a particular country are homogeneous in cultural values. Several of the studies (e.g., Reinig & Mejias, 2004; Sarker, 2005) appear to assume that GVTs with members from countries that are dissimilar on several cultural dimensions (e.g., individualism–collectivism, uncertainty avoidance,

masculinity–femininity) according to research by Hofstede (1980), are in fact diverse in cultural value orientations. They, thereby, assume that the values of individual GVT members are representative of their native countries' cultural values. As a consequence, GVTs may be actually more or less culturally diverse than the researchers may have assumed.

Another common assumption about cultural values is that geographical location equates to a certain set of cultural value orientations. For example, in an experiment using students in the United States and India conducted by Paul and colleagues (2004), the experimental conditions were ostensibly based on the teams' cultural homogeneity (i.e., GVTs with US *or* Indian members only) and cultural heterogeneity (i.e., GVTs with a mix of US *and* Indian members). The authors state that "all students enrolled at the US institution were considered 'US' whereas the students enrolled at the Indian institution were 'Indian'" (pp. 308–309) regardless of students' national origin and/or cultural value orientations. This categorization does not take into consideration the fact that some of the students at the US university may in fact have been of Indian nationality, may have identified more with the Indian culture, or have cultural value orientations that are more in line with average Indian values rather than average US cultural values.

As is obvious from the examples in the preceding text, the conclusions about the functioning of cultural differences in GVTs, which are drawn from studies that assume rather than measure cultural values of GVT members, have the potential to be erroneous. It is, therefore, necessary to measure each member's cultural values and/or cultural and country identification before drawing conclusions about relationships related to cultural values or cultural heterogeneity in GVTs. This will help to tease out the effects that culture truly has on GVT functioning.

*Languages*
Language has been a critical barrier to effective communication in cross-cultural interactions since time immemorial. Yet, surprisingly, it has not been examined very systematically as an input variable in research on GVTs. As the number of native languages of GVT members increases, the level of globalness could also increase. Although most studies do not report the language in which GVT members interacted, it appears that the majority of studies utilized English as the language of the GVTs in their samples. Among the few studies that have addressed language in a GVT (e.g., Kayworth & Leidner, 2000; Overholt, 2002), the focus has been on English language proficiency.

The greater the variance in GVT members' proficiency in a common language, the greater is its globalness. However, how this dimension of globalness operates within a GVT is far from well understood. The issue of language proficiency is predominantly seen as an issue of effective communication. However, differences in language proficiency could also affect power and status within a GVT. For example, in a GVT in which the common language is English, group members from English-speaking countries may enjoy greater power and status over members who are not native English speakers, simply due to their greater proficiency in the language. In such teams, some nonnative English speakers may be hesitant to offer suggestions because they have greater difficulty expressing their thoughts in English.

The predominance of English as the common language in research on GVTs to date also has implications for our understanding of language as a dimension of globalness. Each language is constrained by its own rules, assumptions, expressions, etc., thus affecting how thoughts are expressed. Additional research that is based on samples in which languages other than English are the dominant languages in the GVTs, would enrich our understanding of language as an aspect of GVT globalness. Going further, researchers could also examine how various combinations of languages affect GVT dynamics. Moreover, even when studying teams in which English is the common team language, it would be interesting to examine hidden language barriers facing GVT members from different English-speaking countries (e.g., United States, Ireland, South Africa, Jamaica, India, etc.). Although members of such GVTs may assume that they all speak the same language, there are significant differences in the versions of English used in various English-speaking countries, which can cause communication difficulties and misunderstandings.

*Geographic Locations*

Geographic location as an aspect of GVTs has taken many forms in the literature. A major element of global location within GVTs is the geographic dispersion of team members across time zones. The greater the extent to which a GVT has to work across multiple time zones, the greater its globalness. Thus, for example, a GVT composed of members from multiple countries and cultures, but which operate in the same location and/or time zone (e.g., as is sometimes the case in extant studies of student teams), is less global than a GVT composed of members located in several time zones. Time zone differences affect the extent of overlap in work hours of GVT members, thus affecting the team's interactions and project structure such as meetings and deadlines.

Due to recent trends toward global outsourcing, there is a location-based distinction made between "onshore/onsite" and "offshore/offsite" members of a GVT (e.g., David et al., 2008; Newell et al., 2007; Oshri et al., 2008). Often, the offshore workforce is located in countries with low labor costs, in contrast to the onshore workforce that is located in richer countries. Furthermore, GVTs composed of onshore and offshore members are often connected by a small number of individuals who perform the roles of connectors across the two subgroups. Such teams present an interesting new context in which to examine GVTs, one in which the dynamics of subgroups, social networks, and power can be examined to good effect.

The configuration of global locations represented in a GVT also has significant implications for team functioning, but has not been focused on much in the literature. Polzer and colleagues (2006) provided evidence of location-based faultlines in GVTs, especially when the subgroups within a location were of the same nationality. Similarly, O'Leary and Mortensen (2010) found that the configuration of a GVT (i.e., whether the team was collocated, distributed with one isolate member, imbalanced in terms of unequally sized subgroups in the two locations, and balanced in terms of equal subgroup size in the two locations) had a powerful impact on the team's functioning. Also, in their analysis of three case studies, Gluesing et al. (2003) note the power struggles that can result when members of a GVT are clustered in two locations instead of being geographically scattered, and observe that these negative dynamics are exacerbated when the locations also differ on other dimensions such as organizational function, thereby creating a deep faultline. Other aspects of GVT locational configurations that need to be examined in future research include the location of GVT members relative to the power center of the organization (e.g., distance from company headquarters), the experiences of sole members in remote locations, and the geographic location of the team leader. Additionally, researchers could treat location as a dimension of GVT diversity, as done by Polzer and colleagues (2006), and draw on established research on the configuration of diversity in teams (e.g., Kanter, 1977) to examine the effects of various GVT compositions.

## Virtualness

Of the three dimensions of the definition of GVTs, virtualness has clearly received the most research attention. Much of this research focuses on choice of technologies, characteristics of technologies, and effects of technologies used in GVTs (see discussion of organizational-level inputs in the preceding text). Several researchers have argued that every team in organizations today can be characterized as more or less virtual, since even within supposedly FtF teams, members tend to use email, the phone, instant messaging, and other virtual working technologies in the course of working together (e.g., Bell & Kozlowski, 2002; Kirkman & Mathieu, 2005; Martins et al., 2004). Despite the calls of these researchers for conceptualizing virtualness as a dimension of teams, as with the virtual team literature in general (e.g., see Kirkman et al., in press), researchers examining GVTs continue to compare teams that work FtF to those that work via electronic media. Here we reiterate the call of these researchers and propose that it is important to examine not *if* but *how* and under what circumstances a GVT's virtualness affects team processes or outcomes. This is particularly important for GVTs because their globalness implies that an FtF GVT is very rare in organizations, and therefore, we may be drawing conclusions from contrived experimental situations that do not generalize well to organizations.

Kirkman and Mathieu (2005) proposed that the extent of virtualness of a team depends on: when team members work together (i.e., the extent of synchronicity), how they work together (i.e., the richness of the media used and the level of informational value that the tools provide), and how much of the work is accomplished via technology (i.e., the percentage of the work done via technology, often measured as the ratio of FtF versus virtual meetings). Teams are more virtual as their interactions are asynchronous, the electronic tools are low in richness and informational value, and the proportion of work done via technology is high, while the ratio of FtF to virtual meetings is low (Kirkman & Mathieu, 2005). Given that GVTs are a subset of virtual teams, these dimensions apply well to GVTs. However, there may be nuances to each of these dimensions caused by the globalness of GVTs that need to be factored into future research.

*Synchronicity*
Although virtual teams in general differ on synchronicity of interaction due to the nature of technologies used to communicate (e.g., email is asynchronous, whereas a phone conversation is synchronous), GVTs potentially face the added challenge of asynchronicity caused by the geographic dispersion of team members across time zones. For example, for a GVT with members in San Francisco, Bangalore, and Sydney, the challenges to synchronous interaction are qualitatively different than those facing a virtual team with members in San Francisco, Chicago, and

Atlanta even though the number of time zones represented in both teams is the same.

For widely dispersed GVTs, the window of overlap of the working hours of team members in various locations is narrow or nonexistent, leading to a larger proportion of asynchronous work (e.g., Harvey et al., 2004). Asychronicity in such a circumstance involves long stretches in which individual members or locational subgroups work in isolation, punctuated by occasional structured synchronous meetings. In essence, it is very unlikely that a spontaneous synchronous meeting can occur in most widely dispersed GVTs. How this affects monitoring and backup behavior as well as other team processes related to synchronicity of interactions in a GVT is indeed an interesting question in need of research. Furthermore, given the narrow to nonexistent natural overlaps in working hours in widely dispersed GVTs, issues of power and justice can easily be tied into the scheduling of synchronous interactions. For example, what are the effects of always scheduling whole-GVT conference calls during the team leader's normal workday versus rotating the timing of the call to fit within each team member's normal workday? Also, as team members are forced to work late hours or take calls during what would normally be nonwork hours to enable synchronous communications in a GVT, what effects to these arrangements have on the long-term work–life balance, well being, and attitudes of team members?

*Media and Information Richness*
The influence of technology on GVT processes and outcomes have been well examined (e.g., DeSanctis et al., 2001; Kayworth & Leidner, 2000), as have the antecedents of technology choice and use (e.g., Massey et al., 2001a; Pauleen & Yoong, 2001). However, there are some inconsistencies in the findings to date. For example, a study by Riopelle and colleagues (2003) found that when the task environment changed, GVTs adopted different technologies to fit the new task environment. In contrast, there is evidence that GVTs do not easily change their technology selection and use (Huysman et al., 2003). Therefore, we still do not know exactly how GVTs decide what technologies to use and when to change their use of communication technologies.

Another interesting question relates to how technologies and their uses vary across cultures. There is growing evidence that the choice of communication channels may be affected by national and organizational cultural dispositions toward communication (Massey et al., 2001a; Pauleen, 2003a) and the role of technology in society and business (Riopelle et al., 2003). Massey and colleagues (2001a) found cultural effects on perceptions of and preferences for the Lotus Notes® groupware. Would these relationships hold if a different communication technology or a different GVT task were used? Follow-up to this research should address the following questions in more detail: To what extent do people of different cultures have a preference for different communication technologies? What cultural values determine the choice and use of communication channels? Do people of different cultures use communication technologies in different ways? Future studies could also look at the evolution of media choices made by GVT members over time because they may change as the members' level of familiarity with the technologies and with each other increases.

*FtF Interaction*

There are several ways in which FtF interactions in GVTs may be understood. One obvious element is the proportion of FtF interaction relative to virtual interaction, which has been used as a measure of virtualness in prior research on virtual teams. The literature, however, does not do a good job of clearly accounting for the meaning of various points on this continuum. Does 40% FtF interaction have twice the effects of 20% FtF interaction? Is the difference between no FtF and 10% FtF qualitatively different from the difference between 10% FtF and 20% FtF? In fact, given their greater geographic dispersion, GVTs face a higher likelihood that members may never meet FtF; an interesting question that this raises is: How does the possibility of never meeting other members of a GVT affect an individual's behavior in and attitudes toward the team and the task?

The extent of globalness of GVTs may create other unique issues related to FtF interactions. For example, do GVT members from high-context cultures place greater value on FtF interactions than do members from low-context cultures? Overholt (2002) reported that foreign members of GVTs were more comfortable participating in team meetings when typing rather than speaking in English, due to their greater proficiency in written English. This finding suggests implications for either training in language skills or for a mix of technologies to enable more equal participation across GVT members, which can be tested in future research. Similarly, Uber Grosse (2002) suggested that email as a communication medium provides a psychologically safe context where questions can be asked without embarrassment or losing face. A testable implication of this is that GVT members of cultures where losing face is a serious concern may eschew bringing up risky questions in FtF interactions during which major decisions on GVT tasks are made, thus reducing their influence on team functioning unless email channels are utilized as well. These and other questions linking GVT members' cultural values and preferences to the utilization and outcomes of various FtF and non-FtF processes within GVTs promise interesting and useful findings in future research.

Additionally, the timing of FtF interactions in a GVT is a critical question of both theoretical and practical importance. For example, FtF interaction early in the life of a GVT has been found to be beneficial for the functioning and outcomes of the team (e.g., Pauleen, 2003a; Uber Grosse, 2002). However, the effects of later FtF interactions within the GVT are a lot less clear. Also, although most of the extant studies have focused on whole-team FtF meetings, there are certain circumstances in which some GVT members meet FtF, while others do not. The effects of such uneven FtF contact on GVT dynamics and outcomes would be an interesting avenue for future research.

Finally, the use of FtF interactions has other benefits not often reported on in the GVT literature. Working FtF can enhance team member focus on and attention to the GVT task at hand. In contrast, working via technology (synchronous or asynchronous) can dissipate members' focus on the GVT task, as they are focused simultaneously on other work assignments (Shapiro et al., 2002), or multitask during synchronous GVT interactions (e.g., during team conference calls). Future research should examine the dynamics of attention and focus in GVTs, as well as their antecedents and consequences for team outcomes such as decision quality.

## Teamness

The extent of GVT teamness can be assessed based on, among other things, the type of team (e.g., extent of task interdependence), common goals and accountability, a recognizable team boundary, and the extent to which team members cohere into a unified entity. Although the last of these has been examined in several studies (see discussion of mediators in the preceding text), the others have not been the focus of very much research. Partly, this is due to research methods used, wherein individuals are assigned to teams, as in the studies using student teams, or intact teams in field settings have been selected for study. Therefore, extent of teamness has not been factored explicitly into theorizing and research models.

*Type of Team*

Cohen and Bailey (1997) concluded from their review on traditional teams and groups in organizations that team type matters in predicting the determinants of team processes and effectiveness, and the same may be expected in GVTs. Surprisingly, task type has not been built into research models examining the functioning of GVTs; yet, prior research suggests that the dynamics of teams may differ considerably depending on whether the task is additive, conjunctive, disjunctive, or discretionary (Steiner, 1972), or depending upon whether the team is working on a production, discussion, or problem-solving task (Hackman, Jones, & McGrath, 1967). A notable exception is a study by Riopelle and colleagues (2003) who examined the relationship between the nature of the task (pooled, sequential, reciprocal, or intensive) and the use of communication technologies in GVTs. The limited attention to task type may be driven partly by the nature of research samples used. To date, most of the empirical research on GVTs has been based primarily on case studies and small samples. In instances where experiments were used, almost all studies involved student teams from universities in different countries, typically working on relatively short-term tasks (e.g., Jarvenpaa et al., 1998; Kayworth & Leidner, 2000; Paul et al., 2004).

The use of student teams and the short duration of most studies create certain bounds on GVT research that may prevent theoretical development and testing of more complex relationships as well as limit the generalizability of findings. For example, the political dynamics and status effects that are part of day-to-day life in organizations are difficult to replicate in student teams. Furthermore, although the tasks assigned to student teams are meant to be interdependent (e.g., a team organizational analysis project), there is commonly a great deal of shirking in student teams, whereby a small subset of team members actually performs the task. Thus, both in student teams and field teams, it is advisable to measure the experienced amount of task interdependence and workload sharing. Related to the use of student teams in GVT research is the fact that there are few rigorous longitudinal studies of GVTs. Many GVTs work on organizationally important and complex issues over a considerable duration of time, and longitudinal research studies are required to truly understand their functioning. Long-term studies are particularly important because there is evidence that if GVT members are given enough time to get used to each other and to the communication technology tools, they may interact as effectively as in colocated teams (e.g., Chen et al., 2007; Chidambaram, 1996). Therefore, findings based primarily on short-term teams may create the impression that team dynamics in GVTs are more problematic than they really are (Hertel et al., 2005). Thus, there is a pressing need to study GVTs over longer time periods.

### Common Goals and Accountability

A key aspect of teams that differentiates them from groups in general is that their members have a common team goal. Research on GVTs has examined the development and consequences of common goals to some extent. For example, researchers have found that various factors, such as effective communication in initial team interactions (Munkvold & Zigurs, 2007) and effective GVT leadership (Kayworth & Leidner, 2000) help teams set common goals, and that the existence of superordinate goals facilitates GVT effectiveness (e.g., Vieira da Cunha & Pina e Cunha, 2001; Kerber & Buono, 2004; Rockett et al., 1998).

Future research on common goals in GVTs could examine the mechanisms that are involved in the maintenance of focus on a common goal over time and on the emergence of shared goals and objectives as teams work together. In this regard, the literature on team mental models (e.g., Klimoski & Mohammed, 1994; Rouse & Morris, 1986) could be employed to good effect to understand how GVTs develop common understandings of their task and goals. Additionally, the notion of team cross-understanding – "the extent to which group members have an accurate understanding of one another's mental models" – recently introduced by Huber and Lewis (2010, p. 7) could prove useful in explaining the functioning and outcomes of GVTs.

### Team Boundary

Researchers focusing on traditional teams have identified a recognizable team boundary as a characteristic of teams. In GVTs, however, team configurations, multiple team memberships, and distance can complicate the definition of a team's boundary (e.g., Mortensen & Hinds, 2001). One of the benefits of virtual teams is that they allow organizations to access individuals with specialized expertise for a task regardless of their location and very often, regardless of their organizational affiliation. However, this can lead to unclear team boundaries, whereby specialist members are involved with the GVT on an as-needed basis but do not influence the ongoing work of the team. Therefore, GVT configurations may have important implications for GVT teamness by affecting the nature and perception of team boundaries. Additionally, members of a GVT are often also members of other GVTs. The effects of such global multi-teaming need to be examined in future research (Lu et al., 2006).

Beyond external definitions of team membership and team boundaries of a GVT, team members themselves may face challenges in defining team boundaries for themselves. One obvious hurdle is that with global dispersion and lean communication channels, the lower social presence (Short et al., 1976) of others in the team may make it difficult for team members to develop a sense for the GVT as an entity. Furthermore, physical distance can result in psychological distance (e.g., Snow et al., 1996), thus potentially making it difficult for GVT members to think of each other as working closely together in a team. Related to this point, the recently developed Construal-Level Theory (see Trope & Liberman, 2010) is a promising new theoretical direction that could be tremendously useful in helping researchers to understand how GVT members make sense of their teammates as well as of the team as a whole. We encourage future research to utilize this theory, and the prior research that it builds on, to advance our understanding of the functioning of GVTs.

*Team Entitativity*
The extent to which GVT members gel together into a unified team entity is an important indicator of the teamness of a GVT. As discussed in the section on team mediators in the preceding text, GVTs face several challenges to cohering into an integrated team. An interesting aspect of GVTs that may affect team coherence is the fact that they often span multiple organizations in addition to multiple locations. An example is GVTs composed of client organization employees, onshore outsourced vendor employees, and offshore outsourced vendor employees. Although the teamworks on a common task, getting it to cohere into a single entity may be challenging, and the factors that facilitate such entitativity as well as the effects of varying levels of entitativity on GVT processes and outcomes are interesting topics for future research.

Alternative team arrangements such as inclusion of contractors and offshore vendors potentially create power and status dynamics that have not been researched much in the literature. Levina and Vaast (2008) found that boundaries related to different national and organizational contexts create status differences that interfere with effective collaboration in GVTs. This study makes important contributions to our understanding of GVTs by illuminating the role of status differences. As global outsourcing increases, additional research focused on understanding the role of the relative power of home office versus outsourced vendor employees, of the distribution of power and status within GVTs, and the causes and consequences of these status differences are all potentially fruitful avenues for research on GVTs. In particular, it will be interesting to examine how status distribution and dynamics affect a GVT's ability to function as a coherent team.

## CONCLUSION

As business becomes more global, organizations increasingly use GVTs for various tasks. GVTs now play a critical role in the success of many of today's global organizations and will increasingly do so in the future. Therefore, it is of utmost importance that researchers and managers develop a sound understanding of how to design, train, support, and manage GVTs. As Harvey and colleagues (2004, p. 283) stated, "there is more to GVTs than the technology networking the members together; it is the community behind the technology that creates a successful working unit." Understanding the functioning of that community is important for both researchers and managers.

Our review of the GVT literature suggests that researchers have made considerable progress toward understanding both the technological enablers as well as the social and psychological factors affecting GVT functioning and outcomes. Several effects have been found consistently over multiple studies, and these suggest an emerging agreement in the literature that among the critical success factors for GVTs are: using the appropriate communication technologies that fit the GVTs task, developing and following rules of effective communication, developing trust and a positive team identity via social interaction, and training GVT members on technologies and cultural differences. However, several inconsistencies remain, along with numerous interesting questions that have yet to be examined empirically, which we have outlined in the preceding text. Fortunately, there is a tremendous interest in the topic among researchers from several fields, who have over time developed more sophisticated models getting at various nuances of GVTs. The literature on GVTs is certainly thriving and continues to advance theoretical development as well a set of guidelines for managers charged with designing and managing GVTs.

## REFERENCES

Alexander, S. (2000). Virtual teams going global. *Infoworld,* (November), 55–56.
Anawati, D., & Craig, A. (2006). Behavioral adaptation within cross-cultural virtual teams. *Information & Communications Technology Law, 15*(2), 157.

Ashforth, B. E., Harrison, S. H., & Corley, K. G. (2008). Identification in organizations: An examination of four fundamental questions. *Journal of Management, 34*, 325–374.

Baba, M. L., Gluesing, J., Ratner, H., & Wagner, K. H. (2004). The contexts of knowing: Natural history of a globally distributed team. *Journal of Organizational Behavior, 25*, 547–586.

Bartlett, C., & Ghoshal, S. (1989). *Managing across borders: The transnational solution.* Cambridge, MA: Harvard University Press.

Baskerville, R., & Nandhakumar, J. (2007). Activating and perpetuating virtual teams: Now that we're mobile, where do we go? *IEEE Transactions on Professional Communication, 50*(1), 17–34.

Bell, B. S., & Kozlowski, S. J. (2002). A typology of virtual teams: Implications for effective leadership. *Group & Organization Management, 27*(1), 14–49.

Bennett, M. J. (1986). A developmental approach to training for intercultural sensitivity. *International Journal of Intercultural Relations, 10*(2), 179–195.

Bettenhausen, K. L. (1991). Five years of groups research: What we have learned and what needs to be addressed. *Journal of Management, 17*, 345–381.

Bjørn, P., & Ngwenyama, O. (2009). Virtual team collaboration: Building shared meaning, resolving breakdowns and creating translucence. *Information Systems Journal, 19*(3), 227–253.

Bradner, E., Mark, G., & Hertel, T. D. (2005). Leading global product development teams. *IEEE Transactions on Professional Communication, 48*(1), 68–77.

Carlson, J. R., & Zmud, R. W. (1999). Channel expansion theory and the experiential nature of media richness perceptions. *Academy of Management Journal, 42*, 153–170.

Carmel, E. (1999). *Global software teams: Collaboration across borders and time zones.* New York: Prentice-Hall.

Carmel, E., & Agarwal, R. (2001). Tactical approaches for alleviating distance in global software development. *IEEE Software Journal, 18*(2), 22–29.

Chen, M., Liou, Y., Wang, C. W., Fan, Y. W., & Chi, Y. P. J. (2007). TeamSpirit: Design, implementation, and evaluation of a web-based group decision support system. *Decision Support Systems, 43*, 1186–1202.

Cheng, C. S., & Beaumont, C. (2004). Evaluating the effectiveness of ICT to support globally distributed PBL teams. *ITICSE*, 47–51.

Chidambaram, L. (1996). Relational development in computer-supported groups. *MIS Quarterly, 20*(2), 143–165.

Chudoba, K. M., Wynn, E., Lu, M., & Watson-Manheim, M. B. (2005). How virtual are we? Measuring virtuality and understanding its impact in a global organization. *Information Systems Journal, 15*(4), 279–306.

Cogburn, D. L., Zhang, L., & Khothule, M. (2002). Going global, locally: The Socio-technical influences on performance in distributed collaborative learning teams. *Proceedings of SAICSIT* (pp. 52–64). Republic of South Africa.

Cohen, S. G., & Bailey, D. E. (1997). What makes teams work: Group effectiveness research from the shop floor to the executive suite. *Journal of Management, 23*, 239–290.

Cramton, C. D. (2001). The mutual knowledge problem and its consequences for dispersed collaboration. *Organization Science, 12*, 346–371.

Cramton, C. D., & Webber, S. S. (2005). Relationships among geographic dispersion, team processes, and effectiveness in software development work teams. *Journal of Business Research, 58*(6), 758–765.

Cummings, L. L., & Bromiley, P. (1996). *The organizational trust inventory (OIT): Development and validation.* Thousand Oaks, CA: Sage Publications.

Daft, R. L., & Lengel, R. H. (1984). Information richness: A new approach to managerial behavior and organizational design. In: B. M. Staw & L. L. Cummings (Eds), *Research in organizational behavior* (pp. 191–233). Greenwich, CT: JAI Press.

Daily, B. F., & Teich, J. E. (2001). Perceptions of contributions in multi-cultural groups in non-GDSS and GDSS environments. *European Journal of Operational Research, 134,* 70–83.

David, G. C., Chand, D., Newell, S., & Resende-Santos, J. (2008). Integrated collaboration across distributed sites: The perils of process and the promise of practice. *Journal of Information Technology, 23*(1), 44–54.

Davison, R., & de Vreede, G-J. (2001). The global application of collaborative technologies. *Communications of the AMC, 44*(12), 69–70.

Dekker, D. M., Rutte, C. G., & Van den Berg, P. T. (2008). Cultural differences in the perception of critical interaction behaviors in global virtual teams. *International Journal of Intercultural Relations, 32*(5), 441–452.

DeSanctis, G., & Poole, M. S. (1994). Capturing the complexity in advanced technology use: Adaptive structuration theory. *Organization Science, 5,* 121–147.

DeSanctis, G., Wright, M., & Jiang, L. (2001). Building a global learning community. *Communications of the ACM, 44*(12), 80–82.

Dobbins, G. H., & Zaccaro, S. J. (1986). The effects of group cohesion and leader behavior on subordinate satisfaction. *Group & Organization Studies, 11*(3), 203–219.

Dubé, L., & Paré, G. (2001). Global virtual teams. Association for computing machinery. *Communications of the ACM, 44*(12), 71–74.

Earley, P. C., & Gardner, H. K. (2005). Internal dynamics and cultural intelligence in multinational teams. In: D. L. Shapiro, M. A. Von Glinow & J. L. C. Cheng (Eds), *Managing multinational teams: Global perspectives* (Vol. 18, pp. 1–31). Amsterdam, The Netherlands: Elsevier.

Earley, P. C., & Gibson, C. B. (2002). *Multinational work teams: A new perspective.* Mahway, NJ: Lawrence Erlbaum Associates.

Edwards, H. K., & Sridhar, V. (2005). Analysis of software requirements engineering exercises in a global virtual team setup. *Journal of Global Information Management, 13*(2), 21–41.

Elron, E., & Vigoda-Gadot, E. (2006). Influence and political processes in cyberspace: The case of global virtual teams. *International Journal of Cross Cultural Management, 6*(3), 295–318.

Estienne, M. (1997). The art of cross-cultural management: An alternative approach to training and development. *Journal of European Industrial Training, 21*(1), 14–18.

Evaristo, R. (2003). The management of distributed projects across cultures. *Journal of Global Information Management, 11*(4), 58–70.

Fiol, C. M., & O'Connor, E. J. (2005). Identification in face-to-face, hybrid, and pure virtual team: Untangling the contradictions. *Organization Science, 16,* 19–32.

Forester, G. L., Thoms, P., & Pinto, J. K. (2007). Importance of goal setting in virtual project teams. *Psychological Reports, 100,* 270–274.

Fuller, M. A., Hardin, A. M., & Davison, R. M. (2007). Efficacy in technology-mediated distributed teams. *Journal of Management Information Systems, 23*(3), 209–235.

Gersick, C. J. G. (1988). Time and transition in work teams: Toward a new model of group development. *Academy of Management Journal, 31*, 9–41.

Gibson, C. B., & Manuel, J. A. (2003). Effective multicultural communication processes in virtual teams. In: C. B. Gibson & S. G. Cohen (Eds), *Virtual teams that work: Creating conditions for virtual team effectiveness.* San Fransisco: Jossey-Bass.

Gibson, C. E., & Gibbs, J. E. (2006). Unpacking the concept of virtuality: The effects of geographic dispersion, electronic dependence, dynamic structure, and national diversity on team innovation. *Administrative Science Quarterly, 51*, 451–495.

Gluesing, J. C., Alcordo, T. C., Baba, M. L., Britt, D., Wagner, K. H., McKether, W., Monplaisir, L., Ratner, H. H., & Riopelle, K. (2003). The development of global virtual teams. In: C. B. Gibson & S. G. Cohen (Eds), *Virtual teams that work: Creating conditions for virtual team effectiveness.* San Fransisco: Jossey-Bass.

Griffith, T. L., & Neale, M. A. (2001). Information processing in traditional, hybrid, and virtual teams: From nascent knowledge to transactive memory. *Research in Organizational Behavior, 23*, 379–422.

Griffith, T. L., Sawyer, J. E., & Neale, M. A. (2003). Virtualness and knowledge in teams: Managing the love triangle of organizations, individuals, and information technology. *MIS Quarterly, 27*(2), 265–288.

Gully, S. M., Devine, D. S., & Whitney, D. J. (1995). A meta-analysis of cohesion and performance: Effects of level of analysis and task interdependence. *Small Group Research, 26*, 497–520.

Haas, M. R. (2006). Acquiring and applying knowledge in transnational teams: The roles of cosmopolitans and locals. *Organization Science, 17*, 367–384.

Hackman, J. R., Jones, L. E., & McGrath, J. E. (1967). A set of dimensions for describing the general properties of group generated written passages. *Psychological Bulletin, 67*, 379–390.

Hambrick, D. C., Davidson, S. C., Snell, S. A., & Snow, C. C. (1998). When groups consist of multiple nationalities: Towards a new understanding of the implications. *Organization Studies (Walter de Gruyter GmbH & Co. KG.), 19*(2), 181–205.

Hamner, W. C., & Organ, D. W. (1978). *Organizational behavior: An applied psychological approach.* Dallas, TX: Business Publications.

Hardin, A. M., Fuller, M. A., & Davison, R. M. (2007). I know I can, but can we?: Culture and efficacy beliefs in global virtual teams. *Small Group Research, 38*, 130–155.

Harvey, M., Novicevic, M. M., & Garrison, G. (2004). Challenges to staffing global virtual teams. *Human Resource Management Review, 14*(3), 275–294.

Henttonen, K., & Blomqvist, K. (2005). Managing distance in a global virtual team: The evolution of trust through technology-mediated relational communication. *Strategic Change, 14*(2), 107–119.

Hertel, G., Geister, S., & Konradt, U. (2005). Managing virtual teams: A review of current empirical research. *Human Resource Management Review, 15*, 69–95.

Hinds, P., & Mortensen, M. (2005). Understanding conflict in geographically distributed teams: The moderating effects of shared identity, shared context, and spontaneous communication. *Organization Science, 16*, 290–307.

Hofstede, G. (1980). *Culture's consequences: International differences in work-related values.* Beverly Hills, CA: Sage.

Huber, G. P., & Lewis, K. (2010). Cross-understanding: Implications for group cognition and performance. *Academy of Management Review, 35*(1), 6–26.

Huysman, M., Steinfield, C., Jang, C.-Y., David, K., Huis in 't veld, M., Poot, J., & Mulder, I. (2003). Virtual teams and the appropriation of communication technology: Exploring the concept of media stickiness. *Computer Supported Cooperative Work, 12*, 411–436.

Ilgen, D. R., Hollenbeck, J. R., Johnson, M., & Jundt, D. (2005). Teams in organizations: From input-process-output models to IMOI models. *Annual Review of Psychology, 56*, 517–543.

James, M., & Ward, K. (2001). Leading a multinational team of change agents at Gloxo Wellcome (now GlaxoSmithKline). *Journal of Change Management, 2*(2), 148–159.

Jang, C. (2009). Facilitating trust in virtual teams: The role of awareness. *Competition Forum, 7*(2), 399–408.

Jang, C., Steinfield, C., & Pfaff, B. (2002). Virtual team awareness and groupware support: An evaluation of the TeamSCOPE system. *International Journal of Human-Computer Studies, 56*(1), 109–126Special issue: Awareness and the WWW.

Jarvenpaa, S. L., Knoll, K., & Leidner, D. E. (1998). Is anybody out there? Antecedents of trust in global virtual teams. *Journal of Management Information Systems, 14*(4), 29–64.

Jarvenpaa, S. L., & Leidner, D. E. (1998). Communication and trust in global virtual teams. *Journal of Computer-Mediated Communication, 3*(4) Special issue: Virtual organizations.

Jarvenpaa, S. L., & Leidner, D. E. (1999). Communication and trust in global virtual teams. *Organization Science, 10*, 791–815.

Jarvenpaa, S. L., Shaw, T. R., & Staples, D. S. (2004). Toward contextualized theories of trust: The role of trust in global virtual teams. *Information Systems Research, 15*(3), 250–267.

Joshi, A., Labianca, G., & Caligiuri, P. M. (2002). Getting along long distance: Understanding conflict in a multinational team through network analysis. *Journal of World Business, 37*(4), 277–284.

Joshi, A., Lazarova, M. B., & Liao, H. (2009). Getting everyone on board: The role of inspirational leadership in geographically dispersed teams. *Organization Science, 20*, 240–252.

Joshi, A., & Roh, H. (2009). The role of context in work team diversity research: A meta-analytic review. *Academy of Management Journal, 52*, 599–628.

Kanawattanachai, P., & Yoo, Y. (2002). Dynamic nature of trust in virtual teams. *Journal of Strategic Information Systems, 11*, 187–213.

Kanawattanachai, P., & Yoo, Y. (2007). The impact of knowledge coordination on virtual team performance over time. *MIS Quarterly, 31*, 783–808.

Kankanhalli, A., Tan, B. C. Y., & Wei, K-K. (2007). Conflict and performance in global virtual teams. *Journal of Management Information Systems, 23*(3), 237–274.

Kanter, R. M. (1977). *Men and women of the corporation.* New York: Basic Books.

Katzenbach, J. R., & Smith, D. K. (1993). *The wisdom of teams: Creating the high-performance organization.* Boston: Harvard Business School Press.

Kayworth, T. R., & Leidner, D. E. (2000). The global virtual manager: A prescription for success. *European Management Journal, 18*(2), 183–194.

Kayworth, T. R., & Leidner, D. E. (2001). Leadership effectiveness in global virtual teams. *Journal of Management Information Systems, 18*(3), 7–40.

Kelly, S., & Jones, M. (2001). Groupware and the social infrastructure of communication. *Communications of the ACM, 44*(12), 77–79.

Kerber, K. W., & Buono, A. F. (2004). Leadership challenges in global virtual teams: Lessons from the field. *S.A.M. Advanced Management Journal, 69*(4), 4–10.

Kirkman, B. L., Gibson, C. B., & Kim, K. (in press). Across borders and technologies: Advancements in virtual teams research. In: S. Kozlowski (Ed.), *Oxford handbook of industrial and organizational psychology*. New York: Oxford University Press.

Kirkman, B. L., & Mathieu, J. E. (2005). The dimensions and antecedents of team virtuality. *Journal of Management, 31*, 700–718.

Klimoski, R. J., & Mohammed, S. (1994). Team mental model: Construct or metaphor? *Journal of Management, 20*, 403–437.

Knoll, K. E. (2000). *Communication and cohesiveness in global virtual teams*. Doctoral dissertation. Available at ProQuest dissertations and theses database, AAT 9983268.

Levina, N., & Vaast, E. (2008). Innovating or doing as told? Status differences and overlapping boundaries in offshore collaboration. *MIS Quarterly, 32*(2), 307–332.

Levy, O., Beechler, S., Taylor, S., & Boyacigiller, N. A. (2007). What we talk about when we talk about 'global mindset': Managerial cognition in multinational corporations. *Journal of International Business Studies, 38*, 231–258.

Lu, M., Watson-Manheim, M. B., Chudoba, K., & Wynn, E. (2006). How does virtuality affect team performance in a global organization? Understanding the impact of variety of practices. *Journal of Global Information Technology Management, 9*(1), 4–23.

Majchrzak, A., Malhotra, A., Stamps, J., & Lipnack, J. (2004). Can absence make a team grow stronger? *Harvard Business Review, 82*(5), 131–137.

Malhotra, A., & Majchrzak, A. (2004). Enabling knowledge creation in far-flung teams: Best practices for IT support and knowledge sharing. *Journal of Knowledge Management, 8*(4), 75–88.

Marks, M. A., Mathieu, J. E., & Zaccaro, S. J. (2001). A temporally based framework and taxonomy of team processes. *Academy of Management Review, 26*, 356–376.

Marks, M. A., Zaccaro, S. J., & Mathieu, J. E. (2000). Performance implications of leader briefings and team-interaction training for team adaptation to novel environments. *Journal of Applied Psychology, 85*, 971–986.

Martins, L. L., Gilson, L. L., & Maynard, M. T. (2004). Virtual teams: What do we know and where do we go from here? *Journal of Management, 30*, 805–835.

Martins. L. L., & Shalley, C. E. (in press). Creativity in virtual work: Effects of demographic differences. *Small Group Research*.

Massey, A. P., Hung, C., Montoya-Weiss, M. M., & Ramesh, V. (2001a). When culture and style aren't about clothes: Perceptions of task-technology "fit" in global virtual teams. *Group*, September 30–October 3, Boulder, CO.

Massey, A. P., Montoya-Weiss, M. M., Hung, C., & Ramesh, V. (2001b). Cultural perceptions of task-technology fit. *Communications of the ACM, 44*(12), 83–84.

Massey, A. P., Montoya-Weiss, M. M., & Hung, Y.-T. (2003). Because time matters: Temporal coordination in global virtual teams. *Journal of Management Information Systems, 19*(4), 129–155.

Mathieu, J. E., Heffner, T. S., Goodwin, G. F., Salas, E., & Cannon-Bowers, J. A. (2000). The influence of shared mental models on team process and performance. *Journal of Applied Psychology, 85*, 273–283.

Maznevski, M. L. (1994). *Synergy and performance in multicultural teams*. Unpublished doctoral dissertation. University of Western Ontario, London, Canada.

Maznevski, M. L., & Chudoba, K. M. (2000). Bridging space over time: Global virtual team dynamics and effectiveness. *Organization Science, 11*, 473–492.

McDonough, E. F., III., Kahn, K. B., & Barczak, G. (2001). An investigation of the use of global, virtual, and colocated new product development teams. *The Journal of Product Innovation Management, 18*(2), 110–120.

Metiu, A. (2006). Owning the code: Status closure in distributed groups. *Organization Science, 17,* 418–435.

Mockaitis, A. I., Rose, E. L., & Zettinig, P. (2009). The determinants of trust in multicultural global virtual teams. *Academy of Management Annual Meeting Proceedings,* 1–6.

Monalisa, M., Daim, T., Mirani, F., Dash, P., Khamis, R., & Bhusari, V. (2008). Managing global design teams. *Research Technology Management, 51*(4), 48–59.

Montoya-Weiss, M. M., Massey, A. P., & Song, M. (2001). Getting it together: Temporal coordination and conflict management in global virtual teams. *Academy of Management Journal, 44,* 1251–1262.

Moreland, R. L. (1999). Transactive memory: Learning who knows what in work groups and organizations. In: L. L. Thompson, J. M. Levine & D. M. Messick (Eds), *Shared cognition in organizations: The management of knowledge* (pp. 3–31). Mahwah, NJ: Lawrence Erlbaum.

Mortensen & Hinds, E. (2001). Fuzzy teams: Boundary disagreement in distributed and collocated teams. In: P. Hinds & S. Kiesler (Eds), *Distributed work* (pp. 283–308). Cambridge, MA: MIT Press.

Mullen, B., & Copper, C. (1994). The relation between group cohesiveness and performance: An integration. *Psychological Bulletin, 115,* 210–227.

Munkvold, B. E., & Zigurs, I. (2007). Process and technology challenges in swift-starting virtual teams. *Information & Management, 44,* 287–299.

Newell, S., David, G., & Chand, D. (2007). An analysis of trust among globally distributed work teams in an organizational setting. *Knowledge & Process Management, 14*(3), 158–168. Special issue: Managing knowledge within and across geographic borders: The role of culture.

Oshri, I., van Fenema, P., & Kotlarsky, J. (2008). Knowledge transfer in globally distributed teams: The role of transactive memory. *Information Systems Journal, 18*(6), 593–616.

Overholt, A. (2002). Virtually there? *Fast Company, 56,* 108–114.

O'Hara-Devereaux, M., & Johansen, R. (1994). *Global work: Bridging distance, culture, and time.* San Fransisco: Jossey-Bass Publishers.

O'Leary, M. B., & Mortensen, M. (2010). Go (con)figure: Subgroups, imbalance, and isolates in geographically dispersed teams. *Organization Science, 21,* 115–131.

Panteli, N., & Davison, R. M. (2005). The role of subgroups in the communication patterns of global virtual teams. *IEEE Transactions on Professional Communication, 48*(2), 191–200.

Paul, S., Samarah, I., Seetharaman, P., & Mykytyn, P. P. (2005). An empirical investigation of collaborative conflict management style in group support system-based global virtual teams. *Journal of Management Information Systems, 21*(3), 185–222.

Paul, S., Seetharaman, P., Samarah, I., & Mykytyn, P. P. (2004). Impact of heterogeneity and collaborative conflict management style on the performance of synchronous global virtual teams. *Information & Management, 41*(3), 303–321.

Pauleen, D. J. (2003a). Lessons learned crossing boundaries in an ICT-supported distributed team. *Journal of Global Information Management, 11*(4), 1–19.

Pauleen, D. J. (2003b). Leadership in a global virtual team: An action learning approach. *Leadership & Organization Development Journal, 24*(3), 153–162.

Pauleen, D. J., & Yoong, P. (2001). Relationship building and the use of ICT in boundary-crossing virtual teams: A facilitator's perspective. *Journal of Information Technology, 16,* 205–220.

Perlmutter, H. (1969). The tortuous evolution of the multinational corporation. *Columbia Journal of World Business, 4*(1), 9–18.

Piccoli, G., & Ives, B. (2003). Trust and the unintended effects of behavior control in virtual teams. *MIS Quarterly, 27,* 365–395.

Polzer, J. T., Crisp, C. B., Jarvenpaa, S. L., & Kim, J. W. (2006). Extending the faultline model to geographically dispersed teams: How collocated subgroups can impair group functioning. *Academy of Management Journal, 49,* 679–692.

Powell, A., Piccoli, G., & Ives, B. (2004). Virtual teams: A review of current literature and future research directions. *The DATABASE for Advances in Information Systems, 35*(1), 6–36.

Prasad, K., & Akhilesh, K. B. (2002). Global virtual teams: What impacts their design and performance? *Team Performance Management, 8*(5 and 6), 102–112.

Pratt, M. G. (2001). Social identity dynamics in modern organizations: An organizational psychology/organizational behavior perspective. In: M. Hogg & D. J. Terry (Eds), *Social identity processes in organizational contexts* (pp. 13–30). Philadelphia, PA: Psychology Press.

Qureshi, S., & Zigurs, I. (2001). Paradoxes and prerogatives in global virtual collaboration. *Communications of the ACM, 44*(12), 85–87.

Reinig, B. A., & Mejias, R. J. (2004). The effects of national culture and anonymity on flaming and criticalness in GSS-supported discussions. *Small Group Research, 35,* 698–723.

Riopelle, K., Gluesing, J. C., Alcordo, T. C., Baba, M. L., Britt, D., McKether, W., Monplaisir, L., Ratner, H. H., & Wagner, K. H. (2003). Context, task, and the evolution of technology use in global virtual teams. In: C. B. Gibson & S. G. Cohen (Eds), *Virtual teams that work: Creating conditions for virtual team effectiveness.* San Fransisco: Jossey-Bass.

Rockett, L., Valor, J., Miller, P., & Naude, P. (1998). Technology and virtual teams: Using globally distributed groups in MBA learning. *Campus-Wide Information Systems, 15*(5), 174–182.

Rouse, R., & Morris, N. M. (1986). On looking into the blackbox: Prospects and limits in the search for mental models. *Psychological Bulletin, 100,* 349–363.

Rutkowski, A. F., Saunders, C., Vogel, D., & van Genuchten, M. (2007). "Is it already 4 a.m. in your time zone?" Focus immersion and temporal disassociation in virtual teams. *Small Group Research, 38,* 98–129.

Rutkowski, A. F., Vogel, D. R., van Genuchten, M., Bemelmans, T. M. A., & Favier, M. (2002). E-collaboration: The reality of virtuality. *IEEE Transactions on Professional Communication, 45*(4), 219–230.

Saphiere, D. M. H. (1996). Productive behaviors of global business teams. *International Journal of Intercultural Relations, 20,* 227–259.

Sarker, S. (2005). Knowledge transfer and collaboration in distributed U.S.-Thai teams. *Journal of Computer-Mediated Communication, 10*(4)article 15.

Sarker, S., Sarker, S., Nicholson, D. B., & Joshi, K. D. (2003). Knowledge transfer in virtual systems development teams: An exploratory study of four key enablers. *Proceedings of the 36th Hawaii international conference on system sciences.* Big Island, Hawaii.

Sarker, S., Sarker, S., Nicholson, D. B., & Joshi, K. D. (2005). Knowledge transfer in virtual systems development teams: An exploratory study of four key enablers. *IEEE Transactions on Professional Communication, 48,* 201–218.

Saunders, C., Van Slyke, C., & Vogel, D. R. (2004). My time or yours? Managing time visions in global virtual teams. *Academy of Management Executive, 18,* 19–31.

Shachaf, P. (2008). Cultural diversity and information and communication technology impacts on global virtual teams: An exploratory study. *Information & Management, 45*(2). 131–142.

Shapiro, D. L., Furst, S. A., Spreitzer, G. M., & Von Glinow, M. A. (2002). Transnational teams in the electronic age: Are team identity and high performance at risk? *Journal of Organizational Behavior, 23,* 455–467.

Short, J., Williams, E., & Christie, B. (1976). *The social psychology of telecommunications.* London: Wiley.

Smith-Jentsch, K. A., Campbell, G. E., Milanovich, D. M., & Reynolds, A. M. (2001). Measuring teamwork mental models to support training needs assessment, development, and evaluation: Two empirical studies. *Journal of Organizational Behavior, 22,* 179–194.

Snow, C. C., Snell, S. A., Davison, S. C., & Hambrick, D. C. (1996). Use transnational teams to globalize your company. *Organizational Dynamics, 24,* 50–51.

Solomon, C. M. (1998). Building teams across borders. *Global Workforce,* 12–17.

Stanko, T. L., & Gibson, C. B. (2009). Virtuality here and now: The role of cultural elements in virtual teams. In: R. S. Bhagat & R. M. Steers (Eds), *Cambridge handbook of culture, organization, and work* (pp. 272–304). Cambridge, UK: Cambridge University Press.

Staples, D. S., & Zhao, L. (2006). The effects of cultural diversity in virtual teams versus face-to-face teams. *Group Decision and Negotiation, 15,* 389–406.

Steiner, I. D. (1972). *Group processes and productivity.* New York: Academic Press.

Swigger, K., Alpaslan, F., Brazile, R., & Monticino, M. (2004). Effects of culture on computer-supported international collaborations. *International Journal of Human-Computer Studies, 60,* 365–380.

Tajfel, H. (1981). *Human groups and social categories: Studies in social psychology.* New York: Cambridge University Press.

Thompson, L. (2000). *Making the team: A guide for managers.* Upper Saddle River, NJ: Prentice-Hall, Inc.

Townsend, A. M., DeMarie, S. M., & Hendrickson, A. R. (1998). Virtual teams: Technology and the workplace of the future. *Academy of Management Executive, 12,* 17–29.

Triandis, H. C., & Gelfand, M. J. (1998). Converging measurement of horizontal and vertical individualism and collectivism. *Journal of Personality and Social Psychology, 74,* 118–128.

Trope, Y., & Liberman, N. (2010). Construal-level theory of psychological distance. *Psychological Review, 117*(2), 440–463.

Uber Grosse, C. (2002). Managing communication within virtual intercultural teams. *Business Communication Quarterly, 65*(4), 22–38.

Vieira da Cunha, J., & Pina e Cunha, M. (2001). Brave new (paradoxical) world: Structure and improvisation in virtual teams. *Strategic Change, 10*(6), 337–347.

Vogel, D. R., van Genuchten, M., Lou, D., Verveen, S., van Eekout, M., & Adams, A. (2001). Exploratory research on the role of national and professional cultures in a distributed learning. *IEEE Transactions on Professional Communication, 44*(2), 114–125.

Walther, J. B. (1997). Group and interpersonal effects in international computer-mediated collaboration. *Human Communication Research, 23*(3), 342–369.

Walther, J. B., Slovacek, C. L., & Tidwell, L. C. (2001). Is a picture worth a thousand words? Photographic images in long-term and short-term computer-mediated communication. *Communication Research, 28,* 105–134.

Wiesenfeld, B. M., Raghuram, S., & Garud, R. (1999). Communication modes as determinants of organizational identity in a virtual organization. *Organization Science, 10,* 777–790.

Workman, M. (2004). Goals, relationships, information and processes in global virtual team performance. *International Journal of Management & Decision Making, 5*(4), 348–372.

Yoo, Y., & Kanawattanachai, P. (2001). Developments of transactive memory systems and collective mind in virtual teams. *International Journal of Organizational Analysis, 9,* 187–208.

Zhang, D., Lowry, B. J., Zhou, L., & Fu, X. (2007). The impact of individualism-collectivism, social presence, and group diversity on group decision making under majority influence. *Journal of Management Information Systems, 23,* 53–80.

Zolin, R., Hinds, P. J., Fruchter, R., & Levitt, R. E. (2004). Interpersonal trust in cross-functional, geographically distributed work: A longitudinal study. *Information & Organization, 14*(1), 1–26.

# AN INTEGRATION AND EXTENSION OF INTRINSIC MOTIVATION THEORIES: THE ROLE OF CORE AFFECT

Matt Bloom and Amy E. Colbert

## ABSTRACT

*Intrinsic motivation occurs due to positive reactions that arise directly from engagement in work activities. Scholars have asserted that intrinsic motivation plays an important role in organizational phenomena such as creativity (George, 2007), leadership (Piccolo & Colquitt, 2006), and performance (Gagné & Deci, 2005). We review the research literature on intrinsic motivation and provide an overview and integration of the leading theories. We then develop a conceptual model in which positive affect serves as a primary cause of intrinsic motivation. We discuss how affect alone may induce intrinsic motivation, how affect may lead to nonconscious experiences of intrinsic motivation, and how affect and cognitions may work in concert to produce the strongest and most persistent intrinsic motivation experiences. We conclude by suggesting new avenues for research that might be pursued using this cognitive–affective model of intrinsic motivation.*

Research in Personnel and Human Resources Management, Volume 30, 73–114
Copyright © 2011 by Emerald Group Publishing Limited
All rights of reproduction in any form reserved
ISSN: 0742-7301/doi:10.1108/S0742-7301(2011)0000030004

What is work like for people when it is such a positive experience that they are motivated by the work itself instead of by external rewards? What do people think and feel during such an experience? What factors or conditions are conducive to creating these experiences, and is there anything that organizations and managers can do to influence the likelihood that people will have them? Scholars interested in intrinsic motivation have, for many years, sought answers to questions like these by studying the psychology of encounters when work itself is the source of highly positive, highly motivating experiences for people (e.g., Argyris, 1964; Hackman & Oldham, 1976). Intrinsic motivation occurs when people are motivated to engage in a work activity for its own sake, because of the positive experiences they obtain directly from this engagement, rather than for factors external to the work experience itself, such as rewards and performance incentives (Amabile, 1996; Brief & Aldag, 1977; Gagné & Deci, 2005; Patall, Cooper, & Robinson, 2008).

A rich research literature on intrinsic motivation stretches back at least to Woodworth (1918) and came into its formative years with the work of White (1959), Argyris (1964), Deci (1971), and Porter and Lawler (1968). Woodworth (1918) asserted that "while a man may enter a certain line of business from a purely external economic motive, he develops an interest in the business for its own sake …. The [economic] end furnishes the motive force for the search for means but once the means are found, they are apt to become interesting on their own account" (p. 104). Since this earliest, foundational research, organizational scholars have suggested that intrinsic motivation plays an important role in eliciting the highest levels of work motivation and performance (Argyris, 1964; Porter & Lawler, 1968). Hackman and Oldham (1980) regarded it as the "key (to) understanding both organizational productivity and the quality of employees' work experiences" (p. 20). Thomas and Velthouse (1990) asserted that intrinsic motivation is the essential force behind organizational phenomena such as empowerment and transformational leadership. Some management scholars even suggest that intrinsic motivators are more important to organizations than are extrinsic (e.g., economic) motivators. Simon (1991), for example, asserts that "organizations would be far less effective systems than they actually are if economic rewards were the only means, or even the principal means, of motivation available. In fact, observation of behavior in organizations reveals other powerful motivators that induce employees to accept organizational goals and authority as the bases for their actions" (p. 34).

Our objective is to pursue an enhanced understanding of these "other powerful motivators" through a review and extension of research and theory on intrinsic motivation. Existing theory and research provide a rich understanding of the cognitive dimension of intrinsic motivation (Amabile, 1996; Hackman & Oldham, 1980; Ryan & Deci, 2000; Spreitzer, 1995; Thomas & Velthouse, 1990). We provide an overview of these important theories and an integration of their propositions. We then develop an extension to these theories in which affect – moods and emotions – takes center stage (Barrett, Mesquita, Ochsner, & Gross, 2007; Barsade, Brief, & Spataro, 2003; Brief & Weiss, 2002; Watson, 2000; Weiss & Cropanzano, 1996). Our core proposition is that positive affect is also an important, and sometimes sufficient, cause of intrinsic motivation. Affect is important, in part, because "organizations are affectively laden environments" (Amabile, Barsade, Mueller, & Staw, 2005, p. 367), but also because, we will argue, intrinsic motivation is affectively laden too. A central tenet of existing research is that intrinsic motivation occurs when people find engaging in work to be such a positive experience that no source of external motivation, such as a tangible reward, is required (Amabile, 1996; Deci, 1971; Thomas & Velthouse, 1990; Zhou, 1998). Positive affect, we will argue, is the essence of what makes these experiences so positive and motivating.

In our cognitive–affective model of intrinsic motivation (Fig. 1), we propose that core positive affect influences intrinsic motivation through three pathways. First, when individuals experience positive moods, these moods are often implicit and may not be the subject of further cognitive appraisals (Russell, 2003). This implicit positive affect may be a sufficient cause of intrinsic motivation, leading directly to nonconscious experiences of intrinsic motivation. Second, when positive affect enters cognitive awareness, individuals likely make limited attributions about the causes of the positive affect (Barrett, 2005; Cropanzano, Weiss, Hale, & Reb, 2003). These positive emotional experiences are also expected to lead to higher levels of intrinsic motivation. Finally, emotional meta-experiences (Barrett et al., 2007; Elfenbein, 2007) occur when positive affect triggers more extensive cognitive processing. In these situations, core cognitions and affect work together to influence intrinsic motivation and likely encourage individuals to seek out similar experiences in the future, resulting in more persistent intrinsic motivation. We propose that considering positive affect as an antecedent of intrinsic motivation may help explain its self-generating and self-perpetuating properties.

Intrinsic motivation is likely to be particularly important for under-standing nonmandatory workplace behaviors such as organizational citizenship behaviors, extra-role performance (Podsakoff, MacKenzie, Paine, & Bachrach, 2000), creativity (George, 2007), and proactive behavior

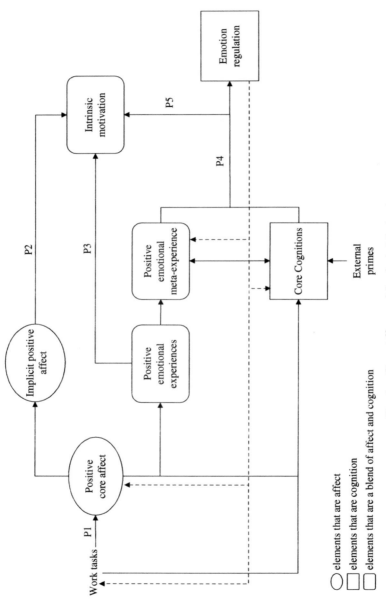

*Fig. 1.* Core Affect and Intrinsic Motivation.

(Grant & Parker, 2009). Research has provided compelling evidence that these nonmandatory behaviors can make significant contributions to organizational performance (e.g., Chuang & Liao, 2010; Podsakoff, Whiting, Podsakoff, & Blume, 2009), and they also have the potential to foster more positive work climates. While research has provided a great deal of insight into how human resource management (HRM) practices can motivate and support mandatory work behaviors, an enhanced understanding of intrinsic motivation will be helpful for designing HRM practices that also support important nonmandatory work contributions (Bloom, 2008). Intrinsic motivation may also change the way in which individuals approach mandatory, or task-related, work behaviors. As Kahn (1990, 1992) noted, individuals vary in terms of their engagement, or the extent to which they invest themselves in their role performances. When a task is intrinsically motivating, people may be more likely to become highly engaged, investing themselves physically, cognitively, or emotionally in the task at hand. Higher levels of engagement have been shown to positively impact both task performance and organizational citizenship behavior (Rich, LePine, & Crawford, 2010). Thus, HRM practices that promote intrinsic motivation may help facilitate higher levels of both mandatory and nonmandatory work contributions. In the final section of this chapter, we discuss more fully how HRM practices may influence intrinsic motivation within organizations.

# RESEARCH ON INTRINSIC MOTIVATION

## *Defining Intrinsic Motivation*

A number of researchers (e.g., Brief & Aldag, 1977; Dyer & Parker, 1975; Thomas & Velthouse, 1990) have expressed concerns about inconsistencies in the way intrinsic motivation has been defined and studied in the research literature. The lack of a consistent definition of intrinsic motivation produces a number of challenges, including confusion about the core construct, diffusion in measures of intrinsic motivation, difficulties in comparing findings across studies, and increased potential for confusion with other constructs, all of which may impede research progress. Based on our review of the literature, we found that definitions of intrinsic motivation vary in breadth. For example, in self-determination theory (SDT), Ryan and Deci (2000) take a relatively narrow perspective on intrinsic motivation, defining it as "doing an activity for the inherent satisfaction of the activity itself" (p. 71). According to SDT, intrinsically motivating activities are those in which the activity itself is assessed as enjoyable or interesting. However, others have taken a broader approach. For example, Thomas and Velthouse (1990) define intrinsic motivation as "positively valued experiences that individuals derive directly from a task" (p. 668), but they specify that the task includes both the activities undertaken by the worker and the purpose toward which those activities are directed. Brief and Aldag (1977) concur with this perspective, noting that intrinsic motivation occurs when "the worker attributes the force of his or her task behaviors to outcomes derived from the task per se; that is, from outcomes which are not mediated by a source external to the task-person situation." These definitions recognize that the reasons people engage in work "for its own sake" may include both activities that are assessed as enjoyable or interesting and activities that have a purpose that is valued by the individual, as well as allowing for other bases of intrinsically motivating work. We believe that this broader definition best reflects the foundational premises upon which the concept of intrinsic motivation is based. Clarifying these premises will, we hope, provide convincing support for adopting this broader definition of intrinsic motivation.

The first premise is that intrinsic motivation arises directly from engagement with a work activity. The referent for the term "intrinsic" is the activity, not the person (Amabile, 1996; George, 2007; Hackman & Oldham, 1980; Thomas & Velthouse, 1990; Zhou, 1998). When work activities are intrinsically motivating, the motivating potential is endogenous to the work activities and motivation arises directly from engaging in the activities. When work activities are extrinsically motivating, the motivating potential is exogenous to the activities; motivation is driven by something outside of engaging in the activities per se (cf. Kruglanski, 1975). In this context, the term "work activity" refers to a set of tasks, roles, and interpersonal interactions associated with sphere of action that are directed toward a common purpose (Brief & Aldag, 1977; Katz & Kahn, 1978; Thomas & Velthouse, 1990). Thus, a work activity may be intrinsically motivating because people find the activity itself to be enjoyable or interesting, because people identify with the roles they fill as a result of engaging in the activity, or because the purpose of the activity is perceived by the individual to be valuable and important. For example, a professor might be intrinsically motivated to hold office hours to review homework assignments because she enjoys helping students learn, identifies with the role of educator, or believes that the development that occurs during these sessions is valuable and important.

In means–ends language, work activities are intrinsically motivating when engaging in the activities themselves is the motivational end, and work activities are extrinsically motivating when they are a means to some other motivational end that is separable from engagement in the activity. One aspect of intrinsic motivation that makes it of such great interest is its ability to induce action simply through the motivating potential of engaging in work. Extrinsic motivation requires a constant source of rewards that are not a direct result of engaging in the activity: when the rewards run out, so does the extrinsic motivation. Intrinsic motivation, on the other hand, may continue for long periods of time because its source – whether enjoyment that arises from the task or a sense that the purpose of the task is valuable – is potentially unlimited. This is the foundation for Hackman and Oldham's (1980) assertion that intrinsic motivation can be self-generating and self-perpetuating.

A second fundamental premise is that activities are intrinsically motivating to the extent they create or invoke experiences that individuals perceive as positive. Existing theories assert that people engage in ongoing assessments and evaluations of the work activities they engage in and form cognitions about the meaning and significance of those activities for their ongoing well-being, goals, and higher order need satisfaction (Hackman & Lawler, 1971; Hackman & Oldham, 1980; Thomas & Velthouse, 1990). Again, intrinsically motivating activities may be perceived as positive because they fulfill the need for enjoyable work or achieving an important purpose. Importantly, it is these "positively valued experiences" (Thomas & Velthouse, 1990, p. 668) or "positive reactions" (Amabile, 1996, p. 115) that are regarded as the core or essence of intrinsic motivation.

A third important premise is that certain characteristics or features of work activities make them more or less likely to evoke the core cognitions that create these positive experiences. This is one of the important insights of early research done by scholars such as Porter and Lawler (1968), Hackman and Oldham (1976, 1980), and Thomas and Velthouse (1990). For example, job characteristics theory (JCT; Hackman & Oldham, 1980) proposes that activities with high levels of skill variety, task identity, task significance, autonomy, and feedback are more likely to result in the positive cognitions that lead to higher levels of intrinsic motivation. Thomas and Velthouse (1990) assert that activities that lead to perceptions of competence, impact, autonomy, and meaningfulness are most conducive to intrinsic motivation. It is important to emphasize that these theories view core cognitions as the proximal cause of intrinsic motivation, while the state of intrinsic motivation itself is framed as the positive experience that ensues as a result of these cognitions. Much of the related management research has sought to understand which features or characteristics of work activities are most conducive to the cognitive precursors of intrinsic motivation (Fried & Ferris, 1987).

Based on these three foundational premises, we define intrinsic motivation as any motivation that occurs due to positive reactions that arise directly from engagement in work activities. Under intrinsic motivation, the rewards are inseparable from engagement in a work activity; engaging in the activity is the motivational end. These positive reactions can take the form of positive cognitions (cf. Brief & Aldag, 1977), a combination of cognitions and affect (Amabile, 1996; Hackman & Oldham, 1980), or, as we propose later in the text, these positive reactions can be exclusively affective. In contrast, motivation is extrinsic when its source is outcomes that are separable from and obtained by engaging in work activities; the activity is a means to obtain other motivational ends.

## Leading Theories of Intrinsic Motivation

Although researchers have proposed a number of theories of intrinsic motivation (e.g., Argyris, 1964; deCharms, 1968; Deci, 1971; Porter & Lawler, 1968), three of these have emerged as the most widely used in research: Hackman and Oldham's (1976, 1980) JCT, Deci and Ryan's (2000) SDT, and Thomas and Velthouse's (1990; Spreitzer, 1995, 1996) psychological empowerment theory (PET). We summarize the core propositions of these theories in the following text. We also provide a brief overview of Csikszentmihalyi's (1990) flow theory because of a resurgence of interest in this view. We summarize the major elements of these theories in Table 1.

### Job Characteristics Theory
Hackman and Oldham (1976) developed JCT to describe how the design of jobs could affect work motivation, but their interest later expanded to include concerns about how work influences human well-being and life fulfillment (Hackman & Oldham, 1980). Although Hackman and Oldham (1976, 1980) use the term internal motivation, rather than intrinsic motivation, their model focuses on motivation that arises directly from work experiences rather than from rewards attached to those experiences. As such, the focus of JCT and the essence of Hackman and Oldham's (1980) notion of internal motivation are consistent with our definition of intrinsic motivation. They define internal motivation as "positive affect ... (that) is

*Table 1.* Summary of Cognitive Models of Intrinsic Motivation.

| Theory | Core Motivational Concept | Core Cognitions |
|---|---|---|
| Job characteristics theory | Internal motivation defined as "positive affect ... (that) is self-reinforcing to the individual, and serves as an incentive for him to continue to try to perform well in the future" (Hackman & Oldham, 1976, p. 256). | • Experienced meaningfulness: the degree to which an individual experiences work as meaningful, valuable, and worthwhile.<br>• Experienced responsibility: the degree to which an individual feels personally accountable for the results of the work he or she does.<br>• Knowledge of results: the degree to which an individual knows and understands, on a continuous basis, how effectively he or she is performing. |
| Self-determination theory | Intrinsic motivation defined as "activities ... that individuals find interesting and would do in the absence of operationally separable consequences" (Deci & Ryan, 2000, p. 233). | • Autonomy: a sense of volition, a sense that one's behavior is self-chosen and endorsed.<br>• Competence: a sense of mastery, a sense that one is effective in what one does.<br>• Relatedness: feeling that one has positive connections with others. |
| Psychological empowerment theory | Intrinsic motivation defined as "positively valued experiences that individuals derive directly from a task" (Thomas & Velthouse, 1990, p. 668). | • Impact: a sense that one has influence or agency to affect outcomes of importance.<br>• Competence: a sense that one can perform a task skillfully.<br>• Meaningfulness: intrinsic caring or valuing the task purpose as judged by the person's own ideals or standards.<br>• Choice: a sense that one is causally responsible for his or her actions, that one is self-determining. |
| Flow theory | Flow defined as "the state in which people are so involved in an activity that nothing else seems to matter, the experience itself is so enjoyable that people will do it even at great cost, for the sheer sake of doing it" (Csikszentmihalyi, 1990, p. 4). | • Flow results when the individual's skills match the challenges of undertaking the activity. |

self-reinforcing to the individual, and serves as an incentive for him to continue to try to perform well in the future" (Hackman & Oldham, 1976, p. 256). According to JCT, job characteristics influence internal motivation through three psychological states or cognitions. First, *experienced meaningfulness* refers to the degree to which an individual experiences work as meaningful and worthwhile, "something that 'counts' in one's own system of values" (Hackman & Oldham, 1980, p. 73). Three job characteristics combine to influence experienced meaningfulness – skill variety, task identity, and task significance. Second, *experienced responsibility* refers to the degree to which an individual feels personally accountable for and proud of the results of the work he or she does. When employees have autonomy in determining how to do their work, they are more likely to feel responsible for the work. Finally, *knowledge of results* is the degree to which an individual knows and understands, on a continuous basis, how effectively he or she is performing. When the job itself provides employees with feedback, they are able to assess their own performance and feel as though they have knowledge of results. JCT continues to be a very influential theory in the motivation literature. Recent research has provided support for many of its propositions (Humphrey, Nahrgang, & Morgeson, 2007).

*Psychological Empowerment Theory*
Thomas and Velthouse's (1990) PET was developed in response to the movement toward empowered workplaces. This movement sought to create workplaces where employees were motivated and energized by the work they were doing and the environment in which they were working, rather than only by the contingent rewards and punishments emphasized by classical approaches to management. Thomas and Velthouse proposed that the positive effects of empowerment emanate from its capacity to foster intrinsic motivation which they define as "positively valued experiences that individuals derive directly from a task" (1990, p. 668). Building on JCT and the work of Conger and Kanungo (1988), Thomas and Velthouse (1990) developed a model that focuses primarily on four core cognitions or activity assessments that facilitate IM. *Competence* refers to a sense of mastery, or a sense that one can perform an activity skillfully. *Choice* refers to the perception that a person is causally responsible for their actions, or self-determining. *Impact* is an individual's sense that they have agency to influence outcomes, that their behavior makes a difference in accomplishing the purpose of the activity or activities. *Meaningfulness* is intrinsic caring or valuing of the purpose of the activity as judged against the person's own ideals and standards. Research indicates that intrinsic motivation as

conceptualized under PET has important relationships with work outcomes including performance, job satisfaction, and work strain (Seibert, Silver, & Randolph, 2004; Spreitzer, Kizilos, & Nason, 1997).

*Self-Determination Theory*
Deci and Ryan's (2000) SDT is one of the most widely studied theories of intrinsic motivation in the psychological research literature (Ryan & Deci, 2000; Sheldon, Turban, Brown, Barrick, & Judge, 2003). Like JCT, a major premise of SDT is that intrinsic motivation results from the positive reactions that arise directly from engaging with work activities and environments. However, according to SDT, the key to intrinsic motivation is the extent to which individuals feel autonomous, "literally, self-authored or endorsed," versus feeling controlled in their motivation (Ryan & Deci, 2000, p. 69). SDT maintains that when individuals believe that they have fully chosen and endorsed what they are thinking and doing, and therefore perceive their thoughts and actions as being self-determined, they are intrinsically motivated. Under extrinsic motivation, individuals perceive that the locus of causality of their thoughts and behaviors is sources outside of themselves and they feel that these external factors are constraining, coercing, or otherwise largely determining what they think and do.

This sense of being autonomous or self-authored in one's motivation emerges when activities and work environments facilitate meeting three basic organismic human needs. *Autonomy* is a sense of volition, a sense that one's behavior is self-chosen and self-authored. *Competence* is a sense of mastery, a belief that one is capable and effective in what one does. *Relatedness* is a feeling that one has positive interpersonal connections with others. Although Deci and Ryan (2000) propose that an activity or experience is intrinsically motivating to the degree that it fosters all three basic cognitions, autonomy is the linchpin of SDT. Intrinsic motivation results primarily from the degree to which individuals believe their behavior results from their own volition and free choice. It is important to note that Deci and Ryan (2000) propose three forms of autonomous motivation. Intrinsic motivation arises from enjoyment of or interest in the activity caused primarily by a heightened sense of autonomy. In contrast, identified motivation occurs when individuals consciously value the goal of an activity so that "action is accepted or owned as personally important," and integrated motivation occurs when the valued goal is fully integrated with one's sense of self (Ryan & Deci, 2000, p. 72). Because identified and integrated motivation is based on the purpose of the activity rather than the activity itself, they are not considered forms of intrinsic motivation in SDT.

However, in most of the empirical research on SDT, these three forms of motivation are treated as indicators of autonomous motivation, and they appear to produce similar outcomes (e.g., Houser-Marko & Sheldon, 2006; Koestner, Otis, Powers, Pelletier, & Gagnon, 2008).

*Flow Theory*
Although Csikszentmihalyi's (1990) flow theory has not been widely applied in empirical research, it has been used to represent the idea of intrinsic motivation in a variety of literatures. Flow is described as "the state in which people are so involved in an activity that nothing else seems to matter, the experience itself is so enjoyable that people will do it even at great cost, for the sheer sake of doing it" (Csikszentmihalyi, 1990, p. 4). Using one's skills to work toward a challenging but important goal is posited to be conducive to experiencing flow states. The combination of skills well-matched to an important challenge is thought to draw people to higher levels of performance or excellence. During flow, people experience a merging of awareness and action and become so deeply involved or completely absorbed in the activity that time seems to stand still, they lose track of the prosaic, and experience "a sense of exhilaration, a deep sense of enjoyment, that is long cherished and that becomes a landmark in memory of what life should be like" (Csikszentmihalyi, 1990, p. 3). This state of deep involvement and stretching of oneself causes people to feel "transported into a new reality" (Csikszentmihalyi, 1990, p. 74) and, at the same time, to perform at unexpectedly high levels.

Because the challenging goal is deemed important by the individual, both progress toward and eventual achievement of the goal are viewed as worthwhile and valuable. During the experience, people are motivated to act because doing so creates powerful positive emotions and creates a compelling sense of accomplishment. Goal achievement builds a sense that something important, difficult, and meaningful has been accomplished and, as a result, reinforces a positive sense of self. Thus, people are motivated both to perpetuate current flow experiences and to seek new ones. Thus, one important nuance offered by flow theory is to conceptualize how and why people might actively seek future experiences of intrinsic motivation. We return to this important idea again in our discussion of affect and intrinsic motivation.

*Integration of Cognitive Theories*
Our brief review of the cognitive theories of intrinsic motivation indicates there are both common and unique elements. An integration of the theories

suggests five primary cognitive antecedents of intrinsic motivation. First, competence is centrally important to all intrinsic motivation theories and is expressly equated with self-efficacy in most. Bandura (1989) has emphasized that self-efficacy is one of the foundations of human motivation, noting "People's self-efficacy beliefs determine their level of motivation, as reflected in how much effort they will exert in an endeavor and how long they will persevere in the face of obstacles" (p. 1176), and a great deal of research supports this claim. Autonomy is also centrally important to all models of intrinsic motivation. It is explicitly included in PET and SDT as a determinant of intrinsic motivation. Hackman and Oldham's (1980) definition of experienced responsibility – "feelings of personal responsibility for work outcomes" and individuals' beliefs that work outcomes depend "substantially on their *own* efforts, initiatives, and decisions" (p. 79) – are consistent with the sense of volition that is the essence of autonomy.

PET includes a unique cognition, impact. We believe that a fuller exploration of this concept will demonstrate that it goes beyond the motivating role of self-efficacy and autonomy in important ways. Impact refers to an individual's beliefs in their capacity to accomplish, through their self-efficacious and self-chosen actions, the *purpose* of the task. The concept of impact corresponds to the social psychological concept of personal control, "an individual's belief that he or she can behave in ways that maximize good outcomes and/or minimize bad outcomes" (Peterson, 1999, p. 288; Gilbert, 2006; Mischel, Cantor, & Feldman, 1996). As such, impact is a belief that one can make a positive difference through one's actions and decisions. As such, impact is distinct and important cognitive precursor of intrinsic motivation.

A fourth concept that is prominent in two theories, JCT and PET, is meaningfulness, which occurs when individuals believe that the work they are doing is important and worthwhile. Both theories assert that mean-ingfulness derives from an individual's personal values, ideals, and beliefs (Hackman & Oldham, 1980). That is, work is experienced as meaningful to the extent that people perceive a strong match or fit between the requirements and purpose of a work role and their own values, ideals, and beliefs (Cantor & Sanderson, 1999; Hackman & Oldham, 1980; Spreitzer, 1996; Thomas & Velthouse, 1990). Deci and Ryan seem to agree that meaningfulness is important when, for example, they define autonomy as "the organismic desire to ... have activity be concordant with one's integrated sense of self" (2000, p. 231). Whereas autonomy focuses on freedom to choose or control behaviors, activities, or tasks, mean-ingfulness focuses on self-endorsing the purpose or reason behind those activities, tasks, or work.

Unique to SDT is the concept of relatedness. Deci and Ryan (2000; Ryan & Deci, 2000) propose that intrinsic motivation is more likely to flourish when the need for relatedness is satisfied. While their conceptualization of relationships is quite broad, ranging from relationships that offer instrumental help and support to those comprising, caring, emotional support, and love (e.g., Ryan & Deci, 2000), they suggest that relatedness plays only a distal or indirect role in creating intrinsic motivation. For example, relatedness may provide a sense of security that potentially increases autonomy and self-efficacy, or it may facilitate the integration of values and regulations, leading to increased perceptions of meaningfulness. However, other research on belongingness and relationships (e.g., Baumeister & Leary, 1995; Gersick, Dutton, & Bartunek, 2000; Reis, Collins, & Berscheid, 2000) suggests that relationships which satisfy the need to belong may be a direct source of intrinsic motivation. Further, in a recent review and extension of research on JCT, Oldham and Hackman (2010) noted that, with the benefit of hindsight, it is clear that social sources of intrinsic motivation deserve more attention. They call for more theory work to identify the specific social factors that are relevant to intrinsic motivation.

Our discussion and integration suggests that self-efficacy, autonomy, impact, meaningfulness, and relatedness are core cognitive elements associated with intrinsic motivation. We propose that affect is also a core element of intrinsic motivation and, furthermore, that it may be a key to richer understanding of intrinsic motivation. For example, we will propose how including affect may provide the basis for understanding different levels of intrinsic motivation. Indeed, the existing cognitive literature suggests this is the case. For example, Amabile (1996) refers to intrinsic motivation as "an inner passion" (p. 78) and Csikszentmihalyi (1990) characterizes it as "a sense of exhilaration, a deep sense of enjoyment that is long cherished" and as an experience that is "so enjoyable that people will do it even at great cost, for the sheer sake of doing it" (p. 3 and 4). Hackman and Oldham (1976) maintain that the core of intrinsic motivation is "positive affect ... (that) is self-reinforcing to the individual" (p. 256). Thus, in the next section, we develop a model of intrinsic motivation that recognizes both its affective and cognitive antecedents.

## THE AFFECTIVE CORE OF INTRINSIC MOTIVATION

People are always in some affective state, but these states are in flux, shifting with changes in external circumstances, the vicissitudes of life, and the individual's internal condition (Barrett et al., 2007; Cropanzano et al., 2003; Elfenbein, 2007; Frijda, 2007; Schwarz & Clore, 2007; Watson, 2000; Zajonc, 1998). Even so, these affective states appear to play a potentially indispensable role in virtually all human motivation (Ashkanasy, Härtel, & Zerbe, 2000; Barsade et al., 2003; Brief & Weiss, 2002; Cropanzano et al., 2003; George & Brief, 1996; Lord, Klimoski, & Kanfer, 2002; Seo, Barrett, & Bartunek, 2004; Weiss & Cropanzano, 1996). A growing body of research provides strong evidence that affect has powerful motivational capacities and at times can inundate people's consciousness, inducing a potent flood of motivation that sweeps them into dramatic courses of action (Csikszentmihalyi, 1990; Kagan, 2009; LeDoux, 1996; Russell, 2003). Empirical research also suggests that a great deal of motivation happens without the involvement of conscious cognitions and, in these situations, affect appears to be the primary motivational impetus (Barsade, Ramarajan, & Westen, 2009; Custers & Aarts, 2005; Izard, 1993; Loewenstein, Weber, Hsee, & Welch, 2001; Zajonc, 1980, 1998). This nonconscious, affect-based motivation can have a powerful influence on human thoughts and behaviors, yet it circumvents the pathways articulated in existing theories of intrinsic motivation that rely on the operation of conscious cognitions.

Core affect theory has emerged as one useful model for exploring a broad range of affect-laden experiences, including the relationship between affect and motivation (Barrett et al., 2007; Clore, Storbeck, Robinson, & Centerbar, 2005; Russell, 2003, 2005; Russell & Barrett, 1999). Seo et al. (2004) used core affect theory to suggest how affect might influence goal setting processes and, following their lead, we build on core affect theory to suggest how affect might play a crucial role in intrinsic motivation. Core affect itself is the feelings of pleasure–displeasure (hedonic tone) and activation–deactivation (activation) that arise from a person's continuous, automatic, nonreflective, and often nonconscious assessments of their own well-being and the potential implications of environmental objects (e.g., people, physical objects, places, conditions, or states of affairs) and events (e.g., salient incidents such as actions of other people or changes in environmental conditions) for their ongoing well-being (Barrett et al., 2007; Russell, 2003, 2005). A person always has core affect, but may not always be consciously aware of it. Nevertheless, it can have a substantial impact on their motivational experiences (Seo et al., 2004). *Positive* core affect, which is the central construct in our model, comprises affective experiences of positive hedonic tone across a range of activation levels, including feeling excited, happy, or contented (see Fig. 2). Positive core affect indicates that objects and events have beneficial, good, or otherwise positive implications

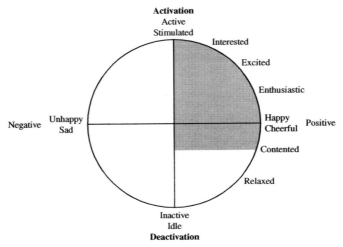

*Fig. 2.*  Core Affect.  *Source:*  Adapted from Russell and Barrett (1999) and
Russell (2003).

for individuals' well-being (Barrett et al., 2007; Russell, 2003; Zajonc, 1998,
2000), and it has been shown to induce approach-oriented, promotion-
focused motivation (Baas, De Dreu, & Nijstad, 2008; Damasio, 1994;
Higgins, 2006; Isen, 2002; Panksepp, 2004; Zajonc, 1998).

   In some cases, core affect is free-floating – people do not think much
about it and make no attributions about its causes – and so it remains
largely in the background, outside of individuals' awareness (Barrett et al.,
2007; Russell, 2003; Watson, 2000). This unattributed core affect is referred
to as an *implicit affective experience* or sometimes more broadly as *mood* to
include times individuals notice, but do not process, their somatic feelings
(Russell, 2003). In other cases individuals notice their core affect and engage
in further appraisals of it. Sometimes these appraisals are minimal and result
simply in people identifying the probable causes of their affect; core affect
theory refers to these as *emotional experiences* (Barrett et al., 2007; Russell,
2003; Scherer, 2001). At still other times individuals engage in more
extensive sensemaking activities or *emotional meta-experiences* during which
they interpret, label, and construct explanations, memories, and schema
about their affective states (Russell, 2003). It is during emotional meta-
experiences that conscious cognitions (i.e., emotional appraisals) play an

important role as people examine perceived causal objects and events more closely to determine their characteristics and likely trajectories, piece together relationships between these perceived causes and their core affect, craft plausible accounts of the reasons for and probable outcomes of their core affect, and categorize their experiences as being of a particular kind of emotion (Roseman & Smith, 1999; Scherer, 2001). When a person says, for example, "I am excited about my new project at work," they are in the midst of an emotional meta-experience. Finally, emotional meta-experiences set into motion *emotion regulation processes* by which people try to control and adjust their affective experiences (Gross & Thompson, 2007; Russell, 2003). For positive core affect, these emotion regulation processes are largely directed toward prolonging, enhancing, and repeating the positive core affective experience (Gross & Thompson, 2007; Hirt, Melton, McDonald, & Harackiewicz, 1996; Wegener & Petty, 1994).

## Core Affect and Intrinsic Motivation

We propose that the fundamental cause of intrinsic motivation is positive core affect. While cognitions can be important codeterminants of intrinsic motivation, we hypothesize that eliciting intrinsic motivation at work requires and begins with a change in core affect to a more positive, activated state that results from certain work experiences. In the next sections, we propose three pathways by which positive core affect may cause intrinsic motivation. We suggest that in some cases positive core affect is a sufficient cause of intrinsic motivation, while in other cases, affect works in concert with cognitions to induce intrinsic motivation (see Fig. 1).

Many scholars assert that the fundamental purpose of affect *is* to motivate and that positive affect induces approach-oriented motivation that causes people to actively and persistently engage with objects and events that appear to be the source of their affect (cf. Brehm, 1999; Custers & Aarts, 2005; Damasio, 1999; Frijda, 2007; LeDoux, 1996; Russell, 2003). Some scholars go further. Izard (1993) asserts that cognitions must elicit affect in order for them to have motivational impact, and Zajonc (1998) asserts that emotions "are sources of energy for action that reason alone cannot generate" (p. 596). Similarly, research indicates that some forms of motivation, such as approach motivation, arise immediately and automatically in response to activities that produce positive affective experiences and which then energizes and directs eager engagement in the activities that have produced positive affect (Carver, 2006; Elliot, 2006; Watson, 2000).

The more intense or activated the affect, the faster and stronger are its motivation-inducing properties (Brehm, 1999; Damasio, 1999).

Research on regulatory focus theory (Higgins, 2000; Brockner & Higgins, 2001) leads to similar conclusions. Studies suggest that positive affective experiences, even at very mild activation levels, foster a promotion-focus wherein people are motivated to move toward and eagerly pursue activities that create positive affect (Brockner & Higgins, 2001; Frijda, 2007; Higgins, 2000, 2006). Regulatory focus research indicates that people not only approach activities that create positive core affect, but they also become more fully engaged in – that is, more "involved, occupied, and interested in" (Higgins, 2006, p. 442) – such activities. This research also indicates that people choose behavioral strategies that help them achieve and sustain their engagement in these activities (Higgins, 2000, 2006).

Our core proposal is that intrinsic motivation begins with a change in core affect and, hence, that all experiences of intrinsic motivation are, at their core, positive affective experiences. We have referenced several lines of research that indicate that the positive core affect that arises directly from engaging with work activities and work environments can have strong, persistent motivational effects.

**Proposition 1.** Intrinsic motivation is elicited when engaging with work activities and work environments induces positive core affect in individuals.

*Implicit Intrinsic Motivation*

We propose that in some cases intrinsic motivation can result from experiences of implicit positive affect (Fig. 1). Studies show that the motivational effects of positive core affect do not require, and often occur without, the involvement of conscious cognitions (Barsade et al., 2009; Cacioppo, Gardner, & Berntson, 1999; Izard, 1993; Loewenstein et al., 2001; Winkielman & Berridge, 2004; Zajonc, 1980, 2000). For example, positive core affect can motivate individuals through nonconscious processes when they are aware of neither their affect nor the factors that are causing their affective experiences (Custers & Aarts, 2005, 2007; Zajonc, 1980, 2000). There is growing evidence of neurological mechanisms that are responsible for the direct impact of positive affect on motivation (Damasio, 1994; Panksepp, 2004; Zajonc, 1998). Gray (1987, 1990) has identified two general motivational systems in the human brain, one of which, the *behavioral activation system* (BAS), initiates appetitive behavior. The BAS is activated by signals of reward, including positive affective experiences, and in turn it initiates approach-oriented motivation and behavior without the involvement of any cognitive mediators (Lord et al., 2002). Researchers have found that these implicit positive affective experiences can influence the actions and goals people decide to pursue, and also the intensity and persistence of their goal-oriented motivation, all without the individual being aware of their affect or, in many cases, without being aware of their motivation (Barsade et al., 2009; Russell, 2003; Winkielman & Berridge, 2004). Research also indicates that affective reactions happen much faster and earlier than do cognitions and so a great deal of human motivation is produced first by affect and shaped later by cognitions (Damasio, 1994; Panksepp, 2004; Zajonc, 1998). In addition, studies show that once affect is activated, it is sufficient for generating and sustaining motivation (Brehm, 1999; Izard, 1993; Zajonc, 2000).

A series of studies by Custers and Aarts (2005, 2007) exemplify the research that suggests a direct link between implicit positive affect and intrinsic motivation. Custers and Aarts (2005) primed subjects with either nonconscious positive or neutral affect by displaying positive or neutral words on a computer screen for 150 ms, too fast to be consciously noticed, but long enough to induce implicit affect. After each affect prime, they showed a mundane activity – cleaning, changing clothes, writing – again for only 150 ms. They then showed subjects each activity again, but this time long enough for the subjects to notice them (2,500 ms) and asked subjects which activities they would be willing to engage in. Results showed that subjects were more willing to engage in activities that had been nonconsciously paired with positive affect than those paired with neutral affect. In a second series of studies (Custers & Aarts, 2007), the goal concept of "socializing" was subliminally primed with positive affect and then participants were given an activity that provided the opportunity to socialize. In two studies they found that participants put more effort into attaining the opportunity to socialize when the goal had been subliminally associated with positive affect. This growing body of research indicates that individuals can be motivated to pursue an activity without knowing why they are so motivated and, in some cases, without realizing they are motivated (Custers & Aarts, 2005; Murphy, Monahan, & Zajonc, 1995; Zajonc, 2000). Intrinsic motivation may be particularly important for understanding when and why individuals sustain engagement with prosaic, even mundane, activities over long periods of time, when performance-reward contingencies may not be salient or strong enough to motivate effort. These experiences might also prove somewhat elusive to measurement, especially using self-report methods, and so in later sections we propose some alternative approaches.

**Proposition 2.** Implicit intrinsic motivation occurs when engaging with work activities and work environments induces implicit positive core affect. Individuals are likely to be unaware of either their positive core affect or their implicit intrinsic motivation.

*Emotion-Based Intrinsic Motivation*

In other cases, positive core affect enters individuals' conscious awareness and is subjected to some limited cognitive appraisal. Essentially, during these *positive emotional experiences*, individuals make attributions about the perceived cause of their affect (Barrett, 2005; Cropanzano et al., 2003; Russell, 2003; Weiss, 2002). These appraisals are automatic, fast, and minimal, and result in little conscious cognition beyond attributions of the cause of an affective experience. In terms of resulting motivation, affect remains the primary motivational force (Roseman & Smith, 1999; Russell, 2003; Scherer, 2001). In these cases, we propose individuals' conscious emotional experiences are sufficient causes for intrinsic motivation (Fig. 1).

Unlike implicit intrinsic motivation experiences, during a positive emotional experience individuals are more likely to consciously evaluate continued engagement with the activity in a positive manner and are, therefore, more inclined to seek out and persist in their engagement with the activity (Desteno, Petty, Wegener, & Rucker, 2000; Lyubomirsky, King, & Diener, 2005; Martin, Ward, Achee, & Wyer, 1993). Research on Damasio's (1994, 1999) "somatic marker" hypothesis indicates that even anticipatory affect – affect experienced as people think about a particular course of action – strongly influences peoples' subsequent behavioral choices.

**Proposition 3.** Emotion-based intrinsic motivation is caused when engaging with work activities and work environments creates positive emotional experiences. Individuals are aware of their positive work experience and are therefore likely to seek ways to continue their engagement in activities they perceive as the source.

*Affective–Cognitive Intrinsic Motivation*

Finally, there are situations in which both affect and cognition play a central role in experiences of intrinsic motivation. During emotional meta-experiences people engage in extensive cognitive processing of their positive core affect, and we propose it is during these experiences that core cognitions play an important role (Fig. 1). Emotional meta-experiences may occur when core affect is sufficiently intense to draw individuals' attention to it. For example, powerful positive emotional experiences that people describe as exuberance, exhilaration, elevation, and awe create abundant physical and mental energy, and people experiencing them feel capable of and compelled to take robust, potent action (Csikszentmihalyi, 1990; Haidt, 2006). People tend to be very aware of these experiences and, because they are so powerful and so positive, people search for causes and explanations of their emotions (Csikszentmihalyi, 1990; Kagan, 2009). Emotional meta-experiences may also occur when individuals have been primed in some way, often by an external source, to more deeply process their core affect (Barrett et al., 2007; Elfenbein, 2007; Russell, 2003). For example, emotional meta-experiences may be primed when employees discuss their work activities with each other, when a salient change draws attention to a task, when people are asked to evaluate their work activities, or when some other trigger evokes close scrutiny of activities. This idea is consistent with affective events theory (AET; Weiss & Cropanzano, 1996), which proposes that people often react emotionally to workplace activities and events. Under AET, events, which are defined as "a change in circumstances, a change in what one is currently experiencing" (p. 31), cause emotional reactions that, in turn, influence people's thoughts, feelings, behaviors, and their motivation. For example, recognizing an employee for superior work is an event that likely has an influence on an individual's affect. In turn, the nature of this affect has implications for the employee's attitudes, motivation, and behavior. We build on AET and propose that these processes can also lead to emotional meta-experiences.

During these emotional meta-experiences, people look for ways to explain, understand, and regulate their positive affective experience (Frijda, 2007; Russell, 2003; Smith & Kirby, 2001). Consistent with feeling-as-information research (Schwarz & Clore, 2007; Seo et al., 2004), when people try to explain their affect-based motivation, they craft post hoc explanations that are heavily informed by, and created to be consistent with, their affective experience. When trying to explain their motivation people ask themselves, "How do I feel about this activity?" and use their affect as the basis for the answers they craft to this question. In the case of positive core affect, these cognitions would be of a form such as, "I like this task," or "I enjoy this activity." The appraisals that people develop to understand their affect can include detailed assessments of the work activities they view as the probable causes of their affective experiences, evaluations of the relevance of these activities for their current goals and activities, appraisals of the susceptibility of these activities to being manipulated or controlled, predictions of the likely outcomes of these activities, and assessments of the potential implications of the activities for their short- and long-term well-being (Scherer, 2001; Smith & Kirby, 2001). It is through emotional meta-experiences that individuals form specific understandings about the nature, causes, and outcomes of their affective experience (Barrett et al., 2007; Russell, 2003, 2005).

We propose that it is also during emotional meta-experiences that the conscious core cognitions identified by existing theories play a central role (Hackman & Oldham, 1980; Spreitzer, 1996; Thomas & Velthouse, 1990). During these experiences, positive affect and conscious core cognitions work in concert to create intrinsic motivation. In some situations, conscious core cognitions form before emotional meta-experiences, such as when they have been primed by an external source. This might occur, for example, when there is a salient change in an activity, when employees discuss their work, or when individuals are asked to report about activities they find enjoyable. In other cases, conscious core cognitions are integral to emotional meta-experiences and the sensemaking efforts that constitute these experiences. We posit that it is likely people will attribute their emotions to activities that are consistent with the core cognitions identified by existing theories – experienced meaningfulness, a sense of impact, efficacy beliefs, perceptions of self-determination, and a sense of relatedness – because these characteristics also create positive affective experiences.

**Proposition 4.** Affective–cognitive intrinsic motivation is caused by the joint effects of positive emotional meta-experiences and conscious core cognitions.

Finally, these experiences of affective–cognitive intrinsic motivation usually induce emotion regulation activities whereby people seek to sustain, enhance, and repeat their positive core affective experiences (dashed feedback loops in Fig. 1; Elfenbein, 2007; Gross, 1998; Gross & Thompson, 2007; Russell, 2003). During emotion regulation, people use a variety of techniques to manage their affective experience including (a) selectively attuning to activity characteristics that may enhance the positive experience, (b) directly shaping work activities or modifying their engagement with activities to enhance and prolong the experience, (c) selecting activities and situations that are likely to create positive core affect, and (d) reappraising the situation – adjusting their cognitions by, for example, carefully choosing from among the several potential meanings of the situation – to enhance their positive core affect (Elfenbein, 2007; Gross, 1998; Gross & Thompson, 2007; Hirt et al., 1996). Because these experiences are conscious and intentional, individuals look for ways to enhance, intensify, prolong, and repeat their motivational experience, both in the current moment and in the future (Frijda, 1999; Gross, 1998; Gross & Thompson, 2007; Russell, 2003; Smith & Kirby, 2001). As a result, people will likely be better equipped to shape their future work experiences in a manner that fosters intrinsic motivation.

Finally, we suggest that emotional regulation activities might be the source of the self-generating and self-perpetuating properties some scholars have attributed to intrinsic motivation (Hackman & Oldham, 1980). The potential for intrinsic motivation to be self-generating and self-perpetuating has been one of its most intriguing and beneficial characteristics largely because of its implications for sustaining motivation over long periods of time. The combined effect of these three psychological processes might create positive cycles by which positive core affect leads to positive core cognitions, which leads to emotional regulation activities that, in turn, enhance positive core affect thereby creating a self-reinforcing relationship.

**Proposition 5.** Positive emotional meta-experiences and core cognitions initiate emotion regulation activities that increase the likelihood of sustaining, enhancing, and repeating intrinsic motivation.

# IMPLICATIONS OF A COGNITIVE–AFFECTIVE MODEL OF INTRINSIC MOTIVATION

## Understanding Intrinsic Motivation

Our enhanced model of intrinsic motivation has a number of implications for research on intrinsic motivation. The first implication is to suggest the central role that affect is likely to play in experiences of intrinsic motivation. While we acknowledge that cognitions can also play a very important role in intrinsic motivation, we have argued that the essence of these experiences is positive affect. We have argued that this perspective is in keeping with even the earliest conceptualizations of intrinsic motivation and that including affect as an essential component of theories of intrinsic motivation is of paramount importance. Our focus on affect is in keeping with a growing body of research that indicates affect plays an important and potentially indispensable role in motivation (Ashkanasy et al., 2000; Barsade et al., 2003; Brief & Weiss, 2002; Cropanzano et al., 2003; George & Brief, 1996; Lord et al., 2002; Seo et al., 2004; Weiss & Cropanzano, 1996). We have described how this new approach may allow researchers to understand some

important, but unexplored, manifestations of intrinsic motivation, such as
the purported self-generating and self-perpetuating properties of intrinsic
motivation that scholars have long ago posited (e.g., Hackman & Oldham,
1980). We have also proposed how affect might lead to nonconscious
experiences of intrinsic motivation. These properties are not addressed by
existing cognitive theories.

Including affect may also provide a basis for exploring new issues, such as
whether there are different levels or intensities of intrinsic motivation.
Again, existing cognitive theories do not suggest how, for example,
differences in individuals' perceptions of meaning, impact, or self-efficacy
might be related to higher or lower levels of intrinsic motivation. Affect
research suggests that the intensity of an emotion – its activation level –
influences the intensity of the ensuing motivation (see Fig. 2; Brehm, 1999;
Seo et al., 2004). Activation creates energy and mobilization such that
people experiencing more activated affective states tend to devote more
effort toward and engage more vigorously in activities associated with the
affective experience (Brehm, 1999; Damasio, 1994; Izard, 1993; Seo et al.,
2004). As activation levels increase, people experience higher levels of energy
and a stronger sense of mobilization, which in turn induce more animated
and vigorous responses (Brehm, 1999; Custers & Aarts, 2005; Russell, 2003;
Seo et al., 2004). This research suggests that the intensity of intrinsic
motivation is likely to vary positively with the intensity of the affect that
underlies it. Less activated affect, such as experiences associated with
enjoyment, are likely to be associated with lower levels of intrinsic
motivation, while emotional experiences such as excitement and exuberance
are likely to be associated with more intense levels of intrinsic motivation.

## Antecedents of Intrinsic Motivation

Another important implication of our cognitive–affective model of intrinsic
motivation is that it suggests researchers can learn more about the kinds of
work situations that foster intrinsic motivation by investigating the affect
induced by different work activities and events. Those activities and events
that consistently evoke positive affect are likely to also induce intrinsic
motivation. While existing research on intrinsic motivation relies on self-
report measures of individuals' cognitions, affect can be measured in a
variety of ways that would allow researchers greater flexibility in their
studies. For example, in addition to traditional self-report measures (e.g.,
the PANAS scale; Watson, Clark, & Tellegen, 1988), affect can be measured

using observational techniques (e.g., analyzing facial expressions), physiological methods (e.g., heart rate, galvanic skin response), as well as high-fidelity self-report methods such as experience sampling techniques. Observational methods, such as Ekman's Facial Action Coding System (Ekman, Friesen, & Hager, 2002) or his more recent Micro Expression method (Ekman, 2008), could be used in lab or field settings to measure how work events influence employees' intrinsic motivation. These observational techniques would allow researchers to study intrinsic motivation without relying exclusively on self-reports. Researchers might, for example, study how events such as performance evaluations, recognition of superior employee performance, or interactions among coworkers shape employee intrinsic motivation by observing changes in employees' facial expressions that reflect their underlying affective state. Alternatively, researchers could use experience sampling methodologies to study how positive core affect varies in accordance with work events or changes in features of work environments and, in turn, how these variations influence observable outcomes of intrinsic motivation such as creative performance, activity performance, time spent on task, and organizational citizenship behaviors (Piccolo & Colquitt, 2006; Shin & Zhou, 2003; Spreitzer, 1996).

This discussion of variation points to another potential implication of our model: it may also be useful for understanding the variability of intrinsic motivation. While many researchers suggest that work motivation varies over the course of time (Kanfer, Chen, & Pritchard, 2008), little is known about variations in the level or duration of intrinsic motivation or the determinants of any such variability. Most cognitive theories do not expressly address this possibility nor has research yet addressed whether the cognitions that are central to these theories vary much, at least over the short-run. Given that the work features that influence these cognitions – such as empowerment, sociopolitical support, transformational leadership, and unit climate (Piccolo & Colquitt, 2006; Spreitzer, 1996) – tend to be fairly stable over time, it seems likely that core cognitions will also be fairly stable. This begs the question of what causes changes in intrinsic motivation. Research suggests that core affect, unlike core cognitions, is much more labile even when conditions do not change (Barrett et al., 2007; Elfenbein, 2007; Russell, 2003). One explanation for this variability is hedonic treadmill effects (Fredrick & Loewenstein, 1999), which have been a staple of affect research for several decades. Hedonic treadmill effects occur when people adjust psychologically to their life or work conditions and respond as if those conditions have changed, even when no objective change has occurred. Using this view, researchers might find that people become accustomed to some work activities, and, even though the characteristics of these activities have not changed, the impact of these activities on employees' intrinsic motivation might diminish over time.

Consider an activity that employees initially find interesting. Over time they may grow to find the activity boring and tedious. Initially this activity would likely induce intrinsic motivation but, even though the activity itself has not changed, hedonic treadmill effects would cause a change in employees' affective response to the activity in such a manner that their intrinsic motivation is eroded over time. Similarly, bringing affect into the study of intrinsic motivation could also help explain why intrinsic motivation might diminish in some situations even when work character-istics have been changed substantially to increase employee motivation. For example, consider efforts to change work activities, such as increasing empowerment, to enhance employees' intrinsic motivation. Initially, increased empowerment may foster intrinsic motivation-related cognitions (e.g., perceptions of self-determination and mastery) and induce positive core affect. Over time, however, as the workers become accustomed to the increased level of empowerment, the affect-related effects might wear off. The empowerment that at one juncture created feelings of excitement and enjoyment may no longer have this effect. As such, after the initial change to create greater empowerment, the employees' level of intrinsic motivation might drop-off somewhat because of declines in positive core affect even as perceptions of empowerment remain relatively stable.

## The Effects of HRM Practices on Intrinsic Motivation

A large body of research has examined the impact of human resource systems and management practices on intrinsic motivation as conceptua-lized by cognitive theories. We believe that our enhanced model of intrinsic motivation may suggest other ways in which organizations can encourage intrinsic motivation in the workplace. For example, much research has examined how reward systems enhance or undermine interest-based intrinsic motivation. Cognitive evaluation theory (Deci & Ryan, 1985) proposes that extrinsic rewards may negatively impact interest-based intrinsic motivation, especially when rewards diminish feelings of autonomy. Although there is still debate about the impact of rewards on intrinsic motivation (Eisenberger, Pierce, & Cameron, 1999), meta-analytic findings have provided support for cognitive evaluation theory. When rewards are given contingent on engaging in a task or completing a task, intrinsic motivation (as assessed by free choice behavior and self-reported interest) tends to be lower than in a no-reward control condition (Deci, Koestner, & Ryan, 1999). Further, rewards given contingent on performance also undermine intrinsic motivation, unless the context is supportive rather than controlling (Deci et al., 1999). However, when rewards are given in an environment that is supportive or when rewards are independent of task engagement or are unexpected, extrinsic rewards do not undermine intrinsic motivation (Deci et al., 1999).

Consistent with cognitive evaluation theory, most research on the impact of rewards on intrinsic motivation defines it as motivation that arises from interest in the activity itself. As Gagné and Deci (2005) noted, little research has examined how extrinsic rewards may impact motivation that arises from the perceived importance of the outcomes of the task (referred to as integrated motivation in SDT; Ryan & Deci, 2000). Further, little research has addressed the link between extrinsic rewards and affect (Brief & Weiss, 2002). Thus, it is possible that extrinsic rewards may impact intrinsic motivation differently when intrinsic motivation is based on meaningfulness or passion and is characterized by highly activated positive affect. Eisenberger et al. (1999) suggested that extrinsic rewards enhance intrinsic motivation "when they convey that task performance helps satisfy needs, wants, or desires" (p. 678). Thus, it is possible that extrinsic rewards enhance intrinsic motivation based on meaningfulness when they convey information about the importance or value of the task. Similarly, group-based extrinsic rewards may enhance intrinsic motivation because such rewards are consistent with a sense of community and shared values. Further, Amabile (1996) proposes that "synergistic" extrinsic motivators, which support perceptions of competence or increase involvement with a task, will also enhance intrinsic motivation. Research clarifying how reward systems can be used to enhance intrinsic motivation is very important given that managers of most organizations try to marshal a bundle of rewards (Milkovich & Newman, 2005), including extrinsic (e.g., compensation and benefits) and intrinsic (e.g., challenging work, great work environment, and good coworkers) to motivate and direct the efforts of their employees. Currently, very little is known about how the effects of the various elements of a total rewards package interact with each other, yet more and more organizations are adopting a total rewards approach to managing workplace motivators (Milkovich & Newman, 2005).

Intrinsic motivation might also enhance the effects of extrinsic motivation. For example, an employee might initially engage in a mundane, mandatory task because of extrinsic motivators. However, if engaging in the task creates positive affect, our model predicts that it will foster implicit intrinsic motivation that, combined with the effects of extrinsic motivation, might then boost the employee's overall motivation to perform the task. Similarly, this combined effect might explain how certain structural features of compensation systems might foster intrinsic motivation and enhance the effects of extrinsic motivators. Compensation researchers have emphasized that communicating the reasons behind a compensation system might boost its motivational power (Milkovich & Newman, 2005). One way this might work would be when the reasons given for the extrinsic motivator enhance employees' perceptions of the importance and meaningfulness of the goals to which it is attached. This might occur, for example, when the bonus is tied to outcomes such as safety or customer satisfaction that reinforce the perceived importance of the goal. According to our model, pursuing a challenging and meaningful goal will create affective–cognitive intrinsic motivation which, in turn, might boost the effects created by the bonus. This completes the loop that begins with Amabile's (1996) synergistic extrinsic motivation by suggesting a positive cycle where the two forms of motivation interact to create higher motivation. Because our model focuses on the affect that is created in this dynamic relationship, it suggests, for example, that if pursuing an incentive creates emotions such as excitement or enthusiasm, intrinsic motivation will also be induced. In such a situation, the two forms of motivation are likely to work in concert. However, this mutually enhancing effect might be disrupted if employees' affect subsides.

Another way in which human resource systems may influence intrinsic motivation is through selection procedures. When employees are selected based on person–job fit, the goal is to match the knowledge, skills, and abilities of the employee with the demands of the job (Kristof-Brown & Guay, 2010). Selecting employees based on demands–abilities fit increases the likelihood that employees perceive themselves to be competent in their jobs, and jobs that fulfill the need for competence are more likely to be viewed as intrinsically motivating (Ryan & Deci, 2000). Similarly, when selection is based on employees' fit with the organization, organizations hire employees whose values or goals are consistent with those of the organization (Kristof-Brown & Guay, 2010). Employees who share the organization's values and goals may have higher intrinsic motivation because of their sense that their work is meaningful and that they belong to the organization. Selection procedures that maximize person–environment fit may also impact intrinsic motivation through their influence on positive affect. When employees fit with the work environment, they may feel as though they are similar to others (Byrne, 1971) or that their needs are being fulfilled, which promotes positive affect at work (Locke, 1976). Thus, selection procedures can place employees in positions in which the potential for intrinsic motivation is high.

Finally, management practices can significantly influence intrinsic motivation in the workplace. When managers create environments that support the fulfillment of autonomy, competence, and relatedness needs, intrinsic motivation that comes from interest in the task and intrinsic motivation that comes from valuing the outcome of the task may be fostered (Ryan & Deci, 2000). For example, when managers give employees the opportunity to voice their perspectives and make choices about the ways in which they do their work, employees have the opportunity to actively craft their work so that they can focus on parts of their job that are most interesting or meaningful to them (Wrzesniewski & Dutton, 2001). Further, specific leadership behaviors, such as transformational leadership, have been shown to shape employees' perceptions of their job characteristics (Piccolo & Colquitt, 2006) and encourage employees to set goals that are higher in self-concordance (Bono & Judge, 2003). Management practices and work environment may also influence positive affect in the workplace (Brief & Weiss, 2002), facilitating higher levels of intrinsic motivation among employees.

## New Frontiers in Research on Intrinsic Motivation

We believe that our cognitive–affective model of intrinsic motivation suggests a number of promising new directions for research. In the following text, we discuss three of these potential new directions. First, we pick up on a theme of intrinsic motivation and employee well-being that Hackman and Oldham (1980) raised in their pioneering work. We discuss how experiences of intrinsic motivation might foster positive psychological states such as subjective well-being and resilience. Second, we suggest links between intrinsic motivation and identity through processes such as the internalization of work goals. Lastly, we push further by exploring the potential moral underpinnings of intrinsic motivation. Research on moral motivations suggests that emotions might play a critical role in moral behaviors and responses (Haidt, 2001). We build on this research by suggesting how moral emotions such as pride might be a source for powerful experiences of intrinsic motivation.

### Intrinsic Motivation and Well-Being

One of the most important of the original purposes of JCT was to understand the impact of jobs on employee well-being, yet this idea has gone largely unstudied. Hackman and Oldham (1980) devoted a considerable proportion of their seminal book to both an analysis and normative reappraisal of management systems in light of their impact on employee well-being. They end their book with a caution that then current trends in management systems might bode poorly for employees. The recent emergence of positive organizational scholarship (Cameron, Dutton, & Quinn, 2003) highlights that employee well-being remains an important research issue. The addition of positive affect as a key cause of intrinsic motivation may create useful theoretical linkages between research on intrinsic motivation and existing research on well-being. For example, a growing body of research indicates that regular experiences of positive affect may foster life satisfaction and subjective well-being (Lyubomirsky et al., 2005), bolster resilience (Ong, Bergeman, Bisconti, & Wallace, 2006; Tugade & Fredrickson, 2004), and create resources useful for coping with life stressors (Folkman & Moskowitz, 2003). Work experiences that foster intrinsic motivation might, therefore, also be conducive to employee well-being, yielding twice the bang (performance and well-being) for the HRM buck.

The cognitive core also provides important theoretical underpinnings for research on intrinsic motivation and well-being. For example, research indicates that possessing a sense that one's life is meaningful and that one has important contributions to make in the world appears to be salutary for physical health (McKnight & Kashdan, 2009; Sherman, Simonton, Latif, & Bracy, 2010) and bolsters life satisfaction (Sheldon & Elliot, 1999). Existing research provides very few insights into how the work factors that are thought to lead to high performance (e.g., compensation, especially incentive pay) might influence employee well-being, but we believe such research is much needed. There is ample literature suggesting that money per se bears little relationship to well-being (Kahneman, Krueger, Schkade, Schwarz, & Stone, 2006) and the pursuit of money might be detrimental to life satisfaction (Sheldon, Ryan, Deci, & Kasser, 2004), but what are the effects of factors such as autonomy, variety, and feedback on employee well-being? Research provides little evidence to address this issue. Studies in educational settings indicate that some forms of feedback foster learning and well-being (e.g., those forms designed to encourage students to focus on developing their abilities), while other forms seem to be detrimental to both (e.g., those that encourage students to focus on earning grades; Meece, Anderman, & Anderman, 2006). There are other intriguing studies that suggest praise might undermine students' intrinsic motivation and also, perhaps, their well-being (Henderlong & Lepper, 2002). We do not know whether similar relationships exist in work settings, so there are many research possibilities for HRM scholars. The research on self-concordance theory (Sheldon & Elliot, 1999), a subtheory of SDT, is already moving in this direction. One of the propositions of this theory is that individuals' well-being will be enhanced when they pursue goals and activities that foster autonomous motivation. Sheldon et al. (2004) found that individuals' well-being was enhanced when they pursued intrinsically oriented goals and it was worsened when they pursued extrinsically oriented goals. This approach can be translated into research on intrinsic motivation and might help advance the important calls for research that Hackman and Oldham (1980) issued 30 years ago.

*Identity and Intrinsic Motivation*
The centrality of meaning to three of the intrinsic motivation theories we reviewed provides a potential link to research on identity. Identities are "the meanings that individuals attach to themselves" and they appear to have important implications for individuals' work performance and work experiences (Dutton, Roberts, & Bednar, 2010, p. 266; Ashforth & Kreiner, 1999). One manifestation of identity, work as a calling, is particularly salient for research on intrinsic motivation (Bunderson & Thompson, 2009). Many lay people expect that those people who feel destined or called by some divine source to their work will also "love what they do." Bunderson and Thompson's (2009) study of zoo keepers suggests that callings might foster intrinsic motivation – zoo keepers who felt more destined to their work also reported finding greater meaning in even the most mundane tasks. This suggests that those with positive identities might be more likely to experience intrinsic motivation. However, they also found that callings may have a dark side: zoo keepers with stronger callings appeared to be more susceptible to manipulation by managers. This research is only suggestive of the links between identity and intrinsic motivation, and there is very little empirical evidence linking the two. Recent theory development by Johnson, Chang, and Yang (2010) provides a potentially useful conceptual foundation for further exploration. Briefly, they propose that employees will experience higher levels of intrinsic motivation when they have internalized organizational values and, therefore, feel more autonomously motivated when they enact those values. Johnson et al. (2010) go on to propose specific manifestations of this intrinsic motivation. Drawing on regulatory focus theory (Brockner & Higgins, 2001), they propose that employees who have integrated their organization's values into their work self-concepts will tend to adopt a promotion-focus at work, which, in turn, induces them to actively

and energetically engage in their work activities. A straightforward proposal based on this model is that employees who have internalized organizational values into their work identities will be more likely to experience intrinsic motivation at work.

Dutton et al.'s (2010) conceptual model may add theoretical richness to this idea. They distinguish several types of positive identities, one of which is a virtue identity that exists when one's identity is infused with notions about good character and proper conduct. This might be the kind of work identity that is held by employees who work for organizations that foster strong identification with strategic mission and values (e.g., some humanitarian organizations, Whole Foods Markets, Starbucks). Such identities might also foster intrinsic motivation because work activities are more likely to be seen as an expression of one's positive, virtuous self-image. However, Crocker and Park (2004) present an important counterpoint in their work on the downsides of pursing self-esteem, an issue of great relevance to identity. They note, "When people have self-validation goals, they react to threats in these domains in ways that undermine learning; relatedness; autonomy and self-regulation; and over time, mental and physical health" (p. 392). The burgeoning work on identity boundaries seems to provide many fruitful opportunities for exploring their relationship to intrinsic motivation.

*The Moral Roots of Intrinsic Motivation*
Psychologists have recently begun to explore the moral underpinnings of motivation and behavior by focusing on the important role played by moral emotions (Haidt, 2001; Tangney, Stuewig, & Mashek, 2007), and there is much to be learned by organizational scholars from this research. The basic premise is that, through socialization processes, people internalize moral standards of good and bad, right and wrong. These internalized standards are primarily enacted through moral emotions that "provide the motivational force – the power and energy – to do good and to avoid doing bad" (Tangney et al., 2007, p. 347; Kroll & Egan, 2004). One important feature of moral emotions is that they are elicited directly by situations, without the interplay of any conscious cognition, and, in turn, directly motivate responses (Bargh, Chen, & Burrows, 1996; Haidt, 2008; Tangney et al., 2007). Haidt (2001) refers to these as "gut feelings in the mind" (p. 825) and proposes they are an important source of motivation. We focus briefly on one moral emotion – pride – to illustrate how moral commitments, enacted through moral emotions, might be an important source of intrinsic motivation.

Pride is most often defined as a positive, self-conscious emotion people experience when they feel responsible for a socially valued outcome (Mascolo & Fischer, 1995; Williams & Desteno, 2008). Pride serves to enhance people's self-worth but, perhaps more importantly, feelings of pride likely serve important motivational functions by reinforcing people's commitment to moral standards and inducing future behavior that is consistent with those standards (Tangney et al., 2007). Pride often arises spontaneously and, when it does, it induces people to engage energetically and persistently in activities they associate with those feelings (Williams & Desteno, 2008; Tangney et al., 2007). Pride might, therefore, cause people to be intrinsically motivated to engage in an activity without any conscious thoughts about the meaning or virtue of such engagement: Simply feeling pride may be enough to initiate and sustain engagement in activities. Organizations that strive to inculcate a strong moral mission through activities such as employee orientations that emphasize the mission, organization-wide celebrations, sharing of organizational stories about extraordinary behavior consistent with the mission, and the like might engender a sense of pride in their employees. When presented with an opportunity to enact that mission, feelings of pride might be elicited spontaneously and, in turn, these feelings might foster intrinsic motivation to engage in those activities. This is only one possible way that HR and management practices might foster intrinsic motivation through their effects on employees' feelings of pride, and there are likely to be others. One interesting idea this suggests is that the key to fostering ethical behavior among employees might be to find ways to foster the right moral emotions, perhaps in addition to trying to inculcate the right moral commitments (e.g., encouraging employees to internalize organizational values), and theories of intrinsic motivation provide important conceptual foundations for understanding for how such emotions might lead to ethical conduct.

Other moral emotions that may induce intrinsic motivation include empathy (Batson, 1991) and elevation (Schnall, Roper, & Fessler, 2010), which have been shown to motivate a variety of helping behaviors directed even at strangers; gratitude (McCullough, Kilpatrick Emmons, & Larson, 2001); compassion (Crocker & Canevello, 2008), which seems to foster a variety of prosocial behaviors including those that appear to be related to building positive work relationships and teams; and joy, which might encourage curiosity, exploration, and engagement in activities associated with innovation (Fredrickson, 2001). The possibility that intrinsic motivation might have moral roots may be one useful way to explore how, why, and when employees engage in ethical behavior.

## CONCLUSION

For many years, researchers interested in intrinsic motivation have sought to understand situations in which people are motivated by work activities themselves, when there is no apparent influence from external motivators and people engage in an activity for the positively valued experience they derive directly from this engagement (Deci, 1971; Thomas & Velthouse, 1990). While other researchers have advanced understanding of the cognitive dimensions of intrinsic motivation, our main objective is to offer a conceptual model that articulates the role that affect plays in intrinsic motivation experiences. Like Hackman and Oldham (1980), we propose that positive affect lies at the core of these intrinsically motivating experiences, but we propose that affect can be a sufficient cause of intrinsic motivation. We have indicated three paths by which affective experiences can induce intrinsic motivation. Although our proposed model accounts for mechanisms through which conscious core cognitions, such as those that play a central role in existing cognitive theories (e.g., Hackman & Oldham, 1980; Thomas & Velthouse, 1990), may influence intrinsic motivation, it also suggests how affect alone can create intrinsic motivation. Our proposed conceptual framework incorporates the large and growing body of research that indicates that affect plays a crucial role in virtually all human motivation, thought, and behavior (Barrett et al., 2007; Brief & Weiss, 2002; Cropanzano et al., 2003; Gollwitzer & Bargh, 1996; Watson, 2000; Weiss & Cropanzano, 1996). In so doing, we hope to offer a conceptual model that better explains nonconscious experiences of intrinsic motivation, the self-generating and self-perpetuating properties of intrinsic motivation, and intraindividual variability in intrinsic motivation. Ultimately, we hope our model will help researchers arrive at a fuller understanding of intrinsic motivation and the conditions which foster it.

## REFERENCES

Amabile, T. (1996). *Creativity in context: Update to the social psychology of creativity*. Boulder, CO: Westview Press.

Amabile, T. M., Barsade, S. G., Mueller, J. S., & Staw, B. M. (2005). Affect and creativity at work. *Administrative Science Quarterly, 50*, 367–403.

Argyris, C. (1964). *Integrating the individual and the organization*. New York: Wiley.

Ashforth, B. E., & Kreiner, G. E. (1999). "How can you do it?": Dirty work and the challenge of constructing a positive identity. *Academy of Management Review, 24*, 413–434.

Ashkanasy, N. M., Härtel, C. E. J., & Zerbe, W. J. (2000). *Emotions in the workplace: Research, theory, and practice.* Westpoint, CT: Quorum.

Baas, M., De Dreu, C. K. W., & Nijstad, B. A. (2008). A meta-analysis of 25 years of mood-creativity research: Hedonic tone, activation, or regulatory focus? *Psychological Bulletin, 134,* 779–806.

Bandura, A. (1989). Human agency in social cognitive theory. *American Psychologist, 44,* 1175–1184.

Bargh, J. A., Chen, M., & Burrows, L. (1996). Automaticity of social behavior: Direct effects of trait construct and stereotype activation on action. *Journal of Personality and Social Psychology, 71,* 230–244.

Barrett, L. F. (2005). Feeling is perceiving: Core affect and conceptualization of the experience of emotion. In: L. F. Barrett, P. M. Nidenthal & P. Winkielman (Eds), *Emotion and consciousness* (pp. 255–286). New York: Guilford Press.

Barrett, L. F., Mesquita, B., Ochsner, K. N., & Gross, J. J. (2007). The experience of emotion. *Annual Review of Psychology, 58,* 373–403.

Barsade, S. G., Brief, A. P., & Spataro, S. E. (2003). The affective revolution in organizational behavior: Emergence of a paradigm. In: J. Greenberg (Ed.), *Organizational behavior: The state of the science* (2nd ed., pp. 3–52). Mahwah, NJ: Erlbaum.

Barsade, S. G., Ramarajan, L., & Westen, D. (2009). Implicit affect in organizations. *Research in Organizational Behavior, 29,* 135–162.

Batson, C. D. (1991). *The altruism question: Toward a social psychological answer.* Hillsdale, NJ: Erlbaum.

Bloom, M. (2008). A century of compensation research. In: J. Barling & C. L. Cooper (Eds), *The SAGE handbook of organizational behavior* (Vol. 1, pp. 300–317). Los Angles: Sage.

Bono, J. E., & Judge, T. A. (2003). Self-concordance at work: Toward understanding the motivational effects of transformational leaders. *Academy of Management Journal, 46,* 554–571.

Brehm, J. W. (1999). The intensity of emotions. *Personality and Social Psychology Review, 3,* 2–22.

Brief, A. P., & Aldag, R. J. (1977). The intrinsic-extrinsic dichotomy: Toward conceptual clarity. *Academy of Management Review, 2,* 496–500.

Brief, A. P., & Weiss, H. M. (2002). Organizational behavior: Affect in the workplace. *Annual Review of Psychology, 53,* 279–307.

Brockner, J., & Higgins, E. T. (2001). Regulatory focus theory: Implications for the study of emotions at work. *Organizational Behavior and Human Decision Processes, 86,* 35–66.

Bunderson, J. S., & Thompson, J. A. (2009). The call of the wild: Zookeepers, callings, and the double-edged sword of deeply meaningful work. *Administrative Science Quarterly, 54,* 32–57.

Byrne, D. (1971). *The attraction paradigm.* Orlando, FL: Academic Press.

Cacioppo, J. T., Gardner, W. L., & Berntson, G. G. (1999). The affect system has parallel and integrative processing components: Form follows function. *Journal of Personality and Social Psychology, 76,* 839–855.

Cameron, K. S., Dutton, J. E., & Quinn, R. E. (Eds). (2003). *Positive organizational scholarship.* San Francisco: Berrett-Koehler.

Cantor, N., & Sanderson, C. A. (1999). Life task participation and well-being: The importance of taking part in daily life. In: D. Kahneman, E. Diener & N. Schwarz (Eds), *Well-being: The foundations of hedonic psychology* (pp. 230–243). New York: Russell Sage Foundation.

Carver, C. S. (2006). Approach, avoidance, and the self-regulation of affect and action. *Motivation and Emotion, 30*, 105–110.

Chuang, C.-H., & Liao, H. (2010). Strategic human resource management in service context: Taking care of business by taking care of employees and customers. *Personnel Psychology, 63*, 153–196.

Clore, G. L., Storbeck, J., Robinson, M. D., & Centerbar, D. B. (2005). Seven sins in the study of unconscious affect. In: L. F. Barrett, P. M. Nidenthal & P. Winkielman (Eds), *Emotion and consciousness* (pp. 384–408). New York: Guilford Press.

Conger, J. A., & Kanungo, R. N. (1988). The empowerment process: Integrating theory and practice. *Academy of Management Review, 13*, 471–482.

Crocker, J., & Canevello, A. (2008). Creating and undermining social support in communal relationships: The role of compassionate and self-image goals. *Journal of Personality and Social Psychology, 95*, 555–575.

Crocker, J., & Park, L. E. (2004). The costly pursuit of self-esteem. *Psychological Bulletin, 130*, 392–414.

Cropanzano, R., Weiss, H. M., Hale, J. M. S., & Reb, J. (2003). The structure of affect: Reconsidering the relationship between negative and positive affectivity. *Journal of Management, 29*, 831–857.

Csikszentmihalyi, M. (1990). *Flow: The psychology of optimal experiences.* New York: HarperPerenniel.

Custers, R., & Aarts, H. (2005). Positive affect as implicit motivator: On the nonconscious operation of behavioral goals. *Journal of Personality and Social Psychology, 89*, 129–142.

Custers, R., & Aarts, H. (2007). In search of the nonconscious sources of goal pursuit: Accessibility and positive affective hedonic tone of the goal state. *Journal of Experimental Social Psychology, 43*, 312–318.

Damasio, A. (1994). *Descartes' error: Emotion, reason, and the human brain.* New York: G. P. Putnam.

Damasio, A. (1999). *The feeling of what happens: Body and emotion in the making of consciousness.* New York: Harcourt Brace.

deCharms, R. (1968). *Personal causation.* New York: Academic Press.

Deci, E. L. (1971). Effects of externally mediated rewards on intrinsic motivation. *Journal of Personality and Social Psychology, 18*, 105–115.

Deci, E. L., Koestner, R., & Ryan, R. M. (1999). A meta-analytic review of experiments examining the effects of extrinsic rewards on intrinsic motivation. *Psychological Bulletin, 125*, 627–668.

Deci, E. L., & Ryan, R. M. (1985). *Intrinsic motivation and self-determination in human behavior.* New York: Plenum Press.

Deci, E. L., & Ryan, R. M. (2000). The 'what' and 'why' of goal pursuits: Human needs and the self-determination of behavior. *Psychological Inquiry, 11*, 227–268.

Desteno, D., Petty, R. E., Wegener, D. T., & Rucker, D. D. (2000). Beyond hedonic tone in the perception of likelihood: The role of emotion specificity. *Journal of Personality and Social Psychology, 78*, 397–416.

Dutton, J. E., Roberts, L. M., & Bednar, J. (2010). Pathways for positive identity construction at work: Four types of positive identity and the building of social resources. *Academy of Management Review, 35*, 265–293.

Dyer, L., & Parker, D. F. (1975). Classifying outcomes in work motivation research: An examination of the intrinsic–extrinsic dichotomy. *Journal of Applied Psychology, 60*, 455–458.

Eisenberger, R., Pierce, W. D., & Cameron, J. (1999). Effects of rewards on intrinsic motivation – negative, neutral, and positive: Comment on Deci, Koestner, and Ryan (1999). *Psychological Bulletin, 125*, 677–691.

Ekman, P. (2008). Micro expression training tool. Available at http://www.mettonline.com.

Ekman, P., Friesen, W. V., & Hager, J. C. (2002). *Facial action coding system.* Salt Lake City, UT: A human face. Available at http://www.face-and-emotion.com/dataface/tools/tools_intro.jsp.

Elfenbein, H. A. (2007). Emotions in organizations. *Academy of Management Annals, 1*, 315–386.

Elliot, A. J. (2006). The hierarchical model of approach-avoidance motivation. *Motivation and Emotion, 30*, 111–116.

Folkman, S., & Moskowitz, J. T. (2003). Positive psychology from a coping perspective. *Psychological Inquiry, 14*, 121–125.

Fredrickson, B. L. (2001). The role of positive emotions in positive psychology. *American Psychologist, 56*, 218–226.

Fried, Y., & Ferris, G. R. (1987). The validity of the job characteristics model: A review and meta-analysis. *Personnel Psychology, 40*, 287–322.

Frijda, N. (1999). Emotions and hedonic experience. In: D. Kahneman, E. Diener & N. Schwarz (Eds), *Well-being: The foundations of a hedonic psychology* (pp. 190–212). New York: Russell Sage Foundation.

Frijda, N. H. (2007). *The laws of emotion.* Mahwah, NJ: L. Erlbaum Associates.

Gagné, M., & Deci, E. L. (2005). Self-determination theory and work motivation. *Journal of Organizational Behavior, 26*, 331–362.

George, J. M. (2007). Creativity in organizations. *Academy of Management Annals, 1*, 439–477.

George, J. M., & Brief, A. P. (1996). Feeling good-doing good: A conceptual analysis of the mood at work-organizational spontaneity relationship. *Psychological Bulletin, 112*, 310–329.

Gersick, C. J. G., Dutton, J. E., & Bartunek, J. M. (2000). Learning from academia: The importance of relationships in professional life. *Academy of Management Journal, 43*, 1026–1044.

Gilbert, D. (2006). *Stumbling on happiness.* New York: Random House.

Gollwitzer, P. M., & Bargh, J. A. (Eds). (1996). *The psychology of action: Linking cognition and motivation to behavior.* New York: Guilford Press.

Grant, A. M., & Parker, S. K. (2009). Redesigning work design theories: The rise of relational and proactive perspectives. *Academy of Management Journal, 3*, 317–375.

Gray, J. A. (1987). *The psychology of fear and stress.* New York: Cambridge University Press.

Gray, J. A. (1990). Brain systems that mediate both emotion and cognition. *Cognition and Emotion, 4*, 269–288.

Gross, J. J. (1998). The emerging field of emotion regulation: An integrative review. *Review of General Psychology, 2*, 271–299.

Gross, J. J., & Thompson, R. A. (2007). Emotion regulation: Conceptual foundations. In: J.J. Gross (Ed.), *Handbook of emotion regulation* (pp. 3–26). New York: Guilford Press.

Hackman, J. R., & Lawler, E. E. (1971). Employee reactions to job characteristics. *Journal of Applied Psychology, 55*, 259–286.

Hackman, J. R., & Oldham, G. R. (1976). Motivation through the design of work: Test of a theory. *Organizational Behavior and Human Performance, 16*, 250–279.

Hackman, J. R., & Oldham, G. R. (1980). *Work redesign*. Reading, MA: Addison-Wesley.

Haidt, J. (2001). The emotional dog and its rational tail. *Psychological Review, 108*, 814–834.

Haidt, J. (2006). *The happiness hypothesis: Finding modern truth in ancient wisdom*. New York: Basic Books.

Haidt, J. (2008). Morality. *Perspectives on Psychological Science, 3*, 65–72.

Henderlong, J., & Lepper, M. R. (2002). The effects of praise on children's intrinsic motivation. *Psychological Bulletin, 128*, 774–795.

Higgins, E. T. (2000). Beyond pleasure and pain. In: E. T. Higgins & A. Kruglanski (Eds), *Motivational science: Social and personality perspectives* (pp. 231–255). New York: Psychology Press.

Higgins, E. T. (2006). Value from hedonic experience and engagement. *Psychological Review, 113*, 439–460.

Hirt, E. R., Melton, R. J., McDonald, H. E., & Harackiewicz, J. M. (1996). Processing goals, activity interest, and the mood-performance relationship: A mediational analysis. *Journal of Personality and Social Psychology, 71*, 245–261.

Houser-Marko, L., & Sheldon, K. M. (2006). Motivating behavioral persistence: The self-as-doer construct. *Personality and Social Psychology Bulletin, 32*, 1037–1049.

Humphrey, S. E., Nahrgang, J. D., & Morgeson, F. P. (2007). Integrating motivational, social, and contextual work design features: A meta-analytic summary and theoretical extension of the work design literature. *Journal of Applied Psychology, 92*, 1332–1356.

Isen, A. M. (2002). Missing in action in the AIM: Positive affect's facilitation of cognitive flexibility, innovation, and problem solving. *Psychology Inquiry, 13*, 57–65.

Izard, C. E. (1993). Four systems for emotion activation: Cognitive and noncognitive processes. *Psychological Review, 100*, 68–90.

Johnson, R. E., Chang, C.-H., & Yang, L. (2010). Commitment and motivation at work: The relevance of employee identity and regulatory focus. *Academy of Management Review, 35*, 226–245.

Kagan, J. (2009). *What is emotion? History, measures, and meanings*. New Haven, CT: Yale University Press.

Kahn, W. A. (1990). Psychological conditions of personal engagement and disengagement at work. *Academy of Management Journal, 33*, 692–724.

Kahn, W. A. (1992). To be fully there: Psychological presence at work. *Human Relations, 45*, 321–349.

Kahneman, D., Krueger, A. B., Schkade, D., Schwarz, N., & Stone, A. A. (2006). Would you be happier if you were richer? A focusing illusion. *Science, 312*, 1908–1910.

Kanfer, R., Chen, G., & Pritchard, R. D. (Eds). (2008). *Work motivation: Past, present, and future*. New York: Psychology Press.

Katz, D., & Kahn, R. L. (1978). *The social psychology of organizations* (2nd ed.). New York: Wiley.

Koestner, R., Otis, N., Powers, T. A., Pelletier, L., & Gagnon, H. (2008). Autonomous motivation, controlled motivation, and goal progress. *Journal of Personality, 76*, 1201–1230.

Kristof-Brown, A. L., & Guay, R. (2010). Person-environment fit. In: S. Zedeck (Ed.), *APA handbook of industrial and organizational psychology* (Vol. 3, pp. 3–50). Washington, DC: American Psychological Association.

Kroll, J., & Egan, E. (2004). Psychiatry, moral worry, and the moral emotions. *Journal of Psychiatric Practice, 10,* 352–360.

Kruglanski, A. W. (1975). The endogenous-exogenous partition in attribution theory. *Psychological Review, 82,* 387–406.

LeDoux, J. (1996). *The emotional brain.* New York: Simon & Schuster.

Locke, E. A. (1976). The nature and causes of job satisfaction. In: M. D. Dunnette (Ed.), *Handbook of industrial and organizational psychology* (pp. 1297–1349). Chicago: Rand-McNally.

Loewenstein, G. F., Weber, E. U., Hsee, C. K., & Welch, N. (2001). Risk as feelings. *Psychological Bulletin, 127,* 267–286.

Lord, R. G., Klimoski, R. J., & Kanfer, R. (Eds). (2002). *Emotions in the workplace: Understanding the structure and role of emotions in organizational behavior.* San Francisco: Jossey-Bass.

Lyubomirsky, S., King, L., & Diener, E. (2005). The benefits of frequent positive affect: Does happiness lead to success? *Psychological Bulletin, 136,* 803–855.

Martin, L. L., Ward, D. W., Achee, J. W., & Wyer, R. S. (1993). Mood as input: People have to interpret the motivational implications of their moods. *Journal of Personality and Social Psychology, 64,* 317–326.

Mascolo, M. F., & Fischer, K. W. (1995). Developmental transformations in appraisals for pride, shame, and guilt. In: J. P. Tangney & K. W. Fischer (Eds), *Self-conscious emotions: The psychology of shame, guilt, embarrassment, and pride* (pp. 64–113). New York: Guilford Press.

McCullough, M. E., Kilpatrick, S. D., Emmons, R. A., & Larson, D. B. (2001). Is gratitude a moral affect? *Psychological Bulletin, 127,* 249–266.

McKnight, P. E., & Kashdan, T. B. (2009). Purpose in life as a system that creates and sustains health and well-being: An integrative, testable theory. *Review of General Psychology, 13,* 242–251.

Meece, J. E., Anderman, E. M., & Anderman, L. H. (2006). Classroom goal structure, student motivation, and academic achievement. *Annual Review of Psychology, 57,* 487–503.

Milkovich, G. T., & Newman, J. M. (2005). *Compensation* (8th ed.). Boston: McGraw-Hill/Irwin.

Mischel, W., Cantor, N., & Feldman, S. (1996). Principles of self-regulation: The nature of willpower and self control. In: E. T. Higgins & A. W. Kruglanski (Eds), *Social psychology: Handbook of basic principles* (pp. 329–360). New York: Guildford Press.

Murphy, S. T., Monahan, J. L., & Zajonc, R. B. (1995). Additivity of nonconscious affect: Combined effects of priming and exposure. *Journal of Personality and Social Psychology, 69,* 589–602.

Ong, A. D., Bergeman, C. S., Bisconti, T. L., & Wallace, K. A. (2006). Psychological resilience, positive emotions, and successful adaptation to stress in later life. *Journal of Personality & Social Psychology, 91,* 730–749.

Panksepp, J. (2004). *Affective neuroscience: The foundations of human and animal emotions.* New York: Oxford University Press.

Patall, E. A., Cooper, H., & Robinson, J. C. (2008). The effects of choice on intrinsic motivation and related outcomes: A meta-analysis of research findings. *Psychological Bulletin, 134,* 270–300.

Peterson, C. (1999). Personal control and well-being. In: D. Kahneman, E. Diener & N. Schwarz (Eds), *Well-being: The foundations of hedonic psychology* (pp. 288–301). New York: Russell Sage Foundation.

Piccolo, R. F., & Colquitt, J. A. (2006). Transformational leadership and job behaviors: The mediating role of core job characteristics. *Academy of Management Journal, 49*, 327–340.

Podsakoff, N. P., Whiting, S. W., Podsakoff, P. M., & Blume, B. D. (2009). Individual- and organizational-level consequences of organizational citizenship behaviors: A meta-analysis. *Journal of Applied Psychology, 94*, 122–141.

Podsakoff, P. M., MacKenzie, S. B., Paine, J. B., & Bachrach, D. G. (2000). Organizational citizenship behaviors: A critical review of the theoretical and empirical literature and suggestions for future research. *Journal of Management, 26*, 513–563.

Porter, L. W., & Lawler, E. E. (1968). *Managerial attitudes and performance*. Homewood, IL: Irwin-Dorsey.

Reis, H. T., Collins, W. A., & Berscheid, E. (2000). The relationship context of human behavior and development. *Psychological Bulletin, 126*, 844–872.

Rich, B. L., LePine, J. A., & Crawford, E. R. (2010). Job engagement: Antecedents and effects on job performance. *Academy of Management Journal, 53*, 617–635.

Roseman, I. A., & Smith, C. A. (1999). Appraisal theory: Overview, assumptions, varieties, controversies. In: K. R. Scherer, A. Schorr & T. Johnstone (Eds), *Appraisal processes in emotion: Theory, methods, research* (pp. 3–19). New York: Oxford University Press.

Russell, J. A. (2003). Core affect and the psychological construction of emotion. *Psychological Review, 110*, 145–172.

Russell, J. A. (2005). Emotion in human consciousness is built on core affect. *Journal of Consciousness Studies, 12*, 26–42.

Russell, J. A., & Barrett, L. F. (1999). Core affect, prototypical emotional episodes, and other things called emotion: Dissecting the elephant. *Journal of Personality and Social Psychology, 76*, 805–819.

Ryan, R. M., & Deci, E. L. (2000). Self-determination theory and the facilitation of intrinsic motivation, social development, and well-being. *American Psychologist, 55*, 68–78.

Scherer, K. R. (2001). Appraisal considered as a process of multilevel sequential checking. In: K. R. Scherer, A. Schorr & A. T. Johnstone (Eds), *Appraisal processes in emotion: Theory, methods, research* (pp. 92–120). New York: Oxford University Press.

Schnall, S., Roper, J., & Fessler, D. M. T. (2010). Elevation leads to altruistic behavior. *Psychological Science, 21*, 315–320.

Schwarz, N., & Clore, G. L. (2007). Feelings and phenomenal experiences. In: A. Kruglanski & E. T. Higgins (Eds), *Social psychology: Handbook of basic principles* (2nd ed., pp. 385–407). New York: Guilford Press.

Seibert, S. E., Silver, S. R., & Randolph, W. A. (2004). Taking empowerment to the next level: A multiple-level model of empowerment, performance, and satisfaction. *Academy of Management Journal, 47*, 332–349.

Seo, M., Barrett, L. F., & Bartunek, J. M. (2004). The role of affective experience in work motivation. *Academy of Management Review, 29*, 423–439.

Sheldon, K. M., & Elliot, A. J. (1999). Goal striving, need satisfaction, and longitudinal well-being: The self-concordance model. *Journal of Personality and Social Psychology, 76*, 482–497.

Sheldon, K. M., Ryan, R. M., Deci, E. L., & Kasser, T. (2004). The independent effects of goal contents and motives on well-being: It's both what you pursue and why you pursue it. *Personality and Social Psychology Bulletin, 30*, 475–486.

Sheldon, K. M., Turban, D. B., Brown, K. G., Barrick, M. R., & Judge, T. A. (2003). Applying self-determination theory to organizational research. In: J. J. Martocchio & G. R. Ferris (Eds),

*Research in personnel and human resources management* (Vol. 22, pp. 357–393). Oxford: Elsevier Science Ltd.

Sherman, A. C., Simonton, S., Latif, U., & Bracy, L. (2010). Effects of global meaning and illness-specific meaning on health outcomes among breast cancer patients. *Journal of Behavioral Medicine, 33,* 364–377.

Shin, J. S., & Zhou, J. (2003). Transformational leadership, conservation, and creativity: Evidence from Korea. *Academy of Management Journal, 46,* 703–714.

Simon, H. A. (1991). Organizations and markets. *Journal of Economic Perspectives, 5,* 25–44.

Smith, C. A., & Kirby, L. D. (2001). Toward delivering on the promise of appraisal theory. In: K. R. Scherer, A. Schorr & T. Johnstone (Eds), *Appraisal processes in emotion: Theory, methods, research* (pp. 121–138). New York: Oxford University Press.

Spreitzer, G. M. (1995). Psychological empowerment in the workplace: Dimensions, measurement and validation. *Academy of Management Journal, 38,* 1442–1465.

Spreitzer, G. M. (1996). Social structural characteristics of psychological empowerment. *Academy of Management Journal, 39,* 483–504.

Spreitzer, G. M., Kizilos, M. A., & Nason, S. W. (1997). A dimensional analysis of the relationship between psychological empowerment and effectiveness, satisfaction, and strain. *Journal of Management, 23,* 679–704.

Tangney, J. P., Stuewig, J., & Mashek, D. J. (2007). Moral emotions and moral behavior. *Annual Review of Psychology, 58,* 345–372.

Thomas, K. W., & Velthouse, B. A. (1990). Cognitive elements of empowerment: An 'interpretive' model of intrinsic activity motivation. *Academy of Management Review, 15,* 666–681.

Tugade, M. M., & Fredrickson, B. L. (2004). Resilient individuals use positive emotions to bounce back from negative emotional experiences. *Journal of Personality and Social Psychology, 86,* 320–333.

Watson, D. (2000). *Mood and temperament.* New York: Guilford Press.

Watson, D., Clark, L. A., & Tellegen, A. (1988). Development and validation of brief measures of positive and negative affect: The PANAS scales. *Journal of Personality and Social Psychology, 54,* 1063–1070.

Weiss, H. M. (2002). Conceptual and empirical foundations for the study of affect at work. In: R. G. Lord, R. J. Klimoski & R. Kanter (Eds), *Emotions in the workplace: Understanding the structure and role of emotions in organizational behavior* (pp. 20–63). San Francisco: Jossey-Bass.

Weiss, H. M., & Cropanzano, R. (1996). Affective events theory: A theoretical discussion of the structure, causes and consequences of affective experiences at work. In: B. M. Staw & L.L. Cummings (Eds), *Research in Organizational Behavior* (Vol. 18, pp. 1–74). Oxford: Elsevier Science/JAI Press.

White, R. W. (1959). Motivation reconsidered: The concept of competence. *Psychological Review, 66,* 297–333.

Williams, L. A., & Desteno, D. (2008). Pride and perseverance: The motivational role of pride. *Journal of Personality and Social Psychology, 94,* 1007–1017.

Winkielman, P., & Berridge, K. (2004). Unconscious emotion. *Current Directions in Psychological Science, 13,* 120–123.

Woodworth, R. S. (1918). *Dynamic psychology.* New York: Columbia University Press.

Wrzesniewski, A., & Dutton, J. E. (2001). Crafting a job: Revisioning employees as active crafters of their work. *Academy of Management Review, 26,* 179–201.

Zajonc, R. B. (1980). Feeling and thinking: Preferences need no inferences. *American Psychologist, 35,* 151–175.
Zajonc, R. B. (1998). Emotions. In: D. T. Gilbert, S. T. Fiske & L. Gardner (Eds), *The handbook of social psychology* (pp. 591–632). New York: McGraw-Hill.
Zajonc, R. B. (2000). Feeling and thinking: Closing the debate over the independence of affect. In: J. P. Forgas (Ed.), *Feeling and thinking: The role of affect in social cognition* (pp. 31–58). New York: Cambridge University Press.
Zhou, J. (1998). Feedback valence, feedback style, activity autonomy, and achievement orientation: Interactive effects on creative performance. *Journal of Applied Psychology, 83,* 261–276.

# MINDFULNESS AT WORK

Theresa M. Glomb, Michelle K. Duffy,
Joyce E. Bono and Tao Yang

## ABSTRACT

*In this chapter, we argue that state and trait mindfulness and mindfulness-based practices in the workplace should enhance employee outcomes. First, we review the existing literature on mindfulness, provide a brief history and definition of the construct, and discuss its beneficial effects on physical and psychological health. Second, we delineate a model of the mental and neurobiological processes by which mindfulness and mindfulness-based practices improve self-regulation of thoughts, emotions, and behaviors, linking them to both performance and employee well-being in the workplace. We especially focus on the power of mindfulness, via improved self-regulation, to enhance social relationships in the workplace, make employees more resilient in the face of challenges, and increase task performance. Third, we outline controversies, questions, and challenges that surround the study of mindfulness, paying special attention to the implications of unresolved issues for understanding the effects of mindfulness at work. We conclude with a discussion of the implications of our propositions for organizations and employees and offer some recommendations for future research on mindfulness in the workplace.*

Research in Personnel and Human Resources Management, Volume 30, 115–157
ISSN: 0742-7301/doi:10.1108/S0742-7301(2011)0000030005

# INTRODUCTION

The concept of mindfulness – awareness and observation of the present moment without reactivity or judgment – has gone mainstream. A Google database search on the term *mindfulness* yielded more than six million links; *mindfulness and work* generated 1.4 million links. Amazon.com lists more than 2,000 books with *mindfulness* in the title or as a keyword. A PsycInfo database search produced 2,221 articles, books, and dissertations with *mindfulness* as a keyword; Medline yielded 640. As the mindfulness concept has grown in popularity, claims about its broad-reaching beneficial effects have increased; yet its meaning has become hazier. Mindfulness could be easily dismissed as nothing more than the latest panacea for a stressed society (Altman, 2010; Lehrer, Woolfolk, & Sime, 2007) or the newest fad in organizational development (e.g., Carroll, 2006; Duerr, 2004a) if there were not also a growing body of scientific research suggesting that mindfulness and the practices associated with it significantly benefit both healthy individuals (including workers), as well as those suffering from physical and psychological problems.

The time is ripe to carefully examine the role that mindfulness might play in the performance and well-being of individuals at work. Accordingly, the purpose of this chapter is to assess the expected effects of mindfulness on employees' task and relational functioning on the job. We review the literature on mindfulness and discuss its roots, definition, and association with critical psychological, physical, and neurological processes. Others have linked mindfulness and work (Dane, 2010; Davidson et al., 2003; Fredrickson, Cohn, Coffey, Pek, & Finkel, 2008; Giluk, 2010), but existing research has lacked a coherent theoretical framework that explains *why* and *how* mindfulness might impact employee performance and well-being. We aim to fill that void.

This chapter has four major sections. First, we present a brief history of mindfulness and a working definition. Second, we provide a broad overview of the literature regarding outcomes that have been associated with mindfulness. Third, we introduce a process model linking mindfulness and mindfulness-based practices with three core and seven secondary processes that explain its effects. In the process section, we explicitly link each process to work variables, including job performance and employee well-being. Our goal is not to link mindfulness to organizational functioning (Weick, Sutcliffe, & Obstfeld, 1999), but rather to show how mindfulness and related practices might affect employees directly, in both task and relational functioning. Fourth, we focus on three areas where we expect mindfulness to most strongly affect employees: improved social relationships, resilience, and task performance and decision making. Finally, we conclude with a discussion of the controversy and confusion surrounding mindfulness, suggestions for future research, and practical implications for organizations.

## History of Mindfulness

Rooted in Buddhist philosophy, the concept of *mindfulness* is the literal translation of the Buddhist word *sati* – "intentness of mind," "wakefulness of mind," and "lucidity of mind" (Davids & Stede, 1959, p. 672) – highlighting intention, awareness, and attention as key constituents of mindfulness. Mindfulness meditation is at the heart of Buddhist tradition and its aim is to deepen conscious awareness of the present moment (Nyanaponika, 1998). Despite these roots, the concept of mindfulness, per se, has no religious connotation (see Hagen, 2003, for a discussion of whether Buddhism is a religion), and mindfulness meditative practices are becoming increasingly popular, not only in Eastern countries but throughout the world (Mitchell, 2002).

The public has become more aware of mindfulness largely because psychologists and medical practitioners have turned to therapeutic use of mindfulness meditation. Over the past three decades, researchers have frequently examined mindfulness meditation for its role in alleviating symptoms of physical and psychological disorders in clinical populations, and as a stress reduction technique in nonclinical populations (Chiesa & Serretti, 2010; Delmonte, 1990). Patients are trained in mindfulness meditation to heighten their awareness and attention to the present by intentionally orienting them to attend to moment-to-moment stimuli, and to accept those stimuli without judgment, elaboration, or attempts to control them (e.g., Baer, 2003; Chambers, Gullone, & Allen, 2009).

Among the most prominent of the therapeutic mindfulness-based interventions is Mindfulness-Based Stress Reduction (MBSR; Kabat-Zinn, 1990), initially developed to assist medical patients. More than 18,000 medical and nonmedical patients have participated in the MBSR program at the University of Massachusetts alone (Center for Mindfulness in Medicine, Health Care, and Society, 2010). Clinical evaluation and academic research have established the health benefits of MBSR in clinical and nonclinical populations (for qualitative reviews, see Baer, 2003; Bishop, 2002; Chiesa & Serretti, 2010; for meta-analyses, see Chiesa & Serretti, 2009; Grossman, Niemann, Schmidt, & Walach, 2004). Furthermore, thousands of health-care professionals have been trained to teach MBSR techniques (Duerr, 2004b). Mindfulness has also emerged as a therapeutic practice in psychology (i.e., Mindfulness-Based Cognitive Therapy [MBCT]; Segal, Williams, & Teasdale, 2002). As a variant of MBSR, MBCT has integrated components of cognitive-behavioral therapy (Beck, Rush, Shaw, & Emery, 1979) with mindfulness meditation. It has been shown effective in reducing clinical symptoms and relapses in patients with psychiatric disorders (for review, see Baer, 2003; Chiesa & Serretti, 2010). Clinical psychologists have found mindfulness practices to benefit both clinical populations and therapists; practices such as meditation may lead therapists to feel more empathy toward patients (Delmonte, 1990) and "enjoy their work more fully" (Germer, 2005, p. 11). Preliminary evidence shows that mindfulness meditation training helped psychotherapists achieve significantly better treatment results for their patients (Grepmair, Mitterlehner, Rother, & Nickel, 2006).

## Definitions

The popular press and the scholarly literature have both used the term *mindfulness* to refer to a variety of related constructs, traits, practices, and processes (e.g., Baer, Smith, Hopkins, Krietemeyer, & Toney, 2006; Bishop et al., 2004; Brown & Ryan, 2003; Brown, Ryan, & Creswell, 2007; Chiesa & Serretti, 2010; Grossman, 2008). Grossman (2008) noted: "Mindfulness is a difficult concept to define, let alone operationalize" (p. 405). Despite surface-level confusion about the nature and meaning of mindfulness, agreement exists on its fundamental nature, defined by Brown and colleagues as "*a receptive attention to and awareness of present events and experience*" (Brown et al., 2007, p. 212, italics in original; see also Brown & Ryan, 2003). Put simply, mindfulness is the process of paying attention to what is happening in the moment – both internal (thoughts, bodily sensations) and external stimuli (physical and social environment) – and observing those stimuli without judgment or evaluation, and without assigning meaning to them. Basic-level examples of mindfulness include experiences such as noticing "the positions of our hands and the sensations of holding a knife and bagel," being aware of "our bodies sitting in the car when we drive," and noticing the traffic, the road, and the passing scenery (Siegel, Germer, & Olendzki, 2009, p. 21). Thus, awareness and attention are at the heart of mindfulness, but mindfulness also involves attending to stimuli without imposing judgments, memories, or other self-relevant cognitive manipulations on them (Brown et al., 2007). In the driving example, mindfulness involves noticing heavy traffic but refraining from evaluating it negatively when it is tied up or moving slowly and from ruminating about what traffic might be like on another route. Our working definition of mindfulness draws heavily from Brown and colleagues (see Brown et al., 2007; Brown & Ryan, 2003). We define mindfulness as *a state of consciousness characterized by receptive attention to and awareness of present events and experiences, without evaluation, judgment, and cognitive filters.* Our definition clearly establishes mindfulness as a state of consciousness, given empirical evidence of considerable within-individual variation in mindfulness over time (Brown & Ryan, 2003) and evidence that mindfulness can be cultivated or enhanced through practices and training such as mindfulness meditation (see Brown & Ryan, 2003), loving-kindness meditation (see Fredrickson et al., 2008), and MBSR and MBCT (see Giluk, 2010).

Although we define mindfulness as a state of consciousness, we also recognize that the average frequency with which individuals experience states of mindfulness may vary from person to person, suggesting that people may have trait-like tendencies toward mindfulness (see Brown et al., 2007; Brown & Cordon, 2009; Brown & Ryan, 2003); indeed one line of research treats mindfulness as a stable individual difference (i.e., trait mindfulness) similar to other personality traits (e.g., Brown & Ryan, 2003; Cardaciotto, Herbert, Forman, Moitra, & Farrow, 2008; Lakey, Campbell, Brown, & Goodie, 2007; Walsh, Balint, Smolira SJ, Fredericksen, & Madsen, 2009; Way, Creswell, Eisenberger, & Lieberman, 2010).

The literature has also examined mindfulness training as a therapeutic technique (e.g., MBSR; Kabat-Zinn, 1990, or MBCT; Segal et al., 2002) that aims to improve the capacity to create more mindful states. One central element of these programs is mindfulness meditation. Our definition suggests that none of these programs nor the mindfulness meditation they incorporate are mindfulness, but rather meditation is a technique used to develop mindfulness (see also Brown et al., 2007; Grossman, 2008). Moreover, we note that mindfulness meditation is just one specific type of meditation and differs from other practices such as concentrative meditation that requires focused attention on a single stimulus such as a word, sound, or candle (see Goleman, 1977; but see also Cahn & Polich, 2006; Germer, 2005; Lutz, Slagter, Dunne, & Davidson, 2008, for the counterargument that concentrative meditation may also develop mindfulness). Thus, mindfulness meditation, but perhaps not all meditation, develops the mindfulness state of nonjudgmental awareness of and attention to internal and external stimuli. In our review of the literature, we use the term *mindfulness treatment* to refer to mindfulness-based therapeutic programs designed to develop the ability to achieve mindful states (e.g., MBSR), the term *mindfulness meditation* to refer to mindfulness-based meditation practices, and the term *trait mindfulness* to refer to stable individual differences in mindfulness.

Despite our efforts to clarify the mindfulness literature, we acknowledge the difficulty of making clean distinctions. For example, it is not clear whether studies of the brain, which document changes in brain activities during mindfulness meditation, are documenting the effects of mindfulness meditation practices or the state of mindfulness achieved during meditation, or both.

There is also an important stream of mindfulness research in the psychological and organizational literature that does not explicitly have roots in Buddhist philosophy. Langer (1989a) defined mindfulness as an "active information processing" mode (p. 138). Although research based on Langer's work uses the term mindfulness, her concept, although related, appears to be a distinct phenomenon from our definition of mindfulness as nonjudgmental attention to and awareness of internal and external stimuli. Both approaches focus on ongoing awareness of and attention to stimuli but diverge in considering what individuals do with observations. Rather than observing without judgment, Langer's conceptualization explicitly includes deliberate cognitive categorization, generating new distinctions, and adapting to changing situations (see Brown et al., 2007; Brown & Ryan, 2003; Langer, 1989b, for a discussion of overlap and distinction of the two mindfulness concepts).

Langer's work on mindfulness is germane because it partially forms the basis of Weick and colleagues' theorizing about collective mindfulness in high-reliability organizations (Weick et al., 1999). These authors draw on both Langer (1989a) and Buddhist mindfulness, and define collective mindfulness as an organizational level attribute that involves "a rich awareness of discriminatory detail and a capacity for action" (Weick et al., 1999, p. 88; see also Weick & Putnam, 2006). Collective mindfulness is construed as the result of a set of organizational practices and processes aimed at observing, categorizing, and responding to unexpected events and errors and it is fundamental to high-reliability organizations; (Weick et al., 1999). Recent work on collective mindfulness (Weick & Sutcliffe, 2006, 2007) has shifted somewhat from a focus on action capacities to awareness. Although there are touchpoints with our conceptualization of mindfulness, Weick and colleagues' work on collective mindfulness operates at the organizational level and is distinct from the individual state level phenomenon of interest here.

### Positive Effects of Mindfulness

What benefits have been established regarding mindfulness and mindfulness-based practices and therapies? First, a burgeoning body of research has reported clear links between mindfulness meditation, mindfulness treatment, and improved physical health. Most of this research has focused on reducing symptoms or distress caused by physical disease. Research has shown that mindfulness treatment (i.e., MBSR, MBCT, and their variants) can reduce pain, decrease symptoms (e.g., Carmody & Baer, 2008; Ljótsson et al., 2010), and increase overall physical health in clinical populations with various health challenges (for qualitative review, see Baer, 2003; for meta-analysis, see Grossman et al., 2004). Mindfulness treatments have also been linked to higher melatonin levels (an indicator of immune function) in nonclinical populations (for review, see Baer, 2003). Mindfulness meditation has been associated with decreased somatic health complaints (Delgado et al., 2010) and improvements in an array of physiological markers including increased cardiac respiratory sinus arrhythmia (RSA; Ditto, Eclache, & Goldman, 2006), increased cardiac output (Ditto et al., 2006), lowered respiratory rate (Delgado et al., 2010), and decreased blood pressure (for qualitative review, see Chiesa & Serretti, 2010) across clinical and healthy populations. Evidence from laboratory settings has suggested that mindfulness is associated with decreased unpleasantness and sensitivity to painful stimuli (Grant & Rainville, 2009; Perlman, Salomons, Davidson, & Lutz, 2010).

Second, mindfulness and mindfulness-based practices have been clearly linked to reduced symptoms of mental, psychological, and psychiatric conditions. Mental health benefits include decreased anxiety (e.g., Biegel, Brown, Shapiro, & Schubert, 2009), depression (e.g., Foley, Baillie, Huxter, Price, & Sinclair, 2010), stress (e.g., Bränström, Kvillemo, Brandberg, & Moskowitz, 2010), psychological distress (e.g., Foley et al., 2010), and overall psychological symptoms (e.g., Carmody & Baer, 2008). Mindfulness treatments have also been associated with reduced anxiety and depression in individuals with chronic conditions such as pain disorders, cancer, diabetes, rheumatoid arthritis, and heart disease (for qualitative review, see Baer, 2003; Chiesa & Serretti, 2010; for meta-analysis, see Bohlmeijer, Prenger, Taal, & Cuijpers, 2010; Grossman et al., 2004; Hofmann, Sawyer,

Witt, & Oh, 2010). Mindfulness meditation has been associated with reduced alcohol and substance abuse (for review, see Chiesa & Serretti, 2010) and lowered anxiety (Sears & Kraus, 2009), depression, worry (Delgado et al., 2010), and stress (for review, see Chiesa & Serretti, 2010) in nonclinical populations. Trait mindfulness has been negatively associated with depressive symptoms in healthy young adults and the relationship was fully mediated by affective regulations (Jimenez, Niles, & Park, 2010).

Third, in addition to the well documented mental and physical health benefits of mindfulness and mindfulness-based practices, literature has examined the power of such practices to promote well-being and human flourishing. In clinical populations with heterogeneous diagnoses, mindfulness treatment has improved psychological well-being (Bränström et al., 2010; Carmody & Baer, 2008), overall well-being (for review, see Chiesa & Serretti, 2010), sleep quality (Biegel et al., 2009; cf. Roth & Robbins, 2004), and overall quality of life (Chiesa & Serretti, 2010; Foley et al., 2010; Ljótsson et al., 2010). In nonclinical populations, positive effects of mindfulness meditation include reduced negative affect (Sears & Kraus, 2009; cf. Delgado et al., 2010), increased hope of goal achievement (Sears & Kraus, 2009), positive emotions and life satisfaction (Fredrickson et al., 2008), overall well-being (Falkenström, 2010), and social connectedness (Hutcherson, Seppala, & Gross, 2008). Trait mindfulness has been positively linked to sleep quality (Howell, Digdon, Buro, & Sheptycki, 2008), emotional well-being (Weinstein, Brown, & Ryan, 2009), overall well-being (Howell, Digdon, & Buro, 2010), and intimate relationship quality (Saavedra, Chapman, & Rogge, 2010). Trait and state mindfulness have been negatively associated with hostility and aggression (Heppner et al., 2008).

Finally, a line of neuroscience research has focused explicitly on the effects of mindfulness-based practices on changes in the brain's activity and structure. This line of research has important implications as it suggests neurobiological changes in the brain as the mechanism by which individuals experience improved well-being and reduction of mental and physical distress as a result of mindfulness. One line of research employed electroencephalographic (EEG) techniques to examine changes in the brain's electrical signals during mindfulness meditation in both novices and long-term meditators. Ongoing mindfulness meditation has been associated with increased alpha activity (cf. Treadway & Lazar, 2009), a marker of relaxation and decreased anxiety, increased theta activity, an indicator of reduced trait and state anxiety, and increased gamma activity, an indicator of affect regulation. Mindfulness meditation has also been associated with increased left prefrontal activation in lateralized EEG, which signals positive affective states, and the absence of alpha-blocking habituation, which indicates mindful awareness of stimuli (for review, see Cahn & Polich, 2006; Chiesa & Serretti, 2010; Treadway & Lazar, 2009).

Other research has used functional magnetic resonance imaging (fMRI) techniques to examine activation of specific brain regions during mindfulness meditation and enduring brain structure changes in experienced meditators. Changes observed during mindfulness meditation include activation in the areas of the brain associated with emotional regulation, attentional regulation, enhanced attentional focus, and heightened awareness of internal bodily sensations (for review, see Cahn & Polich, 2006; Chiesa & Serretti, 2010; Treadway & Lazar, 2009). Researchers have found that long-term meditators show increased thickness of brain regions (e.g., middle prefrontal cortex [mPFC]) associated with internal awareness and attention (for review, see Chiesa & Serretti, 2010; Treadway & Lazar, 2009) and areas associated with reduced pain sensitivity (Grant, Courtemanche, Duerden, Duncan, & Rainville, 2010). Trait mindfulness has been linked to the brain's neural activities. Recent fMRI studies found trait mindfulness is associated with increased prefrontal cortex (PFC) activity (Creswell, Way, Eisenberger, & Lieberman, 2007; Frewen et al., 2010) and decreased amygdala activity (Creswell et al., 2007; cf. Frewen et al., 2010) during affect-related tasks, suggesting better affective regulation among individuals high in dispositional mindfulness, which may explain why such individuals experience less depression (Way et al., 2010). Thus, neurobiology research suggests mindfulness-related changes in brain activities and structures are related to heightened awareness, positive mental experiences, and attentional, affective, and physiological regulation.

# CORE PROCESSES LINKING MINDFULNESS AND SELF-REGULATION

As discussed in the preceding text, a large and growing body of literature affirms that mindfulness and mindfulness-based practices have beneficial effects for a variety of outcomes in clinical and nonclinical populations. Yet scholars and researchers have only recently begun to carefully examine the process and mechanisms behind these effects. Reviews of the mindfulness literature converge in identifying the central outcome of mindfulness: *improved self-regulation* of thoughts, emotions, behaviors, and physiological reactions. As our goal here is to explore the potential effects of mindfulness on employees' functioning at work, we draw from neuroscience, psychology, and medicine to develop propositions about how mindfulness and mindfulness-based practices will influence work behaviors, performance, and well-being. Although there is considerable agreement that mindfulness improves self-regulation, our goal is to dig more deeply into the processes by which that occurs.

In Fig. 1, we present a model linking mindfulness to its outcomes, via a series of core and secondary mental and neurobiological processes. We identify two core mental processes and one core neurobiological process that are affected by mindfulness: (a) a decoupling of the self (i.e., ego) from events, experiences, thoughts, and emotions; (b) a decrease in automaticity of mental processes in which past experiences, schemas, and cognitive habits constrain thinking; and (c) increased awareness and regulation of physiological systems. In addition to these three core processes, we identify seven additional, secondary processes by which mindfulness-based practices are expected to improve employee functioning: (a) decreased rumination, (b) greater empathy, (c) increased response flexibility, (d) improved affective regulation, (e) increased self-determination and greater persistence (f) enhanced working memory, and (g) greater accuracy in affective forecasting. We suggest that, in concert, these three core and seven secondary processes form a series of pathways by which mindfulness and mindfulness-based practices lead to improved self-regulation and, ultimately, higher functioning.

As we describe the secondary processes, we provide evidence from the literature linking them to mindfulness, as well as outlining their expected work-related outcomes. We also draw on interviews the first three authors conducted as part of a larger mindfulness research project. Through a local

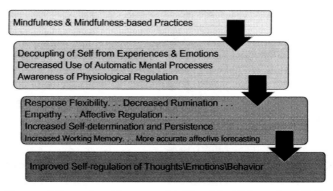

*Fig. 1.* Core and Secondary Processes Linking Mindfulness to Self-Regulation.

meditation center, we recruited 20 employed individuals who had been regularly practicing mindfulness-based practices for at least 1 year. In one-hour interviews, we asked participants how their mindfulness-based practices influenced their attitudes, emotions, thoughts, and behaviors on the job. We use observations from three of these interviews to illustrate the secondary processes in action.

### Decoupling of the Self from Experiences, Events, and Mental Processes

One of the key mechanisms by which mindfulness affects self-regulation is by creating a separation between the self (e.g., ego, self-esteem, self-concept) and events, emotions, and experiences. Mindfulness-based practices aim to train individuals to observe internal and external stimuli objectively, creating meta-awareness. As such, most mindfulness training involves noticing, observing, and naming stimuli without evaluating or assigning meaning to them. This leads individuals to create distance between themselves (and their self-worth) and their thoughts, emotions, and experiences. This process has also been described as "de-centering" in which one "view[s] thoughts as events in the mind rather than necessarily being reflections of reality or accurate self-view" (Feldman, Greeson, & Senville, 2010, p. 1002).

When ego involvement in a negative situation is high, people feel their self-worth is under attack (Kernis, Paradise, Whitaker, Wheatman, & Goldman, 2000), but when the ego is separated from events, negative events are decoupled from the self and become less threatening. For example, before an important sales presentation, a salesperson might interpret thoughts about what could go wrong or potential failure as "just those nerves talking," rather than as a valid indication of inadequacy. The literature has supported the idea that mindfulness and mindfulness-based practices are associated with a decoupling of the self from experiences. Hargus, Crane, Barnhofer, and Williams (2010) found that 8 weeks of mindfulness training was associated with a significant improvement in meta-awareness, demonstrating that mindfulness can help people "learn to uncouple the sensory, directly experienced self from the 'narrative' self" (Williams, 2010, p. 1). Preliminary evidence has indicated that even temporarily heightened mindfulness (via experimental manipulation) increases separation between self-worth and experiences such as interpersonal rejection (Heppner & Kernis, 2007). Although existing neurobiological research has not yet explicitly tested the decoupling hypothesis, Davidson (2010) suggested that the brains of mindfulness practitioners might reveal "decreased connectivity between emotion processing and self-relevant processing" (p. 10) areas of the brain. For example, one study found that when subjects were exposed to a manipulation designed to induce sadness, those who were trained in mindfulness techniques reported just as much sadness as others, but their fMRI scans showed less activity in the brain regions associated with self-referential processing. These differences in neural patterns "may stem from the objectification of emotions as innocuous sensory information rather than as affect laden threats to the self" (Farb et al., 2010, p. 31).

## Decreased Use of Automatic Mental Processes

A second core process by which mindfulness leads to improved self-regulation is via decreased automaticity of mental processes. Through the process of *automaticity*, engrained brain states mold awareness of present-day experiences (Siegel, 2007). Automaticity of thinking can arise from different sources including prior experiences, entrenched mental models, and bodily responses based on prior experiences. Offering individuals a clear survival benefit (i.e., quick information processing and responses), automaticity has the unfortunate consequence of restricting individuals' perceptions and experiences of the present moment. In a sense, automaticity hijacks the ability to fully experience the present moment. Although automaticity provides mental efficiency, it diminishes present-moment awareness, control, and intent (Bargh, 1994). For example, we may find ourselves responding to colleagues without really listening to the conversation because we believe we already know where the conversation is going. We may complete a task without recalling actually doing it or head to the store to get groceries and end up in the parking lot at work, all because of deeply ingrained, automatic responses.

Engaging in mindfulness disrupts automaticity of thought patterns and habits as individuals move from heuristic modes of information processing to more systematic modes (Chaiken, 1980). Through the simple act of observing thoughts arising in the mind, mindful nonjudging awareness allows one to disengage from: (a) automatic thought patterns and (b) perceptual filtering driven by emotions and schemas from the past (Siegel, 2007). As Shapiro and colleagues noted, "We experience what *is* instead of a commentary or story about what is" (Shapiro, Carlson, Astin, & Freedman, 2006, p. 379, italics in original).

As a result, the range of responses is increased because responses are no longer constrained by automaticity. Mindful awareness allows individuals to consciously sense and shape their thoughts and to have greater cognitive flexibility in response to thoughts (Siegel, 2010). The flipside of reduced automaticity is that mindfulness may promote "relatively more thorough attention to the external environment" (Herndon, 2008, p. 33). For example, Radel, Sarrazin, Legrain, and Gobance (2009) showed that students higher in trait mindfulness were immune to a motivational manipulation using unconscious priming; they were less influenced by automatic processes.

### *Awareness of Physiological Regulation*

The third major process through which mindfulness influences self-regulation is through generating bodily awareness and concomitant physiological regulation (Siegel, 2010). Much like the process of "thought observation" described in the preceding text, present-moment nonjudgmental awareness of one's physiological state promotes a more balanced regulation of the body's physiological response systems (e.g., approach–avoidance, fight–flight, inhibition–activation systems). Coordinated by the brain's mPFC via the sympathetic (activation) and parasympathetic (inhibition) nervous system, these physiological response systems are designed to work in balance and coordination with another. When physiological activation reaches too high a threshold, the mPFC is overloaded and unable to modulate the firing of the limbic system, which leads to myriad undesirable affective (i.e., anger, anxiety) and physical consequences (i.e., heart palpitations, gastrointestinal distress) (Siegel, 2007). As Siegel (2010) noted, without the coordination of the activation and inhibition systems people are likely to "burn out, revving up" when they need to slow down (p. 27). When balanced, however, these brain systems can generate feelings of calm, connection, and physical well-being (Cozolino, 2006). Thus, increased attention to and awareness of the body's physiological response systems can help individuals better interpret and respond to messages from the body.

## SECONDARY MINDFULNESS PROCESSES

As presented in Fig. 1, the mental and neurobiological processes associated with mindfulness and mindfulness-based practices lead to more distal processes that influence employees' ability to effectively regulate their thoughts, behaviors, and emotions at work. In this section, we turn our focus explicitly to these processes, with a special emphasis on how these processes might be expected to affect employee performance and well-being at work. We explicitly link each process to one or more of the core processes described in the preceding section. We provide empirical evidence for each process, suggest ways in which the process would affect employees' functioning at work, and, where available, provide illustrations of these processes from our interviews. In Table 1, we provide a summary of the

*Table 1.*  Potential Effects of Secondary Processes of Mindfulness on Employee Performance and Well-Being.

| Mindfulness-Based Process | Possible Work-Related Effects |
|---|---|
| Response flexibility | • Improved decision making<br>• Improved communication |
| Decreased rumination | • Improved coping with stressful events<br>• Faster recovery from negative events<br>• Increased confidence and self-efficacy<br>• Better problem solving<br>• Improved concentrations<br>• More effective use of social support |
| Empathy | • Increased interactional and informational justice<br>• Reduced antisocial behavior<br>• Increased organizational citizenship behaviors<br>• Positive leadership behaviors |
| Affective regulation | • Improved communication<br>• Improved coping with stressful events<br>• Faster recovery from negative events<br>• Fewer accidents |
| Increased self-determination and persistence | • Increased goal-directed effort<br>• Improved task performance<br>• Greater learning<br>• Increased job satisfaction<br>• Increased organizational commitment<br>• Increased performance on creative tasks |
| Increased working memory | • Reduced negative affect<br>• Improved ability to handle multiple demands<br>• Ability to perform under stress |
| More accurate affective forecasting | • Less biased decision making<br>• More accurate expectations<br>• Less frustration and negative emotion |

cognitive and emotional process related to mindfulness and their proposed work-related effects.

### Response Flexibility

[During a meditation retreat] my teacher was talking about a kind of reptilian inherited kind of restlessness – jump! jump! jump! jump! – that we probably inherited because we needed to, and I tend not to respond to that ... which I think is wise. Now when someone comes to me with something [at work], instead of giving a fast glance I find myself staring a lot at people ... just kind of slowing down, you know ... and I try to come to some wisdom before I answer ... and if that turns out not to be wise, or not wisdom, then switching it. But I don't think I'm nearly as impulsive as I would be if I didn't practice, that's for sure.

– Mindfulness Meditator (Participant #3)

*Response flexibility* can be defined as the ability to pause before taking verbal or physical action (Siegel, 2007). Response flexibility occurs when one is able to pause before responding to an environmental stimulus. In the words of our study participant, response flexibility is characterized by a "slowing down" and deeper consideration of the situation ("come to some wisdom") before responding to workplace events and interactions. Allowing time and space to reflect and consider multiple, nonautomatic ways of responding offers more opportunities for optimal outcomes and functioning. Rather than responding to workplace events habitually and invariantly, response flexibility allows one the power to act in alignment with one's goals, needs, and values (Brown et al., 2007). As our interviewee indicated, mindfulness promotes a slowing down of one's response and more thoughtful consideration of how (and whether) to react to work events rather than "jump" impulsively and reactively.

A growing body of evidence suggests that mindfulness plays a significant role in heightened response flexibility across a variety of situations ranging from gambling to interpersonal communication (e.g., Bishop et al., 2004; Chatzisarantis & Hagger, 2007; Lakey et al., 2007; Wenk-Sormaz, 2005). Responding in a flexible manner requires not only a delay in response but also a careful assessment of the situation, the available response options, as well as an ultimate initiation of action (Siegel, 2007). This type of executive self-control is initiated in large part by the mPFC, which, as noted in the preceding text, is activated by mindfulness. All three core processes delineated in the preceding text appear to play a role in generating a capacity for flexible responding. *Physiological regulation and awareness* allows one to assess environmental stimuli without experiencing physiological activation of the fight-or-flight response system in which high levels of physiological arousal overload the mPFC and override the ability to think and to choose reactions (Cozolino, 2006). Mindfulness also facilitates response flexibility through the nonreactive, nonjudging aspects that characterize two of our other core processes – *decoupling* and *decreased automaticity*. Through decoupling and decreased automaticity, individuals recognize that thoughts and reactions to an event are not an objective reality requiring immediate alteration or response (Chambers et al., 2009).

As such, the range and optimization of possible behavioral responses grows. In the workplace, we suspect that increased response flexibility would contribute to a more productive environment in a variety of ways including fewer instances of escalating conflict and displaced aggression in response to perceived threats and disagreements and improved decision making because reactive decision making would be less likely (i.e., escalation of commitment).

## Decreased Rumination

I find that meditation lets you just have an emotion, and it's so hard to not get caught up in them. But you can take a breath and step back and say "Oh! I'm feeling really angry!" And a lot of times that lets you do something different and not just do your habitual response. It's helped with my emotions quite a bit ... But it's also helped me be aware of thought patterns that keep occurring ... that you really get trapped in. And you can spend a lot of time there if you can't step back and say "Oh! Here I am having this argument with myself again!" And I find with both the emotional kind of habits and thought habits ... I think it really helps me to just stop, step back and see it, you know?
                                                                    – Mindfulness Meditator (Participant #1)

When individuals are confronted with events that would normally provoke negative thought patterns, a mindful orientation makes them less likely to engage in rumination – a repetitive and passive focus on symptoms, causes, and consequences of distress (Nolen-Hoeksema, 1991). Because mindfulness leads to a separation of the self from the experience or emotion, and because it reduces automatic responding, individuals who practice mindfulness engage in less rumination, leading them to better cope with stressful events (Broderick, 2005).

Absent the power of mindfulness to decouple and reduce automaticity, rumination will follow certain stimuli as individuals attempt to make sense of and resolve discrepancies between what is happening and what they desire to happen. As our interviewee noted, rumination can "trap" one in a spiral of negative and unproductive thoughts. In a mindful state, individuals are aware of their thoughts, but can separate them from their self-view and avoid evaluating their thoughts as good or bad. Indeed, more adaptive coping with change or with adverse experiences at work was one of the common themes that emerged in our interviews.

In terms of the empirical evidence, a clear link exists between mindfulness and mindfulness-based techniques and decreased rumination among clinical and nonclinical populations. Research has suggested that individuals who participated in mindfulness programs reported less ruminative thinking in response to life events (Ramel, Goldin, Carmona, & McQuaid, 2004), even when the events were similar to those experienced by others who had no mindfulness training (Goldin & Gross, 2010). Trait mindfulness also has been associated with less rumination. Frewen, Evans, Maraj, Dozois, and Partridge (2008) found associations between trait mindfulness [as measured by the Mindful Attention and Awareness Scale (MAAS; Brown & Ryan, 2003) and the Kentucky Inventory of Mindfulness Skills (KIMS; Baer, Smith, & Allen, 2004)] and less difficulty "letting go" of negative automatic thinking (depressive, worry, or social fear cognitions). Verplanken, Friborg, Wang, Trafimow, and Woolf (2007) found moderate negative correlations between the MAAS and a scale of habitual negative thinking as well as rumination.

Individuals who engage in ruminating thought patterns are at greater risk for poor concentration (Ingram & Smith, 1984), depressed mood (Nolen-Hoeksema & Morrow, 1991), low self-efficacy (Brockner & Hulton, 1978) and are more likely to alienate those who might provide social support (Nolen-Hoeksema & Davis, 1999). Conversely, individuals who are less prone to rumination after stressful events report fewer work-related health complaints. Accordingly, we suggest that a reduction in rumination resulting from mindfulness will have broad ranging effects on employees' performance and well-being, via improved confidence, better problem solving, more effective use of social support mechanisms, and better concentration. In addition, a reduction in rumination will lead to faster recovery from negative workplace events.

### Empathy

The other part was ... working with compassion outside of class, like really looking at how damaged my students are and how ... how many holes they have in their life and how wounded they are ... really looking at their pain and their confusion and their traumas and dramas and ... really feeling how hard it is to be a teenager in this world, and really just feeling it, like how inherently shitty their circumstances are ... Once you feel that, then you're not so angry because ... you feel like, well, just try to help them. You know, just try to ... make them smile and just pat them on the back, and try to make their life a little less hard. That becomes the goal ... being friendly and being kind and just understanding that this is really hard for them ... kind of coming at it from their point of view.

— Mindfulness Meditator (Participant #3)

Empathy is the ability to see life from another's perspective. Empathy allows us to be attuned to others, to resonate with them, and to have compassion (Cozolino, 2006). As suggested in the quote above, empathy enabled our interviewee to see how deeply wounded the students were. Our interviewee altered his/her behavior to better connect with them, offering kindness and compassion rather than judgment. Through empathy, individuals are able to consider the larger social picture, moving out of "survival mode" by considering what actions are best for others (Siegel, 2007). How is mindfulness related to empathy? Building on a growing body of work, we see several links between mindful awareness and empathy via its links to decreased automaticity and decoupling and increased physiological awareness and regulation (Block-Lerner, Adair, Plumb, Rhatigan, & Orsillo, 2007; Brems, Fromme, & Johnson, 1992; Brown et al., 2007; Cozolino, 2006; Hughes, Tingle, & Sawin, 1981; Shapiro, Schwartz, & Bonner, 1998; Siegel, 2010; Tipsord, 2009).

As the Dalai Lama (2002, p. 67) noted, "Ultimately, how we act and behave in relation to our fellow humans and the world, depends on how we perceive ourselves." With empathy, one must be able to simultaneously "hold one's own perspective in mind while simultaneously imagining what it is like to be the other" (Cozolino, 2006, p. 203). The ability to perceive the self as it is without the constraints of automaticity is a key feature of mindfulness. Indeed, it is difficult for individuals to be aware of others' perspectives if they are unaware of their own. In essence, nonjudgmental, present-moment awareness (i.e., mindfulness) of one's own internal thoughts facilitates empathy for the internal states of others (Block-Lerner et al., 2007). Through mindfulness generated meta-cognitive awareness, individuals can develop the capacity to understand their own internal emotional processes, which can help them better understand the emotional processes of others (Teasdale et al., 2002). A cycle of mutual reinforcement develops where *intra*personal attunement promotes *inter*personal attunement (Siegel, 2007). A growing body of social neurobiology research indicates that our capacity to be attuned to others depends, in part, on our knowledge of our own mind and internal state (Siegel, 2010).

Second, a growing body of research indicates that *physiological awareness and regulation* promotes empathy (e.g., Cozolino, 2006). In the process of attuning and resonating with others, individuals use subcortical data (i.e., heart rate, limbic system) to guide their responses. The act of empathy requires individuals to experience, emotionally and physiologically, the inner experience of others. As part of the empathy process, the physiological and limbic systems send signals to the body and brain allowing individuals to literally feel what the other person is experiencing.

Third, mindfulness increases our ability to tolerate negative emotions in ourselves and others (Tipsord, 2009). Having true empathy requires a tolerance for and regulation of the negative internal states of others and those that arise in ourselves as a consequence. By observing and not reacting to our own negative states (i.e., decoupling) we can better tolerate our own negative states and the negative states of others. Without the ability to regulate our own negative emotional states, we can become flooded with the negative emotions of others, limiting our ability to remain attuned and compassionate.

Higher levels of empathy are clearly desirable for organizational members at all levels (Kamdar, McAllister, & Turban, 2006; Patient & Skarlicki, 2010). Organizational members who have higher levels of empathy for their colleagues demonstrate higher levels of interactional justice (i.e., lower levels of sexual harassment and antisocial behavior; Douglas & Martinko, 2001; O'Leary-Kelly, Bowes-Sperry, Bates, & Lean, 2009), informational justice (Patient & Skarlicki, 2010), organizational citizenship behaviors (Kamdar et al., 2006; Kidder, 2002), and positive leadership behaviors (Kellett, Humphrey, & Sleeth, 2002; Scott, Colquitt, Paddock, & Judge, 2010). Empathy may be particularly important in certain occupations that require greater compassion. For example, in one study of medical students, an MBSR training program increased self-reported empathy over preprogram levels (Shapiro et al., 1998). Thus, if mindfulness can imbue employees with empathy, we would expect positive organizational and individual outcomes.

## Affective Regulation

... just even being in a positive state of mind ... you know, I've only been here two years after being gone for ten and I hate winter and, just using a practice while walking to the bus of dis-identification with the experience of having it be twenty below, freezing, and it's 5:30 in the morning. You know, I'd instantly just go to agitation. But the practice has taught me just to watch it and even have a sense of humor about it .... . If I go to the bus with agitation and I got to work with agitation, I'm not going to be very productive.
– Mindfulness Meditator (Participant #2)

Affective regulation comprises the reduction of negative emotions as well as the generation and maintenance of positive emotion. Our interviewee captured the essence of affective regulation and its benefits. Rather than be distressed by the cold, by using mindfulness practices this meditator eliminated "agitation" about external conditions beyond their control.

Mindfulness (state and trait) has been linked to both facets of affect regulation (generating positive emotions, down-regulating negative emotions when they arise; e.g., Fredrickson et al., 2008; Giluk, 2009, 2010) in large part because mindfulness enhances the brain circuits responsible for emotional regulation (Davidson, 2000; Siegel, 2007). Specifically, enhanced left prefrontal activation seems to be a critical trigger of positive emotion, approach motivation, and increased ability to modulate negative moods arising from the firing of the limbic system. Building on the growing literature in this area (e.g., Urry et al., 2004), we assert that two core processes – awareness and regulation of one's physiological states combined with decoupling of the self from experiences and emotions – play a key role in affect regulation.

In terms of the influence of mindfulness on *positive emotions*, meta-analytic evidence indicates a positive association between mindfulness and positive mood states (i.e., PA; Giluk, 2009). Although challenging situations deplete important self-regulatory resources (Tice, Baumeister, & Zhang, 2004), positive mood states "restore and replenish" these resources, allowing individuals to persist (Giluk, 2010, p. 55). Greater awareness promoted by mindfulness may enhance the experience of and engagement with positive emotions (Erisman & Roemer, 2010; Tomarken, Davidson, & Henriques, 1990). In other words, a cycle of positivity may develop through mindfulness, as individuals are more likely to notice positive events in their lives and thus experience more positive moods.

According to Brown and his colleagues (2007), mindfulness is also associated with acceptance of emotional states and enhanced ability to repair negative states. Further evidence of the role of mindfulness in regulating negative affect comes from a study by Hariri, Bookheimer, and Mazziotta (2000) in which the simple act of observing a negative emotion and labeling it without judgment decreased limbic system activation, which subsequently reduced felt and expressed negative emotions. It appears that mindfulness driven mPFC activation modulates limbic system activation in response to negative emotions (Siegel, 2007).

In terms of the workplace, a significant body of extant work has documented the benefits of increased positive mood and decreased or regulated negative affective experiences (Bono & Ilies, 2006; Isen, 1987;

Losada, 1999; Lyubomirsky, King, & Diener, 2005; Miner, Glomb, & Hulin, 2005). For example, Lyubomirsky and her colleagues (2005) demonstrated that positive affect generates success in multiple life domains. Likewise, Fredrickson and her colleagues (Cohn, Fredrickson, Brown, Mikels, & Conway, 2009; Fredrickson, 1998; Fredrickson et al., 2008) suggested that positive emotions enable individuals to build important cognitive, physical, and social resources such as resilience. Moreover, employees who tend to experience more positive moods are more sensitive to the reward signals in the environment such as pay raises and other forms of recognition (e.g., Shaw, Duffy, Mitra, Lockhart, & Bowler, 2003).

The regulation and reduction of negative emotion also has clear implications for employee functioning (see Brief & Weiss, 2002). For example, individuals who experience chronically negative mood states are more likely to be victimized at work and to be perpetrators of workplace aggression (e.g., Aquino, Grover, Bradfield, & Allen, 1999; Tepper, Duffy, Henle, & Lambert, 2006). Leaders' negative mood states have been linked to followers' moods and group processing effects as well (Sy, Côté, & Saavedra, 2005).

## Increased Self-Determination and Persistence

I do this job because … it's working with humans, but also it's essential to me that I have a right livelihood you know … that's very important to me. I mean, I don't want a job that wouldn't fall under the category of right livelihood or direct contact with people in need.
– Mindfulness Meditator (Participant #2)

Brown and Ryan (2003) argued that individuals acting mindfully behave in accord with their underlying values and interests. They reported a positive association between the experience of mindful states and feelings of autonomy, a key component of self-determination. Additionally, Shapiro et al. (2006) suggested that the detached observation developed in mindfulness training allows greater recognition of what is valued, and increased likelihood that individuals will choose behaviors in alignment with those values. The reduced automaticity associated with mindfulness leads individuals to "*reflectively* choose what has previously been *reflexively* adopted or conditioned" (Shapiro et al., 2006, p. 380), ultimately creating greater congruence between values and actions, which is at the heart of self-determined behavior. Because mindful individuals better understand their goals and values, and act more congruently with them, their intentions are better predictors of their behavior. This proposition is consistent with the predictions of self-determination theory (Ryan & Deci, 2000) and was supported empirically by Chatzisarantis and Hagger (2007), who found that intentions for physical activity in leisure time predicted actual physical activity among individuals high in trait mindfulness.

Greater alignment between goals and values is also associated with persistence toward goal accomplishment. Self-determined goals elicit more effort (Bono & Judge, 2003; Sheldon & Elliot, 1999) and also lead to greater persistence, even in the face of challenges. Mindfulness also reduces the extent to which people see barriers to goal accomplishment, or obstacles in goal pursuit, as indications of their competency (e.g., decoupling of self from experiences). Challenges often trigger derailing negative, self-critical, reactive, and judgmental thoughts. As individuals attempt to avoid dealing with these challenging threats to self, persistence lags (Teasdale, Segal, & Williams, 1995). By allowing negative thoughts to occur without judgment and reaction, the thoughts and concomitant frustration dissipate, allowing successful goal pursuit (Brown et al., 2007). Empirical evidence has supported the notion that mindfulness plays a significant role in persistence (e.g., Evans, Baer, & Segerstrom, 2009). Rather than being absorbed in a dysfunctional cycle of rumination, mindfulness helps people maintain cognitive focus (Chambers et al., 2009; Chambers, Lo, & Allen, 2008). We suggest this occurs because mindful people are pursuing goals that are important to them, and mindfulness helps them cope more effectively with obstacles.

The implications for increased self-determination and persistence at work are broad reaching. Existing research links goal self-concordance directly to job satisfaction and organizational commitment (Bono & Judge, 2003), increased job satisfaction (Judge, Bono, Erez, & Locke, 2005), and increased effort and performance on creative tasks (Bono & Judge, 2003). Additionally, Sheldon, Turban, Brown, Barrick, and Judge (2003) suggested that self-determination increases goal-commitment and learning efforts, and ultimately increases learning. A series of studies also link goal self-concordance to increased effort, improved goal attainment, and greater satisfaction with goal attainment (Sheldon & Elliot, 1999). In summary, we expect that mindfulness, primarily via reduced automaticity of thought, will lead employees to both be more productive and to experience greater satisfaction from their work.

## Other Secondary Processes

So far we have identified major processes we believe to be central in the operation of mindfulness. However, the literature has provided suggestive evidence for additional processes. In the following text, we detail two such processes: increased working memory capacity and more accurate affective forecasting. Although these issues did not arise directly in our interviews, empirical evidence suggests that mindfulness may increase working memory and improve affective forecasting.

### Increased Working Memory

Working memory or "the cognitive mechanism that allows us to keep a limited amount of information active for a limited period of time" (Elzinga & Roelofs, 2005, p. 98), plays a key role in self-regulatory processes because it is used to manage cognitive demands and to regulate emotions (e.g., Schmeichel, Volokhov, & Demaree, 2008). The existing literature has provided considerable evidence that highly stressful or demanding situations deplete working memory capacity, partly because stressful or other physiologically and emotionally activated situations cause the adrenal glands to release stress hormones (e.g., cortisol) to meet situational demands (e.g., Roozendaal, 2002). Although helpful in activating response systems, elevated cortisol levels in stressful situations have the unfortunate consequence of inhibiting working memory (Oei, Everaerd, Elzinga, Van Well, & Bermond, 2006). Indeed, working memory is considered to be one of the memory functions most affected by cortisol (Elzinga & Roelofs, 2005).

Given the link between mindfulness and physiological balance and awareness, and building on the growing research in this area (e.g., Jha, Stanley, Kiyonaga, Wong, & Gelfand, 2010), we propose that mindfulness meditation will improve working memory in work settings. In a recent study of military employees, Jha and her colleagues (2010) hypothesized and found that mindfulness practices protected working memory from degradation during a stressful predeployment phase for soldiers who completed an 8-week mindfulness training program. Results confirmed an increase in working memory capacity for soldiers who were trained and who practiced and degradations in working memory capacity for those who were trained but did not practice, consistent with expectations for individuals in stressful environments. Jha and her colleagues proposed that mindfulness may help cultivate a "working memory reserve" (p. 62). In addition, they found that the increase in working memory capacity associated with mindfulness training led to reduced negative affect.

Although not a focus of their study, this research is also consistent with the notion that mindfulness is associated with improved self-regulation because it affects the brain's capacity for balanced physiological regulation.

As noted in the preceding text, when individuals become more aware of their bodily states, they are more able to regulate their levels of physiological activation and responses to negative thoughts and emotions. Consequently, unhealthy stress hormone production (i.e., cortisol) is reduced, allowing working memory to function more effectively, which suggests that mindfulness may be especially important for effective performance in the workplace when multiple demands or stress-inducing conditions prevail.

*Improved Accuracy in Affective Forecasting*
Affective forecasting refers to an individual's ability to accurately predict their emotional responses to future events (Wilson & Gilbert, 2003). It has been well established that people are generally poor at anticipating future emotions; they are unable to accurately predict how they will feel following emotionally charged events (Gilbert, Pinel, Wilson, Blumberg, & Wheatley, 1998). They tend to predict they will be happier than they actually are after positive events and to predict that they will be unhappier than they actually are following negative events. Mindfulness may lead to improvements in affective forecasting by reducing the impact bias (i.e., overestimating the emotional impact of a future event), because mindfulness allows people to consider emotions and emotional experiences as separate from the self, and because it reduces automaticity of thought. In one study of a sample of 188 young adults who forecasted their emotions for the weeks following the 2008 presidential election, Emanuel, Updegraff, Kalmbach, and Ciesla (2010) found that trait mindfulness was associated with more moderate affective forecasts and decreased impact bias.

Errors in affective forecasting are important in the workplace because they introduce bias into decision-making processes when individuals overweight their own or others' reactions to future occurrences. More accurate affective forecasting is expected not only to improve employee performance via improved decision making, but is also expected to improve well-being because of greater alignment between expectations and reality, which eliminates the disappointment, negative emotions, and frustration that follow from unmet expectations.

# KEY WORK-RELATED BENEFITS OF MINDFULNESS

Our central purpose in this manuscript was to link mindfulness and mindfulness-based processes to employees' performance and well-being at work. In examining the cognitive, emotional, and neurobiological processes linking mindfulness with improved self-regulatory capacity in the work-place, three central themes emerge. First, mindfulness is associated with factors expected to influence relationship quality. Second, mindfulness is linked to processes indicative of resiliency. Third, mindfulness is linked with processes expected to improve task performance and decision making. In the following sections, we focus explicitly on the ways mindfulness and mindfulness-based practices lead to more positive relational functioning at work, how they build resiliency, and how they improve task performance and decision making. The three outcomes we focus on are inextricably linked, but we discuss them independently because they represent distinct work-related outcomes.

### Improved Social Relationships

There are two things I think that I'm really aware of how [mindfulness] helped me, and one of them is relationships. It's that pause … I mean I can think of instances where I was having a disagreement with either a co-worker or a student, and just being able to, like, just come back to myself and realize … a lot of times what I actually realize is they're upset but I don't think I have to be (laughter). And boy, that can be so helpful. Many times that either just settles it down or at least … at least I'm not all upset about it. I mean I certainly do get upset at times … there's things that happen but … that's one thing with relationships that helps tremendously.
– Mindfulness Meditator (Participant #1)

A fundamental finding of social psychological research is that individuals thrive through positive social connections with others (Baumeister & Leary, 1995). Positive social connections in a work setting are no exception. A growing body of work indicates that positive workplace relationships build critical resources that protect individuals from workplace stressors, and foster employee thriving, communication, creativity, and citizenship behaviors (e.g., Dutton & Heaphy, 2003; Harter, Schmidt, & Hayes, 2002; Thau, Aquino, & Poortvliet, 2007). We submit that mindfulness will promote these positive social connections.

How does mindfulness foster positive social connections in the work-place? Many processes may contribute to improved workplace relationships, but we note the special importance of *empathy* and *response flexibility*, both markers of the internal attunement associated with mindfulness in which one is distinctly aware of one's own physical and emotional signals, which allows enhanced sensitivity to others' signals *without subsequent reactivity* (Davidson, 2000; Siegel, 2007). Thus, individuals who practice mindfulness should be better poised to respond to colleagues with greater acceptance and without unskillful reactivity. In essence, mindfulness promotes healthy ways of relating to others in the workplace (Giluk, 2010), which include taking another's perspective and reducing habitual reactions that may be dysfunctional or promote escalation. As indicated in the preceding quote, the practice has allowed the mindfulness meditator to communicate more openly and to resolve conflict without negative contagion and escalating patterns of tit-for-tat behaviors, instead being more accepting of others and their imperfections.

Recent research has turned to the role of mindfulness in facilitating the quality of interpersonal connections as well (e.g., Hutcherson et al., 2008), and studies suggest that mindfulness training may be related to greater social connectedness (e.g., Cohen & Miller, 2009). This sense of connection may be important for the workplace as individuals higher in social connectedness tend to display more desirable interpersonal behaviors (e.g., OCBs, received and perceived social support) than those lower in social connectedness (Fredrickson et al., 2008). In many ways, positive inter-personal relationships are a critical determinant of optimal organizational functioning (Duffy, Ganster, & Pagon, 2002), thereby underscoring the important role of mindfulness in work relationships.

### Increased Resiliency

… you get really sensitive, like, to people's energy, like … my [boss name], she's the exact opposite of me, she's like really tight … she's retiring this year, she's very old, she's been doing it for way too long and she's burnt out, she's really whipped up and she's very tight. And I notice I respond to her with calmness "Be at ease, be at ease" like this, and I want to walk away because she's so intense! Like her body, and her language. At first when I was really sensitive I just wanted to, like, get out of there! I just couldn't deal with her energy, … but now I've just learned how to, like, just kind of be with it, and it feels good that I can really just listen to her go off and just … and … just stay with her. But not feel drained by her. It was draining listening to her at one point, and now it's just like "Just let it move through me, don't resist and don't kind of like react, respond, just take it all in." And then she feels better because I'm not reacting, I'm not getting caught up in her drama, 'cause that's what sometimes happens, you get caught up in each others' dramas and just kind of whip it up. When you don't, and they vent, you still feel calm, and that way you don't have to avoid. I used to avoid people because I didn't want to deal with their shit. But now I don't have to, it's like "Alright, give me your shit, what's wrong?"

– Mindfulness Meditator (Participant #3)

The desire to avoid unpleasant and challenging situations, such as the one described in the preceding text by our study participant, is common.

Although offering temporary respite from adversarial conditions, in the long-term such avoidance behavior is maladaptive. Withdrawal tendencies (e.g., "I wanted to get out of there!") deprive individuals of the opportunities to achieve goal-relevant behaviors and activities necessary for thriving (Urry et al., 2004). Conversely, a convincing body of evidence suggests that approach tendencies (e.g., engaged thinking and interacting with others and one's environment) are associated with well-being and thriving (Urry et al., 2004). To engage in approach behaviors and experience their associated well-being effects, individuals must be resilient in the face of challenge and difficulties.

How does mindfulness generate resilience? Although resilience is likely to be fostered through several of the mechanisms posited in the preceding text, we highlight the role of two processes associated with mindfulness – affective regulation and persistence. Approach behavior requires persistence as well as the maintenance of positive affect and well-being in the face of adversity (Chambers et al., 2009; Davidson, 2000). Another central feature of resilience is the capacity to be nonreactive to one's thoughts and emotions and to accept them (i.e., decoupling and reduced automaticity). The capacity to regulate negative thoughts and emotions, particularly once they surface, is a key feature of resilience. Davis (2009) wrote, "The capacity to harness positive emotion in daily life may be a key ingredient to resilience, helping individuals to persevere in the face of challenge, speeding recovery from transient life difficulties, and sustaining quality of life in the face of more chronic stressors" (p. 62). As our meditator so eloquently illustrated, mindfulness not only allows us to approach others positively (in this case, a person who is known to be difficult) it also protects us from other's negative emotional states and agitation through appropriate regulation of affect and decreased reactivity. In a work setting, remaining resilient to work challenges and stressors, be they interpersonal or task related, is critical to optimal work functioning.

### Improved Task Performance

I've learned that when your energy is concentrated on ... when you're absorbed in a task like planning, it really feels good. It really feels good to [work task] because you're absorbed in a task, your mind is focusing on one thing, so those are really pleasurable because you're not scattered, your mind's not scattered

And I also do try and walk really slowly sometimes, or just tell myself "I'm going to do this really slowly" instead of always feeling like I'm being really pushed to rush which we always generally are, but ... and that actually does help, you know, it kinda

just ... something still gets done (laughter), you know? And ... and a lot of times if you
do it slowly it actually gets done well!
                                        – Mindfulness Meditator (Participant #3)

Many processes described in this chapter are likely to have downstream
effects on task performance, but the way that mindfulness affects
performance is likely to depend heavily on the type of tasks required of a
job. For example, for jobs with hefty interpersonal interactions, we might
expect empathy to play a major role. For occupations with high emotional
content, we might expect decreased rumination and improved affective
regulation to be the critical pathways to performance. For jobs that are not
routinized and have high task complexity, response flexibility may be key.
Although some processes (e.g., increased self-determination and persistence)
can be expected to beneficially affect many job types, we believe that the role
of mindfulness in performance largely depends on the task and contextual
features of the work.

The effects of the attentional component of mindfulness on task
performance have been thoughtfully considered by Dane (2010). Dane
suggested that wide attentional breadth, such as that present in a state of
mindfulness, may inhibit or promote task performance depending on the
task environment and level of expertise. Specifically, maintaining a wide
external attentional breadth is useful in dynamic task environments as it
allows for attention to a wide range of stimuli. However, in fairly static
environments, wide external attentional breadth might inhibit performance
as one loses focus on their tasks. Herndon (2008) found that trait
mindfulness was associated with fewer cognitive failures (i.e., forgetting,
distraction, blunders), which suggests that if mindfulness is associated with
greater attention to external stimuli, and therefore, fewer cognitive failures,
then a variety of favorable work outcomes are likely to follow including
increased performance and fewer accidents.

Mindfulness also attunes individuals to internal processes such that an
individual is more attentive to their nonconscious or automatic thoughts,
feelings, and perceptions, often in the form of gut feelings or reactions. Dane
(2010) argued that these intuitions may promote task performance when
expertise is high. Mindfulness is also expected to impact job performance
through improved decision making. When heuristic processing is reduced
and attention to internal and external stimuli is increased, decision biases
such as anchoring and fundamental attribution error should be decreased
(Hammond, Keeney, & Raiffa, 2006).

As we consider the links of mindfulness to task performance, we recognize
that mindfulness might be antithetical to the evolutionary development and

efficient functioning of the human brain, which is designed to rapidly process and categorize a large volume of stimuli. Automaticity is functional and at first blush, it might seem as if mindfulness may make one less efficient and less productive, as individuals are no longer able to rapidly process stimuli. However, we might reconcile these seemingly contradictory ideas by considering that mindfulness may help tune our minds so that automaticity becomes more functional and redirects attention to the appropriate environmental stimuli, allowing individuals to respond more skillfully rather than automatically. There is much room for future research testing our propositions about the effects of mindfulness on performance at work.

# CONTROVERSIES, QUESTIONS, AND CHALLENGES

Although this chapter focuses on carefully examining the processes by which mindfulness and mindfulness-based practices might influence employees' functioning at work, we would be remiss if we did not address several controversies, questions, and challenges in the general mindfulness literature to determine how seriously they challenge the link between mindfulness and work.

## *Mindfulness vs. Mindfulness-Based Practices and Programs*

In conjunction with our foray into the mindfulness literature, the first three authors completed an 8-week mindfulness training program modeled after the Kabat-Zinn MBSR program. Our reasons were twofold. As scholars, we wanted to better understand the ideas of mindfulness and the MBSR approach to cultivating mindfulness. As individuals, we were attracted to the possibilities of stress reduction and other benefits associated with MBSR programs. Although each had different experiences, we all found that the processes described in the preceding text and illustrated by our interviewees resonated with our experiences in mindfulness training. We felt that cultivating mindfulness via MBSR training benefitted our work and personal lives in many ways. Despite these experiences, we believe much remains to be known about the "active ingredients" that led to these benefits, especially whether they were attributable to mindfulness.

Mindfulness-based stress reduction curriculums include, as one aspect, practices designed to develop participant mindfulness. However, especially in a work-related discussion, we must recognize that these programs are, first and foremost, for reducing stress. Indeed, the practices are designed to help individuals relax mentally (guided imagery) and release tension physically (yoga and Qigong). Some, but not all, of these techniques are expected to improve mindfulness. Moreover, because they are conducted in small group sessions with regular sharing among participants, they also provide social support and sometimes lead to ongoing social relationships with the concomitant benefits. Participants may also change various behaviors (e.g., reducing commitments, better time management) over the course of an MBSR program (Kabat-Zinn, 1990, 1994). Although these practices (i.e., mental relaxation, reduced physical tensions, social support, better time management) and their direct benefits are not necessarily related to mindfulness, they would be expected to benefit work outcomes. It is beyond our scope here to analyze which MBSR benefits are due to mindfulness and which result from other processes such as relaxation or social support (see Bishop, 2002; Dimidjian & Linehan, 2003; Dobkin, 2008; Roemer & Orsillo, 2003, for a debate of whether mindfulness is the key ingredient of mindfulness-based practices), and we caution against unthinkingly choosing MBSR-type programs at work if the ultimate goal is to increase mindfulness. As Shapiro et al. (2006) noted, "Dismantle studies are necessary to separate and compare the various active ingredients in mindfulness-based interventions such as social support, relaxation, and cognitive behavioral elements" (p. 374).

Furthermore, questions surface about distinguishing mindfulness from existing self-regulatory concepts. Masicampo and Baumeister (2010) questioned whether mindfulness is substantively different from self-control. Given the difficulty of measuring mindfulness itself (as a state of consciousness), most research has focused on the beneficial effects of mindfulness-based practices or therapies. These effects are generally attributed to improved self-regulation of emotions, thoughts, and behaviors. Brown et al. (2007) argued that mindfulness improves autonomous self-control, which is associated with more effective self-regulation. Masicampo and Baumeister (2010) also questioned whether there is anything unique about mindfulness as a technique for developing self-control.

We suggest this is a question for neuroscience. Neuroimaging studies that link brain activity to self-reported states of mindfulness may be one way to validate self-reports (e.g., Davidson, 2010) and differentiate mindfulness from other self-regulatory strategies. We do not know whether brain activities or structural changes are the same for all practices that improve self-regulation. Perhaps mindfulness-based techniques are unique; perhaps they are not.

From the standpoint of basic research, it is critical to the advancement of knowledge that we continue efforts to separate mindfulness and related states, traits, meditation, and programs. But, from the standpoint of work, it may be more valuable to focus on the outcomes (and mediating processes) by which mindfulness-based practices lead to improved self-regulation of thoughts, emotions, and behaviors. An underlying assumption here is that organizations might implement mindfulness-based programs as part of their wellness initiatives. Thus, the focus of organizational research might be to understand the effects of mindfulness training rather than mindfulness itself, and to identify features of the work environment that support mindfulness.

### *Bringing Mindfulness Training into Work Organizations*

Given the impressive outcomes associated with mindfulness and mindfulness-based practices, especially in the clinical domain, it is easy to think of mindfulness practices as a cure-all. Indeed, already we see research (Giluk, 2010; Tipsord, 2009) – with mixed results – linking MBSR to a variety of work-related outcomes including experienced empathy, affect, citizenship behavior, relationship quality, and job performance. Although we warn against the tendency to view mindfulness and mindfulness-based practices as a panacea, we also recognize its demonstrated efficacy for a number of important work-related outcomes, particularly for stress reduction. According to the National Institute for Occupational Safety and Health (1999), about one-third of workers experience high levels of stress. Work stress has been identified as a major cause of employee turnover and burnout and has been linked to many physical and psychological complaints, including headaches, higher incidence of cardiovascular disease, and increased health insurance claims (Schnall, Dobson, & Rosskam, 2009). Along with emerging neurobiological studies linking mindfulness-based practices to changes in the activity and structure of the brain, research presents compelling evidence that mindfulness-based practices may be a fruitful addition to organizational wellness programs.

Although the evidence for mindfulness is compelling, we also recognize that much of the existing literature has been conducted outside the work environment, with little attention to the contextual features of work. Many examinations have used student samples or patient populations seeking treatment for medical or psychological symptoms. Thus, the generalizability of current research findings to employees in organizations is uncertain. Nevertheless, initial research evaluating the efficacy of mindfulness-based training programs for leaders is promising (Shambhala Sun Foundation, 2010a). For instance, leaders participating in the mindfulness training program in General Mills have experienced dramatic improvement of listening attentiveness and decision-making quality (General Mills, 2010). Additional research using rigorous methodologies is needed.

We also considered the possibility that organizations might experience unintended consequences from mindfulness. Given that mindfulness increases individuals' ability to control their thoughts, emotions, and behaviors, to be more aware of their personal goals and values, and to be more attuned to others' needs, a more mindful employee may act in ways that are counter to the organization's best interests, by favoring family, personal connections, or a slower work pace. For example, in the case of citizenship behaviors, an organization might benefit because a mindful employee is more likely to notice that a coworker needs help (via greater attention to the employee and increased empathy), but the mindful employee may also be more attuned to costs associated with helping (e.g., less time for family) or more aware of task goals and, as a result, choose not to help. This small example raises an important issue: The behaviors of more mindful employees will be more intentional, but they may not always lead to self-regulation that is consistent with organizational goals.

We also suspect that mindfulness is easier to cultivate in certain occupations or organizational contexts. One might argue that mindfulness is diametrically opposed to organizational cultures that value working fast, multitasking, and being hyper busy. Perhaps mindfulness would improve work quality but decrease quantity of work. There are a number of interesting questions to ask: What would an organizational culture that promotes mindfulness look like? How do people enter into mindful states at work? Do certain conditions in the work environment make a mindful state more likely?

We also believe that there may be certain conditions where the effects of mindfulness will be particularly strong, including situations when employees are dealing with challenging roles, when emotional regulation is required, or during times of transition. For example, mindfulness might be helpful in cross cultural situations when response flexibility and affective regulation are critical. Mindful, nonjudgmental attention to cultural differences might improve the odds of successful expatriate adjustment, because conscious awareness of differences should result in better adaptation to cultural norms, and because of the increased resilience and improved social relationships that we expect to result from a more mindful orientation. A similar rationale would apply to employees in new roles, such as moving into a new organization, department, or transitioning into management. Cultivating mindfulness might also be beneficial for organizations during periods of large-scale change. Consider the benefits of increased empathy, response flexibility, and affective regulation along with decreased rumination in times of uncertainty and stress such as during a downsizing, restructuring, or merger. The advantages of mindfulness programs might be heightened in such contexts.

Before organizations adopt existing mindfulness training programs, they should carefully consider their goals. If the goal is to develop mindfulness among employees, they should consider multiple techniques for training employees to be more mindful. Kabat-Zinn (2005) discussed MBSR as "scaffolding," but other techniques to cultivate mindfulness are also possible. If the goal is to develop improved self-regulatory capabilities, results might be obtained via self-control building exercises, or via increases in self-determination at work (e.g., Bono & Judge, 2003). Focusing directly on self-regulation would eliminate uneasiness that might exist in organizations about the Buddhist roots of mindfulness. Deciding on the ultimate goal of an organizational intervention is critical, as there is no reason to believe that self-regulation exercises will lead to the same benefits as mindfulness training, especially those associated with empathy, or those that result from changes in the structure of the brain. Further, research has suggested that other relaxation or meditation exercises (i.e., loving-kindness meditation designed to increase feelings of social connection and progressive muscle relaxation designed for physical relaxation) do not evidence the decentering that occurs in mindful exercises (Feldman et al., 2010). Clearly, there is a need for research on optimal ways to increase mindfulness at work and to delineate the effects of different interventions. It may also be that optimal practices for each of these outcomes vary for different individuals.

It is also important to note that in some organizations, core tenants of original mindfulness training programs are being removed for the organizational audience. For example, programs are not touted as stress reduction programs, given that stress has become a way of life in most organizations and a badge of honor in many. Nor do some work-related programs retain a link to Buddhism or any other philosophical underpinnings. Thus, it seems reasonable to assume that programs must be tailored to work settings, and adoption of any program must carefully consider the elements of the program and the organization's specific goals. Google's "Search Inside Yourself" program provides one example of a setting where mindfulness has been positioned not as a stress reduction program or one with Buddhist links, but as a program designed to promote autonomy, creativity, and joy of work – all in alignment with organizational goals and values. Although Google's program includes the same meditative and contemplative techniques present in other mindfulness programs, there are also topics tailored to organizational settings such as mindful emailing, mindful listening, and dealing with difficult conversations (Shambhala Sun Foundation, 2010b). Indeed, customized mindfulness programs and practices have been increasingly popular in a variety of companies such as Apple, McKinsey, and Deutsche Bank (Mindfulnet, 2011). However, it is hard to know whether such tailoring to suit organizational purposes undermines the core principles of mindfulness or its outcomes. In the words of one of our interviewees:

> what I notice is ... the secularization of mindfulness, I mean, there's some good things about that as people are getting interested and it's helping them reduce stress, and it's making them more effective. That's all good. But I'm a little bit worried about the longevity, if they see it as a tool, if it's seen as like another tactic, strategy ... a lot of times people have a very short span of attention for that because it takes years of practice. When it's [mindfulness meditation] connected to more of a spiritual ... religious teachings, like the Dharma, then it's much more transformative, like it's more of a personal transformation, it's much deeper. And then it's more sustainable because you have that ... it's not just about being effective at work, it's about your life, it's about how to be happy in your life, so then it's much deeper and it's much more transformative. Then I think there's a chance for it to be sustainable in the workplace. But, in the workplace you have different religions, different creeds, and you could never pull that off. You'd have to secularize the practice. And you lose something when you secularize it, you know, you lose something. ... it just seems light, and fluffy. It's not, it doesn't penetrate ... it just feels really ... surface. Mindfulness is really powerful.
>
> – Mindfulness Meditator (Participant #3)

# CONCLUSION

Both the words of our participants and the research literature suggest that mindfulness is powerful and considering the ways that mindfulness might improve people's work lives is exciting. In this chapter, we reviewed the existing literature on mindfulness and explicitly link it to a variety of core and secondary processes that are expected to improve work outcomes, including improved social relationships, resilience, and performance. We see the potential for many positive outcomes associated with mindfulness at work, but note that few studies directly test our propositions in work settings or with employee samples. Building on the strong foundation of existing research, it is time to test the efficacy of mindfulness-based practices in a series of carefully designed field experiments or quasi-experiments in work settings.

# REFERENCES

Altman, D. (2010). *The mindfulness code: Keys for overcoming stress, anxiety, fear, and unhappiness.* Novato, CA: New World Library.

Aquino, K., Grover, S. L., Bradfield, M., & Allen, D. G. (1999). The effects of negative affectivity, hierarchical status, and self-determination on workplace victimization. *Academy of Management Journal, 42,* 260–272.

Baer, R. A. (2003). Mindfulness training as a clinical intervention: A conceptual and empirical review. *Clinical Psychology: Science and Practice, 10,* 125–143.

Baer, R. A., Smith, G. T., & Allen, K. B. (2004). Assessment of mindfulness by self-report: The Kentucky Inventory of Mindfulness Skills. *Assessment, 11,* 191–206.

Baer, R. A., Smith, G. T., Hopkins, J., Krietemeyer, J., & Toney, L. (2006). Using self-report assessment methods to explore facets of mindfulness. *Assessment, 13,* 27–45.

Bargh, J. A. (1994). The four horsemen of automaticity: Awareness, efficiency, intention, and control in social cognition. In: R. S. Wyer, Jr. & T. K. Srull (Eds), *Handbook of social cognition* (2nd ed., pp. 1–40). Hillsdale, NJ: Erlbaum.

Baumeister, R. F., & Leary, M. R. (1995). The need to belong: Desire for interpersonal attachments as a fundamental human motivation. *Psychological Bulletin, 117,* 497–529.

Beck, A. T., Rush, A. J., Shaw, B. F., & Emery, G. (1979). *Cognitive therapy of depression.* New York: Guilford Press.

Biegel, G. M., Brown, K. W., Shapiro, S. L., & Schubert, C. M. (2009). Mindfulness-based stress reduction for the treatment of adolescent psychiatric outpatients: A randomized clinical trial. *Journal of Consulting and Clinical Psychology, 77,* 855–866.

Bishop, S. R. (2002). What do we really know about mindfulness-based stress reduction? *Psychosomatic Medicine, 64,* 71–83.

Bishop, S. R., Lau, M., Shapiro, S., Carlson, L., Anderson, N. D., Carmody, J., Segal, Z. V., Abbey, S., Speca, M., Velting, D., & Devins, G. (2004). Mindfulness: A proposed operational definition. *Clinical Psychology: Science and Practice, 11,* 230–241.

Block-Lerner, J., Adair, C., Plumb, J. C., Rhatigan, D. L., & Orsillo, S. M. (2007). The case for mindfulness-based approaches in the cultivation of empathy: Does nonjudgmental, present-moment awareness increase capacity for perspective-taking and empathic concern? *Journal of Marital and Family Therapy, 33,* 501–516.

Bohlmeijer, E., Prenger, R., Taal, E., & Cuijpers, P. (2010). The effects of mindfulness-based stress reduction therapy on mental health of adults with a chronic medical disease: A meta-analysis. *Journal of Psychosomatic Research, 68,* 539–544.

Bono, J. E., & Ilies, R. (2006). Charisma, positive emotions and mood contagion. *Leadership Quarterly, 17,* 317–334.

Bono, J. E., & Judge, T. A. (2003). Self-concordance at work: Toward understanding the motivational effects of transformational leaders. *Academy of Management Journal, 46,* 554–571.

Bränström, R., Kvillemo, P., Brandberg, Y., & Moskowitz, J. T. (2010). Self-report mindfulness as a mediator of psychological well-being in a stress reduction intervention for cancer patients – A randomized study. *Annals of Behavioral Medicine, 39,* 151–161.

Brems, C., Fromme, D. K., & Johnson, M. E. (1992). Group modification of empathic verbalizations and self-disclosure. *The Journal of Social Psychology, 132,* 189–200.

Brief, A. P., & Weiss, H. M. (2002). Organizational behavior: Affect in the workplace. *Annual Review of Psychology, 53,* 279–307.

Brockner, J., & Hulton, A. B. (1978). How to reverse the vicious cycle of low self-esteem: The importance of attentional focus. *Journal of Experimental Social Psychology, 14,* 564–578.

Broderick, P. C. (2005). Mindfulness and coping with dysphoric mood: Contrasts with rumination and distraction. *Cognitive Therapy & Research, 29,* 501–510.

Brown, K. W., & Cordon, S. (2009). Toward a phenomenology of mindfulness: Subjective experience and emotional correlates. In: F. Didonna (Ed.), *Clinical handbook of mindfulness* (pp. 59–81). New York: Springer.

Brown, K. W., & Ryan, R. M. (2003). The benefits of being present: Mindfulness and its role in psychological well-being. *Journal of Personality and Social Psychology, 84,* 822–848.

Brown, K. W., Ryan, R. M., & Creswell, J. D. (2007). Mindfulness: Theoretical foundations and evidence for its salutary effects. *Psychological Inquiry, 18,* 211–237.

Cahn, B. R., & Polich, J. (2006). Meditation states and traits: EEG, ERP, and neuroimaging studies. *Psychological Bulletin, 132,* 180–211.

Cardaciotto, L., Herbert, J. D., Forman, E. M., Moitra, E., & Farrow, V. (2008). The assessment of present-moment awareness and acceptance: The Philadelphia Mindfulness Scale. *Assessment, 15,* 204–223.

Carmody, J., & Baer, R. A. (2008). Relationships between mindfulness practice and levels of mindfulness, medical and psychological symptoms and well-being in a mindfulness-based stress reduction program. *Journal of Behavioral Medicine, 31,* 23–33.

Carroll, M. (2006). *Awake at work: 35 practical Buddhist principles for discovering clarity and balance in the midst of work's chaos* (2nd ed.). Boston: Shambhala.

Center for Mindfulness in Medicine, Health Care, and Society, University of Massachusetts Medical School. (2010). Stress reduction program. Available at http://www.umassmed.edu/Content.aspx?id=41254&LinkIdentifier=id. Retrieved on December 30, 2010.

Chaiken, S. (1980). Heuristic versus systematic information processing and the use of source versus message cues in persuasion. *Journal of Personality and Social Psychology, 39,* 752–766.

Chambers, R., Gullone, E., & Allen, N. B. (2009). Mindful emotion regulation: An integrative review. *Clinical Psychology Review, 29,* 560–572.

Chambers, R., Lo, B. C. Y., & Allen, N. B. (2008). The impact of intensive mindfulness training on attentional control, cognitive style, and affect. *Cognitive Therapy and Research, 32,* 303–322.

Chatzisarantis, N. L. D., & Hagger, M. S. (2007). Mindfulness and the intention-behavior relationship within the theory of planned behavior. *Personality and Social Psychology Bulletin, 33,* 663–676.

Chiesa, A., & Serretti, A. (2009). Mindfulness-based stress reduction for stress management in healthy people: A review and meta-analysis. *Journal of Alternative and Complementary Medicine, 15,* 593–600.

Chiesa, A., & Serretti, A. (2010). A systematic review of neurobiological and clinical features of mindfulness meditations. *Psychological Medicine: A Journal of Research in Psychiatry and the Allied Sciences, 40,* 1239–1252.

Cohen, J. S., & Miller, L. J. (2009). Interpersonal mindfulness training for well-being: A pilot study with psychology graduate students. *Teachers College Record, 111,* 2760–2774.

Cohn, M. A., Fredrickson, B. L., Brown, S. L., Mikels, J. A., & Conway, A. M. (2009). Happiness unpacked: Positive emotions increase life satisfaction by building resilience. *Emotion, 9,* 361–368.

Cozolino, L. (2006). *The neuroscience of human relationships: Attachment and the developing social brain.* New York: Norton.

Creswell, J. D., Way, B. M., Eisenberger, N. I., & Lieberman, M. D. (2007). Neural correlates of dispositional mindfulness during affect labeling. *Psychosomatic Medicine, 69,* 560–565.

Dalai Lama. (2002). *Live in a better way: Reflections on truth, love, and happiness.* New York: Penguin Compass.

Dane, E. (2010). Reconsidering the trade-off between expertise and flexibility: A cognitive entrenchment perspective. *Academy of Management Review, 35,* 579–603.

Davids, T. W. R., & Stede, W. (Eds). (1959). *The Pali Text Society's Pali-English dictionary.* London: Luzac & Company, Ltd.

Davidson, R. J. (2000). Affective style, psychopathology, and resilience: Brain mechanisms and plasticity. *American Psychologist, 55,* 1196–1214.

Davidson, R. J. (2010). Empirical explorations of mindfulness: Conceptual and methodological conundrums. *Emotion, 10,* 8–11.

Davidson, R. J., Kabat-Zinn, J., Schumacher, J., Rosenkranz, M., Muller, D., Santorelli, S. F., Urbanowski, F., Harrington, A., Bonus, K., & Sheridan, J. F. (2003). Alterations in brain and immune function produced by mindfulness meditation. *Psychosomatic Medicine, 65,* 564–570.

Davis, M. C. (2009). Building emotional resilience to promote health. *American Journal of Lifestyle Medicine, 3,* 60–63.

Delgado, L. C., Guerra, P., Perakakis, P., Vera, M. N., del Paso, G. R., & Vila, J. (2010). Treating chronic worry: Psychological and physiological effects of a training programme based on mindfulness. *Behaviour Research and Therapy, 48,* 873–882.

Delmonte, M. M. (1990). The relevance of meditation to clinical practice: An overview. *Applied Psychology: An International Review, 39,* 331–354.

Dimidjian, S., & Linehan, M. M. (2003). Defining an agenda for future research on the clinical application of mindfulness practice. *Clinical Psychology: Science and Practice, 10,* 166–171.

Ditto, B., Eclache, M., & Goldman, N. (2006). Short-term autonomic and cardiovascular effects of mindfulness body scan meditation. *Annals of Behavioral Medicine, 32,* 227–234.

Dobkin, P. L. (2008). Mindfulness-based stress reduction: What processes are at work? *Complementary Therapies in Clinical Practice, 14,* 8–16.

Douglas, S. C., & Martinko, M. J. (2001). Exploring the role of individual differences in the prediction of workplace aggression. *Journal of Applied Psychology, 86,* 547–559.

Duerr, M. (2004a). The contemplative organization. *Journal of Organizational Change Management, 17,* 43–61.

Duerr, M. (2004b). A powerful silence: The role of meditation and other contemplative practices in American life and work. Retrieved from the Center for Contemplative Mind in Society (http://www.contemplativemind.org).

Duffy, M. K., Ganster, D., & Pagon, M. (2002). Social undermining in the workplace. *Academy of Management Journal, 45,* 331–351.

Dutton, J. E., & Heaphy, E. D. (2003). The power of high-quality connections. In: K.S. Cameron, J. E. Dutton & R. E. Quinn (Eds), *Positive organizational scholarship: Foundations of a new discipline* (pp. 263–278). San Francisco: Berrett-Koehler Publishers.

Elzinga, B. M., & Roelofs, K. (2005). Cortisol-induced impairments of working memory require acute sympathetic activation. *Behavioral Neuroscience, 119,* 98–103.

Emanuel, A. S., Updegraff, J. A., Kalmbach, D. A., & Ciesla, J. A. (2010). The role of mindfulness facets in affective forecasting. *Personality and Individual Differences, 49,* 815–818.

Erisman, S. M., & Roemer, L. (2010). A preliminary investigation of the effects of experimentally induced mindfulness on emotional responding to film clips. *Emotion, 10,* 72–82.

Evans, D. R., Baer, R. A., & Segerstrom, S. C. (2009). The effects of mindfulness and self-consciousness on persistence. *Personality and Individual Differences, 47,* 379–382.

Falkenström, F. (2010). Studying mindfulness in experienced meditators: A quasi-experimental approach. *Personality and Individual Differences, 48,* 305–310.

Farb, N. A. S., Anderson, A. K., Mayberg, H., Bean, J., McKeon, D., & Segal, Z. V. (2010). Minding one's emotions: Mindfulness training alters the neural expression of sadness. *Emotion, 10,* 25–33.

Feldman, G., Greeson, J., & Senville, J. (2010). Differential effects of mindful breathing, progressive muscle relaxation, and loving-kindness meditation on decentering and negative reactions to repetitive thoughts. *Behaviour Research and Therapy, 48,* 1002–1011.

Foley, E., Baillie, A., Huxter, M., Price, M., & Sinclair, E. (2010). Mindfulness-based cognitive therapy for individuals whose lives have been affected by cancer: A randomized controlled trial. *Journal of Consulting and Clinical Psychology, 78,* 72–79.

Fredrickson, B. L. (1998). What good are positive emotions? *Review of General Psychology, 2,* 300–319.

Fredrickson, B. L., Cohn, M. A., Coffey, K. A., Pek, J., & Finkel, S. M. (2008). Open hearts build lives: Positive emotions, induced through loving-kindness meditation, build consequential personal resources. *Journal of Personality and Social Psychology, 95,* 1045–1062.

Frewen, P. A., Dozois, D. J. A., Neufeld, R. W. J., Lane, R. D., Densmore, M., Stevens, T. K., & Lanius, R. A. (2010). Individual differences in trait mindfulness predict dorsomedial prefrontal and amygdala response during emotional imagery: An fMRI study. *Personality and Individual Differences, 49,* 479–484.

Frewen, P. A., Evans, E. M., Maraj, N., Dozois, D. J. A., & Partridge, K. (2008). Letting go: Mindfulness and negative automatic thinking. *Cognitive Therapy and Research, 32,* 758–774.

General Mills. (2010). Leadership program helps train the mind. Available at http://www.generalmills.com/Home/Media/Inside_General_Mills_archive/leadership_6_8_2010. Retrieved on February 22, 2011.

Germer, C. K. (2005). Mindfulness: What is it? What does it matter? In: C. K. Germer, R.D. Siegel & P. R. Fulton (Eds), *Mindfulness and psychotherapy* (pp. 3–27). New York, NY: Guilford Press.

Gilbert, D. T., Pinel, E. C., Wilson, T. D., Blumberg, S. J., & Wheatley, T. P. (1998). Immune neglect: A source of durability bias in affective forecasting. *Journal of Personality and Social Psychology, 75,* 617–638.

Giluk, T. L. (2009). Mindfulness, Big Five personality, and affect: A meta-analysis. *Personality and Individual Differences, 47,* 805–811.

Giluk, T. L. (2010). *Mindfulness-based stress reduction: Facilitating work outcomes through experienced affect and high-quality relationships.* Doctoral dissertation. Available at Iowa Research Online.

Goldin, P. R., & Gross, J. J. (2010). Effects of mindfulness-based stress reduction (MBSR) on emotion regulation in social anxiety disorder. *Emotion, 10,* 83–91.

Goleman, D. (1977). *The varieties of the meditative experience.* New York: Dutton.

Grant, J. A., Courtemanche, J., Duerden, E. G., Duncan, G. H., & Rainville, P. (2010). Cortical thickness and pain sensitivity in Zen meditators. *Emotion, 10,* 43–53.

Grant, J. A., & Rainville, P. (2009). Pain sensitivity and analgesic effects of mindful states in Zen meditators: A cross-sectional study. *Psychosomatic Medicine, 71,* 106–114.

Grepmair, L., Mitterlehner, F., Rother, W., & Nickel, M. (2006). Promotion of mindfulness in psychotherapists in training and treatment results of their patients. *Journal of Psychosomatic Research, 60,* 649–650.

Grossman, P. (2008). On measuring mindfulness in psychosomatic and psychological research. *Journal of Psychosomatic Research, 64,* 405–408.

Grossman, P., Niemann, L., Schmidt, S., & Walach, H. (2004). Mindfulness-based stress reduction and health benefits: A meta-analysis. *Journal of Psychosomatic Research, 57,* 35–43.

Hagen, S. (2003). *Buddhism is not what you think: Finding freedom beyond beliefs.* New York: HarperCollins Publishers.

Hammond, J. S., Keeney, R. L., & Raiffa, H. (2006). The hidden traps in decision making. *Harvard Business Review, 84,* 118–126.

Hargus, E., Crane, C., Barnhofer, T., & Williams, J. M. G. (2010). Effects of mindfulness on meta-awareness and specificity of describing prodromal symptoms in suicidal depression. *Emotion, 10,* 34–42.

Hariri, A. R., Bookheimer, S. Y., & Mazziotta, J. C. (2000). Modulating emotional responses: Effects of a neocortical network on the limbic system. *NeuroReport: For Rapid Communication of Neuroscience Research, 11,* 43–48.

Harter, J. K., Schmidt, F. L., & Hayes, T. L. (2002). Business-unit-level relationship between employee satisfaction, employee engagement, and business outcomes: A meta-analysis. *Journal of Applied Psychology, 87,* 268–279.

Heppner, W. L., & Kernis, M. H. (2007). "Quiet ego" functioning: The complementary roles of mindfulness, authenticity, and secure high self-esteem. *Psychological Inquiry, 18,* 248–251.

Heppner, W. L., Kernis, M. H., Lakey, C. E., Campbell, W. K., Goldman, B. M., Davis, P. J., & Cascio, E. V. (2008). Mindfulness as a means of reducing aggressive behavior: Dispositional and situational evidence. *Aggressive Behavior, 34,* 486–496.

Herndon, F. (2008). Testing mindfulness with perceptual and cognitive factors: External vs. internal encoding, and the cognitive failures questionnaire. *Personality and Individual Differences, 44,* 32–41.

Hofmann, S. G., Sawyer, A. T., Witt, A. A., & Oh, D. (2010). The effect of mindfulness-based therapy on anxiety and depression: A meta-analytic review. *Journal of Consulting and Clinical Psychology, 78,* 169–183.

Howell, A. J., Digdon, N. L., & Buro, K. (2010). Mindfulness predicts sleep-related self-regulation and well-being. *Personality and Individual Differences, 48,* 419–424.

Howell, A. J., Digdon, N. L., Buro, K., & Sheptycki, A. R. (2008). Relations among mindfulness, well-being, and sleep. *Personality and Individual Differences, 45,* 773–777.

Hughes, R., Tingle, B. A., & Sawin, D. B. (1981). Development of empathic understanding in children. *Child Development, 52,* 122–128.

Hutcherson, C. A., Seppala, E. M., & Gross, J. J. (2008). Loving-kindness meditation increases social connectedness. *Emotion, 8,* 720–724.

Ingram, R. E., & Smith, T. W. (1984). Depression and internal versus external focus of attention. *Cognitive Therapy and Research, 8,* 139–151.

Isen, A. M. (1987). Positive affect, cognitive processes, and social behavior. *Advances in Experimental Social Psychology, 20,* 203–253.

Jha, A. P., Stanley, E. A., Kiyonaga, A., Wong, L., & Gelfand, L. (2010). Examining the protective effects of mindfulness training on working memory capacity and affective experience. *Emotion, 10,* 54–64.

Jimenez, S. S., Niles, B. L., & Park, C. L. (2010). A mindfulness model of affect regulation and depressive symptoms: Positive emotions, mood regulation expectancies, and self-acceptance as regulatory mechanisms. *Personality and Individual Differences, 49,* 645–650.

Judge, T. A., Bono, J. E., Erez, A., & Locke, E. A. (2005). Core self-evaluations and job and life satisfaction: The role of self-concordance and goal attainment. *Journal of Applied Psychology, 90,* 257–268.

Kabat-Zinn, J. (1990). *Full catastrophe living: Using the wisdom of your body and mind to face stress, pain, and illness.* New York, NY: Delacorte Press.

Kabat-Zinn, J. (1994). *Wherever you go, there you are: Mindfulness meditation in everyday life.* New York, NY: Hyperion.

Kabat-Zinn, J. (2005). *Coming to our senses: Healing ourselves and the world through mindfulness.* New York, NY: Hyperion.

Kamdar, D., McAllister, D. J., & Turban, D. B. (2006). "All in a day's work": How follower individual differences and justice perceptions predict OCB role definitions and behavior. *Journal of Applied Psychology, 91,* 841–855.

Kellett, J. B., Humphrey, R. H., & Sleeth, R. G. (2002). Empathy and complex task performance: Two routes to leadership. *Leadership Quarterly, 13,* 523–544.

Kernis, M. H., Paradise, A. W., Whitaker, D. J., Wheatman, S. R., & Goldman, B. N. (2000). Master of one's psychological domain? Not likely if one's self-esteem is unstable. *Personality and Social Psychology Bulletin, 26,* 1297–1305.

Kidder, D. L. (2002). The influence of gender on the performance of organizational citizenship behaviors. *Journal of Management, 28,* 629–648.

Lakey, C. E., Campbell, W. K., Brown, K. W., & Goodie, A. S. (2007). Dispositional mindfulness as a predictor of the severity of gambling outcomes. *Personality and Individual Differences, 43,* 1698–1710.

Langer, E. J. (1989a). Minding matters: The consequences of mindlessness-mindfulness. *Advances in Experimental Social Psychology, 22,* 137–173.

Langer, E. J. (1989b). *Mindfulness.* Reading, MA: Addison-Wesley.

Lehrer, P. M., Woolfolk, R. L., & Sime, W. E. (Eds). (2007). *Principles and practice of stress management* (3rd ed.). New York: Guilford Press.

Ljótsson, B., Falk, L., Vesterlund, A. W., Hedman, E., Lindfors, P., Rück, C., Hursti, T., Andréewitch, S., Jansson, L., Lindefors, N., & Andersson, G. (2010). Internet-delivered exposure and mindfulness based therapy for irritable bowel syndrome – A randomized controlled trial. *Behaviour Research and Therapy, 48,* 531–539.

Losada, M. (1999). The complex dynamics of high performance teams. *Mathematical and Computer Modelling, 30,* 179–192.

Lutz, A., Slagter, H. A., Dunne, J. D., & Davidson, R. J. (2008). Attention regulation and monitoring in meditation. *Trends in Cognitive Sciences, 12,* 163–169.

Lyubomirsky, S., King, L., & Diener, E. (2005). The benefits of frequent positive affect: Does happiness lead to success? *Psychological Bulletin, 131,* 803–855.

Masicampo, E. J. & Baumeister, R. F. (2010). Unfulfilled goals interfere with tasks that require executive functions. *Journal of Experimental Social Psychology*, doi: 10.1016/j.jesp.2010.10.011.

Mindfulnet. (2011). Mindfulness in the workplace. Available at http://www.mindfulnet.org/page9.htm. Retrieved on February 23, 2011.

Miner, A. G., Glomb, T. M., & Hulin, C. (2005). Experience sampling mood and its correlates at work. *Journal of Occupational and Organizational Psychology*, 78, 171–193.

Mitchell, D. W. (2002). *Buddhism: Introducing the Buddhist experience*. New York: Oxford University Press.

National Institute for Occupational Safety and Health. (1999). *Stress at work*. DHHS [NIOSH] Publication no. 99-101. Cincinnati, OH: Publications Dissemination, EID

Nolen-Hoeksema, S. (1991). Responses to depression and their effects on the duration of depressive episodes. *Journal of Abnormal Psychology*, 100, 569–582.

Nolen-Hoeksema, S., & Davis, C. G. (1999). "Thanks for sharing that": Ruminators and their social support networks. *Journal of Personality and Social Psychology*, 77, 801–814.

Nolen-Hoeksema, S., & Morrow, J. (1991). A prospective study of depression and posttraumatic stress symptoms after a natural disaster: The 1989 Loma Prieta earthquake. *Journal of Personality and Social Psychology*, 61, 115–121.

Nyanaponika, T. (1998). In: B. Bodhi (Ed.), *Abhidhamma studies: Buddhist explorations of consciousness and time* (4th ed.). Boston, MA: Wisdom Publications.

Oei, N. Y. L., Everaerd, W. T. A. M., Elzinga, B. M., Van Well, S., & Bermond, B. (2006). Psychosocial stress impairs working memory at high loads: An association with cortisol levels and memory retrieval. *Stress: The International Journal on the Biology of Stress*, 9, 133–141.

O'Leary-Kelly, A. M., Bowes-Sperry, L., Bates, C. A., & Lean, E. R. (2009). Sexual harassment at work: A decade (plus) of progress. *Journal of Management*, 35, 503–536.

Patient, D. L., & Skarlicki, D. P. (2010). Increasing interpersonal and informational justice when communicating negative news: The role of the manager's empathic concern and moral development. *Journal of Management*, 36, 555–578.

Perlman, D. M., Salomons, T. V., Davidson, R. J., & Lutz, A. (2010). Differential effects on pain intensity and unpleasantness of two meditation practices. *Emotion*, 10, 65–71.

Radel, R., Sarrazin, P., Legrain, P., & Gobance, L. (2009). Subliminal priming of motivational orientation in educational settings: Effect on academic performance moderated by mindfulness. *Journal of Research in Personality*, 43, 695–698.

Ramel, W., Goldin, P. R., Carmona, P. E., & McQuaid, J. R. (2004). The effects of mindfulness meditation on cognitive processes and affect in patients with past depression. *Cognitive Therapy and Research*, 28, 433–455.

Roemer, L., & Orsillo, S. M. (2003). Mindfulness: A promising intervention strategy in need of further study. *Clinical Psychology: Science and Practice*, 10, 172–178.

Roozendaal, B. (2002). Stress and memory: Opposing effects of glucocorticoids on memory consolidation and memory retrieval. *Neurobiology of Learning and Memory*, 78, 578–595.

Roth, B., & Robbins, D. (2004). Mindfulness-based stress reduction and health-related quality of life: Findings from a bilingual inner-city patient population. *Psychosomatic Medicine*, 66, 113–123.

Ryan, R. M., & Deci, E. L. (2000). Self-determination theory and the facilitation of intrinsic motivation, social development, and well-being. *American Psychologist*, 55, 68–78.

Saavedra, M. C., Chapman, K. E., & Rogge, R. D. (2010). Clarifying links between attachment and relationship quality: Hostile conflict and mindfulness as moderators. *Journal of Family Psychology, 24*, 380–390.

Schmeichel, B. J., Volokhov, R. N., & Demaree, H. A. (2008). Working memory capacity and the self-regulation of emotional expression and experience. *Journal of Personality and Social Psychology, 95*, 1526–1540.

Schnall, P. L., Dobson, M., & Rosskam, E. (Eds). (2009). *Unhealthy work: Causes, consequences, cures.* Amityville, NY: Baywood Publishing.

Scott, B. A., Colquitt, J. A., Paddock, E. L., & Judge, T. A. (2010). A daily investigation of the role of manager empathy on employee well-being. *Organizational Behavior and Human Decision Processes, 113*, 127–140.

Sears, S., & Kraus, S. (2009). I think therefore I am: Cognitive distortions and coping style as mediators for the effects of mindfulness meditation on anxiety, positive and negative affect, and hope. *Journal of Clinical Psychology, 65*, 561–573.

Segal, Z. V., Williams, M. G., & Teasdale, J. D. (2002). *Mindfulness-based cognitive therapy for depression: A new approach to preventing relapse.* New York, NY: Guilford Press.

Shambhala Sun Foundation. (2010a). Finding the space to lead. Available at http://mindful.org/at-work/leadership/finding-the-space-to-lead. Retrieved on December 31, 2010.

Shambhala Sun Foundation. (2010b). Google searches. Available at http://mindful.org/at-work/in-the-workplace/google-searches. Retrieved on December 31, 2010.

Shapiro, S. L., Carlson, L. E., Astin, J. A., & Freedman, B. (2006). Mechanisms of mindfulness. *Journal of Clinical Psychology, 62*, 373–386.

Shapiro, S. L., Schwartz, G. E., & Bonner, G. (1998). Effects of mindfulness-based stress reduction on medical and premedical students. *Journal of Behavioral Medicine, 21*, 581–599.

Shaw, J. D., Duffy, M. K., Mitra, A., Lockhart, D. E., & Bowler, M. (2003). Reactions to merit pay increases: A longitudinal test of a signal sensitivity perspective. *Journal of Applied Psychology, 88*, 538–544.

Sheldon, K. M., & Elliot, A. J. (1999). Goal striving, need satisfaction, and longitudinal well-being: The self-concordance model. *Journal of Personality and Social Psychology, 76*, 482–497.

Sheldon, K. M., Turban, D. B., Brown, K. G., Barrick, M. R., & Judge, T. A. (2003). Applying self-determination theory to organizational research. *Research in Personnel and Human Resources Management, 22*, 357–393.

Siegel, D. J. (2007). *The mindful brain: Reflection and attunement in the cultivation of well-being.* New York: Norton.

Siegel, D. J. (2010). *Mindsight: The new science of personal transformation.* New York: Bantam.

Siegel, R. D., Germer, C. K., & Olendzki, A. (2009). Mindfulness: What is it? Where did it come from? In: F. Didonna (Ed.), *Clinical handbook of mindfulness* (pp. 17–35). New York: Springer.

Sy, T., Côté, S., & Saavedra, R. (2005). The contagious leader: Impact of the leader's mood on the mood of group members, group affective tone, and group processes. *Journal of Applied Psychology, 90*, 295–305.

Teasdale, J. D., Moore, R. G., Hayhurst, H., Pope, M., Williams, S., & Segal, Z. V. (2002). Metacognitive awareness and prevention of relapse in depression: Empirical evidence. *Journal of Consulting and Clinical Psychology, 70*, 275–287.

Teasdale, J. D., Segal, Z., & Williams, J. M. G. (1995). How does cognitive therapy prevent depressive relapse and why should attentional control (mindfulness) training help? *Behaviour Research and Therapy, 33,* 25–39.

Tepper, B. J., Duffy, M. K., Henle, C. A., & Lambert, L. S. (2006). Procedural injustice, victim precipitation, and abusive supervision. *Personnel Psychology, 59,* 101–123.

Thau, S., Aquino, K., & Poortvliet, P. M. (2007). Self-defeating behaviors in organizations: The relationship between thwarted belonging and interpersonal work behaviors. *Journal of Applied Psychology, 92,* 840–847.

Tice, D. M., Baumeister, R. F., & Zhang, L. (2004). The role of emotion in self-regulation: Differing roles of positive and negative emotion. In: P. Philippot & R. S. Feldman (Eds), *The regulation of emotion* (pp. 213–226). Mahwah, NJ: Lawrence Erlbaum.

Tipsord, J. (2009). *The effects of mindfulness training and individual difference in mindfulness on social perception and empathy.* Unpublished doctoral dissertation, University of Oregon, Portland, OR.

Tomarken, A. J., Davidson, R. J., & Henriques, J. B. (1990). Resting frontal brain asymmetry predicts affective responses to films. *Journal of Personality and Social Psychology, 59,* 791–801.

Treadway, M. T., & Lazar, S. W. (2009). The neurobiology of mindfulness. In: F. Didonna (Ed.), *Clinical handbook of mindfulness* (pp. 45–57). New York: Springer.

Urry, H. L., Nitschke, J. B., Dolski, I., Jackson, D. C., Dalton, K. M., Mueller, C. J., Rosenkranz, M. A., Ryff, C. D., Singer, B. H., & Davidson, R. J. (2004). Making a life worth living: Neural correlates of well-being. *Psychological Science, 15,* 367–372.

Verplanken, B., Friborg, O., Wang, C. E., Trafimow, D., & Woolf, K. (2007). Mental habits: Metacognitive reflection on negative self-thinking. *Journal of Personality and Social Psychology, 92,* 526–541.

Walsh, J. J., Balint, M. G., Smolira SJ, D. R., Fredericksen, L. K., & Madsen, S. (2009). Predicting individual differences in mindfulness: The role of trait anxiety, attachment anxiety and attentional control. *Personality and Individual Differences, 46,* 94–99.

Way, B. M., Creswell, J. D., Eisenberger, N. I., & Lieberman, M. D. (2010). Dispositional mindfulness and depressive symptomatology: Correlations with limbic and self-referential neural activity during rest. *Emotion, 10,* 12–24.

Weick, K. E., & Putnam, T. (2006). Organizing for mindfulness: Eastern wisdom and Western knowledge. *Journal of Management Inquiry, 15,* 275–287.

Weick, K. E., & Sutcliffe, K. M. (2006). Mindfulness and the quality of organizational attention. *Organization Science, 17,* 514–524.

Weick, K. E., & Sutcliffe, K. M. (2007). *Managing the unexpected: Resilient performance in an age of uncertainty* (2nd ed.). San Francisco, CA: Jossey-Bass.

Weick, K. E., Sutcliffe, K. M., & Obstfeld, D. (1999). Organizing for high reliability: Processes of collective mindfulness. *Research in Organizational Behavior, 21,* 81–123.

Weinstein, N., Brown, K. W., & Ryan, R. M. (2009). A multi-method examination of the effects of mindfulness on stress attribution, coping, and emotional well-being. *Journal of Research in Personality, 43,* 374–385.

Wenk-Sormaz, H. (2005). Meditation can reduce habitual responding. *Alternative Therapies in Health and Medicine, 11,* 42–58.

Williams, J. M. G. (2010). Mindfulness and psychological process. *Emotion, 10,* 1–7.

Wilson, T. D., & Gilbert, D. T. (2003). Affective forecasting. *Advances in Experimental Social Psychology, 35,* 345–411.

# SOCIOEMOTIONAL WEALTH AND HUMAN RESOURCE MANAGEMENT (HRM) IN FAMILY-CONTROLLED FIRMS

Cristina Cruz, Shainaz Firfiray and
Luis R. Gomez-Mejia

## ABSTRACT

*This chapter takes a socioemotional wealth (SEW) perspective to explain the adoption of human resource (HR) practices in family-controlled firms. Previous studies on human resource management (HRM) in family firms have focused only on a small range of HR practices and have rarely utilized strong conceptual frameworks. As a result, these studies have overlooked important factors that contribute to the distinctiveness of HRM in these organizations. Based on ample evidence that shows family businesses' preference for non-economically motivated objectives collectively labeled as SEW, we propose that the presence of SEW influences HR practices in family firms.*

*Consequently, we reexamine existing empirical evidence of the determinants of HRM in family-controlled firms under the SEW approach. We also reinterpret existing theoretical models of family-controlled firms and their implications for HRM under the SEW umbrella. Our final goal is to establish an integrated framework through a set of sound propositions on*

Research in Personnel and Human Resources Management, Volume 30, 159–217
ISSN: 0742-7301/doi:10.1108/S0742-7301(2011)0000030006

*HRM in family businesses. By integrating the literature, we aim to fill theoretical gaps in our understanding of the determinants of HR practices in the family business context and direct future research in this area.*

## INTRODUCTION

Family-controlled firms represent at least 70 percent of all firms in the United States and close to 85 percent of firms around the world, employing a vast majority of people in both industrialized and nonindustrialized nations (Sirmon & Hitt, 2003). Research on these firms has grown rapidly over the past decade, reflecting the important role they play in national economies and world trade. The extant scholarship on family-owned firms has revealed the tremendous impact that family control has on managerial behavior and strategic choices (Anderson, Mansi, & Reeb, 2003; Mishra & McConaughy, 1999; Gomez-Mejia, Haynes, Nunez-Nickel, Jacobson, & Moyano-Fuentes, 2007; Gomez-Mejia, Makri, & Larraza, 2010b). However, there has been little systematic exploration of how family ownership influences human resource management (HRM) practices. This chapter intends to fill some of these gaps and suggests some propositions to guide future research.

We use the terms "family-controlled" and "family-owned" firms interchangeably, given that there is no consensus in the literature as to what the precise definition of a "family firm" is or should be. Often the family shares ownership with other parties (such as individual shareholders and institutional investors), particularly if the firm is publicly traded. Sometimes a family owner is an executive in the firm, but this is not always the case (especially in firms that have moved beyond the first generation). In some firms, the family has two or more family members in the Board of Directors, but in other firms the family prefers to have nonfamily members in the board to represent its interests and thus give the board more symbolic legitimacy. Also, the exact meaning of a family firm may be context dependent. While five percent family ownership may be appropriate to designate a firm as family controlled among the Fortune 500 firms, a family ownership of 20 percent or more may be more appropriate for smaller firms in most "non-Anglo-Saxon" countries around the world (La Porta, Lopez-de-Silanes, & Shleifer, 1999). While there is disagreement about the operational definition of a family firm, there is broad consensus that these are organizations in which a family plays a major role (either as owners actively involved in the firm's affairs and/or as managers).

Hence, for our purposes we define family firms as those where a family exercises a controlling interest, even if other stakeholders (such as banks and institutional investors) may be present.

A common thread across much of the family business literature is that the overlap between the institutions of family and business generates a distinct way of managing the firm (Astrachan & Kolenko, 1994; Covin, 1994a, 1994b). Managing human capital in family-owned firms is a complex task since family members simultaneously participate in both business and family relationships in their personal and professional lives. Moreover, the interaction of family owners, family managers, professional managers, and family employees is often fraught with conflict and unclear demarcations of authority and responsibilities. These features of family-owned firms create a unique context for managing human resources as compared to non-family-owned firms, with both positive and negative implications.

Despite this, as noted above, academic interest by HR scholars in the special milieu of family-owned firms has been rather limited. Most of the writings on HRM in family-owned firms have been descriptive and normative without much attention devoted to theory building or rigorous empirical analysis. On the other hand, over the past decade, some researchers have enriched the literature on family-owned firms by challenging widely held assumptions about family firms' governance, owner's preferences, and their unique sources of value creation. However, these rigorous efforts toward understanding family dynamics have been mainly focused on governance, succession, and strategic decision-making issues. The way these dynamics affect HRM is not yet well understood.

The aim of this chapter is to provide an integrated framework for the study of the determinants of HR practices in family-owned firms by capitalizing on "what we already know" about the sources and consequences of the uniqueness of family-owned firms. In particular, we build on the notion that families have a leaning toward or preferences for non-economically motivated objectives, which Gomez-Mejia et al. (2007) collectively labeled as "socioemotional wealth" (SEW) or "affective endowments." Extant evidence shows that the presence of SEW has idiosyncratic effects on family-owned firms' behavior, including aspects that influence HR practices (Sirmon & Hitt, 2003; Gomez-Mejia, Nunez-Nickel, & Gutierrez, 2001). Based on this evidence, we propose that the presence of SEW in family-controlled firms has a considerable impact on the way in which family and nonfamily employees are selected, trained, compensated, evaluated, and retained. Consequently, we aim to revisit existing theoretical and empirical studies that deal with the management of human resources in family-owned firms under the lens of the SEW approach. By integrating the literature, we hope to bring some coherence into the growing but varied and occasionally contradictory scholarship on HRM in family-owned businesses, thereby setting the stage for generating more creative, cumulative, and insightful findings into this area.

This chapter is divided into five parts. The first part revisits the concept of HRM and its key dimensions and the main theoretical frameworks that attempt to explain each dimension. The second part summarizes the main findings from empirical studies that investigate HRM in family-owned firms. The third part reviews the theoretical implications for HRM that stem from the various theoretical frameworks that have been applied to the family business field. Finally, in the fourth and fifth sections, we propose to use the SEW approach as an umbrella to create an integrated framework for explaining the uniqueness of HRM in family-owned firms and identify a set of propositions to guide future empirical and theoretical research in this field.

# DIMENSIONS OF HUMAN RESOURCE MANAGEMENT (HRM)

The field of HRM has emerged from the conceptual, empirical, and practical intersection of several disciplines including psychology, sociology, economics, and management/organization sciences (Ferris, Hall, Royle, & Martocchio, 2004). It largely started out as a "problem-driven" academic area of study with scholars attempting to solve practical HRM issues, such as absenteeism and turnover.

HRM is defined as the process of attracting, developing, and maintaining a workforce that supports and helps advance the mission, the objectives, and the strategies of the organization (Gomez-Mejia, Balkin, & Cardy, 2012). An organization's HRM can be viewed either as a collection of multiple, discrete practices with no explicit or discernible link between them or as a more strategic approach that views HRM as an integrated and coherent bundle of mutually reinforcing practices. Considering that HR practices are rarely, if ever, used in isolation, failure to consider all of the HR practices in unison neglects potentially important "gestalt" effects because it is the combination of practices in a bundle, rather than individual practices, that shapes the pattern of interactions between and among managers and employees (Wu & Chaturvedi, 2009; Toh, Morgeson, & Campion, 2008; Cutcher-Gershenfeld, 1991; Lepak, Liao, Chung, & Harden, 2006).

A commonly used framework classifies HR practices into a threefold taxonomy: (a) employee skills (practices aimed at recruitment, training, and employee development), (b) employee performance and reward systems (practices that elicit high levels of effort), and (c) employee involvement and communication (practices that enable employee communication, voice, and influence) (Wright & Boswell, 2002). This classification follows the underlying logic of the HRM literature that HR practices are likely to contribute to improved economic performance only when employees possess the requisite knowledge and skills, when employees are motivated to apply this skill and knowledge through discretionary effort, and when employees contribute to such discretionary effort (Nishii, Lepak, & Schneider, 2008; Levine & Tyson, 1990; Bailey, 1992; MacDuffie, 1995).

Some theorists have called for empirical research on the utility of this three-dimensional categorization (Wright & Boswell, 2002; Boselie, Dietz, & Boone, 2005). In response to these calls, Subramony's (2009) study provided evidence for the efficacy of this classification and contributed to the literature by providing empirical evidence for both synergistic effects (significantly stronger effect sizes for bundles than their constituent individual practices) and positive relationships between the three proposed HRM bundles and business outcomes. Consequently, we will follow this classification to examine HRM in family-owned firms. Each of these dimensions is briefly described in the subsequent pages.

### *Employee Skills: Practices Aimed at Recruitment, Selection, Training, and Employee Development*

Skill-enhancing practices are primarily related to **recruitment, selection, training and development** and focus on increasing the collective knowledge, ability, and skill levels (collective human capital) of the workforce (Kuvaas, 2007; Ostroff & Bowen, 2000).

Regarding practices aimed at **recruiting and selecting employees**, existent research suggests that organizations must decide on four types of questions: (a) What methods should firms use to recruit and select new employees? (b) What employee and job characteristics should a firm examine when deciding whom to hire, and how should these characteristics be assessed? (c) Should managers consider how a potential employee fits with the organizational culture in addition to that employee's fit with the job? (d) Who should take the decision to select new employees? (Gomez-Mejia et al., 2012).

As an answer to the first question, evidence shows that companies may use formal or informal methods to recruit and select employees. Informal methods used by job seekers may take several forms. The most common of these involves obtaining information on job vacancies from family members, relatives, or friends. Generally, informal methods of job search are conceptually distinct in that the interpersonal channels conveying information were not established specifically for the purpose of job matching. On the other hand, formal recruitment procedures would typically involve employers publicizing available job openings, assembling limited information about a pool of eligible applicants through job applications, gathering more detailed information about job applicants through face-to-face interviews, targeting suitable candidates for job offers (Ma & Allen, 2009; Marsden & Gorman, 2001), and finally selecting the most able candidates.

The second and third questions regarding the characteristics that should be considered when recruiting and selecting an employee focus the debate on whether a firm values employee fit with the job or employee fit with the organization. These two types of fit are labeled as person–job fit (P–J) and person–organization (P–O) fit. P–J fit refers to the compatibility between the characteristics of a person and those of a specific job (e.g., Edwards, 1991; O'Reilly, Chatman, & Caldwell, 1991). The P–J fit perspective includes the traditional view of selection, which emphasizes the matching of employee knowledge, skills, and abilities (KSAs) and other qualities to job demands (Ployhart, Schneider, & Schmitt, 2006). On the other hand, P–O fit is defined as "the compatibility between people and organizations that occurs when (a) at least one entity provides what the other needs, (b) they share similar fundamental characteristics, or (c) both" (Kristof, 1996, p. 4). The notion of P–O fit is rooted in the assumption that individuals will be most successful in organizations that share their personalities.

Finally, with regard to who should make the final decision about the selection process, evidence suggests that in many organizations the HR department routinely makes staffing decisions, particularly for entry-level jobs. However, in some cases, firms also involve other stakeholders in the process such as line managers, top managers, and/or board members. Less frequently, decision-making in staffing practices is highly centralized, with the founder or at most a small group of people making selection decisions.

The employee skills dimension also acknowledges that, in order to continually hone the skills of its workforce and compete effectively, organizations need to make adequate investments in **training and development**

**activities for their employees**. While training activities are focused on enabling employees to learn specific skills and correct performance deficits, development activities enable employees to acquire a broad range of skills through planned activities and experience and place an emphasis on the long-term growth of an individual (Gomez-Mejia et al., 2012). Frequently, development activities take the form of mentoring, which is a long-term relationship commitment between a senior person (mentor) and a junior person (mentee) in which a junior person is given personal and professional development support by the senior person (Haggard, Dougherty, Turban, & Wilbanks, in press; Ratwani, Zaccaro, Garven, & Geller, 2010; McCauley & Douglas, 2004).

Once employees develop a sense of competence and self-efficacy in the workplace, the next step is to keep them motivated so that they help the organization in attaining desired objectives. This leads us to the next conceptual dimension that is mainly concerned with factors that influence employees to perform in a desired manner.

## Employee Performance and Reward Systems

Employee performance and reward systems help galvanize employee efforts toward the accomplishment of organizational goals and provide them with the incentives necessary to engage in high levels of performance ( Jones, Kalmi, & Kauhanen, 2010; Takeuchi, Chen, & Lepak, 2009). Practices such as performance appraisals that assess individual and group performance and link these appraisals tightly with incentive systems, internal promotion systems that focus on employee merit, and other forms of incentives intended to align the interests of employees with those of the shareholders usually form an organization's motivation-enhancing efforts (Subramony, 2009; Huselid, 1995).

From a theoretical point of view, scholars in the area of employee performance and reward systems have extensively studied the issue of incentive alignment through the lens of agency theory (Jensen & Meckling, 1976; Fama & Jensen, 1983). This stream of research has been most concerned with describing the governance mechanisms that solve the agency problem, which is reflected in the divergent interests between principals (owners) and agents (managers). The key idea within much of the agency literature is that losses to principals resulting from interest divergence may be curbed either by imposing control structures upon the agent or through well-planned compensation systems.

Although agency theory is the dominant paradigm underlying most governance research, its key limitation lies in its assumption about individualistic utility motivations resulting in principal–agent divergence, which may not hold true for all managers. The stewardship perspective emerged as a response to this key inadequacy of agency theory to account for human behaviors that may not be explained through a "self-serving" view of people. The stewardship perspective posits that executives as stewards of the firm will act in the best interests of their principals (Donaldson & Davis, 1991). Consequently, their motivation is more intrinsic, directed toward obtaining satisfaction by effectively performing exigent work, and thereby gaining recognition from peers and superiors (Donaldson & Davis, 1991).

These two antagonistic views of managerial behavior will be reflected in the final design of an employee's compensation package. Indeed, organizations face several choices in the design of employee compensation such as the following: paying market versus below-market rates; paying the same amount on a predictable basis (e.g., monthly paycheck) or providing a substantial portion of an employee's income on a variable basis; providing long- or short-term pay; providing monetary rewards involving tangible cash or benefit payment to employees such as merit pay adjustments, annual bonuses, employee stock ownership plans, or nonmonetary rewards of an intangible nature involving employment security, recognition, increased responsibility, and gift exchanges; using equity versus non-equity-based incentives; using higher versus lower performance contingent pay systems; and so on (Gomez-Mejia, Berrone, & Franco-Santos, 2010a).

### Employee Involvement and Communication

This dimension refers to the broad pattern of employee management practices, including **employee involvement and systems of direct communication** that target the individual worker (Heery & Noon, 2001; Kim, MacDuffie, & Pil, 2010). Employee involvement refers to interventions that seek to increase members' input into decisions that affect organizational performance and employee well-being. Within the workplace, these interventions can take the form of programs designed to increase employee knowledge, power, information, and rewards (Cummings & Worley, 2009). Communication involves the process of information exchange among two or more parties and can take many forms in a work setting, such as written or spoken orders, informal chatter, electronic messages, printed reports or procedure manuals, announcements posted on bulletin boards, or Web-based communication. The effective flow of communication is crucial to an organization's ability to operate smoothly and productively (Riggio, 2007). Collectively, employee involvement and communication systems are concerned with maintaining employee–employer relationships that contribute to satisfaction, productivity, motivation, and morale.

Research within this area has predominantly been done using the social exchange framework. Extant literature clearly distinguishes social exchange relationships from those based on purely economic exchanges, in that the former are based on a series of mutual obligations, which are often unspecified and in which the standards for measuring contributions are often unclear (Blau, 1964). A clear implication of the social exchange theory for HRM is that employees have beliefs and expectations about a series of reciprocal obligations in the employee–organization relationship that are referred to as psychological contracts (Rousseau, 1989). The social exchange theory and the concept of psychological contracts provide vital insights into the mechanisms that affect employees' fairness perceptions of their contractual arrangements with the organization, which may ultimately impact their attitudes and behavior toward the organization (Rosen, Harris, & Kacmar, in press; Masterson, Lewis, Goldman, & Taylor, 2000).

Consistent with the social exchange perspective, extant research suggests that employee participation and communication initiatives can affect employees' beliefs pertaining to the organization's commitment to the welfare of its workforce (Eisenberger, Huntington, Hutchison, & Sowa, 1986), which leads them to reciprocate by developing positive emotional bonds with the organization (Pazy & Ganzach, 2009; Shore & Tetrick, 1991; Shore & Wayne, 1993) and exert discretionary effort on behalf of the firm (Eisenberger, Armeli, Rexwinkel, Lynch, & Rhoades, 2001; Piercy, Cravens, Lane, & Vorhies, 2006). Nevertheless, studies that investigate the impact of employee participation on job attitudes have found inconsistent results. While some scholars have found improvements in job satisfaction or performance (Liao, Toya, Lepak, & Hong, 2009; Mohr & Zoghi, 2008; Cawley, Keeping, & Levy, 1998; Steel, Dilla, Lloyd, Mento, & Ovalle, 1985), others have suggested that the efficacy of participation provides only mixed support for evidence of improvement in employee satisfaction or performance (Frenkel & Lee, 2010; Schweiger & Leana, 1986; Yukl, 1989).

In response to these inconsistencies, several scholars have investigated the role of justice mechanisms on the relationship between employee participation programs and employee outcomes. Justice within the context of organizations comes in three forms: distributive, procedural, and interactional. Distributive justice refers to an employee's perception of the fairness of his or her own outcomes, such as pay (Adams, 1965). Procedural justice is defined as an employee's evaluation of the perceived fairness of rules and processes used by the organization to distribute outcomes to all employees within the organization (Thibaut & Walker, 1975). Interactional justice refers to an employee's evaluation of the perceived fairness of interpersonal treatment from his or her own superiors (Bies & Moag, 1986), and includes an organization's leaders treating employees with respect, dignity, sensitivity, and sincerity. Of these three forms, procedural justice, because of its emphasis on process control, and voice (Thibaut & Walker, 1975) is the most relevant to the study of employee involvement.

Extant research has confirmed the influence of justice on the relationship between employee participation and employee outcomes. For instance, Roberson, Moye, and Locke (1999) showed that procedural justice fully mediated the relationship between participation and task satisfaction, suggesting that "reactions to procedures are a significant factor in determining employee satisfaction" (p. 591). In a similar vein, a study by Earley and Lind (1987) has shown that allowing workers control in the way tasks are assigned enhances procedural justice judgments and, ultimately, performance. In addition, Douhitt and Aiello (2001) showed that participation (input or no input regarding work tasks and reward structure to be used) positively affects employees' procedural justice judgments and performance.

# HR PRACTICES IN FAMILY-CONTROLLED FIRMS: WHAT WE KNOW FROM EMPIRICAL EVIDENCE

Having presented the typology and reviewed some of the most important developments in the HRM literature for each of the identified dimensions, we now turn our attention to what all this means in the specific context of family-owned firms. As mentioned above, despite the importance given to the management of human resources for the success of family business, research dealing directly with HR practices in family-owned firms is scarce and fragmented. Moreover, in most cases, the empirical evidence provided by these studies is inconclusive with different studies providing inconsistent results. Multiple factors contribute to the contradictory nature of these results. First, as noted earlier, there is a lack of consistency in defining family businesses. Operational definitions vary considerably (Anderson & Reeb, 2003; Bartholomeusz & Tanewski, 2006; Cucculelli & Micucci, 2008), leading to major differences in classifying and identifying family-owned firms (Astrachan, Allen, Spinelli, Wittmeyer, & Glucksman, 2003). Second, researchers have faced difficulties in pinpointing the source of distinctiveness of family businesses (Hoy, 2003; Wortman, 1994). These problems are compounded by the fact that most family-owned firms are not publicly traded, so data on these firms is difficult to obtain. Third, most HRM scholars are trained in issues that confront large, complex organizations with formalized HR programs, and this background is of limited use in the case of most family-owned firms. Lastly, most mainstream management journals are likely to view HR practices in family-owned firms as too phenomenological to be of theoretical value to a broader academic audience. In fact until the early 2000s, one could not find a single paper on family-owned firms in "top tier" management journals (such as *Academy of Management Journal, Academy of Management Review*, and *Administrative Science Quarterly*), much less on HR practices in family-owned firms.

Given the above caveats, two sets of empirical studies can be found in the literature: the first set compares HR practices of family versus nonfamily companies; the second set examines differences in HR practices among family-owned firms. To be consistent with our proposed taxonomy, we will examine this evidence grouped in accordance with the three dimensions of employee skills, employee performance and reward systems, and employee involvement and communication.

*Empirical Evidence on HR Practices: Family- versus Non-family-owned Firms*

This first set of studies is based on the maxim that organizational characteristics or contingencies shape a firm's HR practices. Given that an overwhelming majority of family-owned firms tend to be smaller and less complex than non-family-owned firms, an important bulk of evidence pertaining to HRM dimensions in family-owned firms has been derived from studies focusing on the distinctiveness of HRM in small to medium-sized enterprises (SMEs). Evidence suggests that smaller firms make less use of professional HR practices in comparison to larger firms (Barron, Black, & Loewenstein, 1987; Hornsby & Kuratko, 1990). For example, prior research has shown that smaller firms make less use of formalized recruitment practices (Aldrich & Langton, 1998), provide less training to their employees (Koch & McGrath, 1996; Westhead & Storey, 1997, 1999), and are less likely to use formalized performance appraisals (Jackson, Schuler, & Rivero, 1989).

However, differences in HR practices used by family- and non-family-owned firms cannot be exclusively attributed to variations in firm size and its associated differences in organizational complexity or resource availability. Existent studies also demonstrate that there is a unique effect derived from the presence of a family group within the organization (De Kok, Uhlaner, & Thurik, 2006). For instance, it has been shown that while both family- and non-family-owned firms adopt more formalized HR practices as they experience growth (e.g., Leon-Guerrero, McCann, & Haley, 1998; Reid, Morrow, Kelly, Adams, & McCartan, 2000), family-owned firms, in general, employ less complex HR practices than non-family-owned firms. For instance Reid and Adams (2001), using a sample of 300 Irish SMEs ranging in size from 20 to 100 employees, found that family SMEs are less likely to have professional HR practices, including the use of references, appraisal systems, a peer appraisal process, training assessment, or merit-based pay. A similar finding is corroborated by De Kok et al. (2006) using a sample of 700 Dutch SMEs.

Other studies that compare HR practices between family- and non-family-owned firms have focused on the study of a single HRM practice. With some exceptions (i.e., Miller, Le Breton-Miller, & Scholnick, 2008), most of these studies also confirm the use of less complex and informal nature of HRM in family-owned firms.

With regard to practices aimed at **attracting and developing employee skills,** existent research indicates that family-owned firms tend to avoid clear criteria for selecting and recruiting employees to management positions, and consequently, jobs are filled by friends and relatives, frequently based upon personal referrals (Gersick, Davis, Hampton, & Lansberg, 1997). For instance, in the case of new ventures, Aldrich and Langton (1998) found that 25 percent of the firms in their sample employed family members at the time of start-up. The importance of family members as a source of employment has also been emphasized in the case of micro- and small firms (Cruz, Justo, & De Castro, 2011; Wheelock & Baines, 1998; Scase & Goffee, 1987; Adkins, 1995) and in the context of hostile environments (Dyer & Mortensen, 2006). Although this evidence highlights the importance of family employment, it also shows that the prevalence of nonfamily executives in management teams increases relative to the size of the family business. For instance, Klein (2000) used a random sample ($n = 1,158$) of all German companies with a turnover of more than 1 million euros and found high involvement of nonfamily executives: 44 percent of all management boards in the sample were completely controlled by family members, 42 percent had a mixed management team, and 14 percent had a pure nonfamily management (Klein, 2000, p. 170). Similarly, Cruz, Gomez-Mejia, & Becerra (2010), using a sample of 122 Spanish firms with more than 50 employees, found that in 29 percent of the cases, the Top Management Team (TMT) (excluding the CEO) were just made of nonfamily members and that in 11 percent of the cases, both the CEO and the TMT were not related to the owning family. Anderson and Reeb (2003) also showed that 55 percent of the 141 large, quoted family businesses in the S&P 500 had a nonfamily CEO. Similar results were reported by Gomez-Mejia, Larraza, and Makri (2003) in a study using a sample of publicly listed US family owned US firms.

Researchers have also examined whether family-owned firms conduct more **training** than non-family-owned firms as well as the type of training they provide to their employees (formal versus informal). As mentioned above, although most studies agree that family businesses engage less in training activities, Miller, Le Breton-Miller, and Scholnick (2008) found an opposite result using a sample of 676 Canadian small-family and nonfamily businesses. With regard to the type of training provided, Kotey and Folker (2007) examined the main and interaction effects of size and firm type (family versus nonfamily) on a variety of informal and formal training programs in SMEs. Their results point to the prevalence of informal training for all firm sizes and an increase in adoption of formal, structured, and development-oriented training with increasing firm size. However, this pattern was evident for non-family-owned firms but not for family-owned ones. For family-owned firms, formal training programs increased significantly only during the critical growth phase (20–49 employees).

The importance of **mentoring relationships** has also been highlighted in the family business literature. For instance, Fiegener, Brown, Prince, and File (1996) confirmed that CEOs of family-owned firms are able to transmit the strategic vision and mission of the business through close incumbent/ successor relationships, which are supplemented with a long period of mentoring. In contrast, CEOs in non-family-owned firms have less opportunity to build close incumbent–successor relationships of the same depth. The close relationship between the successor and the incumbent in family-owned firms is often a source of advantage over non-family-owned firms, as successors' training develops through a lifetime of learning experiences inside the business, which will not occur in nonfamily organizations. The same study also analyzes promotion decisions. Results confirm the existence of difference in the use of these practices between family and nonfamily firms, with the latter emphasizing outside work experience and university training in promotion decisions to a higher extent than the former.

The family dimension has also been shown to influence the design of HR practices **related to employee performance and reward systems.** For instance,

Carrasco-Hernandez and Sanchez-Marin (2007), using a sample of 836 Spanish firms, showed that *pay level* is lower in family-owned and -managed firms than in both non-family-managed and professionally managed family-owned firms. Regarding the use of incentive pay, it is reported that few family business owners allow nonfamily members to possess shares in the family business (Hennerkes, 1998). Anderson and Reeb (2003) found that pay premiums or financial returns in nonfamily businesses exceed those of family businesses by about 10 percent, and according to Werner and Tosi (1995), such premiums can reach 15.4–29.5 percent.

Lastly, empirical evidence on the differences between family- and non-family-owned firms in terms of **employee involvement and communication systems** is almost nonexistent. The literature suggests that family-owned firms are prone to relationship conflicts (Zellweger & Astrachan, 2008), which may have severe implications for family and firm functioning. Indeed, it has been suggested that relationship conflicts in family-owned firms may not only rip apart controlling families but also threaten the survival of the family business (Davis & Harveston, 2001) by creating incentives to sell out ownership stakes (Beckhard & Dyer, 1983; Levinson, 1971). Moreover, prior research has shown that relationship conflicts negatively influence family-owned firms' performance (Eddleston & Kellermanns, 2007). With regard to employee participation, a study by Howorth, Westhead, and Wright (2004) reveals that access to key information is more difficult in family businesses than in nonfamily ones, especially for those employees who do not belong to the family. Prior research has also shown that family-owned firms take a different approach with respect to employee involvement and other forms of participation strategies that are meant to elicit worker effort. In a study by Harris and Reid (2008), it was found that family-owned firms were four times less likely to use joint consultation committees and were more than four times more likely to have no direct communication or consultation with their employees. These findings suggest that employee involvement may be seen as a threat to the culture of the family business as it has the potential to challenge the way a business is run by family members.

### Empirical Evidence on HR Practices: Differences Within Family-Controlled Firms

Another set of studies have examined differences in HR practices within family businesses. The vast majority of this research has looked at differences between family and nonfamily employees. In this respect, extant evidence confirms that the presence or absence of family ties is an important determinant in the development of HRM policies and practices in a family business. For instance, an in-depth analysis of the MassMutual data by Astrachan and Kolenko (1994) found significant differences in HR practices for family versus nonfamily employees. In particular, they found that employee reviews, compensation plans, appraisal, and personal development plans were used significantly more frequently in family-owned firms for nonfamily employees than for family members. In a similar vein, Aldrich and Langton (1998) found a negative relationship between the number of family members who work in a firm and the use of formal HR practices.

Empirical evidence also found some differences within family-owned firms when examining individual practices. Following our proposed taxonomy, we first found some evidence pertaining to differences in practices aimed at **attracting and developing employee skills.** In this regard, Matlay (2002) studied how training needs and related issues were perceived in the context of family-owned small businesses. His results, based on 120 case studies conducted in the UK, showed that these needs were perceived in two distinct ways: the requirements of family members were addressed mostly in terms of individual career development, while the needs of nonfamily employees were viewed strictly as firm-specific HRM issues. Evidence also suggests that training needs differ across family and nonfamily employees because junior generation members of family-owned firms, as compared to their peers who come from nonfamily business settings, were found to have lesser clarity about their abilities, talents, goals, and career interests (Eckrich & Loughead, 1996).

The family business literature has also examined the influence of the presence or absence of family ties in the design of practices related to **employee performance and reward system**s. A primary conclusion of these studies is that, regardless of the motive, the use of incentive compensation for family executives in family-owned firms is quite common (Chrisman & Chang, 2007; Schulze, Lubatkin, Dino, & Buchholtz, 2001; Cruz et al., 2010). However, there exist important differences in the use of incentives for family and nonfamily employees. Gomez-Mejia et al. (2001) using a sample comprising 276 newspapers published in Spain show that the overwhelming factor that determines the sensitivity of executive tenure to performance and business risk is family status. The links between performance, business risk, and executive tenure were stronger when agents had no family ties to principals. Similarly, in a related empirical study with 253 family-controlled US firms, Gomez-Mejia et al. (2003) demonstrated that although executives with family ties to owners receive lower total pay than professional managers, this pay disadvantage was lowered as business risk increased. The importance of family ties in determining the nature of the contract is also highlighted by Cruz et al. (2010). Using Spanish data gathered from interviews with 122 CEOs from family-owned firms, the authors found that the level of CEO's trustworthiness on TMT members influenced contract design, and in turn, this trustworthiness was determined by the presence of family ties between the CEO and the TMT. Moreover, they also found that while the proportion of variable pay differed only modestly as a function of family status, it was strongly related to firm performance for nonfamily executives. Consequently, the authors conclude that family altruism manifests not in higher pay but rather in a greater risk protection. Evidence on longer tenures and removal of compensation risk leads many authors to conclude that family managers are entrenched in their companies (Gomez-Mejia et al., 2001). The findings of Cruz et al. (2010) in Spanish firms also suggest that perceptions of justice may play a role in the design of executive compensation contracts in family-owned firms; the family may want to make it look as if family and nonfamily executives are treated equally when in fact this may not be the case (for instance, while pay mix may be the same for both groups, variable pay may be more sensitive to firm performance among the nonfamily executives). Similar results were found by Gomez-Mejia et al. (2003) among large publicly traded American firms.

Some evidence also suggests that the presence of family ties influences HR practices that deal with **employee involvement and communication** within the organization. For instance, Kets de Vries (1993) held in-depth interviews with family owners of more than 300 firms and found that delegating responsibility to outsiders tends to be discouraged. Similar arguments can be found in Kepner (1983), Gersick et al. (1997), Schulze, Lubatkin, and Dino (2003), Gomez-Mejia et al. (2007), and Jones, Makri, and Gomez-Mejia, (2008), among others.

Evidence also exists with regard to the influence of family ties in employee's perceptions of justice within the organization. Poza, Alfred, and Maheshwari (1997) studied 26 family businesses as part of the Discovery Research program at Case Western. They found that nonfamily managers were significantly less satisfied with the management's ability to handle growth and the extent to which the necessary processes were in place to facilitate growth. Further, nonfamily managers were significantly less satisfied with the fairness of the compensation system and more satisfied with feedback from performance appraisals.

Lastly, the literature also suggests that other organizational character-istics apart from family ties may explain the differences in the adoption of

HR practices within family-owned firms. In this regard, firm size is frequently pointed out as an important contingency. In particular, studies demonstrate that small family businesses are less experienced in recruiting nonfamily executives than larger family businesses (Bhattacharya & Ravikumar, 2004). Similarly, they also show that the larger and more complex the family business is, the more the number of executives with a higher level of professionalism and external knowledge are required (Klein, 2000). Moreover, variables such as family ownership and the presence of institutional investors have also been shown to influence executive compensation policies in family-owned firms (Gomez-Mejia et al., 2003). Research also confirms a negative relationship between family-owned firm governance and the use of professional HR practices (Fiegener et al., 1996; Reid & Adams, 2001; Cyr, Johnson, & Welbourne, 2000).

## HRM IN FAMILY-CONTROLLED FIRMS: WHAT WE CAN LEARN FROM RELATED TOPICS IN THE FAMILY BUSINESS LITERATURE

The empirical evidence reviewed so far has clearly demonstrated that the family dimension has an impact on the way companies attract, select, train, motivate, and involve their employees in the organization. However, most of these studies are descriptive and empirically driven, and they do not provide a theoretical explanation for the source of distinctiveness of the family dimension and its impact on the design of HR practices. In contrast to this scarcity of theory-based research on HRM in the family business context, since the mid-1990s, research on family-owned firms pertaining to topics such as family business governance, succession, or culture has increasingly become more theoretically grounded. Scholars from mainstream disciplines have started to recognize the unique characteristics of these firms and begun to view them as a fertile ground for theory building and empirical research. By applying the dominant theoretical frameworks from their respective disciplines to the study of family-owned firms, they have to a great degree contributed to enriching our theoretical understanding of the family business phenomena.

Our aim is to use this existing knowledge to enhance our understanding of HRM in family firms. This is why in this section we will revisit these theoretical frameworks and their implications for HRM in family-owned firms. As in the empirical review, we will classify our review into the aforementioned categories of HR practices: **employee skills, employee performance and reward systems, and employee involvement and communication.** Moreover, because many of these theoretical models have been applied to explain various types of family business behavior, the discussion is organized around common themes that overlap with two or more theories.

### Family Business Succession

Although not directly linked to HRM, succession studies have provided many insights mainly about the process of **attracting and developing** employee skills, and dealing with **employee involvement and communication practices** in family-owned firms. According to Le Breton-Miller, Miller, and Steier (2004), succession planning and the nurturing of a successor from within the family are among the most critical decisions ever taken by the patriarch or current family business leader. Indeed, research shows that failure to provide for succession is the primary cause for the demise of family-owned businesses (Hershon, 1975; Lansberg, 1983; Danco, 1987). Therefore, it is not surprising that since the inception of academic research on family-owned firms in the early 1980s, family business succession has been a leading topic (Dyer & Sanchez, 1998; Sharma, Chua, & Chrisman, 2000).

Although a number of factors influencing succession have been suggested (e.g., Handler & Kram, 1988; Harveston, Davis, & Lyden, 1997; Sharma, Chrisman, & Chua, 1997), the literature is highly fragmented. Most of the theoretical models on family business succession are grounded in the **resource-based view (RBV) of the firm** (Barney, 1991). Under this view, family involvement contributes to the building of competitive advantage for the firm through the development of tacit knowledge and higher stocks of social capital (Sirmon & Hitt, 2003). The problem with family businesses is that unlike in other firms, this idiosyncratic knowledge, which includes aspects such as personal business contacts and networks, knowledge about the local conditions, and the internal operations of the family business (Lee, Lim, & Lim, 2003), is often individual specific rather than firm specific (Castanias & Helfat, 1991, 1992). The profitability of family businesses, therefore, often depends on the extent of the idiosyncratic knowledge possessed by the heads of their businesses (Barach, Gantisky, Carlson, & Doochin, 1988; Rosenzweig & Wolpin, 1985) and, indeed, may be accessible only to family members and trusted agents. Consequently, research in this area emphasizes the importance of transferring the tacit embedded knowledge across generations to enhance the competitive advantage of family-owned firms (Cabrera-Suárez, De Saá-Pérez, & Garcia-Almeida, 2001). Therefore, the implementation of HR practices aimed at **developing employee skills** (those of the successor in this case) in family-owned firms should be designed to facilitate this transition.

The succession literature also highlights the central role of the founder in the development of successor skills. Ample evidence recognizes that, due to their long tenures and the centrality of their position in the family and the firm, founders exert considerable influence on the culture and performance of their firms (Anderson et al., 2003; Garcia-Alvarez, Lopez-Sintas, & Gonzalvo, 2002; Kelly, Athanassiou, & Crittenden, 2000; McConaughy, 2000). This influence could last long beyond their tenure (Davis & Harveston, 1999). For instance, Garcia-Alvarez et al. (2002) suggested that the founders' view of the role of business in their family influences the mode and process of socialization that they use for the next-generation of family members. In their study, those founders who perceived their business as a means to support their family communicated higher values of group orientation to their successors, who were found to join the firm at a young age, at lower position, and with low levels of formal education. On the other hand, founders who viewed the business as an end in itself encouraged successors to achieve high levels of formal education and acquire professional experience outside the business before joining the family-owned firm at senior levels.

Another related stream of research analyzes the succession process from the successors' perspective. In this regard, a bunch of studies suggest that certain characteristics of a successor affect the selection process and the smoothness and efficacy of a succession. These include sensitivity to the founder's needs (Lansberg, 1988), patience, and diplomacy (Jonovic, 1989); understanding the organization's intricacies and culture (Horton, 1982); and congruence between the successor's power in the family and the business (Holland & Boulton, 1984). As per our discussion above, all these features point toward a higher preference for using the extent of P–O fit as a criterion for choosing a successor. Moreover, findings of prior studies concur in that positive firm performance by family successors is associated with successor's development and intergenerational relationship, succession planning, successor's potential capability, commitment to the firm, and successor's business skills (Handler, 1989; King 2003; Wang, Watkings, Harris, & Spicer, 2004).

Understanding successor's motivation and career goals is also an important topic within succession studies that has implications for practices toward **attracting and developing employee (successor) skills** in family firms. As mentioned earlier, compared to their peers who come from nonfamily business settings, junior generation members of family-owned firms were found to have less clarity about their abilities, talents, goals, and career interests (Eckrich & Loughead, 1996). Although this could be a reflection of vocational clarity, some scholars have interpreted this result as a product of the socialization processes that inculcate a sense of obligation among juniors to pursue a career in their firms (Sharma, 2004). This also has implications for a better understanding of HR practices dealing with **employee involvement** in family-owned firms. In a related study, drawing on the organizational commitment literature, Sharma and Irving (2005) have developed a theoretical model to understand the behavioral and perfor- mance implications of the junior family members based on their reasons for pursuing a career in their family-owned firms. Behavioral and performance variations are expected depending on whether juniors join their family- owned firms because they want to, from a sense of obligation, due to involved opportunity costs, or from a sense of need. It is imperative that family business owners take into account these expectations when designing their HRM processes and practices.

*Family Business Governance*

The dominance of agency theory in the field of family business governance (as it happens in conventional governance studies) is one of the main reasons why theory development on family-owned firms' governance was hampered until the late 1990s. For decades, researchers were inclined to view being family owned and managed as a highly desirable governance structure (Daily & Dollinger, 1992; Galve-Górriz & Salas-Fumás, 1996; Jensen & Meckling, 1976; Mishra, Randoy, & Jensen, 2001). The existence of kin relationships was generally believed to lessen self-interest and foster commitment of those inside the family business (Chrisman, Chua, & Litz, 2004; Davis, 1983; Gersick et al., 1997). Moreover, families endow firms with tangible and intangible benefits such as unique identities (Berrone, Cruz, Gomez-Mejia, & Larraza, 2010; Gersick et al., 1997; Rosenblatt, de Mik, Anderson, & Johnson, 1985), strong involvement (Jorissen, Laveren, Martens, & Reheul, 2005), and long-term orientation (Casson, 1999; Kets de Vries, 1993). From an agency theory perspective, this has a positive effect on family-owned firm governance because it limits moral hazard among family members by reducing goal divergence and information asymmetry (Fama &

Jensen, 1983; Daily & Dollinger, 1992; Lubatkin, Durand, & Ling, 2007a). From an HRM perspective, these positive effects influence the design of HR practices related to employee (family) **performance and reward systems** since they imply that the design of costly mechanisms to monitor and motivate employees (in particular top managers) was unnecessary or even detrimental to these firms' performance (DeAngelo & DeAngelo, 1985; Fama & Jensen, 1983).

This posture has changed recently, in view of accumulating findings from studies conducted around the globe on the role of family businesses, their distinctive characteristics, and the specific agency problems they encounter (Bartholomeusz & Tanewski, 2006; La Porta et al., 1999; Morck & Yeung, 2003, 2004). Collectively, this research has identified a unique set of agency problems within family-owned firms that result from the inclusion of noneconomic factors in the utility function that the family attempts to maximize (Gomez-Mejia et al., 2003), from altruism among family members (Lubatkin, Schulze, Ling, & Dino, 2005), and from lack of self-control among decision makers (Schulze et al., 2001). Although not explicitly addressed, these agency problems affect the design and implementation of employee reward practices. For instance, they can result in the design of unfair compensation and performance evaluation systems (Chua, Chrisman, & Bergiel, 2009; Jorissen et al., 2005), overpaid relatives (Jorissen et al., 2005), and managerial entrenchment (Gomez-Mejia et al., 2001). The latter is commonplace in some family-owned firms: in a sample of publicly traded American firms, McConaughy (2000) found the tenure of family business leaders to be almost three times longer than that of nonfamily executives (17.6 years versus 6.43 years). Cruz et al. (2010) found similar results. Lastly, agency problems within family firms may also affect HR practices that deal with **employee involvement** since existing studies suggest that they can also lead to nepotism (Sharma et al., 1997) and scapegoating of nonfamily executives and employees (Gomez-Mejia et al., 2001).

Still, the use of agency theory to analyze phenomena within family-owned firms has been heavily criticized since it fails to capture the cooperative behaviors that, despite emotional tensions, are common among family-owned firm members (Eddleston & Kellermanns, 2007). For some authors, the coincidence of ownership and control in the same hands makes the stewardship perspective more adequate, since family business managers are more apt to act as stewards of the company's goals and interests (Miller et al., 2008; Zahra, 2003). Altruism has been identified as a key component of stewardship behavior in family-owned firms (Zahra, 2003). Altruistic behaviors also affect **employee reward systems** since they create a self-reinforcing system of incentives that encourages family members to be thoughtful and "selfless" toward one another (Van den Berghe & Carchon, 2003). It also affects the HR dimension that deals with **employee involvement and communication** by giving rise to a sense of collective ownership among family members that encourages higher participation among family members (Eddleston & Kellermanns, 2007) and increases communication and cooperation, thereby reducing information asymmetries (Schulze, Lubatkin, & Dino, 2002). However, although there is some empirical evidence that suggests that altruism in family-owned firms may reduce conflicts (Chrisman et al., 2004), altruism needs to be reciprocal to have such a positive influence. Among the negative effects of asymmetric altruism that may affect HRM in family-owned firms, scholars cite problems in effectively monitoring family members (Schulze et al., 2003), inability to attract the best nonfamily managers (Gomez-Mejia et al., 2001), and the placement of family members in positions for which they are not best qualified (Burkart, Panunzi, & Shleifer, 2003).

The study by Cruz et al. (2010) has used the trust literature as a bridge to reconcile both theoretical perspectives. According to the authors, whether the agency or the stewardship position is correct depends on how the principal perceives the benevolence of the agent. Using a sample of 122 family-owned firms, the authors found that as perceived agent benevolence increased, the agency contract became less control oriented and more concerned about the welfare of agents (which has greater affinity to the stewardship view). In short, this study argued that neither the agency nor the stewardship positions accurately describe corporate governance within family-owned firms. Instead, much depends on the perceived benevolence of agents, which is a positive function of congruence in family status and a negative function of family exposure to opportunistic agent behaviors. Consequently, we believe that employee benevolence levels must be given consideration when designing **HR practices** within an organization.

### Family Social Capital

A related topic that affects HRM and that has been largely researched in the past few years is the concept of family social capital. Extant research suggests that the relationships among family members create an ideal environment in which to create social capital (Coleman, 1988). Indeed, for many family-owned firms, social capital residing in familial relationships has been suggested as an important element of competitive success (Arregle,

Hitt, Sirmon, & Very, 2007). By modeling trust, the family provides the foundation of moral behavior on which its guidelines for cooperation and coordination as well as principles of reciprocity and exchange are developed (Bubolz, 2001). Therefore, family-owned firms must take into account their family's social capital when designing and implementing HR practices aimed at **rewarding and measuring employee performance**.

Family social capital would also affect other nonfamily employees since the literature also suggests that the reciprocal bonds seen within family businesses are not exclusively restricted to family members but are likely to be extended to a wide set of constituents. For instance, family-owned firms often have time-honored vendors and suppliers, and relationships with them may be viewed as, or may actually be, family relationships (Uhlaner, 2006). Thus, the sense of belonging, self, and identity derived from the firms is often shared by nonfamily employees and close customers.

The enduring long-term relationships with internal and external stakeholders that family-owned firms enjoy are more often than not beneficial to the accumulation of social capital (Arregle et al., 2007) and can also impact the design of practices that an organization uses to develop healthy **employee involvement and communication practices**. For instance, a study of 58 enduring cases with median age of 104 years revealed that the interplay of strong ties within the internal community and the connection with external stakeholders enables these firms to sustain their viability across generations (Miller & Le Breton-Miller, 2005).

## Professionalization: Dealing with Nonfamily Employees

The literature suggests that family-owned firm owners have a tendency to rely exclusively on family members because they often find it difficult to delegate to outsiders, have insufficient knowledge of formal management techniques, fear losing control, or believe that professionalization is an unnecessary cost (Dyer, 1989; Sharma et al., 1997). In turn, nonfamily managers frequently decide to stay away from family-owned firms because these firms are likely to offer outsiders limited potential for professional growth and exclude them from succession (Chua, Chrisman, & Sharma, 2003; Covin, 1994a; Gallo & Vilaseca, 1998; Klein, 2000). Despite this, it also recognizes that **attracting** qualified nonfamily employees and **developing their skills** and **motivating** them toward value-creating attitudes and behaviors can be major factors in the success or failure of family-owned firms (Chrisman, Chua, & Litz, 2003; Chua et al., 2003). Consequently, several research efforts have been devoted to understanding the role of nonfamily managers in family-owned firms.

In addition, scholars have devoted lots of research efforts to understand the differences between family and nonfamily employees. Gomez-Mejia et al. (2003) noted that family managers face higher exit barriers and greater organizational commitment than nonfamily managers, since their human capital is firm specific, and incur higher personal risk as a result of business failure (what they call "the family handcuff"). On the other hand, they are less worried about employment risk and short-term financial results (Gomez-Mejia et al., 2001; Sharma & Irving, 2005; Ward, 1987). Litz (1995) and Casson (1999) also added that the idea of the family business as something to pass through generations gives family managers a longer decision horizon as compared with nonfamily ones. For nonfamily employees, the relationship with the firm is more utilitarian and distant (Lubatkin et al., 2005). Authors also claim that nonfamily managers are more vulnerable than family managers as external business risk increases, since they may be more easily scapegoated for disappointing results beyond their control (Gomez-Mejia et al., 2001; Cruz et al., 2010). Based on these differences, scholars have analyzed the advantages and disadvantages of family versus nonfamily employment. Again, RBV and agency theory have been the predominant theoretical frameworks in the field. Empirical findings from these studies were explained in the previous section.

Lastly, scholars have also indirectly studied **employee involvement and communication practices** when dealing with nonfamily employees. Lubatkin, Ling, and Schulze (2007b) use behavioral economics and distributive justice theories to suggest that nonfamily employees' perceptions of fairness, in terms of resource allocation exhibited by controlling owners, will be dependent on the extent of self-control exhibited by these individuals. If they are perceived to make decisions that gratify immediate needs of family members as opposed to promoting long-term value for the family-owned firm, they will be perceived as unjust. Such perceptions are likely to lead to dissatisfaction among nonfamily employees and reduce the likelihood of high performance or long tenures of these employees. In a similar vein, Barnett and Kellermanns (2006), integrating mainstream theories of justice, developed a conceptual model to specify how the extent of family influence affects the fairness of HR practices toward nonfamily employees. The authors conclude that fair HR practices will be more or less likely depending on the nature and extent of family influence inherent in the firm. As in the case of the succession literature, studies also suggest the importance of the founder's role in determining this perception of fairness. For instance,

Lubatkin et al. (2007b) distinguish "far-sighted" founders from those suffering from "myopic altruism." While the first ones are able to withhold immediate gratification of each and every need of family members in favor of actions that enhance long-term value for the family and the firm, myopic altruists find it difficult to take such actions, thereby violating rules of procedural and distributive justice, leading to their being perceived as unjust by family and nonfamily members.

## Family Business Culture

When considered in the context of family businesses, researchers agree that culture takes an even more complex dimension. A family business's culture is the product of beliefs, values, and goals embedded in its history and social ties so family values assume the role of organizational cultural values (Hall, Melin, & Nordqvist, 2001). Moreover, because of the dominant role of the founder, not only during the entrepreneurial period but also potentially through successive stages, values and owner motivations are powerful cultural drivers.

This distinctiveness of the family business culture has important implications for the design and implementation of the three aforementioned categories of HR practices. First, the family culture embedded in family organizations may influence practices to **attract and motivate** employees by offering a sense of transcendent meaning to their participants – whether or not they are in the family, because family organizations embody the legacies of their owners (Aronoff & Ward, 1995). It also suggests the prospect of a type of organizing process that is less impersonal, in which attachments developed between people in the company are not only instrumental or rationally oriented but also molded by elements like friendship, goodwill, caring, and kinship (Colli, 2003).

The presence of a unified organizational family culture also affects **employee involvement and communication practices** since it permits easy coordination without the need of formal mechanisms through shared and internalized norms and values. Indeed some authors suggest that in certain companies, family culture is so intensive that the companies continued to rely on informal coordination mechanisms even as they were growing rapidly (McCollom, 1988). In turn, this may also inspire high-trust relationships. If interpersonal relationships are structured around values and beliefs that are weakly formalized and codified, organizational and family members are fated to coordinate their relationships and transactions on mutual trust (Astrachan, 1988).

Lastly, another aspect of family culture that relates to HR practices is the centralization of decision-making. Both anecdotal and empirical evidence suggest that decision-making tends to be highly centralized in family-owned firms as owners are unwilling to dilute their personal power and control (Pondy, 1969). Kets de Vries (1996) found that family-firm founders exhibit stronger requirements for control. Founders are less likely to delegate power, and family-owned firms tend to be centralized and controlled by the founder's beliefs (Kets de Vries, 1996). Goffee and Scase (1985), Hall (1988), Tagiuri and Davis (1996), and Poza et al. (1997) also find that decision-making is centered with the top family members in family-owned firms. These findings have crucial implications for the adoption of **employee involvement** programs as firms that are highly centralized and autocratic in terms of their organizational culture will be unwilling to devolve authority to lower-level employees.

### *Differences in Strategic Decision-Making Between Family- and Non-Family-Owned Firms*

Another important field of study in the family business arena has focused on identifying major differences in strategic decision-making processes and outcomes between family- and non-family-owned firms. In that sense, a wealth of empirical findings confirms the existence of important differences between the two types of firms.

For instance, in terms of diversification, a number of empirical studies have shown that family-owned firms tend to diversify less frequently than non-family-owned firms (Anderson & Reeb, 2003), both domestically and internationally (Gomez-Mejia et al., 2010b). Research on strategic alliances in family-owned firms has shown that they do not pursue alliances with other organizations as much as non-family-owned firms (Gallo, Tapies, & Cappuyns, 2004). It also shows that they are less willing to join a cooperative as compared to non-family-controlled firms even when it represents a rather lucrative option (Gomez-Mejia et al., 2007). There also exist remarkable differences in the speed and style with which family-owned businesses proceed in their international ventures. For instance, Gallo and Estape (1992) found that family-owned businesses tend to internationalize later and much more slowly than non-family-owned firms. Similar findings were reported by Gomez-Mejia et al. (2010b). In terms of innovation, Gomez-Mejia, Hoskisson, Makri, Sirmon, and Campbell (2011) showed that in high-technology industries, family-controlled firms tend to invest less in R&D and engage in lower technological diversification than non-family-controlled firms. Similarly, Mishra and McConaughy (1999) showed that family-owned firms use less debt in their capital structure. Lastly, Berrone et al. (2010) demonstrated that family-owned firms exhibit better environmental performance than their nonfamily counterparts.

Scholars have proposed several explanations for these empirical findings including the notion of risk bearing, which stems from a concentration of family wealth in a single business (Anderson & Reeb, 2003; Mishra & McConaughy, 1999; James, 1999), the emotional attachment to the business (Nicholson & Björnberg, 2008; Thomsen & Pedersen, 2000), or the transgenerational view (James, 1999). Recently, in a set of related papers, Gomez-Mejia et al. (2007, 2010b) have proposed the concept of SEW as a framework to integrate all of these existing theoretical explanations. The concept of SEW was first defined by Gomez-Mejia et al. (2007) as the stock of affect-related value that a family derives from its controlling position in a particular firm. It includes aspects such as the ability to exercise authority (Schulze et al., 2003); the satisfaction of needs for belonging, affect, and intimacy (Kepner, 1983); the perpetuation of family values through the business (Handler, 1990); the preservation of the family dynasty (Casson, 1999); the conservation of the family's social capital (Arregle et al., 2007); the fulfillment of family obligations based on blood ties rather than on strict criteria of competence (Athanassiou, Crittenden, Kelly, & Marquez, 2002); and the opportunity to be altruistic to family members (Schulze et al., 2003). Losing this SEW implies loss of intimacy, reduced status, and/or failure to meet the family's expectations. The study of Gomez-Mejia et al. (2007) first introduced the SEW concept within the theoretical framework of the Behavioral Agency Model or BAM (Wiseman & Gomez-Mejia, 1998). The BAM integrates elements of prospect theory, behavioral theory of the firm, and agency theory. Fundamental to the BAM is the notion that firms make choices depending on the referent point of dominant principals. These principals will make decisions so as to preserve their accumulated endowment within the firm. In particular, from BAM's perspective, an individual who perceives a subjective threat to his or her endowment (what is considered important for personal welfare that is already accrued and can be counted on) is more willing to undertake risky actions to preserve that endowment. To the extent that SEW preservation is a key objective of family owners, Gomez-Mejia et al. (2007) hypothesized that for family-owned firms, the most important reference point when framing major decision choices is the perceived threat to SEW. Therefore, when threats to SEW are present, that is, when the family-owned firm faces the dilemma of choosing between an action that would reduce economic risk and confer financial gains (but a subsequent deficit of SEW) and the alternative of protecting SEW (but with uncertain economic benefits), they would tend to favor the latter (Gomez-Mejia et al., 2007). That is why family-owned firms in the study by Gomez-Mejia et al. (2007) decided not to join a cooperative since joining may imply a loss of the family's SEW (such as loss of a distinct family image). It would also explain why they diversify less since diversification implies going beyond the competitive advantage of the family (Stein, 1989), making SEW losses more probable (Gomez-Mejia et al., 2010b). In a similar vein, SEW has also been shown to account for better environmental performance of family-owned firms as demonstrated by Berrone et al. (2010). According to the authors, family-owned firms would place a greater value on the legitimacy afforded by environmental initiatives because the gains in legitimacy would translate into a socioemotional reward that compensates the cost and uncertainty involved in pursuing environment-friendly policies. Moreover, given the greater levels of identification that the owning family has with the firm, a negative image of the firm as a result of poor environmental performance would be personalized, directly implying a loss of the family's SEW.

Therefore, the SEW perspective posits that any strategic decision-making process in family-owned firms can be explained under the logic of preserving the socioemotional endowment. Given that **HR practices** are a reflection of the strategic decisions made by firms (Gomez-Mejia et al., 2012), we contend that family owners will also follow this "decision making process based on a SEW logic" when making decisions pertaining to HRM. Indeed, a study by Gomez-Mejia et al. (2010b) explicitly recognizes that the adoption of SEW as a frame of reference will lead family-owned firms to be reluctant to **attract and select** nonfamily managers whose presence may damage the family's socioemotional endowment. In the next section, we will explain how this emphasis on SEW preservation will affect each of the three proposed categories of related HR practices.

# A SOCIOEMOTIONAL WEALTH PRESERVATION APPROACH TO UNDERSTANDING HRM IN FAMILY-OWNED FIRMS

Our review of the extant literature suggests that regardless of the theoretical model, scholars agree on the distinctiveness of family-owned firms. More

***Table 1.*** Family Business Research and Its Relationship with HRM.

| Main topics | Theoretical models | HRM dimensions | | |
|---|---|---|---|---|
| | | Employee skills | Employee performance and reward systems | Employee involvement and communication |
| Sucesssion | RBV | X | | X |
| Family business governance | Agency Theory/ RBV/stewardship | | X | X |
| Professionalization | Agency Theory/ RBV/distributive justice | X | X | X |
| Family social capital | Social capital/social networks | X | X | X |
| Family culture | RBV | X | X | X |
| Strategic decisión-making | BAM | X | | |

importantly, although not directly linked to HRM in family-owned firms, all the reviewed studies highlight some unique aspects of family human capital and family contracting. Table 1 summarizes much of the ensuing theoretical discussion of each of the reviewed topic and its relationship with our proposed taxonomy of HR practices. The first column shows the key themes as they have been grouped in the previous section. The second column provides a list of the major theories or model used for each of the topics. The remaining columns show the three categories of HR-related practices identified earlier.

An examination of Table 1 makes evident the absence of a theoretical paradigm to explain the sources and consequences of the distinctiveness of HRM in family-owned firms. Nevertheless, from the previous discussion it has also emerged that, regardless of the topic, all existing theoretical explanations draw on the importance of socioemotional factors in the ability of family-owned firms to obtain, retain, and develop human capital. For instance, in the case of family business succession and family business culture, our review showed how the intentions to transfer the firm through generations could lead the family-owned firm to invest in the development of family members' managerial capabilities (Cabrera-Suárez et al., 2001; Sirmon & Hitt, 2003), providing a just work environment for nonfamily employees (Barnett & Kellermanns, 2006) and an effective transmission of values throughout the organization (Handler, 1990). Similarly, in the case of family governance, we mentioned how the presence of emotions derived from kinship ties creates a sense of belonging and identity with the firm (Kepner, 1983), fosters the development of social capital (Arregle et al., 2007), and leads family members to display altruistic behavior (Schulze et al., 2003). On the other hand, our review suggests that socioemotional aspects may also have negative consequences for HRM including scapegoating (Gomez-Mejia et al., 2001), unjust compensation and performance evaluation (Chua et al., 2009), and/or nepotism (Sharma et al., 1997). Indeed, as we have showed throughout the review, although not directly linked with HRM, the literature on family business is full of anecdotal evidence that shows that family connections have many nonrational consequences allowing unconditional love and concern to conflict with business values of profitability and efficiency (Dyer, 1988), power based on ascribed rather than achieved status (Dyer, 1994), difficulty in dealing objectively with a family member's performance and qualifications (Crane, 1985), and a lack of rational systems based on merit (Kanter, 1989).

Based on that evidence, we propose to use the SEW approach as an integrated framework for developing a theory of HRM in family-owned firms. As mentioned before, since HR practices are a reflection of the strategic decisions made by firms, we argue that family owners would also follow the SEW logic when faced with decisions pertaining to attracting, retaining, motivating, or increasing employee involvement and communication within the organization. That is, when faced with any of these decisions, family owners will frame the problem in terms of an assessment of how the action will impact the firm's socioemotional endowment. If they perceive that there could be a potential threat to that endowment, the family will tend to make decisions that are not driven by an economic logic and will be inclined to put the firm at risk if this is what it takes to preserve that endowment. Therefore, independent of financial and (economic) risk considerations, family owners would favor HRM strategies that enhance the family's noneconomic utilities and/or prevent SEW losses.

Consequently, we will reexamine existing empirical evidence on the determinants of HRM in family-owned firms under the lens of the SEW approach. We will also reinterpret existing theoretical models of family-owned firms and their implications for HRM under the SEW umbrella. Our final goal would be to establish an integrated framework through a set of sound propositions to guide future research on HRM in family-owned firms. Consistent with our proposed taxonomy of related HR practices, we divide our propositions into three groups: (a) propositions dealing with attracting and developing employee skills, (b) propositions dealing with designing employee performance and reward systems, and (c) propositions dealing with employee involvement and communication practices in family-owned firms.

### Attracting and Developing Employees' Skills in Family-Owned Firms Under the SEW Logic

As explained earlier, skill-enhancing practices are primarily related to recruitment, selection, training, and development of employees (Ostroff & Bowen, 2000). In the following paragraphs, we discuss how the SEW logic will impact these activities within family businesses.

*Recruitment*
As mentioned before, when making decisions regarding recruitment, organizations can look for two types of fit: P–J fit, or the compatibility between the characteristics of a person and those of a specific job, and P–O fit, or the compatibility between the person and the organization (Kristof-Brown, Barrick, & Stevens, 2005). We believe that when SEW is the frame of reference, family-owned firms will show a higher likelihood of selecting employees on the basis of P–O rather than P–J fit. While P–J fit is crucial to ensure that the new hires will perform competently on the job, an emphasis on SEW preservation would imply that the firm will take the requisite steps to ensure that the people being hired will uphold the values and cultural ethos of the firm. The company may often need to trade off employee capabilities and job-specific knowledge in favor of person–organization compatibility because they believe such efforts will serve to protect the firm's SEW and will be in the long-term interest of the firm. Moreover, firms with SEW as the frame of reference are likely to hold the view that lower levels of fit with the job can be addressed post selection through on-the-job training, whereas poor compatibility with the organization's core philosophy is difficult to remedy upon selection and could be really damaging for the SEW. Therefore,

> **Proposition 1.** Because family-owned firms are more likely to use SEW as the frame of reference, the recruitment process will tend to show a greater reliance on P–O fit than on P–J fit.

Extending the arguments of the previous proposition, we argue that when a family-owned firm uses SEW as the frame of reference and wishes to ensure the compatibility of the employees with the organization, it is more likely to show a lower use of formal recruitment methods (e.g., advertising vacancies, use of assessment centers, formal interviews, etc.). Although it has been recognized that the possibility of obtaining a better P–J fit is more likely when more formal recruitment sources are utilized as it helps in reaching a larger potential pool of job applicants (Schwab, 1982; Hunter & Schmidt, 1982), the same set of practices may not prove as effectual in achieving P–O fit (Gorter & Van Ommeren, 1999; Holzer, 1987). Informal recruitment practices are more likely to focus on a narrow pool of candidates that share the family's values and culture, reflecting a prototype of what an ideal employee should be like (in essence, considering as a selection criterion how the prospective employee may contribute to the family's SEW). Formally stated,

**Proposition 2.** Because family-owned firms are more likely to use SEW as a frame of reference, they are less likely to rely on formal recruitment methods.

From the previous propositions, it becomes evident that with regard to acquisition of human resources in family-owned firms, because of their higher likelihood of using SEW as the frame of reference, family owners and management will be more concerned with knowing, in advance, how well a given individual will fit with the organization once hired. Insights about a person's ability to fit with the company's culture cannot be readily obtained during the recruitment process owing to problems of adverse selection and provision of misleading information during the selection process. Therefore, one would expect the family to use its social networks as a means to recruit people with better fit to the organization. Existing evidence suggests that since the two parties already know each other and the mutual attraction is based on perceived similarity, people recruited through social networks are believed to fit well with the organization (Leung, 2003; Brass, 1995). Moreover, theoretical work also suggests that social networks act as excellent channels for the transmission of information between job applicants and potential employers (Montgomery, 1991; Saloner, 1985; Simon & Warner, 1992), and thus, act as a vehicle for the preservation of a family's SEW. The following proposition captures this argument:

**Proposition 3.** Because family-owned firms are more likely to use SEW as a frame of reference, they will tend to emphasize social networks in the recruiting process.

*Selection*

Logically, a recruitment process based on P–O fit, coupled with an emphasis on the use of social networks as a recruitment method for firms that use SEW as a frame of reference, will result in a higher percentage of hires within the family and a higher percentage of hired employees with social ties to the owning family. But there exist additional SEW arguments that reinforce this preference toward family employment and/or employees with social ties. First of all, recruiting family members is more likely contribute to SEW enhancement. Being part of the family business not only provides the family employee with a means of subsistence, but also enhances the person's self-concept based on long-term identification with the firm (Westhead, Cowling, & Howorth, 2001). Moreover, providing a means of livelihood for family members gives a strong justification for the very existence of a family-owned firm and perpetuates a cycle that triggers a distinct sense of identification among family employees, which enriches SEW (Gomez-Mejia et al., 2007). This also reinforces the self-image of the family founder or elder family member who can extend largess to other family members via the provision of secure employment. Second, recruitment of an outsider could lead to SEW losses through three main drivers. Hiring someone who is an expert in specialized knowledge areas beyond the comprehension of the family owners increases information asymmetries (Gomez-Mejia et al., 2011). It also increases behavioral uncertainty since predicting employees' behaviors becomes more difficult when recruiting an outsider (Cruz et al., 2010). Lastly, it increases goals conflicts owing to divergent motivations and career goals of family and nonfamily employees (Gomez-Mejia et al., 2001).

Moreover, recent research by Cruz et al. (2011) combines the family embeddedness perspective with the SEW approach to suggest that the presence of SEW imprints family employment based on kinship ties with two features that have a direct positive impact on a firm's performance. First of all, SEW provides kinship ties with some of the same collective benefits as those that arise in closed networks including the development of "collective social capital" that results in a group-based identity (Coleman, 1990), and promotes shared behavioral norms (Rowley, Behrens, & Krackhardt, 2000) and cooperation (Walker, Kogut, & Shan, 1997). It also endows kinship ties with the dyadic, interpersonal advantages that the relational embeddedness approach has attributed to the presence of strong (versus weak) ties (Nahapiet & Ghoshal, 1998). Among these benefits of strong ties, scholars have emphasized the formation of relational trust (Coleman, 1990) and feelings of closeness and interpersonal solidarity (Uzzi, 1997).

In such a scenario, family owners are faced with the task of striking a balance between the benefits proffered by the nonfamily employee in terms of specialized knowledge and expertise and the potential erosion of SEW that may arise from the increased information asymmetries and goal conflict between outsiders and family members, which results in greater behavioral uncertainty. They may also be faced with the loss of potential benefits implied in hiring someone with family ties. So, when SEW is used as a frame of reference, the perceived benefits of hiring outsiders are not likely to counteract the potential loss in SEW. Therefore,

**Proposition 4.** Because family-owned firms are more likely to use SEW as a frame of reference, they will have a higher percentage of hires with family ties, based on either a blood nexus or strong social ties to the owning family.

The SEW logic would also influence a family firm's posture toward the selection of a successor. In particular, we would expect that using SEW as a frame of reference will increase the likelihood of choosing a successor within the family. When this is the case, the idiosyncratic knowledge of family members becomes a much more relevant asset that would impinge on the choice of a family successor (Cabrera-Suárez, 2005; Cabrera-Suárez et al., 2001; Lee et al., 2003; Sharma & Irving, 2005). Second, a family successor would reinforce family power and influence in the company, which is a key element of SEW. Even in contexts where nonfamily successors are perceived as more suited to become leaders, they are unlikely to as closely identify with the family-owned firm and may harbor selfish interests. Family successors, on the other hand, closely identify with the firm and are expected to work in its long-term interest. Trusting the successor's loyalty to the family is, therefore, an important criterion of successions in these organizations (Donckels & Lambrecht, 1999; Matthews, Moore, & Fialko, 1999). The credibility of the successor to the family is crucial to his or her successful integration into the business, because without credibility, the successor cannot attain legitimacy (Barach et al., 1988, p. 50). Thus, owing to a stronger belief in the family successor's efficacy in maintaining the family-owned firm's SEW and the SEW costs associated with nonfamily succession, it seems reasonable to expect that family-owned firms that use SEW as a frame of reference will prefer to choose a family successor.

**Proposition 5.** Because family-owned firms are more likely to use SEW as the frame of reference, they are more likely to choose successors who are family members.

Lastly, in relation to the selection process, we also expect that when the family-owned firm uses gains or losses in SEW as a frame of reference, decision-making with regard to selection would be highly centralized. As per Proposition 1, preservation of SEW implies that the family wants to ensure that the new hire fits with the organization's beliefs and values that are mainly derived from the family's vision. Consequently, decision-making pertaining to the selection process would be highly centralized, with the authority resting with top management team members belonging to the owning family. Indeed, control and influence are an integral part of SEW (Berrone, Cruz, & Gomez-Mejia, 2011), and family-owned firms that strive to preserve their SEW are more likely to perpetuate owners' direct or indirect control and influence over any of the firm's affairs irrespective of financial considerations (Gomez-Mejia et al., 2007). Therefore,

**Proposition 6.** Because family-owned firms are more likely to use SEW as a frame of reference, they will have a more centralized selection process, with family members playing a key decision-making role.

*Training and Development*
When family businesses use SEW as a frame of reference, they adopt a long-term orientation that affects all activities of the firm. In such an instance, the company is seen as a long-term family investment to be bequeathed to descendents (Berrone et al., 2010). Indeed, Zellweger and Astrachan (2008) proposed this transgenerational sustainability as one of the central aspects of SEW. Moreover, an emphasis on SEW preservation implies supporting and developing family members (Gersick et al., 1997; Davis & Harveston, 2001), and rewarding them for merely being members of the family, not for specific deeds (Dyer, 1992). Consequently, we would expect family-owned firms to put a greater emphasis on development activities (designed to enhance the long-term growth of an individual) than on training activities (which are more short term and job focused). Moreover, the implementation of long-term focused developmental plans may help to instill new employees with the norms and values of the organization, thus strengthening his or her identity with the firm and fostering the family's SEW. Formally stated,

**Proposition 7.** Because family-owned firms are more likely to use SEW as a frame of reference, they will tend to invest more in (long-term) career development activities than in training activities.

As frequently mentioned in the family business literature, the choice and nurturing of a successor are two of the most critical decisions ever taken by family owners (Le Breton-Miller et al., 2004). Therefore, we expect that the use of SEW as a frame of reference would affect not only the selection of the successor but also those practices aimed at developing his or her skills within the organization. In particular, we expect family-owned firms that use SEW as the frame of reference to be more likely to emphasize the use of mentoring relationships with successors, because mentoring can infuse protégés with the norms and values of the organization and the junior employee absorbs, imbibes, and internalizes the tacit aspects of the organization's values, thus strengthening his or her identity with the firm (Kram, 1983). Moreover, if firms want to preserve their affective endowment, they must ensure that protégés receive explicit and tacit knowledge for successfully running the family business, such as tricks of the trade, specific know-how about the firm, and valuable advice about the industry in which the firm operates (Lansberg & Astrachan, 1994; Morris, Williams, Allen, & Avila, 1997). For successors, mentoring relationships can help reduce the job stress arising from role overload, role ambiguity, and role conflicts, which can have an adverse effect on turnover (Major, Kozlowski, Chao, & Gardner, 1995). If the junior successor fails to adjust to the demands and expectations of the new role, a premature exit may increase the risk that another family successor cannot be found, thereby eroding the firm's SEW. If the successor is adequately socialized to the role demands and expectations, owing to the mentoring received from the incumbent, family members, or other stakeholders, his or her role commitment and identification increases (Lee, 2008), thus preserving the firm's SEW and enhancing the likelihood of success in the succession process.

**Proposition 8.** Because family-owned firms are more likely to use SEW as a frame of reference, they will tend to show a greater proclivity to mentor potential successors.

### Employee Performance and Reward Systems in Family-Owned Firms under the SEW Logic

Emphasis on SEW preservation implies that the firm strives for other nonfinancial goals and gives these goals a high priority. Therefore, the incentive system in the company will vary a lot depending on the frame of reference that the firm is using. It is expected that companies that use SEW as a frame of reference will show a below-market pay strategy. In such companies, the owner will place a strong emphasis on an employee's security, promotional opportunities, and other perquisites usually reserved for family members and employees will trade off a higher salary in return for nonfinancial rewards. Much of this can be explained by the patriarchal nature of family-owned firms, where job security in exchange for family loyalty replaces the need for strong incentives.

The argument also holds for nonfamily employees since those who accept employment at family-owned firms will hold somewhat different distributive justice expectations than those held by typical employees at public firms (Lubatkin et al., 2007b). Nonfamily employees who seek employment at family-owned firms are not so naïve as to expect that they will be treated by the family owners "like family" when it comes to allocating resources, promotional opportunities, and other perquisites. For example, most nonfamily employees will understand that the controlling family members are generally unwilling to cede control of the firm to outsiders and, therefore, are less likely to use stock and stock options as part of the compensation package. This implies that family-owned firms are more likely to attract nonfamily employees who are less motivated by economic rewards, and more by other rewards, such as the promise of lifetime job security and an informal work environment.

In this regard, we also expect that when family-owned firms seek to preserve their SEW, they will place a higher emphasis on internal equity versus external equity in the design of compensation contracts. Internal equity can be achieved if organizational rewards are distributed in proportion to job value (as per job evaluation), whereas external equity can be accomplished by pegging the organization's pay for a specific job position to the going rate in the market (Gomez-Mejia et al., 2010a). While traditional internal equity strategies rely on job content, productivity, and individual performance measures for the design of compensation contracts (Gomez-Mejia et al., 2012), the unique context of family-owned firms adds greater complexity to this design. The concerns of family employees and their perceptions of justice must be factored in when trying to understand internal equity pay strategies within a family-owned firm. What family members perceive they are owed and must similarly return to each other may be very different from the reciprocal obligations perceived by nonfamily members in the same family business. Owing to the idiosyncratic knowledge possessed by family employees, this group of employees will represent greater value to the family-owned firm than to nonfamily employees. Prior research also suggests that family firms use subjective criteria for defining wage levels (Gomez-Mejia et al., 2010a). Because family employees establish relational contracts with the firm, the exact terms of which may not be known, we expect that pay differentials will exist between family and nonfamily employees occupying same or similar jobs within the family-owned firm. Furthermore, nonfamily employees will not hesitate to leave the firm if they perceive they are being undervalued by the firm, whereas family employees in most instances cannot leave the organization as a coping strategy. Nevertheless, family employees' perceptions of injustice can have long-term negative consequences for the firm and may threaten a firm's SEW and continuance of the organization as a family-owned firm. Building on these arguments, we derive the following propositions:

**Proposition 9.** Because family-owned firms are more likely to use SEW as the frame of reference, they will tend to adopt a below-market pay policy or at best "a matching market" pay policy.

**Proposition 10.** Because family-owned firms use SEW as a frame of reference, they will tend to place a greater emphasis on nonmonetary rewards.

**Proposition 11.** Because family-owned firms use SEW as a frame of reference, they will tend to place a greater emphasis on internal equity (versus external market equity) in the design of compensation contracts.

Moreover in these companies, owners will also try to insulate family members' pay from poor performance (Cruz et al., 2010), and consequently, they will use a greater percentage of fixed versus variable pay. The lower use of performance contingent and variable pay may be attributed to the fact that family owners have strong faith in the ability of family employees to work in the interest of the firm, so it is not essential to make them accountable for every performance lapse as these may result from factors beyond their control. It is also a signal of trustworthiness and of reciprocal obligations that do not need to be enforced throughout a formal contract (Cruz et al., 2010). Therefore,

**Proposition 12.** Because family-owned firms use SEW as a frame of reference, they will tend to place a lower emphasis on variable (versus fixed) pay.

A strong focus on SEW preservation will also be negatively related to stock-related compensation. In case of family executives, their commitment to preserve their socioemotional endowment acts as an implicit incentive mechanism. Family ties, loyalty, insurance, and stability derived from their SEW are expected to be effective in lengthening the horizons of managers and in providing incentives for family managers to make efficient long-term investments in the family business (James, 1999). Emphasis on SEW preservation also implies a strong identification between the family employee and the company (Berrone et al., 2010), so the benefits of equity-based compensation are reduced in such a case. Indeed, as Gomez Mejia et al. (2003) suggested, providing long-term incentives to an already heavily long-term oriented CEO could increase executive entrenchment.

However, a long-term orientation may not be too obvious in the case of nonfamily executives. Although family-owned firms that emphasize SEW have an interest in creating a common fate between owners and nonfamily managers, granting equity to outsiders may also imply renouncing power and influence within the company. It also "waters down" family ownership. When balancing both, family-owned firms may probably decide to protect their SEW by not giving equity-based incentives to outsiders even when this may imply ignoring the benefits in terms of SEW gains of aligning interest between the nonfamily executive and the family owners.

Formally stated,

**Proposition 13.** Because family-owned firms use SEW as a frame of reference, they will tend to place a lower emphasis on the use of equity-based incentives.

Firms that desire to preserve their SEW will also use less traditional methods in evaluating employees' performance. For these companies, contracts are mainly trust based, rooted in positive norms of reciprocity (Cruz et al., 2010). For owners, the contract is a way to reciprocate the employees for their loyalty, protect their interests, show consideration and sensitivity to their needs, and refrain from the use of fear (for instance, threats of termination) as a deterrent to opportunism. Therefore, we would expect that when firms use SEW as a frame of reference, the company will exhibit less dependence on extrinsic controls (e.g., reliance on quantitative performance indicators to punish or reward agents). The main goal is to make the employee feel valued, well treated, and protected so that SEW can be enhanced. Similarly, family-owned firms that use SEW as the frame of reference will seek to demonstrate altruistic behaviors toward family employees and attempt to shield them from the censure that is typically associated with poor performance. As mentioned before, an emphasis on SEW preservation implies rewarding people for merely being members of the family or a close and loyal employee, not for specific deeds (Dyer, 1992). Moreover, when preservation of SEW becomes a priority, the performance of a family CEO may also be judged based on fulfillment of family obligations (Beehr, Drexler, & Faulkner, 1997).

Because use of formal appraisal systems can bring the shortcomings of family or close employees to the fore, family-owned firms that strive to preserve their SEW will refrain from using them because it may damage their SEW. Moreover, inconsistencies in the use of formal appraisals for family and nonfamily employees can aggravate perceptions of injustice that exist within family-owned firms. Hence, in family-owned firms that aim to preserve their SEW, the positive effects of implementing objective measures to assess employee performance will not outweigh the possible losses in SEW that may result from the implementation of such practices.

The previous arguments can be summarized in the following propositions:

**Proposition 14.** Because family-owned firms use SEW as a frame of reference, they are less likely to use formal appraisal systems.

**Proposition 15.** Because family-owned firms use SEW as a frame of reference, they will tend to place a greater emphasis on the use of qualitative measures for evaluating employee performance

### Employee Involvement and Communication Practices in Family-Owned Firms under the SEW Logic

As explained before, this HR dimension refers to the broad pattern of employee management practices of employee involvement and direct communication that target the individual worker (Heery & Noon, 2001).

We believe that family-owned firms that use SEW as a frame of reference will be characterized by the use of more informal communication channels for the following reasons: First, the use of informal communication channels facilitates the development of a familial organizational atmosphere, which in turn enhances the family's SEW. Therefore, even in large family-owned firms, family owners and managers will place greater emphasis on informal interactions in order to strengthen the family ethos by personally conveying the culture and values of the family business. Also, prior evidence by Guest and Conway (2001) shows that informal communication channels are regarded as most effective in aiding employee retention, an outcome that can aid in the preservation of SEW. In particular, family owners may use informal interactions as a way to overcome nonfamily managers' regular complaints about their lack of voice in the formal governance structures of the company, which are mainly controlled by the family. Similarly, family owners may use informal channels to try to alleviate employee role ambiguity since evidence suggests that when communication channels are open and information asymmetries are lowered, individual roles are expected to be clearer for employees and unrealistic role expectations can be prevented (Davis, Schoorman, & Donaldson, 1997). Thus, we expect that family-owned firms that use SEW as the frame of reference will show higher use of informal communication channels. Formally stated,

**Proposition 16.** Because family-owned firms use SEW as a frame of reference, they will tend to place a greater emphasis on informal communication channels.

Regarding practices aimed at employee participation, a significant challenge that family-owned businesses face is effectively managing and fostering a strong sense of involvement and participation among both family and nonfamily employees (Chua et al., 2003). In the case of family employees, Eddleston and Kellermanns (2007) state that an effective participative strategy process can enable family members to openly express their opinions. Absence of a participative strategy in family-owned firms leads to politics and hostility in workplaces (Eisenhardt & Bourgeois, 1988) that can generate role ambiguity and role conflict. However, a participative strategy can lower role ambiguity and conflict in family-owned firms up to an optimum level.

Nonfamily members, on the other hand, may oftentimes find themselves in complex and uncertain situations because they are part of the business system but not the family system (Mitchell, Morse, & Sharma, 2003). Uncertainties with regard to their workplace status may emerge from a variety of issues such as how decisions are made (Blondel, Carlock, & Heyden, 2000), a perceived environment of bias and favoritism (Schulze et al., 2003; Lubatkin et al., 2005), the direct involvement and influence of family members (Astrachan, Klein, & Smyrnois, 2002), as well as fairness and procedural justice issues (Cropanzano & Greenberg, 1997; Barnett & Kellermanns, 2006). Family-owned firms must adopt measures to reassure nonfamily employees of the obligations the firm has toward them.

Many forms of employee participation and involvement can provide opportunities for workers' input on issues of interest to workers. Such a strategy can also hinder status ambiguity, create a sense of psychological attachment with the organization, and foster the preservation of SEW. Given that firms with SEW as the frame of reference will be most concerned with preserving the firm's SEW, and measures that reassure both family and nonfamily employees and infuse a sense of involvement in them can enhance a firm's SEW, we argue that when SEW is the frame of reference, employee participation for both family and nonfamily employees will be encouraged.

**Proposition 17.** Because family-owned firms use SEW as a frame of reference, they will tend to promote employee participation.

We also expect an emphasis on SEW preservation to have an effect on the symbolic as well as substantive responses of family-owned firms to employee concerns. Our argument is rooted in institutional theory, according to which institutional pressures that demand compliance with established norms also dictate that firms respond effectively to employee needs, since responding to employee needs and concerns has long been recognized as a means of fostering the image of a caring workplace (Oliver, 1997). As we have shown, evidence suggests that family owners tend to be sensitive about their firm's external image (Lyman, 1991) and possess a keen desire to project and perpetuate a positive family image and reputation (Sharma & Manikuti, 2005; Westhead et al., 2001) and to be perceived as good corporate citizens (Berrone et al., 2010). Consequently, owing to the emotional repercussions that poor social performance and public condemnation as a result of not addressing employee concerns can have for family SEW, family-owned firms show high levels of symbolic as well as substantive responses to employee concerns.

**Proposition 18.** Because family-owned firms use SEW as a frame of reference, they will tend to exhibit higher levels of symbolic and substantive responses to employee concerns.

However, high levels of sensitivity to employee concerns may not result in better employee perceptions of organizational justice for family-owned firms for several reasons. First of all, in this particular context, the desire to protect a firm's SEW and family altruism often adds to the dilemma of making just distributive decisions. Family altruism motivates parents to be generous to their children and children to be considerate of one another, fostering a set of interdependent relationships among family members that help to preserve SEW. A direct implication of family altruism for HRM in family-owned firms is that compensation, promotion, and succession policies that pertain to family members may have little to do with their contribution to the organization. For instance, some family employees may receive preferential treatment in the distribution of rewards irrespective of their contributions to firm success. In terms of justice theory, these "rewards" are distributed based on nonequity notions of fairness (Adams, 1965). And since equity is the dominant notion of justice in organizations (Bierhoff, Cohen, & Greenberg, 1986), such distribution can be deemed unjust.

Arriving at fair distributive decisions is further complicated by the fact that different groups of family and nonfamily employees will differ in terms of what is perceived as just. While nonfamily employees are often cognizant of the family-owned firm's altruism principle (Gersick et al., 1997), yet there are times when this conduct can exceed the nonfamily employee's zone of indifference. On the other hand, diligent family employees may feel bereft if their rewards are on par with that of less assiduous family employees. Formally stated,

**Proposition 19.** Because family-owned firms use SEW as a frame of reference, they will tend to have poorer perceptions of distributive justice among family and nonfamily employees.

We also expect having SEW as a frame of reference would affect individuals' perceptions about the fairness of formal procedures governing decisions, namely procedural justice concerns (Greenberg, 1987). As already mentioned, like societies, organizations are communities of individuals that are very sensitive to procedural justice because fair processes can engender trust, commitment, and harmony (Greenberg, 1990). In the context of firms that use SEW as the frame of reference, family altruism can cause inconsistencies in the application of organizational rules pertaining to recruitment, performance evaluations, and ethical standards depending on the family or nonfamily status of an employee. For example, family owners may not take corrective action when a family employee violates organizational rules nor take seriously the opinions of nonfamily employees. Even among family employees, organizational processes may not be viewed as equitable especially when certain family members are granted greater voice in decision-making processes whereas the opinions of others are discounted. For example, when members of the younger generation attempt to freely express their novel ideas, they find that they are too often criticized for challenging management's proven formula for success. The older generation may perceive the younger one as dismissive of the older generation's business achievements and disregard their ideas, leaving the younger generation with a feeling of disenfranchisement. Simply put, family owners often run their businesses as family fiefdoms and believe that they are in a better position than others to decide what is best for their firms. Therefore we expect that procedural decisions may be subjected to the owning family's personal biases and needs. Although such behavior may be perceived as fair and just by some family employees, it will trigger notions of injustice among other family employees who are excluded from participating in organizational decision-making. On the other hand, nonfamily employees' perceptions of injustice may be affected by their ability to distinguish between decisions in the workplace social system and those in the family social system (Greenhaus & Powell, 2006). Nonfamily employees may not always be content merely being members of the workplace social system and may have a grouse against the owning family for not giving them enough voice or not treating them as part of their family's social system (Carsrud, 2006). As a result, we expect that in family-owned firms that use SEW as the frame of reference, family altruism will confound fair application of organizational procedures and lead to a decrease in perceptions of procedural justice. Consequently,

**Proposition 20.** Because family-owned firms use SEW as a frame of reference, they will tend to have poorer perceptions of procedural justice among family and nonfamily employees.

Lastly, individuals' fairness judgments are also based on the quality of interpersonal treatment received during the execution of a procedure, a concept that has been labeled interactional justice (Bies & Moag, 1986). It has been hypothesized that interactional justice perceptions would primarily impact attitudes and behaviors toward the person carrying out the treatment, unlike procedural justice perceptions, which are thought to impact reactions to the organization. In the context of family-owned firms, the aim to preserve SEW and family altruism will thwart fair application of organizational procedures and lead to a decrease in perceptions of procedural justice. Given that unfair application of procedures will be attributed to members of the owning family, a sense of interactional injustice will also permeate the organization because of poor perceptions of interactional justice with regard to the owning family among the aggrieved parties.

**Proposition 21.** Because family-owned firms are more likely to use SEW as the frame of reference, they will tend to have poorer perceptions of interactional justice among family employees and nonfamily employees.

### *Explaining HR Practices in Family Firms When SEW Is Challenged as the Frame of Reference*

The previous propositions have been derived under the logic that, in the case of family principals, the emphasis on preserving SEW endowment becomes critical. Hence, the family frames decisions with regard to HRM in terms of how actions will impact socioemotional endowment. Thus, when there is a threat to that endowment, the family is willing to make decisions that are not driven by an economic logic to preserve their SEW.

However, some of the empirical evidence on family firms' strategic behavior mentioned above also suggests that the importance of SEW as a reference point may change depending on the external threats that a firm faces. For instance, when a performance hazard dually jeopardizes SEW and the firm's viability, the loss framing of the family owners shifts from SEW preservation to firm survival, since losing the firm would also imply losing both SEW and financial welfare. Under these circumstances, family owners will be more willing to make economically driven strategic choices. This argument is used by Gomez-Mejia et al. (2011) to explain why the willingness to invest in R&D for family-owned firms is greater as performance indicators deteriorate. These changes in the family owners' loss framing would also affect decisions pertaining to HRM. For instance, we would expect that when faced with poor performance, families would be more willing to recruit outsiders hoping that their specialized knowledge and skills would help them achieve a turnaround. Deteriorating performance may also make more evident the potential disadvantages of family employment in terms of restricted access to new information and new ways of doing things (Coleman, 1988) and of "relational inertia" (Gargiulo & Benassi, 2000), which impedes the development of new knowledge (Granovetter, 1985).

We also expect that this change in the frame of reference may occur when firms are competing in high-technology intensive industries. This type of industry demands a highly specialized human capital. In most cases, hiring a family member is not even a choice since they may not possess the expertise needed. Hiring a family member could jeopardize SEW up to the point of threatening the survival of the company. In these cases, the relevance of general and technical industry-specific knowledge is so crucial that the desire to preserve the firm's SEW takes a backseat and family owners will be willing to implement the necessary HR practices to attract and retain the most suitable candidates. These arguments lead us to establish the following proposition:

**Proposition 22.** Family-owned firms are more likely to compromise on the use of SEW as a determinant criterion for adopting HR practices under conditions of poor performance or when the firm faces a major competitive threat.

Evidence so far has also demonstrated that emphasis on SEW preservation is reduced as the firm moves through generations (Gomez-Mejia et al., 2007), since the degree of family identification, influence, and personal investment in the firm changes as the firm transitions from one generation to the other

(Athanassiou et al., 2002; Gersick, Lansberg, Desjardins, & Dunn, 1999; Mishra & McConaughy, 1999; Chua et al., 2003; Schulze et al., 2003). Based on that, we also argue that decisions regarding HR practices would be more financially driven as the family-owned firm moves from founding-family-controlled and -managed firm to a firm that is owned by an extended family and is professionally managed. This would naturally explain the abundant anecdotal evidence that shows how the degree of a family-owned firm's professionalization increases as a firm moves through generations. Therefore,

**Proposition 23.** Family-owned firms are more likely to compromise on the use of SEW as a determinant criterion for adopting HR practices as the firm moves through generations.

Lastly, we also expect HR practices to be a reflection of the family's power and influence within the organization. The SEW approach states that since problem framing and willingness to take risks depend on subjective utilities of the decision makers, family owners need to have enough discretion within the organization to impose their goals of SEW preservation (Berrone et al., 2010). Therefore, family owners need sufficient power within the company to impose desired HR policies. In this sense, we would expect decisions regarding HR policies in family-owned firms to become more financially oriented as the family influence declines within the organization. This could happen, for instance, when ownership changes occur in the family-owned firm with the majority of shares held by large institutional shareholders rather than by dispersed minority shareholders. Because well-planned HR practices can enhance a firm's reputation, institutional investors are likely to use their influence over a firm's managers to professionalize and adopt more performance-oriented HR practices. These arguments lead to our last proposition:

**Proposition 24.** Family-owned firms are less likely to use SEW as a determinant criterion for adopting HR practices as family influence decreases in the organization.

## CONCLUDING COMMENTS

As argued in this chapter, family-owned firms are likely to be guided by a different set of criteria in adopting HR practices. This uniqueness cannot be explained by other variables associated with family ownership such as firm size, industry, or entrepreneurship. We suggest that the main difference between family- and non-family-owned firms revolves around the importance of preserving the family's SEW among the former. Because family business owners place a high priority on preserving this endowment, this will be reflected in the adoption of various HR practices belonging to the three categories of employee skills, employee performance and reward systems, and employee involvement and communications. The main challenge for the future will be to empirically test some of the propositions that are developed here.

# REFERENCES

Adams, J. S. (1965). Inequity in social exchange. In: L. Berkowitz (Ed.), *Advances in experimental social psychology* (Vol. 2, pp. 267–299). New York: Academic Press.

Adkins, L. (1995). *Gendered work: Sexuality, family and the labour market.* Buckingham: OU Press.

Aldrich, H., & Langton, N. (1998). *Human resource management practices and organizational life cycles. Frontier of entrepreneurship research* (pp. 349–357). Babson Park, MA: Batson College Center for Entrepreneurial Studies.

Anderson, R., Mansi, S., & Reeb, D. (2003). Founding family ownership and the agency cost of debt. *Journal of Financial Economics, 68,* 263–285.

Anderson, R. C., & Reeb, D. M. (2003). Founding-family ownership and firm performance: Evidence from the S&P 500. *The Journal of Finance, LVIII,* 1301–1328.

Aronoff, C. E., & Ward, J. L. (1995). Family-owned businesses: A thing of the past or a model for the future?. *Family Business Review, 8,* 121–130.

Arregle, J. L., Hitt, M. A., Sirmon, D., & Very, P. (2007). The development of organizational social capital and its performance implications: Insights from family-owned firms. *Journal of Management Studies, 44,* 73–95.

Astrachan, J. H. (1988). Family-owned firm and community culture. *Family Business Review, 1,* 165–189.

Astrachan, J. H., Allen, E., Spinelli, S., Wittmeyer, C., & Glucksman, S. (2003). *American family business survey 2002.* New York: George and Robin Raymond Family Business Institute.

Astrachan, J. H., Klein, S. B., & Smyrnois, K. X. (2002). The F-Pec scale of family influence: A proposal for solving the family business definition problem. *Family Business Review, 15,* 45–58.

Astrachan, J. H., & Kolenko, T. A. (1994). A neglected factor explaining family business success: Human resource practices. *Family Business Review, 7,* 251–262.

Athanassiou, N., Crittenden, W. F., Kelly, L. M., & Marquez, P. (2002). Founder centrality effects on the Mexican family-owned firm's top management group: Firm culture, strategic vision and goals, and firm performance. *Journal of World Business, 37,* 139–150.

Bailey, T. (1992). *Discretionary effort and the organization of work: Employee participation and work reform since Hawthorne.* Columbia University: Sloan Foundation.

Barach, J. A., Gantisky, J., Carlson, J. A., & Doochin, B. A. (1988). Entry of the next generation: Strategic challenge for family business. *Journal of Small Business Management, 26,* 49–56.

Barnett, T., & Kellermanns, F. W. (2006). Are we family and are we treated as family? Nonfamily employees' perceptions of justice in the family-owned firm. *Entrepreneurship: Theory & Practice, 30,* 837–854.

Barney, J. (1991). Firm resources and sustained competitive advantage. *Journal of Management, 17,* 99–120.

Barron, J. M., Black, D. A., & Loewenstein, M. A. (1987). Employer size: The implications for search, training, capital investment, starting wages, and wage growth. *Journal of Labor Economics, 5,* 76–89.

Bartholomeusz, S., & Tanewski, G. A. (2006). The relationship between family-owned firms and corporate governance. *Journal of Small Business Management, 44,* 245–267.

Beckhard, R., & Dyer, W. G., Jr. (1983). Managing change in the family-owned firm – issues and strategies. *Sloan Management Review, 24,* 59–65.

Beehr, T. A., Drexler, J. A., Jr., & Faulkner, S. (1997). Working in small family businesses: Empirical comparisons to non-family businesses. *Journal of Organizational Behavior, 18,* 297–312.

Berrone, P., Cruz, C., & Gomez-Mejia, L. R. (2011). Socioemotional wealth in family firms: A review and a future research agenda. *Family Business Review* (forthcoming).

Berrone, P., Cruz, C., Gomez-Mejia, L. R., & Larraza, M. (2010). Socio-emotional wealth and corporate responses to institutional pressures: Do family controlled firms pollute less? *Administrative Science Quarterly, 55,* 82–113.

Bhattacharya, U., & Ravikumar, B. (2004). From cronies to professionals: The evolution of family-owned firms. In: E. Klein (Ed.), *Capital formation, governance and banking.* Hauppauge, New York: Financial Institutions and Service Series, Nova Science Publishers.

Bierhoff, H. W., Cohen, R. L., & Greenberg, J. (1986). *Justice in social relations.* New York: Plenum.

Bies, R. J., & Moag, J. F. (1986). Interactional justice: Communication criteria of fairness. In: B. H. Sheppard & M. H. Bazerman (Eds), *Research on negotiations in organizations* (Vol. 1, pp. 43–55). Greenwich, CT: JAI Press.

Blau, P. M. (1964). *Exchange and power in social life.* New York: Wiley.

Blondel, C., Carlock, R. S., & Heyden, L. V. d. (2000). Fair process: Seeking justice in family-owned firms. In: P. Poutziouris (Ed.), *Tradition or enterprise in the new economy* (pp. 33–46). Manchester: The University of Manchester Business School.

Boselie, P., Dietz, G., & Boone, C. (2005). Commonalities and contradictions in HRM and performance research. *Human Resource Management Journal, 15,* 67–94.

Brass, D. J. (1995). A social network perspective on human resource management. *Research in Personnel and Human Resource Management, 13,* 39–79.

Bubolz, M. M. (2001). Family as source, user and builder of human capital. *Journal of Socioeconomics, 30,* 129–131.

Burkart, M., Panunzi, F., & Shleifer, A. (2003). Family-owned firms. *Journal of Finance, 58,* 2167–2201.

Cabrera-Suárez, K. (2005). Leadership transfer and the successor's development in the family-owned firm. *Leadership Quarterly, 16,* 71–96.

Cabrera-Suárez, K., De Saá-Pérez, P., & Garcia-Almeida, D. (2001). The succession process from a resource and knowledge-based view of the firm. *Family Business Review, 14,* 37–48.

Carrasco-Hernandez, A., & Sanchez-Marin, G. (2007). The determinants of employee compensation in family-owned firms: Empirical evidence. *Family Business Review, 20,* 215–228.

Carsrud, A. L. (2006). "Are we family and are we treated as family? Nonfamily employees' perceptions of justice in the family firm": It all depends on perceptions of family, fairness, equity and justice. *Entrepreneurship Theory and Practice, 30*, 855–860.

Casson, M. (1999). The economics of family-owned firm. *Scandinavian Economic History Review, 47*, 10–23.

Castanias, R. P., & Helfat, C. E. (1991). Managerial resources and rents. *Journal of Management, 17*, 155–171.

Castanias, R. P., & Helfat, C. E. (1992). Managerial and windfall rents in the market for corporate control. *Journal of Economic Behavior and Organization, 18*, 153–184.

Cawley, B. D., Keeping, L. M., & Levy, P. E. (1998). Participation in the performance appraisal process and employee reactions: A meta-analytic review of field investigations. *Journal of Applied Psychology, 83*, 615–633.

Chrisman, J. J., & Chang, E. P. C. (2007). Are family managers agents or stewards? An exploratory study in privately held family-owned firms. *Journal of Business Research, 60*, 1030–1038.

Chrisman, J. J., Chua, J. H., & Litz, R. (2003). A unified systems perspective of family-owned firm performance: An extension and integration. *Journal of Business Venturing, 18*, 467–472.

Chrisman, J. J., Chua, J. H., & Litz, R. (2004). Comparing the agency costs of family and non-family-owned firms: Conceptual issues and exploratory evidence. *Entrepreneurship Theory and Practice, 28*, 335–354.

Chua, J. H., Chrisman, J. J., & Bergiel, E. B. (2009). An agency theoretic analysis of the professionalized family-owned firm. *Entrepreneurship: Theory & Practice, 33*, 355–372.

Chua, J. H., Chrisman, J. J., & Sharma, P. (2003). Succession and nonsuccession concerns of family-owned firms and agency relationships with nonfamily managers. *Family Business Review, 16*, 89–107.

Coleman, J. S. (1988). Social capital in the creation of human capital. *American Journal of Sociology, 94*, 95–120.

Coleman, J. S. (1990). *Foundations of social theory*. Cambridge, MA: Harvard University Press.

Colli, A. (2003). *The history of family business, 1850–2000*. Cambridge: Cambridge University Press.

Covin, T. J. (1994a). Profiling preference for employment in family-owned firms. *Family Business Review, 7*, 287–296.

Covin, T. J. (1994b). Perceptions of family-owned firms: The impact of gender and educational level. *Journal of Small Business Management, 32*, 29–39.

Crane, M. (1985). How to keep families from feuding. In: P. C. Rosenblatt, L. deMik, R. M. Anderson & P. A. Johnson (Eds), *The family in business* (pp. 458–463). San Francisco: Jossey-Bass.

Cropanzano, R., & Greenberg, J. (1997). Progress in organizational justice: 'Tunneling through the maze'. In: L. T. Robertson & C. L. Cooper (Eds), *International review of industrial and organizational psychology* (pp. 317–372). New York: Wiley.

Cruz, C., Gomez-Mejia, L. R., & Becerra, M. (2010). Perceptions of benevolence and the design of agency contracts: CEO-TMT relationships in family-owned firms. *Academy of Management Journal, 53*, 69–89.

Cruz, C., Justo, R., & De Castro, J. (2011). Does family employment enhance MSEs performance? Integrating socioemotional wealth and family embeddedness perspectives. *Journal of Business Venturing, 26* (forthcoming).

Cucculelli, M., & Micucci, G. (2008). Family succession and firm performance: Evidence from Italian family-owned firms. *Journal of Corporate Finance, 14*, 17–31.

Cummings, T. G., & Worley, C. G. (2009). *Organization development and change* (9th ed.). Mason, OH: South-Western Cengage Learning.

Cutcher-Gershenfeld, J. (1991). The impact on economic performance of a transformation in workplace relations. *Industrial and Labor Relations Review, 44*, 241–260.

Cyr, L. A., Johnson, D. E., & Welbourne, T. M. (2000). Human resources in initial public offering firms: Do venture capitalists make a difference? *Entrepreneurship: Theory and Practice, 25*, 77–91.

Daily, C. M., & Dollinger, M. J. (1992). An empirical examination of ownership structure in family and professionally managed firms. *Family Business Review, 5*, 117–136.

Danco, L. A. (1987). Foreword. In: J. L. Ward (Ed.), *Keeping the family business healthy: How to plan for continuing growth, profitability, and family leadership.* San Francisco: Jossey-Bass.

Davis, J. H., Schoorman, F. D., & Donaldson, L. (1997). Toward a stewardship theory of management. *Academy of Management Review, 22*, 20–47.

Davis, P. (1983). Realizing the potential of family businesses. *Organizational Dynamics, 12*, 47–56.

Davis, P. S., & Harveston, P. D. (1999). In the founder's shadow: Conflict in the family-owned firm. *Family Business Review, 12*, 311–324.

Davis, P. S., & Harveston, P. D. (2001). The phenomenon of substantive conflict in the family-owned firm: A cross-generational study. *Journal of Small Business Management, 39*, 14–30.

DeAngelo, H., & DeAngelo, L. (1985). Managerial ownership of voting rights: A study of public corporations with dual classes of common stock. *Journal of Financial Economics, 14*, 33–69.

De Kok, J. M. P., Uhlaner, L. M., & Thurik, A. R. (2006). Professional HRM practices in family-owned-managed enterprises. *Journal of Small Business Management, 44*, 441–460.

Donaldson, L., & Davis, J. (1991). Stewardship theory or agency theory: CEO governance and shareholder returns. *Australian Journal of Management, 16*, 49–64.

Donckels, R., & Lambrecht, J. (1999). The re-emergence of family-based enterprises in east central Europe: What can be learned from family business research in the Western world? *Family Business Review, 12*, 171–188.

Douhitt, E. A., & Aiello, J. R. (2001). The role of participation and control in the effects of computer monitoring on fairness perceptions, task satisfaction, and performance. *Journal of Applied Psychology, 86*, 867–874.

Dyer, W. G., Jr. (1988). Culture and continuity in family-owned firms. *Family Business Review, 1*, 37–50.

Dyer, W. G., Jr. (1989). Integrating professional management into a family-owned business. *Family Business Review, 2*, 221–235.

Dyer, W. G., Jr. (1992). *The entrepreneurial experience: Confronting career dilemmas of the start-up executive.* San Francisco: Jossey-Bass.

Dyer, W. G., Jr. (1994). Potential contributions of organizational behavior to the study of family-owned businesses. *Family Business Review, 7*, 109–131.

Dyer, W. G., Jr., & Mortensen, S. P. (2006). Entrepreneurship and family business in a hostile environment: The case of Lithuania. *Family Business Review, 18*, 247–258.

Dyer, W. G., Jr., & Sanchez, M. (1998). Current state of family business theory and practice as reflected in the Family Business Review 1988-1997. *Family Business Review, 11*, 287–295.

Earley, P. C., & Lind, E. A. (1987). Procedural justice and participation in task selection: The role of control in mediating justice judgments. *Journal of Personality and Social Psychology, 52*, 1148–1160.

Eckrich, C., & Loughead, T. (1996). Effects of family business membership and psychological separation on the career development of late adolescents. *Family Business Review, 9*, 369–386.

Eddleston, K. A., & Kellermanns, F. W. (2007). Destructive and productive family relationships: A stewardship theory perspective. *Journal of Business Venturing, 22*, 545–565.

Edwards, J. R. (1991). Person-job fit: A conceptual integration, literature review, and methodological critique. In: C. L. R. I. T. Cooper (Ed.), *International review of industrial and organizational psychology* (Vol. 6, pp. 283–357). Chichester: Wiley.

Eisenberger, R., Armeli, S., Rexwinkel, B., Lynch, P. D., & Rhoades, L. (2001). Reciprocation of perceived organizational support. *Journal of Applied Psychology, 86*, 42–51.

Eisenberger, R., Huntington, R., Hutchison, S., & Sowa, D. (1986). Perceived organizational support. *Journal of Applied Psychology, 71*, 500–507.

Eisenhardt, K., & Bourgeois, L. J., III. (1988). Politics of strategic decision making in high-velocity environments: Toward a Midrange Theory. *Academy of Management Journal, 31*, 737–770.

Fama, E., & Jensen, M. (1983). Separation of ownership and control. *Journal of Law and Economics, 26*, 301–325.

Ferris, G. R., Hall, A. T., Royle, M. T., & Martocchio, J. J. (2004). Theoretical developments in the field of human resource management: Issues and challenges for the future. *Organizational Analysis, 12*, 231–254.

Fiegener, M. K., Brown, B. M., Prince, R. A., & File, K. M. (1996). Passing on strategic vision. *Journal of Small Business Management, 34*, 15–26.

Frenkel, S. J., & Lee, B. H. (2010). Do high performance work practices work in South Korea? *Industrial Relations Journal, 41*, 479–504.

Gallo, M. A., & Estape, M. J. (1992). *Internationalization of the family business*, Research paper No. 230, IESE Business School. Barcelona: IESE.

Gallo, M. A., Tapies, J., & Cappuyns, K. (2004). Comparison of family and nonfamily business. *Family Business Review, 17*, 303–318.

Gallo, M. A., & Vilaseca, A. (1998). A financial perspective on structure, conduct and performance in the family-owned firm: An empirical study. *Family Business Review, 11*, 35–47.

Galve-Górriz, C., & Salas-Fumás, V. (1996). Ownership structure and firm performance: Some empirical evidence from Spain. *Managerial and Decision Economics, 17*, 575–586.

Garcia-Alvarez, E., Lopez-Sintas, J., & Gonzalvo, P. S. (2002). Socialization patterns of successors in first- to second-generation family businesses. *Family Business Review, 15*, 189–203.

Gargiulo, M., & Benassi, M. (2000). Trapped in your own net? Network cohesion, structural holes, and the adaptation of social capital. *Organization Science, 11*, 183–196.

Gersick, K. E., Davis, J. A., Hampton, M. M., & Lansberg, I. (1997). *Generation to generation: Life cycles of the family business*. Boston, MA: Harvard Business School Press.

Gersick, K. E., Lansberg, I., Desjardins, M., & Dunn, B. (1999). Staging and transitions: Managing change in the family business. *Family Business Review, 12,* 287–297.

Goffee, R., & Scase, R. (1985). Proprietorial control in family-owned firms—some functions of "quasi-organic" management systems. *Journal of Management Studies, 22,* 53–68.

Gomez-Mejia, L. R., Balkin, D. B., & Cardy, R. L. (2012). *Managing human resources.* New York: Pearson-Prentice Hall.

Gomez-Mejia, L. R., Berrone, P., & Franco-Santos, M. (2010a). *Compensation and organizational performance – theory, research and practice.* New York: M.E. Sharpe.

Gomez-Mejia, L. R., Haynes, K. T., Nunez-Nickel, M., Jacobson, K. J. L., & Moyano-Fuentes, J. (2007). Socio-emotional wealth and business risks in family-controlled firms: Evidence from Spanish olive oil mills. *Administrative Science Quarterly, 52,* 106–137.

Gomez-Mejia, L. R., Hoskisson, R., Makri, M., Sirmon, D., & Campbell, J. (2011). *Innovation and the preservation of socioemotional wealth in family controlled high technology firms.* Unpublished technical report. Management Department, Texas A & M University, College Station, Texas.

Gomez-Mejia, L. R., Larraza, M., & Makri, M. (2003). The determinants of executive compensation in family-controlled public corporations. *Academy of Management Journal, 46,* 226–237.

Gomez-Mejia, L. R., Makri, M., & Larraza, M. (2010b). Diversification decisions in family-controlled firms. *Journal of Management Studies, 47,* 223–252.

Gomez-Mejia, L. R., Nunez-Nickel, M., & Gutierrez, I. (2001). The role of family ties in agency contracts. *Academy of Management Journal, 44,* 81–95.

Gorter, C., & Van Ommeren, J. N. (1999). Sequencing, timing and filling rates of recruitment methods. *Applied Economics, 31,* 1149–1160.

Granovetter, M. (1985). Economic action and social structure: The problem of embeddedness. *American Journal of Sociology, 91,* 481–510.

Greenberg, J. (1987). A taxonomy of organizational justice theories. *Academy of Management Review, 12,* 9–22.

Greenberg, J. (1990). Organizational justice: Yesterday, today, and tomorrow. *Journal of Management, 16,* 399–432.

Greenhaus, J. H., & Powell, G. N. (2006). When work and family are allies: A theory of work-family enrichment. *Academy of Management Review, 31,* 72–92.

Guest, D., & Conway, N. (2001). Communicating the psychological contract: An employer perspective. *Human Resource Management Journal, 12,* 22–38.

Haggard, D. L., Dougherty, T. W., Turban, D. B., & Wilbanks, J. E. (in press). Who is a mentor? A review of evolving definitions and implications for research. *Journal of Management* (forthcoming).

Hall, A., Melin, L., & Nordqvist, M. (2001). Entrepreneurship as radical change in the family business: Exploring the role of cultural patterns. *Family Business Review, 14,* 193–208.

Hall, P. D. (1988). A historical overview of family firms in the United States. *Family Business Review, 1,* 51–68.

Handler, W. C. (1989). Methodological issues and considerations in studying family businesses. *Family Business Review, 2,* 257–276.

Handler, W. C. (1990). Succession in family-owned firms: A mutual role adjustment between entrepreneur and next generation family members. *Entrepreneurship: Theory & Practice, 15,* 37–51.

Handler, W. C., & Kram, K. E. (1988). Succession in family-owned firms: The problem of resistance. *Family Business Review, 1*, 361–381.

Harris, R., & Reid, R. (2008). Barriers to growth in family-owned smaller businesses. In: R. Barrett & S. Mayson (Eds), *International handbook of entrepreneurship and HRM*. Cheltenham: Edward Elgar Publishing.

Harveston, P., Davis, P., & Lyden, J. (1997). Succession planning in family business: The impact of owner gender. *Family Business Review, 10*, 373–396.

Heery, E., & Noon, M. (2001). *A dictionary of human resource management*. Oxford: Oxford University Press.

Hennerkes, B. H. (1998). *Familienunternehmen sichern und optimieren*. Frankfurt, Germany: Campus Verlag.

Hershon, S. (1975). *The problem of management succession in the family business*. Unpublished Dissertation, Harvard Business School.

Holland, P. G., & Boulton, W. R. (1984). Balancing the family and the business in a family business. *Business Horizons, 27*, 16–21.

Holzer, H. J. (1987). *Hiring procedures in the firm: Their economic determinants and outcomes*. NBER Working Paper No. 2185. National Bureau of Economic Research.

Hornsby, J. S., & Kuratko, D. K. (1990). Human resource management in small firms: Critical issues for the 1990. *Journal of Small Business Management, 28*, 9–18.

Horton, T. P. (1982). The baton of succession. *Management Review, July*, 2–3.

Howorth, C., Westhead, P., & Wright, M. (2004). Buyouts, information asymmetry and the family management dyad. *Journal of Business Venturing, 19*, 509–524.

Hoy, F. (2003). Legitimizing family business scholarship in organizational research and education. *Entrepreneurship: Theory and Practice, 27*, 417–422.

Hunter, J. E., & Schmidt, F. L. (1982). Ability tests: Economic benefits versus the issue of fairness. *Industrial Relations, 21*, 293–308.

Huselid, M. A. (1995). The impact of human resource practices on turnover, productivity, and corporate financial performance. *Academy of Management Journal, 38*, 635–672.

Jackson, S. E., Schuler, R. S., & Rivero, J. C. (1989). Organizational characteristics as predictors of personnel practices. *Personnel Psychology, 42*, 727–786.

James, H. S. (1999). Owner as manager, extended horizons and the family-owned firm. *International Journal of the Economics of Business, 6*, 41–55.

Jensen, M. C., & Meckling, W. H. (1976). Theory of the firm: Managerial behavior, agency costs and ownership structure. *Journal of Financial Economics, 3*, 305–360.

Jones, C. D., Makri, M., & Gomez-Mejia, L. R. (2008). Affiliate directors and perceived risk bearing in publicly traded, family controlled firms: The case of diversification. *Entrepreneurship: Theory and Practice, 32*, 1007–1026.

Jones, D. C., Kalmi, P., & Kauhanen, A. (2010). How does employee involvement stack up? The effects of human resource management policies on performance in a retail firm. *Industrial Relations, 49*, 1–21.

Jonovic, D. L. (1989). Outside review in a wider context: An alternative to the classic board. *Family Business Review, 2*, 125–140.

Jorissen, A., Laveren, E., Martens, R., & Reheul, A. (2005). Real versus sample-based differences in comparative family business research. *Family Business Review, 18*, 229–246.

Kanter, R. M. (1989). Work and family in the United States: A critical review and agenda for research and policy. *Family Business Review, 2*, 77–114.

Kelly, L. M., Athanassiou, N., & Crittenden, W. F. (2000). Founder centrality and strategic behaviour in the family-owned firm. *Entrepreneurship Theory and Practice, 25*, 27–42.

Kepner, E. (1983). The family and the firm: A coevolutionary perspective. *Organizational Dynamics, 12*, 57–70.

Kets de Vries, M. (1993). The dynamics of family controlled firms: The good news and the bad news. *Organizational Dynamics, 21*, 59–68.

Kets de Vries, M. F. R. (1996). *Family business: Human dilemmas in family-owned firms.* London: International Thompson Business Press.

Kim, J., MacDuffie, J., & Pil, F. (2010). Employee voice and organizational performance: Team versus representative influence. *Human Relations, 63*, 371–394.

King, S. (2003). Organizational performance and conceptual capability: The relationship between organizational performance and successors' capability in a family-owned firm. *Family Business Review, 16*, 173–182.

Klein, S. B. (2000). Family businesses in Germany: Significance and structure. *Family Business Review, 13*, 157–181.

Koch, M. J., & McGrath, R. G. (1996). Improving labor productivity: Human resource management policies do matter. *Strategic Management Journal, 17*, 335–354.

Kotey, B., & Folker, C. (2007). Employee training in SMEs: Effect of size and firm type-family and non-family. *Journal of Small Business Management, 45*, 214–238.

Kram, K. E. (1983). Phases of the mentoring relationship. *Academy of Management Journal, 26*, 608–625.

Kristof, A. L. (1996). Person-organization fit: An integrative review of its conceptualizations, measurement, and implications. *Personnel Psychology, 49*, 1–49.

Kristof-Brown, A., Barrick, M. R., & Stevens, C. K. (2005). When opposites attract: A multi-sample demonstration of complementary person-team fit on extraversion. *Journal of Personality, 73*, 935–957.

Kuvaas, B. (2007). An exploration of how the employee–organization relationship affects the linkage between perception of developmental human resource practices and employee outcomes. *Journal of Management Studies, 45*, 1–25.

Lansberg, I. (1988). The succession conspiracy. *Family Business Review, 1*, 119–143.

Lansberg, I., & Astrachan, J. H. (1994). Influence of family relationships on succession planning and training: The importance of mediating factors. *Family Business Review, 7*, 39–59.

Lansberg, I. S. (1983). Managing human resources in family-owned firms: The problem of institutional overlap. *Organizational Dynamics, 12*, 39–46.

La Porta, R., Lopez-de-Silanes, F., & Shleifer, A. (1999). Corporate ownership around the world. *Journal of Finance, LIV,* 471–517.

Le Breton-Miller, I., Miller, D., & Steier, L. P. (2004). Toward an integrative model of effective FOB succession. *Entrepreneurship: Theory and Practice, 28*, 305–328.

Lee, S. (2008). A theoretical framework on the role of HRM practices in family business succession. In: P. H. Phan & J. E. Butler (Eds), *Theoretical developments and future research in family business* (pp. 261–285). Charlotte, NC: Information Age Publishing.

Lee, K. S., Lim, G. H., & Lim, W. S. (2003). Family business succession: Appropriation risk and choice of successor. *Academy of Management Review, 28*, 657–666.

Leon-Guerrero, A., McCann, J. E., & Haley, J. D. (1998). A study of practice utilisation in family-owned firms. *Family Business Review, 11*, 107–120.

Lepak, D. P., Liao, H., Chung, Y., & Harden, E. E. (2006). A conceptual review of human resource management systems in strategic human resource management. *Research in Personnel and Human Resource Management, 25,* 217–271.

Leung, A. (2003). Different ties for different needs: Recruitment practices of entrepreneurial firms at different developmental phases. *Human Resource Management, 42,* 303–320.

Levine, D., & Tyson, L. (1990). Participation, productivity and the firm's environment. In: A.S. Blinder (Ed.), *Paying for productivity* (pp. 183–243). Washington, DC: Brookings Institutions.

Levinson, H. (1971). Conflicts that plague the family business. *Harvard Business Review, 49,* 90–98.

Liao, H., Toya, K., Lepak, D. P., & Hong, Y. (2009). Do they see eye to eye? Management and employee perspectives of high-performance work systems and influence processes on service quality. *Journal of Applied Psychology, 94,* 371–391.

Litz, R. (1995). The family business: Toward definitional clarity. *Family Business Review, 8,* 71–81.

Lubatkin, M. H., Durand, R., & Ling, Y. (2007a). The missing lens in family-owned firm governance theory: A self-other typology of parental altruism. *Journal of Business Research, 60,* 1022–1029.

Lubatkin, M. H., Ling, Y., & Schulze, B. (2007b). An organizational justice-based view of self-control and agency costs in family-owned firms. *Journal of Management Studies, 44,* 955–971.

Lubatkin, M. H., Schulze, W. S., Ling, Y., & Dino, R. N. (2005). The effects of parental altruism on the governance of family-managed firms. *Journal of Organizational Behavior, 26,* 313–330.

Lyman, A. R. (1991). Customer service: Does family ownership make a difference?. *Family Business Review, 4,* 303–324.

Ma, R., & Allen, D. G. (2009). Recruiting across cultures: A value-based model of recruitment. *Human Resource Management Review, 19,* 334–346.

MacDuffie, J. P. (1995). Human resource bundles and manufacturing performance: Organizational logic and flexible production systems in the world auto industry. *Industrial and Labor Relations Review, 48,* 197–221.

Major, D. A., Kozlowski, S. W. J., Chao, G. T., & Gardner, P. D. (1995). A longitudinal investigation of newcomer expectations, early socialization outcomes, and the moderating effects of role development factors. *Journal of Applied Psychology, 80,* 418–431.

Marsden, P. V., & Gorman, E. H. (2001). Social networks, job changes, and recruitment. In: I. Berg & A. L. Kalleberg (Eds), *Sourcebook of labor markets: Evolving structures and processes* (pp. 467–502). New York: Kluwer Academic Publishers.

Masterson, S. S., Lewis, K., Goldman, B. M., & Taylor, M. S. (2000). Integrating justice and social exchange: The differing effects of fair procedures and treatments on work relationships. *Academy of Management Journal, 43,* 738–748.

Matlay, H. (2002). HRD strategies in small, family and non-family businesses: a critical perspective. In: D. Fletcher (Ed.), *Understanding the small family business* (pp. 138–153). London: Routledge.

Matthews, C. H., Moore, T. W., & Fialko, A. S. (1999). Succession in the family-owned firm: A cognitive categorization perspective. *Family Business Review, 12,* 159–169.

McCauley, C. D., & Douglas, C. A. (2004). Developmental relationships. In: C. D. McCauley, R. S. Moxley & E. Van Velsor (Eds), *The center for creative leadership: Handbook of leadership development* (pp. 160–193). San Francisco: Jossey-Bass.

McCollom, M. (1988). Integration in the family-owned firm: When the family system replaces controls and culture. *Family Business Review, 1,* 399–417.

McConaughy, D. L. (2000). Family CEOs vs non-family CEOs in the family-controlled firm: An examination of level and sensitivity of pay to performance. *Family Business Review, 13,* 121–131.

Miller, D., & Le Breton-Miller, I. (2005). *Managing for the long run: Lessons in competitive advantage from great family businesses.* Boston, MA: Harvard Business School Press.

Miller, D., Le Breton-Miller, I., & Scholnick, B. (2008). Stewardship vs. stagnation: An empirical comparison of small family and non-family businesses. *Journal of Management Studies, 45,* 52–78.

Mishra, C. S., & McConaughy, D. L. (1999). Founding family control and capital structure: The risk of loss of control and the aversion to debt. *Entrepreneurship: Theory and Practice, 23,* 53–64.

Mishra, C. S., Randoy, T., & Jensen, J. I. (2001). The effect of founding family influence on firm value and corporate governance. *Journal of International Financial Management and Accounting, 12,* 235–259.

Mitchell, R. K., Morse, E. A., & Sharma, P. (2003). The transacting cognitions of nonfamily employees in the family businesses setting. *Journal of Business Venturing, 18,* 533–551.

Mohr, R. D., & Zoghi, C. (2008). High Involvement work design and job satisfaction. *Industrial and Labor Relations Review, 61,* 275–296.

Montgomery, J. (1991). Social networks and labor market outcomes: Toward an economic analysis. *American Economic Review, 81,* 1408–1418.

Morck, R., & Yeung, B. (2003). Agency problems in large family business groups. *Entrepreneurship: Theory and Practice, 27,* 367–382.

Morck, R., & Yeung, B. (2004). Family control and the rent seeking society. *Entrepreneurship: Theory and Practice, 28,* 391–409.

Morris, M. H., Williams, R. O., Allen, J. A., & Avila, R. A. (1997). Correlates of success in family business transitions. *Journal of Business Venturing, 12,* 385–401.

Nahapiet, J., & Ghoshal, S. (1998). Social capital, intellectual capital, and the organizational advantage. *Academy of Management Review, 23,* 242–266.

Nicholson, N., & Björnberg, A. (2008). The shape of things to come – emotional ownership and the next generation in the family-owned firm. In: J. Tapies & J. Ward (Eds), *Family values and value creation: The fostering of enduring values within family – owned businesses.* New York: Palgrave Macmillan.

Nishii, L. H., Lepak, D. P., & Schneider, B. (2008). Employee attributions of the "why" of HR practices: Their effects on employee attitudes and behaviors, and customer satisfaction. *Personnel Psychology, 61,* 503–545.

Oliver, C. (1997). Sustainable competitive advantage: Combining institutional and resource-based views. *Strategic Management Journal, 18,* 697–713.

O'Reilly, C. A., Chatman, J., & Caldwell, D. F. (1991). People and organizational culture: A profile comparison approach to assessing person-organization fit. *Academy of Management Journal, 34,* 487–516.

Ostroff, C., & Bowen, D. E. (2000). Moving HR to a higher level. In: K. J. Klein & S. W. Kozlowski (Eds), *Multilevel theory, research, and methods in organizations: Foundations, extensions, and new directions* (pp. 211–266). San Francisco: Jossey-Bass.

Pazy, A., & Ganzach, Y. (2009). Pay contingency and the effects of perceived organizational and supervisor support on performance and commitment. *Journal of Management, 35,* 1007–1025.

Piercy, N. F., Cravens, D. W., Lane, N., & Vorhies, D. W. (2006). Driving organizational citizenship behaviors and salesperson in-role behavior performance: The role of management control and perceived organizational support. *Journal of Academy of Marketing Science, 34,* 244–262.

Ployhart, R. E., Schneider, B., & Schmitt, N. (2006). *Staffing organizations: Contemporary practice and theory.* Mahwah, NJ: Lawrence Erlbaum Associates.

Pondy, L. (1969). Effects of size, complexity and ownership on administrative intensity. *Administrative Science Quarterly, 14,* 47–60.

Poza, E. J., Alfred, T., & Maheshwari, A. (1997). Stakeholder perceptions of culture and management practices in family and family-owned firms. *Family Business Review, 10,* 135–155.

Ratwani, K. L., Zaccaro, S. J., Garven, S., & Geller, D. S. (2010). In: M. G. Rothstein & R.J. Burke (Eds), *The role of developmental social networks in effective leader self-learning processes.* Cheltenham: Edward Elgar.

Reid, R., Morrow, T., Kelly, B., Adams, J., & McCartan, P. (2000). Human resource management practices in SMEs: A comparative analysis of family and non-family-owned firms. *Irish Business and Administration Research, 21,* 157–181.

Reid, R. S., & Adams, J. S. (2001). Human resource management: A survey of practices within family and non-family-owned firms. *Journal of European Industrial Training, 25,* 310–320.

Riggio, R. (2007). *Introduction to industrial/organizational psychology* (5th ed.). Upper Saddle River, NJ: Pearson Education.

Roberson, Q. M., Moye, N. A., & Locke, E. A. (1999). Identifying a missing link between participation and satisfaction: The mediating role of procedural justice perceptions. *Journal of Applied Psychology, 84,* 585–593.

Rosen, C. C., Harris, K. J., & Kacmar, K. M. (in press). LMX, context perceptions, and performance: An uncertainty management perspective, *Journal of Management* (forthcoming).

Rosenblatt, P. C., de Mik, L., Anderson, R. M., & Johnson, P. A. (1985). *The family in business.* San Francisco: Jossey-Bass.

Rosenzweig, M. R., & Wolpin, K. I. (1985). Specific experience, household structure, and intergenerational transfers: Farm family land and labor arrangements in developing countries. *Quarterly Journal of Economics, 100,* 961–987.

Rousseau, D. M. (1989). Psychological and implied contracts in organizations. *Employee Rights and Responsibilities Journal, 2,* 121–139.

Rowley, T., Behrens, D., & Krackhardt, D. (2000). Redundant governance structures: An analysis of structural and relational embeddedness in the steel and semiconductor industries. *Strategic Management Journal, 21,* 369–386.

Saloner, G. (1985). Old boy networks as screening mechanism. *Journal of Labor Economics, 3,* 255–267.

Scase, R., & Goffee, R. (1987). *The real world of the small business owner* (2nd ed.). London: Routledge.

Schulze, W. S., Lubatkin, M. H., & Dino, R. N. (2002). Altruism, agency, and the competitiveness of family-owned firms. *Managerial and Decision Economics, 23,* 247–259.

Schulze, W. S., Lubatkin, M. H., & Dino, R. N. (2003). Exploring the agency consequences of ownership dispersion among the directors of private family-owned firms. *Academy of Management Journal, 46*, 174–194.

Schulze, W. S., Lubatkin, M. H., Dino, R. N., & Buchholtz, A. K. (2001). Agency relationships in family-owned firms: Theory and evidence. *Organization Science, 12*, 99–116.

Schwab, D. P. (1982). Recruiting and organizational participation. In: K. Rowland & G. Ferris (Eds), *Personnel management* (pp. 103–127). Boston, MA: Allyn & Bacon.

Schweiger, D. M., & Leana, C. R. (1986). Participation in decision making. In: E. A. Locke (Ed.), *Generalizing from laboratory to field settings* (pp. 147–166). Lexington, MA: Lexington Books.

Sharma, P. (2004). An overview of family business studies: Current status and directions for the future. *Family Business Review, 17*, 1–36.

Sharma, P., Chrisman, J., & Chua, J. (1997). Strategic management of the family business: Past research and future challenges. *Family Business Review, 10*, 1–35.

Sharma, P., Chua, J. H., & Chrisman, J. J. (2000). Perceptions about the extent of succession planning in Canadian family firms. *Canadian Journal of Administrative Sciences, 17*, 233–244.

Sharma, P., & Irving, P. G. (2005). Four bases of family business successor commitment: Antecedents and consequences. *Entrepreneurship: Theory and Practice, 30*, 13–33.

Sharma, P., & Manikuti, S. (2005). Strategic divestments in family-owned firms: Role of family structure and community culture. *Entrepreneurship: Theory and Practice, 29*, 293–311.

Shore, L. M., & Tetrick, L. E. (1991). A construct validity study of the survey of perceived organizational support. *Journal of Applied Psychology, 76*, 637–643.

Shore, L. M., & Wayne, S. J. (1993). Commitment and employee behavior: Comparison of affective commitment and continuance commitment with perceived organizational support. *Journal of Applied Psychology, 78*, 774–780.

Simon, J. C., & Warner, T. (1992). Matchmaker, matchmaker: The effect of the old boy networks on job match quality, earnings and tenure. *Journal of Labor Economics, 10*, 306–330.

Sirmon, D., & Hitt, M. A. (2003). Creating wealth in family business through managing resources. *Entrepreneurship: Theory and Practice, 27*, 339–358.

Steel, R. P., Dilla, B. L., Lloyd, R. F., Mento, A. T., & Ovalle, N. K. (1985). Factors influencing the success and failure of two quality circles programs. *Journal of Management, 11*, 99–119.

Stein, J. (1989). Efficient capital markets, inefficient firms: A model of myopic corporate behavior. *Quarterly Journal of Economics, 103*, 655–669.

Subramony, M. (2009). A meta-analytic investigation of the relationship between HRM bundles and firm performance. *Human Resource Management, 48*, 745–768.

Tagiuri, R., & Davis, J. (1996). Bivalent attributes of the family-owned firm. *Family Business Review, 9*, 199–208.

Takeuchi, R., Chen, G., & Lepak, D. P. (2009). Through the looking glass of a social system: Cross-level effects of high-performance work systems on employees' attitudes. *Personnel Psychology, 62*, 1–29.

Thibaut, J., & Walker, L. (1975). *Procedural justice: A psychological analysis.* Hillsdale, NJ: Erlbaum.

Thomsen, S., & Pedersen, T. (2000). Ownership structure and economic performance in the largest European companies. *Strategic Management Journal, 21*, 689–705.

Toh, S., Morgeson, F. P., & Campion, M. A. (2008). Human resource configurations: Investigating fit with the organizational context. *Journal of Applied Psychology, 93,* 864–882.

Uhlaner, L. M. (2006). Business family as a team: Underlying force for sustained competitive advantage. In: P. Poutziouris, K. Smyrnios & S. Klein (Eds), *Handbook of research on family business.* Cheltenham: Edward Elgar Publishers.

Uzzi, B. (1997). Social structure and competition in interfirm networks: The paradox of embeddedness. *Administrative Science Quarterly, 42,* 35–67.

Van den Berghe, L. A. A., & Carchon, S. (2003). Agency relations within the family business system: An exploratory approach. *Corporate Governance: An International Review, 11,* 171–179.

Walker, G., Kogut, B., & Shan, W. (1997). Social capital, structural holes and the formation of an industry network. *Organization Science, 8,* 109–125.

Wang, Y., Watkings, D., Harris, N., & Spicer, K. (2004). The relationship between succession issues and business performance. *International Journal of Entrepreneurial Behavior & Research, 10,* 59–84.

Ward, J. L. (1987). *Keeping the family business healthy: How to plan for continuing growth, profitability, and family leadership.* San Francisco: Jossey-Bass.

Werner, S., & Tosi, H. L. (1995). Other people's money: The effects of ownership on compensation strategy and managerial pay. *Academy of Management Journal, 38,* 1672–1691.

Westhead, P., Cowling, M., & Howorth, C. (2001). The development of family companies: Management and ownership imperatives. *Family Business Review, 14,* 369–385.

Westhead, P., & Storey, D. (1997). *Training provision and the development of SMEs.* Research Report No. 26. London: HMSO.

Westhead, P., & Storey, D. J. (1999). Training provision and the development of small and medium sized enterprises: A critical review. *Scottish Journal of Adult and Continuing Education Lifelong Learning, 5,* 35–41.

Wheelock, J., & Baines, S. (1998). Dependency or self-reliance? The contradictory case of work in the UK small business families. *Journal of Family and Economic Issues, 19,* 53–74.

Wiseman, R. M., & Gomez-Mejia, L. R. (1998). A behavioral agency model of managerial risk taking. *Academy of Management Review, 22,* 133–153.

Wortman, M. S., Jr. (1994). Theoretical foundations for family-owned business: A conceptual and research-based paradigm. *Family Business Review, 7,* 3–27.

Wright, P. M., & Boswell, W. R. (2002). Desegregating HRM: A review and synthesis of micro and macro human resource management research. *Journal of Management, 28,* 247–276.

Wu, P., & Chaturvedi, S. (2009). The role of procedural justice and power distance in the relationship between high performance work systems and employee attitudes: A multilevel perspective. *Journal of Management, 35,* 1228–1247.

Yukl, G. (1989). Managerial leadership: A review of theory and research. *Journal of Management, 15,* 251–289.

Zahra, S. A. (2003). International expansion of U.S. manufacturing family businesses: The effect of ownership and involvement. *Journal of Business Venturing, 19,* 495–512.

Zellweger, T. M., & Astrachan, J. H. (2008). On the emotional value of owning a firm. *Family Business Review, 21,* 347–363.

# AN UNCERTAINTY REDUCTION MODEL OF RELATIONAL DEMOGRAPHY

## Prithviraj Chattopadhyay, Elizabeth George and Carmen Kaman Ng

## ABSTRACT

*In this chapter, we review relational demography literature underpinned by the similarity–attraction paradigm and status characteristics and social identity theories. We then develop an uncertainty reduction model of relational demography, which describes a two-stage process of uncertainty emergence and reduction in a workgroup setting. The first stage depicts how structural features of the workgroup (workgroup composition) and occupation (the legitimacy of its status hierarchy) induce two forms of uncertainty: uncertainty about group norms and uncertainty about instrumental outcomes. The second part of the model illustrates employees' choice of uncertainty reduction strategies, depending on the type of uncertainty they experience, and the status of their demographic categories. Implications for theory and practice are discussed.*

Research in Personnel and Human Resources Management, Volume 30, 219–251
Copyright © 2011 by Emerald Group Publishing Limited
ISSN: 0742-7301/doi:10.1108/S0742-7301(2011)0000030007

# INTRODUCTION

Organizations have become more diverse in terms of the demographic composition of their members. We work with colleagues who differ from us on a range of attributes such as gender, age, race, and functional background. Relational demography scholars have examined how demographic dissimilarity influences organizationally relevant outcomes such as employees' identification with their workgroup (Chattopadhyay, George, & Shulman, 2008; Gonzalez & DeNisi, 2009), organizational commitment (Liao, Joshi, & Chuang, 2004; Tsui, Egan, & O'Reilly, 1992), workgroup involvement (Hobman, Bordia, & Gallois, 2004), job performance (Chatman, Boisnier, Spataro, Anderson, & Berdahl, 2008; Joshi, Liao, & Jackson, 2006), citizenship behavior (Chattopadhyay, 1999; Riordan & Shore, 1997), withdrawal (Sacco & Schmitt, 2005), perceived discrimination (Avery, McKay, & Wilson, 2008), as well as affect at work (Chatman & O'Reilly, 2004; Chattopadhyay, Finn, & Ashkanasy, 2010).

Despite the many empirical studies, the results are mixed, and the social psychological process by which individuals are affected by being demographically different from peers are not fully understood yet (Lawrence, 1997; Riordan, 2000). Social identity theory (Tajfel & Turner, 1979, 1986) and self-categorization theory (Turner, 1975; Turner, Hogg, Oakes, Reicher, & Wetherell, 1987) – collectively referred to here as the social identity perspective – have been used most frequently by relational demography researchers. These two theories propose that individuals aim to enhance their social identity, as well as reduce their uncertainty, through group membership. Researchers, however, have mainly focused on the self-enhancement motive (e.g., Chattopadhyay, Tluchowska, & George, 2004b; Tsui et al., 1992), and ignored the uncertainty reduction motive (see Chattopadhyay, George, & Lawrence, 2004a; Goldberg, Riordan, & Schaffer, 2010, for exceptions). As a result, theoretical propositions regarding the role of uncertainty reduction are not fully articulated yet, and our understanding of the effects of relational demography remains incomplete. Furthermore, the idea of uncertainty reduction itself remains underdeveloped within the social identity perspective, so we take preliminary steps to theorize and elaborate on this idea.

Our goal in this chapter is to develop a fuller understanding of the role of uncertainty reduction (Hogg, 2001; Hogg & Abrams, 1993) in relational demography theorizing. Uncertainty reduction is considered a core motive of social identification, along with the self-enhancement motive (Hogg, 2007; Hogg & Abrams, 2003; Reid & Hogg, 2005), and is "perhaps an even more fundamental motive than self-enhancement" (Hogg, 2001, p. 332). We think it deserves a more central place in the relational demography literature and accordingly we highlight why uncertainty reduction is an indispensible theoretical concept in understanding relational demography effects. We contend that one reason for the mixed empirical findings from previous relational demography research focusing solely on self-enhancement is the use of underspecified models that have ignored this key human motivation.

The central feature of this chapter is an uncertainty reduction model of relational demography that describes a two-stage process of uncertainty emergence and reduction in a workgroup setting. The first stage depicts how structural features of the workgroup (workgroup composition) and occupation (legitimacy of status hierarchy) induce two forms of uncertainty: uncertainty about group norms as well as uncertainty about instrumental outcomes. The second part of the model illustrates employees' choice of uncertainty reduction strategies, depending on the type of uncertainty they experience, and the status of their demographic categories. We start with a critical historical overview of relational demography research to point out the merit of exploring the role of uncertainty reduction. We then draw on status characteristics theory (Berger, Cohen, & Zelditch, 1972; Berger, Fisek, Norman, & Zelditch, 1977) and research on strategic interpretation (Chattopadhyay, Glick, & Huber, 2001; George, Chattopadhyay, Sitkin, & Barden, 2006) in addition to the social identity perspective to develop a detailed account of the uncertainty reduction model of relational demography. The final part of the chapter explores implications of our model for both theory and practice.

## SYMMETRIC TO ASYMMETRIC EFFECTS IN RELATIONAL DEMOGRAPHY RESEARCH

Originating in the late 1980s, the notion of relational demography has generated considerable research interest after the pioneering work of Tsui and her colleagues (Tsui & O'Reilly, 1989; Tsui et al., 1992). These researchers introduced to the organizational literature the idea that the experiences of individuals working in diverse groups differ based on their demographic characteristics *relative to* those of their workgroup colleagues. Multiple theoretical perspectives have underpinned relational demography research. While earlier theoretical perspectives (e.g., the similarity–attraction paradigm) assume that all group members respond to dissimilarity in the same way (i.e., symmetric effects are obtained), later perspectives (e.g., status characteristics theory) acknowledge that dissimilarity produces different outcomes for individuals from different demographic categories (i.e., asymmetric effects are obtained). Further advancing our understanding of asymmetrical effects, researchers using a social identity theory perspective have specified the contextual factors that determine how a member from a particular demographic category reacts to dissimilarity. But, as we will argue later, these perspectives together do not provide a comprehensive understanding of how dissimilarity in a workgroup influences employees' attitudes and behaviors. We discuss these developments in detail in the following text.

### The Similarity–Attraction Paradigm and Tokenism Theory

The similarity–attraction paradigm (Byrne, 1971) and tokenism theory (Kanter, 1977, 1978) are the two earliest theories used in relational demography studies (Jackson, Brett, Sessa, Cooper, Julin, & Peyronnin, 1991; Riordan & Shore, 1997; Tsui et al., 1992). The similarity–attraction paradigm basically states that group members who are similar in demographic characteristics will be attracted toward each other because they assume deeper underlying similarities (e.g., in values and beliefs) and form positive expectations of future interactions. Thus, the more dissimilar the individual relative to other group members, the less interpersonal attraction and behavioral integration may be expected. Tokenism theory focuses on groups with more skewed demographic composition, and proposes that "token" group members (those comprising 15% or less of the demographic category in a workgroup) face high levels of stereotyping and blocked opportunities to advance, and thus react negatively to dissimilarity. In other words, both perspectives suggest the same thesis: An individual who is more demographically dissimilar to the rest of the workgroup will exhibit less positive work outcomes. This relationship is illustrated in Fig. 1a.

Empirical studies, however, often find asymmetric relational demographic effects that are inconsistent with the similarity–attraction paradigm and tokenism theory. While these two perspectives assume that everyone will react negatively to dissimilarity, scholars find that employees from different demographic categories react differently to dissimilarity. Tsui et al. (1992), for example, found that for whites, increasing race dissimilarity from workgroup members was related to lower levels of psychological commitment and a lower intent to stay in the workgroup, while for nonwhites, race

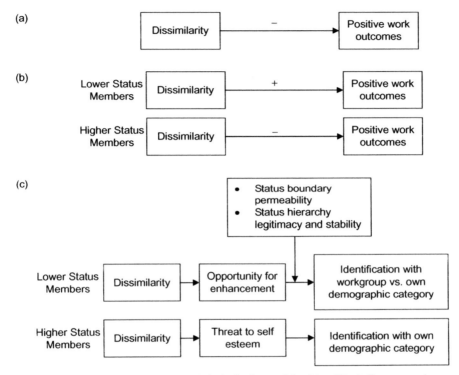

*Fig. 1.* The Relationship between Dissimilarity and Positive Work Outcomes (e.g., Workgroup Identification, Commitment, Citizenship Behaviors) Predicted by (a) the Similarity–Attraction Paradigm, (b) Status Characteristics Theory, and (c) the Self-Enhancement Motive of the Social Identity Perspective.

dissimilarity had no effects on these outcome variables. Similarly, Chattopadhyay (1999) found that race dissimilarity negatively influenced peer relations for white employees in minority-dominated groups, but not for minority employees in white-dominated groups and Chattopadhyay et al. (2004a) found nationality and sex dissimilarity to positively influence non-Australians and women, respectively, with regard to prototype valence, prototype clarity, and self-prototypicality. Similarly, tokenism theory has also ignored potential asymmetric effects (Fairhurst & Snavely, 1983), whereas empirical results show, for example, that male tokens may not share the negative experiences of their female counterparts (Budig, 2002; Cohen & Swim, 1995; McDonald, Toussaint, & Schweiger, 2004). In the light of these asymmetric effects, clearly we need more nuanced theoretical perspectives to understand and predict the effects of dissimilarity in a workgroup.

## Status Characteristics Theory

Status characteristics theory (Berger et al., 1972, 1977) was adopted by some researchers in an attempt to explain asymmetrical dissimilarity effects (e.g., Chatman & O'Reilly, 2004; Mueller, Finley, Iverson, & Price, 1999). According to this theory, a status characteristic is any personal attribute that reflects an individual's status and consequently influences others' evaluations about the focal individual relative to others. A status characteristic can be specific (i.e., limited to a particular situation or task), or diffuse (i.e., applicable to a wide range of situations and tasks). Demographic characteristics like gender, race, and age are some examples of diffuse characteristics that derive from outside of the immediate task situation but are perceived at the societal level to be associated with expectations of competence (Ridgeway & Smith-Lovin, 1999; Ridgeway & Walker, 1995). Status characteristic theory therefore implies that dissimilarity in diffuse status characteristics is associated with status differentiation between an individual and his/her peers.

The theory further predicts that status differentiation creates inequalities in group interactions such that individuals prefer to interact with higher status members who are expected to be more competent (Cohen & Zhou, 1991; Humphreys & Berger, 1981). Therefore, lower status workgroup members (e.g., nonwhites or females) tend to respond positively to demographic dissimilarity, as high dissimilarity means more higher status members in the workgroup, while higher status members (e.g., white males) react negatively to demography dissimilarity (see Fig. 1b). In other words, status characteristic theory goes beyond the emphasis on absolute dissimilarity in the similarity–attraction paradigm to address the valence associated with such dissimilarity. Individuals will interpret whether demographic dissimilarity is advantageous or detrimental to themselves, and as a result their identification with their workgroup, and their interactions with workgroup members, will be affected.

Status characteristics theory advances relational demography theorizing by bringing the notion of status differentiation associated with demographic variables to our attention, as well as providing a theoretical basis for related asymmetrical effects. However, it has not emerged as a significant perspective in the mainstream relational demography research, partially because it does not fully capture the entire range of empirical findings. For example, Chattopadhyay et al. (2008) found that women did not respond positively to increased demographic dissimilarity in their workgroups despite the fact that men were considered a higher status category in the empirical setting in which they conducted their study. These authors, like others, relied on other theoretical perspectives to provide more fine-grained predictions (Chattopadhyay et al., 2004b; Hogg & Terry, 2000). In particular, the social identity perspective is useful in understanding relational demography effects as it explicitly considers how contextual differences related to the status hierarchy shape the status of each demographic category.

## MORE TEXTURED ANALYSIS: SOCIAL IDENTITY THEORY AND SELF-CATEGORIZATION THEORY

Social identity theory (Tajfel & Turner, 1979, 1986) and the associated self-categorization theory (Turner, 1975; Turner et al., 1987) have been used by relational demography researchers to explain dissimilarity-related effects (e.g., Chattopadhyay et al., 2004a). These theories (in particular self-categorization theory, which has a relatively intragroup focus compared to the intergroup focus of social identity theory) suggest that individuals identify with social groups through a process of *self-categorization* in which individuals assimilate their cognition, behaviors, and feelings to the *group prototype* – their cognitive representation of the features that best define their group and distinguish it from other groups in a specific context. As a result of self-categorization, individuals are *depersonalized* such that all members are now processed as interchangeable embodiments of the group prototype, and individuals' self-conception is based on their social identity as a group member.

Social identification can satisfy two motives that drive individual's identity construction activities: First, *self-enhancement* – a motive to maintain or enhance self-esteem – can be achieved when a group prototype is evaluated favorably relative to other groups (referred to as out-groups in social identity theory) (Hogg & Hains, 1996; Tajfel & Turner, 1986). Second, *uncertainty reduction* – a motive to reduce the subjective uncertainty that individuals experience in social interactions – is satisfied by assimilating ones' self to the group prototype that describes and prescribes group members' perceptions, attitudes, and behaviors (Hogg, 2001; Hogg & Terry, 2000).

Workgroups form a salient basis of categorization in the work context (Hogg & Terry, 2000; van Knippenberg & Ellemers, 2003). Self-categorization theory suggests that upon joining a workgroup, an employee first cognitively forms a prototype of this workgroup, which may well include demographic characteristics, e.g., males around mid-30s who are ambitious and achievement oriented. If the individual identifies with the group then he or she adjusts his attitude and behavior to match the group prototype. Membership in the workgroup could help enhance the individual's self-esteem if this group is perceived to be better than other workgroups in the organizational domain, for example, in terms of achieving organizational goals, being friendly, or having the lowest accident rates. Being a member of the workgroup could also help reduce subjective uncertainty as the prototype provides information on how other workgroup members respond to the social environment, and helps to guide the focal employee's perceptions, attitudes, and behaviors. The more the workgroup can enhance the employee's self-esteem and reduce subjective uncertainty, the higher the employee's identification with the workgroup. On the other hand, if membership in a social group increases self-esteem threat and uncertainty, members will engage in coping behaviors to restore self-esteem and reduce uncertainty and decrease identification with that group.

Most relational demography researchers have argued that workgroup composition shapes group identification by affecting the opportunity for self-enhancement, but have ignored the uncertainty reduction motive for group identification (e.g., Chattopadhyay, 1999; Chattopadhyay et al., 2008; Liao et al., 2004; Pelled, Ledford, & Mohrman, 1999; Riordan & Shore, 1997; but see Chattopadhyay et al., 2004a, and Goldberg et al., 2010, for exceptions). We first illustrate how predictions from the self-enhancement motive advanced previous relational demography theorizing and then present our uncertainty reduction model of relational demography.

### Predictions from the Self-Enhancement Motive

The self-enhancement motive suggests that individuals prefer to identify with social groups with positive qualities. For group members who belong to a lower status social category, greater dissimilarity from their group members means a greater proportion of members from the higher status category, which makes the workgroup more prestigious, enabling identity enhancement for those identifying with the workgroup. Lower status members therefore will react positively to dissimilarity. For higher status members, however, greater dissimilarity makes the workgroup a less attractive target for identification, and might even threaten their self-esteem. They thus identify less with the workgroup and more with their higher status demographic categories.

This prediction based on the self-enhancement motive again goes beyond similarity–attraction paradigm's predicted universal negative reaction to dissimilarity, as demographic dissimilarity can be advantageous to individuals by offering the opportunity for self-enhancement. Although at first glance this prediction seems to coincide with that from status characteristic theory, social identity perspective actually further proposes moderating conditions, as illustrate in Fig. 1c.

Lower status members would identify with workgroups dominated by higher status members only when they perceive the demographical status boundary to be permeable, i.e., when "they believe that they can become members of workgroups associated with higher status categories and be accepted by the higher status category members as one of them" (Chattopadhyay et al., 2004b, p. 189). This permeability across categories is a psychological perception of the possibility of movement across boundaries, rather than a change of objective reality. For example, a female workgroup member will perceive the boundary between the higher status category and the lower status category is permeable when she anticipates that she will be seen as "one of the boys" and is accepted as a full-fledged member of the group by her male colleagues. In such a case, the woman will identify with the higher status male-dominated workgroup to achieve self-enhancement (this strategy of identifying with the higher status category, rather than ones' own lower status category, is referred to as social mobility, Tajfel & Turner, 1979).

When members of lower status categories perceive the status hierarchy to be impermeable, they seek other means of identity enhancement rather than via workgroup identification. These means might include directly challenging the higher status category's superiority (referred to as the social competition strategy, Tajfel & Turner, 1979) when lower status category members perceive the status hierarchy to be unstable and illegitimate. However, if they perceive the status hierarchy to be stable, legitimate, and impermeable, lower status members might adopt a social creativity strategy (Tajfel & Turner, 1979) where they redefine the dimension of social comparison such that their own demographic category is favorably evaluated on status-irrelevant dimensions, but avoid directly challenging the outgroup's superior status. In a study of professional dissimilarity in surgical teams (a context where the status hierarchy of professions is stable, legitimate, and impermeable), for example, Chattopadhyay et al. (2010) found that lower status members (e.g., nurses) enhance their self-images by defining themselves as *warm and likable* rather than challenging the *competence* of higher status members (e.g., surgeons).

In sum, drawing on the self-enhancement motive in the social identity perspective, researchers to date have suggested that demographic dissimilarity can lead to various work-related outcomes depending on how individuals can maintain and enhance their social identities. Having completed our review of the relational demography literature, we now turn to developing our two-stage uncertainty reduction model of relational demography.

# THE TWO-STAGE UNCERTAINTY REDUCTION MODEL OF RELATIONAL DEMOGRAPHY

Uncertainty about oneself and other people is aversive because it is associated with reduced control or reduced resources needed for survival (Fiske & Taylor, 1991; Lopes, 1987; Sorrentino & Roney, 1986). Social identity theory proposes that human beings strive to resolve feelings of uncertainty, especially when the uncertainty is self-relevant in a particular context (Hogg, 2007; Hogg & Mullin, 1999), but it does not specify what types of uncertainty are most relevant to individuals in groups. We propose to fill that gap by arguing, based on the literature on groups, that two types of uncertainty are most relevant to workgroup experience, specifically group members experience uncertainty related to behaviors and outcomes.

Upon joining a workgroup, employees seek information about workgroup norms that define what behaviors are expected and sanctioned by group members (Chatman, 2010; Flynn & Chatman, 2003; Hackman, 1992). Group members experience uncertainty if the group or the environment fails to offer a clear norm that guides workgroup members' behaviors. We term this form of uncertainty *norm uncertainty*, which is related to the clarity of workgroup behavioral norms. Workgroup members also have shared goals where the attainment of group goals is linked to rewards earned by individual group members (Hackman, 1983). Employees may feel uncertain about the group's ability and competence to reach the group goal, thus affecting their individual reward. In other words, individuals feel uncertain about the instrumental outcomes that they can obtain as a result of workgroup membership. We term this form of uncertainty *instrumental uncertainty*.

The plausibility of norm and instrumental uncertainties as two key dimensions of workgroup experience is reflected in fairness research. Employees care about fair procedures because these procedures increase predictability and control over instrumental outcomes, thus reducing uncertainty regarding distributive issues (self-interest model: Lind & Tyler, 1988). Procedural justice also matters because it says something about "the formal and informal social processes that regulate much of the group's activities" (group value model: Lind & Tyler, 1988, p. 231).

The two types of uncertainty are independent such that group members may experience one type of uncertainty without the other. Workgroup norms can be about how to dress to work or appropriate conversational styles, which do not have direct implications on instrumental outcomes. An employee can be sure about the behavioral norms but not the instrumental outcome. On the contrary, an employee joining a historically high-performing workgroup can feel quite certain that the group will continue to perform well, but might nevertheless be uncertain about how to behave in the workgroup.

In the following sections, we present a two-stage uncertainty reduction model of relational demography (see Fig. 2). The first stage of the model deals with how workgroup composition in terms of status-related demographic variables, combined with contextual factors related to the

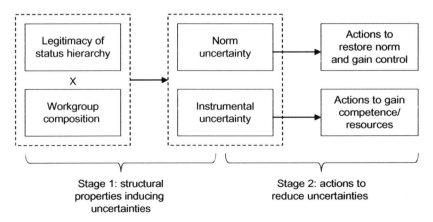

*Fig. 2.* The Uncertainty Reduction Model of Relational Demography.

status hierarchy, can lead to norm uncertainty as well as instrumental uncertainty. The second stage of the model then deals with how individuals adopt various coping strategies to reduce the uncertainty. We incorporate status hierarchy characteristics into our model because the social identity perspective suggests that individuals perceive and react to the status of their own and others' demographic categories based on the manner in which status is distributed. The nature of the status hierarchy (e.g., its legitimacy or the extent to which it is permeable) varies across organizations, industries, as well as occupations, such that the extent to which social identity motives are satisfied is dependent on the nature of status hierarchy in a specific situation (DiTomaso, Post, & Parks-Yancy, 2007; Joshi & Roh, 2009; Reskin, McBrier, & Kmec, 1999). We extend this perspective, focusing on the occupational status hierarchy to illustrate how status hierarchy characteristics help to shape uncertainty emergence and reduction in relational demography research. We note that our arguments are equally valid for hierarchies in various units at different levels, such as organizations and industries.

## STAGE 1: UNCERTAINTY EMERGENCE

*Emergence of Norm Uncertainty*

Norms are socially shared standards against which the appropriateness of behavior can be evaluated. They specify what group members can and cannot do (Birenbaum & Sagarin, 1976; Hackman, 1992). Social identity theorists have argued that group norms are reflected in the shared group prototype that not only describes members' actual behaviors but also prescribes how members ought to behave (Hogg & Terry, 2000). Thus, employees are less likely to experience norm uncertainty when the workgroup prototype is clear and consensual.

What are the workgroup-relevant factors that determine prototype content as well as prototype clarity? Workgroup member' construction of a group prototype stems from both an idealized sense of what a group should be as well as their own experiences of being in that group. A clear group prototype exists when the individual is able to clearly and confidently describe the essential features of the group (Hogg & Hains, 1996). We argue that individuals are more able to do this when the composition of their workgroup is consistent with the norms of the occupation. The more group membership deviates from these norms, the more difficult it is for individuals to construct a clear prototype of the group. In the following sections we explain the role of the occupation and the workgroup in the construction of the group prototype. We focus on one demographic feature associated with occupations, i.e., the sex typing of jobs, in order to both illustrate and simplify our arguments. We expect that our theorizing could be related to other demographic features associated with occupations such as race or age for historical or status-related reasons rather than functional reasons.

*Numerical Majority and Prototype Construction*
The demographic composition of the workgroup influences the content and clarity of workgroup prototype. As argued by relational demography researchers (e.g., Chattopadhyay, 1999; Tsui et al., 1992), demographic categories such as sex and race tend to be salient in organizational contexts and characteristics of demographic categories become associated with groups where members belong to those categories. Specifically, when there is a numerical majority from a particular demographic category in a workgroup, the workgroup prototype usually reflects the majority category and is infused with the values and beliefs typically associated with that category. When there is no clear majority (i.e., half of the workgroup members come from one demographic category and the other half is from a different demographic category), it would be hard for workgroup members to construct a clear prototype as a significant number of peers differs from them in terms of demographic characteristics.

>  **Proposition 1a.** Presence of numerical majority facilitates the creation of a clear workgroup prototype, such that salient characteristics of the majority demographic category are expected to be characteristic of the workgroup prototype; while no clear majority results in an unclear workgroup prototype.

*Legitimacy of Status Hierarchy and Prototype Construction*
The historical dominance of demographic categories in an occupation plays a role in prototype formation. When a single demographic group dominates an occupation, the occupational prototype is associated with that demographic category and negative stereotype-based categorization processes against underrepresented groups are likely (Fiske, 1993; Reskin et al., 1999). For example, occupations become sex-typed as "male" or "female" according to the gender of the typical incumbent (Bielby & Baron, 1986; Chatman et al., 2008), and people often use the employee's gender to judge

their competence (Eagly & Steffen, 1984; Propp, 1995) such that females
are stereotyped to be poor performers in a male sex-typed job, and vice
versa. Even in instances where male tokens in female-dominated industries are seen to perform well, they tend to move on to supervisory
positions (Barnett, Baron, & Stuart, 2000); those left behind in lower level
positions, for example, as team members rather than supervisors, may be
regarded as less competent. Further, if the success of male tokens in female
occupations is attributed to a broader social acceptance of male superiority in a gender-based status hierarchy, then those remaining in lower
level jobs may be viewed as less competent for their inability to leverage
their traditional advantage. Irrespective of the reason, members of the
dominant category are regarded as more competent, and consequently a
workgroup that has those individuals as members is valued. But whether
or not this association holds true depends on the *legitimacy* of status
hierarchy.

Social identity theory suggests that any status hierarchy can vary on the
degree to which it is considered legitimate or not. Legitimacy in this context
has two aspects. The first is the extent to which category members perceive
that "the status accorded their category reflects these members' true status
on qualities that are accepted within that context as being relevant to status
distribution" (Chattopadhyay et al., 2004b, p. 191). This dimension of
legitimacy parallels the idea of distributive justice (Greenberg, 1987). The
second aspect of legitimacy is the extent to which category members perceive
the process used for distribution of status is transparent and fair
(Chattopadhyay et al., 2004b). This parallels the idea of procedural justice
(Lind & Tyler, 1988). In terms of our focus here, these two ideas translate to
whether members from the nonhistorically dominant category accept that
they should be associated with lower competency and lower status in that
occupation, and accept that the process through which this status is
accorded is fair.

Sometimes the status hierarchy remains unchallenged, and consequently is
legitimatized (Ridgeway, Boyle, Kuipers, & Robinson, 1998). In that case
there will be a tendency for others to treat the category that has a lower status
as less competent in that occupation (Barnett et al., 2000; Baron &
Newman, 1990; Cassirer & Reskin, 2000). Confronted with the reality of
their situation, lower status category members are either likely to accept that
they are indeed less competent by engaging in a discourse of system
justification (Jost & Hunyady, 2002) or at best accept that this is what "most
others" believe. When the status hierarchy is legitimate, employees accept
that the workgroup prototype should be built around the norms of the higher

status category, i.e., the historically dominant category. The prototype thus sets up normative expectations among group members, such that workgroup members are expected to act in accordance with the norm of the higher status demographic category.

At other times, however, challenges to the status hierarchy do occur, and individuals who previously accepted their lower status reject the negative evaluation accorded to their demographic categories, and regard the status hierarchy as illegitimate (Berger, Ridgeway, Fisek, & Norman, 1998). As a result, the historically dominant category is less likely to be perceived as the prototype, and it becomes unclear what demographic characteristics can be descriptive of the prototype.

**Proposition 1b.** Legitimate status hierarchy facilitates a clear workgroup prototype, such that salient characteristics of the higher status demographic category are expected to be characteristic of the workgroup prototype; while illegitimate status hierarchy results in unclear prototype.

### The Combined Effects of Status Legitimacy and Numerical Majority on Norm Uncertainty

The two above-mentioned propositions depict the independent effects of status legitimacy and numerical majority on prototype content and clarity. Now let us explore the combined effect of those two factors on prototype construction, and thus on norm uncertainty. The combined effect of status legitimacy and numerical majority on norm uncertainty is presented in Table 1.

As described in Proposition 1b, a legitimate status hierarchy in general results in a workgroup prototype that is characterized by the higher status demographic category. This relationship is expected to hold true when the higher status demographic category dominates the workgroup, because the prototype prescribed by societal (occupational) expectations coincides with that prescribed by numerical majority. Workgroup members in this condition therefore accept norms associated with higher status members as group norms. Since group norms in this condition are clear, norm uncertainty is low.

When there is no clear numerical majority in the workgroup, workgroup composition fails to provide a clear prototype (as described in Proposition 1a). However, if the status hierarchy is considered legitimate, then the higher status category (even if it is not in the absolute numerical majority) would inform the workgroup prototype. In this case, workgroup members are clear about the prototype, resulting in low norm uncertainty.

**Table 1.** Sources of Uncertainty and Coping Strategies to Reduce Norm and Instrumental Uncertainty.

| Workgroup Composition | Legitimacy of Status Hierarchy | |
|---|---|---|
| | Legitimate | Illegitimate |
| Numerical majority is of higher status | Norm uncertainty: *Low*, clear norm from occupation and numerical majority<br><br>Instrumental uncertainty: *Low* | Norm uncertainty: *Low*, clear workgroup norm from numerical majority<br><br>Instrumental uncertainty: *High*, unsure of what resource is need for goal achievement<br><br>Engage in defining available resources as the competence needed for completion of critical tasks and gaining status[a] |
| No clear numerical majority | Norm uncertainty: *Low*, clear norm from occupation<br><br>Instrumental uncertainty: *Moderate*<br><br>Meritorious members of both higher and lower status categories engage in social mobility, i.e., joining workgroups with greater proportion of higher status members. Less meritorious employees engage in social creativity, i.e., portray available status-irrelevant resources as critical to group performance[a] | Norm uncertainty: *High*, unclear norm from both occupation and workgroup composition<br><br>Identify with alternate social groups, i.e., own demographic categories, and adhere to norm of their own demographic categories[b]<br><br>Instrumental uncertainty: *High*, unsure of what resource is need for goal achievement<br><br>Engage in defining available resources as the competence needed for completion of critical tasks and gaining status[a] |

| Numerical majority is of lower status | Norm uncertainty: *High*, because occupation norm conflicts with norm from numerical majority | Instrumental uncertainty: *High*, lack of needed resources in the workgroup | Norm uncertainty: *Low*, clear workgroup norm from numerical majority | Instrumental uncertainty: *High*, unsure of what resource is need for goal achievement |
|---|---|---|---|---|
| | Identify with alternate social groups, i.e., the occupation, and adhere to the occupation norm, which is also the norm of the higher status demographic category[b] | Meritorious members of both higher and lower status categories engage in social mobility, i.e., joining workgroups with greater proportion of higher status members. Less meritorious employees engage in social creativity, i.e., portray available status-irrelevant resources as critical to group performance[a] | | Engage in defining available resources as the competence needed for completion of critical tasks and gaining status[a] |

[a]The coping strategy to reduce instrumental uncertainty.
[b]The coping strategy to reduce norm uncertainty.

Finally, when status hierarchy is legitimate and when the lower status category dominates the workgroup, there is conflict between the prototype prescribed by societal expectations about occupation (higher status category) and the prototype prescribed by numerical majority in the group (lower status category). The conflict makes prototype unclear, and thus workgroup members are uncertain about what norms they should adhere to (those of the higher status members or those of the numerical majority), and how to behave. For example, we expect to see greater norm uncertainty in a team of male nurses than in a team of female nurses. In summary, we propose the following proposition.

**Proposition 1c.** Legitimate occupational status hierarchy results in low norm uncertainty, except when the workgroup is dominated by lower status members.

What is the degree of norm uncertainty when status hierarchy is illegitimate? As we argue in Proposition 1b, illegitimate status hierarchy results in unclear prototype, because the status hierarchy associated with the dominant category is being challenged. Under this condition, societal expectations about the occupation fail to facilitate workgroup prototype construction, and group members have to turn to workgroup composition for guidance. For those workgroups that have a clear numerical majority of any one demographic category, the demographic characteristic of the dominant category is expected to characterize the workgroup prototype (as describe in Proposition 1a). Members from these workgroups are clear about the workgroup prototype, and experience low norm uncertainty. In contrast, members from workgroups with no numerical majority are still unclear about the prototype, thus experiencing high norm uncertainty.

**Proposition 1d.** Illegitimacy of status hierarchy results in high norm uncertainty, except when there is numerical majority in the workgroup.


*Emergence of Instrumental Uncertainty*

Besides norm uncertainty, workgroup members may also be uncertain regarding the instrumental reward they can obtain as a result of workgroup membership. In modern organizational life, rewards are usually based on both individual-based and team-based performance, with an emphasis on the latter for those working in teams (Hackman, 1983). For example, in a research and development team, all workgroup members will receive higher reward if the team invents new products successfully, in addition to being rewarded for individual performance.

Workgroup members experience lower instrumental uncertainty when they perceive that the group (and its group members) possesses the competence to achieve the group goal; and experience higher instrumental uncertainty either when they perceive a lack of the needed competence in the group, or when they are not sure what competence leads to goal achievement. We argue that members' expectation regarding group competence, and thus instrumental uncertainty, are influenced by both the legitimacy of status hierarchy and the workgroup composition. The combined effect is discussed in the following text, and is presented in Table 1.

*The Effects of Status Legitimacy and Workgroup Composition on Instrumental Uncertainty*

According to status characteristics theory, diffuse status characteristics like gender, race, and age are associated with expectations regarding competence (Ridgeway & Smith-Lovin, 1999; Ridgeway & Walker, 1995). Intergroup perception research also suggests that demographic categories are evaluated in terms of their competence (Bergsieker, Shelton, & Richeson, 2010; Fiske, Cuddy, & Glick, 2007). Taken together, these two streams of research suggest that demographic characteristics are used as a basis of competence evaluation.

As we mentioned earlier, the historically dominant demographic category is usually regarded as more competent in an occupation. When this evaluation, and the associated status differential, is perceived to be legitimate, all group members accept that the higher status members do possess higher task-relevant competence to achieve the group's goals (Kalkhoff & Barnum, 2000; Kirchmeyer, 1993; Oldmeadow, Platow, Foddy, & Anderson, 2003; Propp, 1995). Therefore, employees perceive that workgroups with high proportion of higher status members are better able to provide them instrumental outcome, leading to lower instrumental uncertainty.

**Proposition 2a.** When the status hierarchy is legitimate, higher proportion of lower status members in a workgroup relates to higher instrumental uncertainty.

The above-mentioned relationship between workgroup composition and instrumental uncertainty is unlikely to be true when the status hierarchy is perceived to be illegitimate. Delegitimizing the status hierarchy weakens the link between demographic category and competence expectations, such that members (both lower and higher status members) are more doubtful that demographic status is reflective of the competence necessary for group goal attainment. Therefore, regardless of workgroup composition, members experience high instrumental uncertainty.

**Proposition 2b.** Illegitimacy of status hierarchy results in high instrumental uncertainty regardless of the workgroup composition.

## STAGE 2: UNCERTAINTY REDUCTION

Uncertainty is aversive, and thus human beings strive to resolve uncertainty (Hogg, 2001, 2007; Hogg & Abrams, 1993). While the first stage of our model describes how workgroup members may experience norm uncertainty and instrumental uncertainty, the second stage of the model deals with how employees adopt various coping strategies to reduce the uncertainties. We draw upon research on strategic interpretation (Chattopadhyay et al., 2001; George et al., 2006) to suggest that norm and instrumental uncertainty are related to lack of control and resource, respectively, and that as a consequence, responses to them should be predicted by two different theories. Specifically, we draw on their ideas that individuals react in opposite ways when they experience uncertainty related to how to behave in various situations (norm uncertainty) and uncertainty related to whether valued outcomes will be achieved (instrumental uncertainty). Following the above-mentioned researchers, we argue that uncertainty related to how to behave leads to a risk-averse threat-rigidity response (Staw, Sandelands, & Dutton, 1981) as team members act to regain a sense of certainty over their behavior through acting in familiar ways. As predicted by prospect theory (Kahneman & Tversky, 1979), instrumental uncertainty leads to risk-seeking behaviors – team members who perceive they may not be able to achieve team outcomes behave in risky ways to recoup the loss associated with nonachievement of team goals.

Norms are a useful tool for workgroups to regulate members' behaviors such that deviant behaviors will be punished (Birenbaum & Sagarin, 1976; Hackman, 1992). In other words, high norm uncertainty signals that the workgroup has limited control over group members' action. Threat-rigidity theory suggests that decision-makers who perceive little control over situations and are uncertain regarding how to behave tend to be risk averse, and rigidly pursue familiar or well-learned strategies (Staw et al.,

1981). In our context, the risk-averse coping strategies might include attempting to borrow norms from another source so as to restore order to the group (e.g., adhere to norms of the occupation, or to norms of their own demographic categories).

**Proposition 3a.** Under norm uncertainty, employees adopt risk-averse coping strategies to restore norms for themselves.

The experience of instrumental uncertainty is associated with a perceived lack of competence to attain group goals. Without the specific legitimate competence of higher status members, instrumental rewards are believed to be in jeopardy. We argue that groups need competent members to attain their goals, and workgroup members who experience instrumental uncertainty perceive their groups lack adequate resources to attain their goals. Research on strategic interpretation (Chattopadhyay et al., 2001; George et al., 2006) suggests that resource-related loss is better dealt with by prospect theory (Kahneman & Tversky, 1979). Prospect theory postulates that decision-makers in the face of resource loss tend to take riskier actions. So, rather than accepting the status quo that their groups are less competent (the safe option where no changes are required; Kahneman, Knetsch, & Thaler, 1991), workgroup member engage in various risky strategies such as changing to a group with higher instrumental certainty or changing the criteria used to define competence to reduce perceptions of instrumental uncertainty.

**Proposition 3b.** Under instrumental uncertainty, employees adopt risk-seeking coping strategies to gain competence and resources.

The two generic strategies to reduce norm uncertainty and instrumental uncertainty are presented in Fig. 2. In the following sections, we elaborate how each generic strategy manifests under different conditions of status hierarchy legitimacy and workgroup composition. The details are presented in Table 1.

*Reduction of Norm Uncertainty*

Proposition 3a suggests that when employees are uncertain about the norms of their workgroup, they adopt norms from other sources to reduce their norm uncertainty. Specifically, employees would become less identified with the workgroup, and more identified with the alternate social group whose norms they adopted. These alternate social groups can be *superordinate* to the workgroup (Gaertner & Dovidio, 2000; e.g., the occupation) or *cross-cutting* the workgroup (Hornsey & Hogg, 1999; e.g., employees' own demographic category). Employees' actual choice of identification target will depend on their unique situation.

As discussed in Proposition 1c, employees experience high norm uncertainty when the status hierarchy is legitimate but the workgroup is dominated by lower status members. For instance, investment bankers in a female-dominated workgroup experience high uncertainty regarding the workgroup norm because the occupational norm specified (i.e., norm of masculinity, McDowell, 1997) is in conflict with the norm specified by group composition (i.e., norm of femininity). Higher status members (males) in this group could reduce norm uncertainty by identifying with either the occupation or their demographic category. These two groups coincide in being associated with traditionally higher status group members and are characterized by a clear norm of masculinity. Lower status members (females) will prefer to identify with the occupation rather than their own demographic category because uncertainty is reduced more through identification with the more legitimate occupation than their own, less legitimate demographic category. Females in this case are therefore more likely to adhere to the occupational norm of masculinity, and try to become "one of the boys" (Fine, 1987).

Another case where higher norm uncertainty is experienced is when the occupational status hierarchy is illegitimate and no clear numerical majority exists in the workgroup (Proposition 1d). Because neither the occupation nor workgroup composition provides normative guidance, employees therefore can only fall back on their demographic category to guide their behavior. Returning to our previous example of investment banker, if the sex typing of jobs in the occupation is considered illegitimate, there are no occupational norms to help guide behaviors, and thus employees from workgroups with no clear majority can only resort to their demographic category for norms.

## Reduction of Instrumental Uncertainty

We have argued that employees experience instrumental uncertainty if a substantial proportion of members in their group do not possess the competency needed to complete tasks (as defined according to a legitimate status hierarchy, Proposition 2a) or if there is no legitimate status hierarchy that signals what is the needed competency (Proposition 2b). Employees experiencing instrumental uncertainty tend to adopt risk-seeking coping strategies to gain competence and resources, rather than accepting the status quo that their workgroups are less competent (Proposition 3b). Possible strategies that might challenge the status quo include *social mobility* (which for higher status members like men involves joining a workgroup with greater proportions of higher status members and for lower status members like women involves taking on the values and beliefs of higher status members in order to be accepted by them), and *social creativity* (reframing the needed competency in a way that favors the workgroup). We discuss these in the following text.

*Social mobility* is more likely when both higher and lower status group members perceive the status hierarchy to be legitimate and unlikely to change, so the relative status of their categories remain unchanged, yet a few lower status individuals of exceptional merit are accepted by those of higher status as long as the former completely accept the values, beliefs, and behaviors of the latter as their own (Tajfel & Turner, 1986). Thus, in male-typed occupations, talented women or talented men who have "lost" status through working in female-dominated workgroups may aspire to be socially mobile when they perceive the status hierarchy to be permeable. For men who have the talent and ability to move upward, social mobility is relatively easier than for women as their own values and behaviors are naturally inclined to match those of men in a higher status workgroup. The risk for men lies in changing from a workgroup where they are recognized to be competent to one where they may over-reach their level of competence. For the few women of exceptional merit, in addition to this risk, social mobility involves making significant changes to their values and beliefs, reshaping their identity to fit in with male colleagues, and dissociating with other women (Chattopadhyay et al., 2004a, 2004b; see also George, Chattopadhyay, & Zhang, forthcoming; Reynolds & Turner, 2001). These changes may adversely affect their mental well-being.

However, in a group experiencing instrumental uncertainty, the majority of members are unlikely to have the competence to successfully engage in social mobility. The inability to be deemed competent under a legitimate status hierarchy motivates social creativity (Chattopadhyay et al., 2004b, 2010; Tajfel & Turner, 1979). Social creativity in this instance involves creating new criteria to judge the group's performance. These criteria are not directly related to completing critical organizational tasks and thus also not directly related to consolidating or maintaining status in the organization. Going back to our banking example, if the performance of the group is evaluated in terms of revenue and male bankers are deemed to be competent in generating revenue, then a group of predominantly female bankers might reduce their instrumental uncertainty by redefining their group's goal as long-term financial sustainability, rather than short-term revenue generation. This strategy requires a tacit understanding between high- and low-status group members, where high-status group members are prepared to acknowledge the superiority of low-status colleagues on criteria not directly related to consolidating status in the organization, in exchange for their own unchallenged superiority on status-relevant criteria. In this example, long-term financial sustainability may be useful to the organization, but possessing the resources to achieve it is not rewarded with status establishment.

We have so far described the coping strategies involved in resolving the instrumental uncertainty that exists when the status hierarchy is legitimate. Employees can also experience high instrumental uncertainty when the status hierarchy is illegitimate (as suggested in Proposition 2b). Delegitimizing the status hierarchy makes all employees uncertain about what competences are needed for task completion and goal attainment. The illegitimacy of the existing hierarchy provides employees an opportunity to challenge established ways of defining task-relevant competence (i.e., engage in social competition), and to suggest that a competence possessed by their workgroup (i.e., the competence of the workgroup majority) is necessary to successfully accomplish group tasks and therefore to establishing and maintaining status in the relevant context.

To illustrate, let us consider a situation where mathematical skills possessed by male investment bankers were previously being regarded as the needed competence for goal attainment. As the status hierarchy becomes illegitimate, mathematical skills may no longer be regarded as the key to goal attainment and status consolidation. Employees can then portray other skills as the needed competence, and their choice of the new needed competence will depend on what are the available competences in their workgroups as that is the quickest way to reduce uncertainty in this situation. Those from a male-dominated group may retain mathematical skills (stereotypically a male skill) as the needed competence, while those from a female-dominated group may propose building relationships with clients (a female skill) as the most necessary competence for sustained success. Employees from a half-male–half-female workgroup may even redefine the status hierarchy using other demographic characteristics such as functional background, and suggest, for example, that all of their current workgroup members are of the functional background that is best qualified for goal achievement.

# IMPLICATIONS OF THE TWO-STAGE UNCERTAINTY REDUCTION MODEL

Researchers have developed relational demography models based on various theoretical perspectives, such as similarity–attraction paradigm, status characteristic theory, and social identity perspective. While models based on the social identity perspective (Chattopadhyay et al., 2004b; Tsui et al., 1992) have provided fine-grained prediction about demographic dissimilarity effects, they do not capture the full complexity of the social identity perspective. In this chapter, we have incorporated a previously ignored social identification motive – uncertainty reduction – into relational demography theorizing, and elaborated on the uncertainty-related process that underpin effects related to workgroup demography. To this end, a two-stage uncertainty reduction model of relational demography has been proposed. In the first stage of the model, we focused on how workgroup composition and status hierarchy legitimacy jointly influence employees' uncertainties regarding the workgroup norm and instrumental rewards. In the second stage, our analysis indicated that the choice of employee uncertainty reduction strategy depends on the type of uncertainty experienced, workgroup composition, status hierarchy legitimacy, as well as the focal employee's demographic characteristic. In the remainder of this chapter, we discuss the research and practical implications of our model.

## Agenda for Future Research

Our model provides an additional theoretical lens to understand why demographic composition or dissimilarity can have various effects on employee workgroup identification and other work-related outcomes depending on the type and degree of uncertainty emerges and the employee's choice of uncertainty reduction strategy. If we accept that uncertainty reduction is a key motivation for group identification, we may speculate that previous empirical results that cannot be explained by the self-enhancement mechanism alone might be due to the construction of underspecified models that failed to incorporate the uncertainty reduction mechanism suggested here. We therefore suggest that future research should also measure the variables specified in our model in order to gain a fuller understanding of the phenomenon of identification with diverse workgroups.

Empirical testing of our model would require operationalization of several key variables. The first set of variables we need to measure is the (norm and instrumental) uncertainties experienced by workgroup members. Direct measures of norm uncertainty have been devised from Zitek and Hebl's (2007) norm clarity measure, or Jackson's (1965, 1966) formulation of norm intensity. Instrumental uncertainty could be assessed by the pre-aggregated collective efficacy scale (Chen & Bliese, 2002; Jex & Bliese, 1999), which reflects members' belief in the workgroup's capability to achieve the group goal. We may also take an indirect approach and measure norm uncertainty and instrumental uncertainty by asking workgroup members to describe their workgroup prototype. Since norm uncertainty stems from prototype clarity, measures of prototype clarity developed by Fielding and Hogg (1997), where participants are asked to rate the ease of generating prototype descriptions and their confidence regarding the accuracy of the descriptions, can be a proxy of norm uncertainty. Instrumental uncertainty can be coded from the generated prototype descriptions in terms of the positive and negative statements regarding the group's task performance and competence (Chattopadhyay et al., 2004a).

A second set of key constructs is the uncertainty reduction strategies, including identification with alternate social identities, social mobility, and social creativity. Identification with alternate social identities, such as with an employee's occupation or gender, can be directly measured by the scale developed by Mael and Ashforth (1992) (see also Johnson, Morgeson, Ilgen, Meyer, & Lloyd, 2006), or by the match between the values ascribed to social categories and those contained within employee self-definitions. Coping strategies to reduce instrumental uncertainty, on the other hand, are better measured using in-depth interviews or behavioral observation. A reported shift in perceived needed competence would signify the use of a social creativity strategy. Increased self-efficacy in the needed competence together with unwillingness to accept the status hierarchy would signify the use of a social competition strategy.

Besides survey-based field studies, our ideas could be tested using experimental designs. Social identity researchers have used experiments to examine processes related to uncertainty reduction (Grieve & Hogg, 1999; Mullin & Hogg, 1998; Reid & Hogg, 2005). We could manipulate the demographic composition of the workgroup as well as the legitimacy of the status hierarchy, and then take measurement about levels of uncertainty and coping strategies.

## Implications for Human Resources Management

For human resource managers, one implication of our uncertainty reduction model is clear: since employees display aversion to uncertainty, organizations should help employees to reduce their norm and instrumental uncertainty in order to enhance the performance of their workgroups. While we have suggested several tactics individual workgroup members could use to reduce uncertainty (e.g., social mobility, social creativity, identification with the occupation instead of the workgroup), several human resources interventions could also be helpful in this regard.

Workgroup members may suffer from norm uncertainty when there is no clear norm in their workgroups. Instead of being able to focus on their task, employees in these situations may waste their time and mental resources figuring out how they ought to behave. Managers could articulate and propagate organizational norms of acceptable modes of interaction within workgroups, thus enabling dissimilar members to interact smoothly and perform effectively (Chatman, 2010; Flynn & Chatman, 2003).

With regard to the reduction of instrumental uncertainty, our model suggests that human resources managers should take into account workgroup composition and status hierarchy legitimacy when determining training needs for workgroups and individual members. For example, if instrumental uncertainty is due to the lack of legitimate, needed competence in the workgroup, managers should provide training on the needed competence, especially to employees from the lower status category. But when uncertainty arises because of perceived illegitimacy of the status hierarchy (i.e., when workgroup members are unsure of what competence is needed to achieve their group tasks), managers should work with the group to explore what competences may legitimately be deemed as being most useful and available within the group in carrying forward group tasks, and provide training on leveraging this competence. This is consistent with Van Knippenberg, De Dreu, and Homan's (2004) proposal of using information elaboration as a mechanism to increase individual group members' understanding of how diversity in the group can help the group attain its goals.

# CONCLUSION

Despite the enormous number of empirical studies on relational demography, the effects of demographic dissimilarity on individuals and the associated social psychological process are not fully understood yet

(Lawrence, 1997; Riordan, 2000). In this chapter, we reviewed the major contemporary perspectives on relational demography, and pointed out that the role of uncertainty reduction is too important to be ignored. We presented a model that examines the processes of uncertainty emergence and reduction in workgroups. Our uncertainty reduction model, together with other models based on the self-enhancement motive, should provide a fuller explanation of relational demography effects within a social categorization theory framework. We hope our guidelines on the empirical testing of our model facilitate future research in this direction.

## ACKNOWLEDGMENTS

The work on this chapter was funded in part by a grant from the Hong Kong RGC (Grant #640609).

## REFERENCES

Avery, D. R., McKay, P. F., & Wilson, D. C. (2008). What are the odds? How demographic similarity affects the prevalence of perceived employment discrimination. *Journal of Applied Psychology, 93*(2), 235–249.

Barnett, W., Baron, J., & Stuart, T. (2000). Avenues of attainment: Occupational demography and organizational careers in the California civil service. *American Journal of Sociology, 106*, 88–144.

Baron, J. N., & Newman, A. (1990). For what it's worth: Organizations, occupations, and the value of work done by women and nonwhites. *American Sociological Review, 55*, 155–175.

Berger, J., Cohen, B. P., & Zelditch, M. (1972). Status characteristics and social interaction. *American Sociological Review, 37*, 241–255.

Berger, J., Fisek, M. H., Norman, R., & Zelditch, M. (1977). *Status characteristics in social interaction: An expectation states approach.* New York: Elsevier.

Berger, J., Ridgeway, C. L., Fisek, M. H., & Norman, R. Z. (1998). The legitimation and delegitimation of power and prestige orders. *American Sociological Review, 63*(3), 379–405.

Bergsieker, H. B., Shelton, J. N., & Richeson, J. A. (2010). To be liked versus respected: Divergent goals in interracial interactions. *Journal of Personality and Social Psychology, 99*(2), 248–264.

Bielby, W. T., & Baron, J. N. (1986). Men and women at work: Sex segregation and statistical discrimination. *American Journal of Sociology, 91*, 759–799.

Birenbaum, A., & Sagarin, E. (1976). *Norms and human behavior.* New York: Praeger.

Budig, M. J. (2002). Male advantage and the gender composition of jobs: Who rides the glass escalator? *Social Problems, 49*(2), 258–277.

Byrne, D. E. (1971). *The attraction paradigm.* New York: Academic Press.

Cassirer, N., & Reskin, B. F. (2000). High hopes: Organizational location, employment experiences, and women's and men's promotion aspirations. *Work and Occupations, 27*, 438–463.

Chatman, J. A. (2010). Norms in mixed sex and mixed race work groups. *Academy of Management Annals, 4*, 447–484.

Chatman, J. A., Boisnier, A. D., Spataro, S. E., Anderson, C., & Berdahl, J. L. (2008). Being distinctive versus being conspicuous: The effects of numeric status and sex-stereotyped tasks on individual performance in groups. *Organizational Behavior and Human Decision Processes, 107*, 141–160.

Chatman, J. A., & O'Reilly, C. A. (2004). Asymmetric reactions to work group sex diversity among men and women. *Academy of Management Journal, 47*(2), 193–208.

Chattopadhyay, P. (1999). Beyond direct and symmetrical effects: The influence of demographic dissimilarity on organizational citizenship behavior. *Academy of Management Journal, 42*, 273–287.

Chattopadhyay, P., Finn, C., & Ashkanasy, N. M. (2010). Affective responses to professional dissimilarity: A matter of status. *Academy of Management Journal, 53*, 808–826.

Chattopadhyay, P., George, E., & Lawrence, S. A. (2004a). Why does dissimilarity matter? Exploring self-categorization, self-enhancement, and uncertainty reduction. *Journal of Applied Psychology, 89*(5), 892–900.

Chattopadhyay, P., George, E., & Shulman, A. D. (2008). The asymmetrical influence of sex dissimilarity in distributive vs. colocated work groups. *Organization Science, 19*(4), 581–593.

Chattopadhyay, P., Glick, W. H., & Huber, G. P. (2001). Organizational actions in response to threats and opportunities. *Academy of Management Journal, 44*, 937–955.

Chattopadhyay, P., Tluchowska, M., & George, E. (2004b). Identifying the ingroup: A closer look at the influence of demographic dissimilarity on employee social identity. *Academy of Management Review, 29*(2), 180–202.

Chen, G., & Bliese, P. D. (2002). The role of different levels of leadership in predicting self and collective efficacy: Evidence for discontinuity. *Journal of Applied Psychology, 87*, 549–556.

Cohen, B. P., & Zhou, X. (1991). Status processes in enduring work groups. *American Sociological Review, 56*(2), 179–188.

Cohen, L. L., & Swim, J. K. (1995). The differential impact of gender rations on women and men: Tokenism, self-confidence, and expectations. *Personality and Social Psychology Bulletin, 21*, 876–883.

DiTomaso, N., Post, C., & Parks-Yancy, R. (2007). Workforce diversity and inequality: Power, status, and numbers. *Annual Review of Sociology, 33*, 473–501.

Eagly, A. H., & Steffen, V. J. (1984). Gender stereotypes stem from the distribution of women and men into social roles. *Journal of Personality and Social Psychology, 46*, 735–754.

Fairhurst, G. T., & Snavely, B. K. (1983). Majority and token minority group relationships: Power acquisition and communication. *Academy of Management Review, 8*(2), 292–300.

Fielding, K. S., & Hogg, M. A. (1997). Social identity, self-categorization, and leadership: A field study of small interactive groups. *Group Dynamics, 1*, 39–51.

Fine, G. A. (1987). One of the boys, women in male-dominated settings. In: M. S. Kimmel (Ed.), *Changing men: New directions in research on men and masculinity* (pp. 131–147). Newbury Park, CA: Sage.

Fiske, S. T. (1993). Controlling other people: The impact of power on stereotyping. *American Psychologist, 48*, 621–628.

Fiske, S. T., Cuddy, A. J. C., & Glick, P. (2007). Universal dimensions of social cognition: Warmth and competence. *Trends in Cognitive Sciences*, *11*, 77–83.

Fiske, S. T., & Taylor, S. E. (1991). *Social cognition* (2nd ed.). New York: McGraw-Hill.

Flynn, F. J., & Chatman, J. A. (2003). "What's the norm here?" Social categorization as a basis for group norm development. In: J. T. Polzer, E. Mannix & M. A. Neale (Eds), *Research in managing groups and teams* (pp. 135–160). London: JAI Press, Elsevier Science.

Gaertner, S. L., & Dovidio, J. F. (2000). *Reducing intergroup bias: The common ingroup identity model*. Philadelphia, PA: Psychology Press/Taylor & Francis.

George, E., Chattopadhyay, P., Sitkin, S. B., & Barden, J. (2006). Cognitive underpinnings of institutional persistence and change: A framing perspective. *The Academy of Management Review*, *31*(2), 347–365.

George, E., Chattopadhyay, P., & Zhang, L. L. (forthcoming). Helping hand or competition? The moderating influence of permeability on the relationship between blended workgroups and employee attitudes and behaviors. *Organization Science*.

Goldberg, C. B., Riordan, C., & Schaffer, B. S. (2010). Does social identity theory underlie relational demography? A test of the moderating effects of uncertainty reduction and status enhancement on similarity effects. *Human Relations*, *63*(7), 903–926.

Gonzalez, J. A., & DeNisi, A. S. (2009). Cross-level effects of demography and diversity climate on organizational attachment and firm effectiveness. *Journal of Organizational Behavior*, *30*, 21–40.

Greenberg, J. (1987). A taxonomy of organizational justice theories. *Academy of Management Review*, *12*, 9–22.

Grieve, P. G., & Hogg, M. A. (1999). Subjective uncertainty and intergroup discrimination in the minimal group situation. *Personality and Social Psychology Bulletin*, *25*, 926–940.

Hackman, J. R. (1983). *A normative model of work team effectiveness*. Technical Report no. 2. New Haven, CT: Yale University, School of Organization & Management.

Hackman, J. R. (1992). Group influences on individuals in organizations. In: M. D. Dunnette & L. M. Hough (Eds), *Handbook of industrial and organizational psychology* (Vol. 3, pp. 199–267). Palo Alto: Consulting Psychologists Press.

Hobman, E., Bordia, P., & Gallois, C. (2004). Perceived dissimilarity and work group involvement: The moderating effects of group openness to diversity. *Group and Organization Management*, *29*, 560–587.

Hogg, M. A. (2001). Self-categorization and subjective uncertainty resolution: Cognitive and motivational facets of social identity and group membership. In: J. P. Forgas, K. D. Williams & L. Wheeler (Eds), *The social mind: Cognitive and motivational aspects of interpersonal behavior* (pp. 323–349). New York: Cambridge University Press.

Hogg, M. A. (2007). Uncertainty-identity theory. In: M. P. Zanna (Ed.), *Advances in experimental social psychology* (Vol. 39, pp. 69–126). San Diego, CA: Academic Press.

Hogg, M. A., & Abrams, D. (1993). Towards a single process uncertainty reduction model of social motivation in groups. In: M. A. Hogg & D. Abrams (Eds), *Group motivation: Social psychological perspectives* (pp. 173–190). London: Harvester-Wheatsheaf.

Hogg, M. A., & Abrams, D. (2003). Intergroup behavior and social identity. In: M. A. Hogg & J. Cooper (Eds), *The Sage handbook of social psychology* (pp. 407–431). London: Sage.

Hogg, M. A., & Hains, S. C. (1996). Intergroup relations and group solidarity: Effects of group identification and social beliefs on depersonalized attraction. *Journal of Personality and Social Psychology*, *70*, 295–309.

Hogg, M. A., & Mullin, B. A. (1999). Joining groups to reduce uncertainty: Subjective uncertainty reduction and group identification. In: D. Abrams & M. A. Hogg (Eds), *Social identity and social cognition* (pp. 249–279). Oxford, UK: Blackwell.

Hogg, M. A., & Terry, D. J. (2000). Social identity and self-categorization processes in organizational contexts. *The Academy of Management Review, 25*(1), 121–140.

Hornsey, M. J., & Hogg, M. A. (1999). Subgroup differentiation as a response to an overly-inclusive group: A test of optimal distinctiveness theory. *European Journal of Social Psychology, 29*, 543–550.

Humphreys, P., & Berger, J. (1981). Theoretical consequences of the status characteristics formulation. *American Journal of Sociology, 86*, 953–983.

Jackson, J. (1965). Structural characteristics of norms. In: I. D. Steiner & M. F. Fishbein (Eds), *Current studies on social psychology* (pp. 301–309). New York: Holt, Rinehart & Winston.

Jackson, J. (1966). Conceptual and measurement model for norms and roles. *Pacific Sociological Review, 9*, 35–47.

Jackson, S. E., Brett, J. F., Sessa, V. I., Cooper, D. M., Julin, J. A., & Peyronnin, K. (1991). Some differences make a difference: Individual dissimilarity and group heterogeneity as correlates of recruitment, promotions, and turnover. *Journal of Applied Psychology, 76*, 675–689.

Jex, S. M., & Bliese, P. D. (1999). Efficacy beliefs as a moderator of the impact of work-related stressors: A multilevel study. *Journal of Applied Psychology, 84*, 349–361.

Johnson, M. D., Morgeson, F. P., Ilgen, D. R., Meyer, C. J., & Lloyd, J. W. (2006). Multiple professional identities: Examining differences in identification across work-related targets. *Journal of Applied Psychology, 91*(2), 498–506.

Joshi, A., Liao, H., & Jackson, S. E. (2006). Cross-level effects of workplace diversity on sales performance and pay. *Academy of Management Journal, 49*(3), 459–481.

Joshi, A., & Roh, H. (2009). The role of context in work team diversity research: A meta-analytic review. *Academy of Management Journal, 52*(3), 599–627.

Jost, J. T., & Hunyady, O. (2002). The psychology of system justification and the palliative function of ideology. *European Review of Social Psychology, 13*, 111–153.

Kahneman, D., Knetsch, J. L., & Thaler, R. H. (1991). Anomalies: The endowment effect, loss aversion, and status quo bias. *Journal of Economic Perspectives, 5*(1), 193–206.

Kahneman, D., & Tversky, A. (1979). Prospect theory: An analysis of decision under risk. *Econometrica, 47*(2), 263–292.

Kalkhoff, W., & Barnum, C. (2000). The effects of status-organizing and social identity processes on patterns of social influence. *Social Psychology Quarterly, 63*(2), 95–115.

Kanter, R. M. (1977). *Men and women of the corporation.* New York: Basic Books.

Kanter, R. M. (1978). Some effects of proportions on group life: Skewed sex ratios and responses to token women. *American Journal of Sociology, 82*, 965–990.

Kirchmeyer, C. (1993). Multicultural task groups: An account of the low contribution level of minorities. *Small Group Research, 24*, 127–148.

Lawrence, B. (1997). The black box of organizational demography. *Organization Science, 8*, 1–22.

Liao, H., Joshi, A., & Chuang, A. (2004). Sticking out like a sore thumb: Employee dissimilarity and deviance at work. *Personnel Psychology, 57*, 969–1000.

Lind, E. A., & Tyler, T. R. (1988). *The social psychology of procedural justice.* New York: Plenum Press.

Lopes, L. L. (1987). Between hope and fear: The psychology of risk. *Advances in Experimental Psychology*, *20*, 255–295.

Mael, F. A., & Ashforth, B. E. (1992). Alumni and their alma mater: A partial test of the reformulated model of organizational identification. *Journal of Organizational Behavior*, *13*, 103–123.

McDonald, T. W., Toussaint, L. L., & Schweiger, J. A. (2004). The influence of social status on token women leaders' expectations about leading male-dominated groups. *Sex Roles*, *50*(5 and 6), 401–409.

McDowell, L. (1997). *Capital culture. Gender at work in the city*. Oxford: Wiley Blackwell.

Mueller, C. W., Finley, A., Iverson, R. D., & Price, J. L. (1999). The effects of group racial composition on job satisfaction, organizational commitment, and career commitment: The case of teachers. *Work and Occupations*, *26*(2), 187–219.

Mullin, B. A., & Hogg, M. A. (1998). Dimensions of subjective uncertainty in social identification and minimal intergroup discrimination. *British Journal of Social Psychology*, *37*, 345–465.

Oldmeadow, J., Platow, M. J., Foddy, M., & Anderson, D. (2003). Self-categorization, status, and social influence. *Social Psychology Quarterly*, *66*, 138–152.

Pelled, L. H., Ledford, G. E., & Mohrman, S. A. (1999). Demographic dissimilarity and workplace inclusion. *Journal of Management Studies*, *36*(7), 1013–1031.

Propp, K. M. (1995). An experimental examination of biological sex as a status cue in decision-making groups and its influence on information use. *Small Group Research*, *26*, 451–474.

Reid, S. A., & Hogg, M. A. (2005). Uncertainty reduction, self-enhancement, and ingroup identification. *Personality and Social Psychology Bulletin*, *31*(6), 804–817.

Reskin, B. F., McBrier, D. B., & Kmec, J. (1999). The determinants and consequences of workplace sex and race composition. *Annual Review of Sociology*, *25*, 355–361.

Reynolds, K. J., & Turner, J. C. (2001). Understanding prejudice, discrimination and social conflict: A social identity perspective. In: K. J. Reynolds & M. Augoustinos (Eds), *Us and them: Understanding the psychology of prejudice and racism* (pp. 159–178). London, UK: Sage.

Ridgeway, C. L., Boyle, E. H., Kuipers, K. J., & Robinson, D. T. (1998). How do status beliefs develop? The role of resources and interactional experience. *American Sociological Review*, *63*(3), 331–350.

Ridgeway, C. L., & Smith-Lovin, L. (1999). The gender system and interaction. *Annual Review of Sociology*, *25*, 191–216.

Ridgeway, C. L., & Walker, H. A. (1995). Status structures. In: K. S. Cook, G. A. Fine & J. House (Eds), *Sociological perspectives on social psychology* (pp. 281–310). Boston: Allyn and Bacon.

Riordan, C. M. (2000). Relational demography within groups: Past developments, contradictions, and new directions. In: K. M. Rowland & G. R. Ferris (Eds), *Research in personnel and human resource management* (Vol. 19, pp. 131–173). Greenwich, CT: JAI Press.

Riordan, C. M., & Shore, L. M. (1997). Demographic diversity and employee attitudes: An empirical examination of relational demography within work units. *Journal of Applied Psychology*, *82*(3), 342–358.

Sacco, J. M., & Schmitt, N. (2005). A dynamic multilevel model of demographic diversity and misfit effects. *Journal of Applied Psychology, 90*(2), 203–231.

Sorrentino, R. M., & Roney, C. J. R. (1986). Uncertainty orientation, motivation and cognition. In: R. M. Sorrentino & E. T. Higgins (Eds), *The handbook of motivation and cognition: Foundations of social behavior* (Vol. 1, pp. 379–403). New York: Guilford.

Staw, B. M., Sandelands, L. E., & Dutton, J. E. (1981). Threat-rigidity effects in organizational behavior: A multi-level analysis. *Administrative Science Quarterly, 26*, 501–524.

Tajfel, H., & Turner, J. C. (1979). An integrative theory of intergroup conflict. In: W. G. Austin & S. Worchel (Eds), *The social psychology of intergroup relations* (pp. 33–47). Monterey, CA: Brooks/Cole.

Tajfel, H., & Turner, J. C. (1986). The social identity theory of inter-group behavior. In: S. Worchel & W. G. Austin (Eds), *Psychology of intergroup relations* (pp. 7–24). Chicago: Nelson-Hall.

Tsui, A. S., Egan, T. D., & O'Reilly, C. A. (1992). Being different: Relational demography and organizational attachment. *Administrative Science Quarterly, 37*(4), 549–579.

Tsui, A. S., & O'Reilly, C. A. (1989). Beyond simple demographic effects: The importance of relational demography in superior-subordinate dyads. *Academy of Management Journal, 32*(2), 402–423.

Turner, J. C. (1975). Social comparison and social identity: Some prospects for intergroup behaviour. *European Journal of Social Psychology, 5*, 5–34.

Turner, J. C., Hogg, M. A., Oakes, P. J., Reicher, S. D., & Wetherell, M. S. (1987). *Rediscovering the social group: A self-categorization theory.* Oxford, UK: Blackwell.

Van Knippenberg, D., De Drey, C., & Homans, A. (2004). Work group diversity and group performance: An integrative model and research agenda. *Journal of Applied Psychology, 89*(6), 1008–1022.

van Knippenberg, D., & Ellemers, N. (2003). Social identity and group performance: Identification as the key to group-oriented efforts. In: S. A. Haslam, D. van Knippenberg, M. J. Platow & N. Ellemers (Eds), *Social identity at work: Developing theory for organizational practice* (pp. 29–42). New York and Hove, UK: Psychology Press.

Zitek, E. M., & Hebl, M. R. (2007). The role of social norm clarity in the influenced expression of prejudice over time. *Journal of Experimental Social Psychology, 43*(6), 867–876.

# REBRANDING EMPLOYMENT BRANDING: ESTABLISHING A NEW RESEARCH AGENDA TO EXPLORE THE ATTRIBUTES, ANTECEDENTS, AND CONSEQUENCES OF WORKERS' EMPLOYMENT BRAND KNOWLEDGE

Timothy M. Gardner, Niclas L. Erhardt and Carlos Martin-Rios

## ABSTRACT

*Two primary approaches have been used to study employment brands and branding. First, there is a long history of the study of organizational attraction. Second, in the past 10–15 years, there has been growth in a hybrid stream of research combining branding concepts from the consumer psychology literature with I/O psychology frameworks of organizational attraction and applicant job search behavior. In this chapter, we take an entirely different approach and suggest that the theoretical models built around product/service brand knowledge can readily accommodate employment brands and branding without*

Research in Personnel and Human Resources Management, Volume 30, 253–304
ISSN: 0742-7301/doi:10.1108/S0742-7301(2011)0000030008

*hybridizing the framework with I/O psychology. This merging of employment brand with product and service brands is accomplished simply by recognizing employment as an economic exchange between workers and employers and recognizing workers as cognitive and emotional beings that vary in their talents and have their own vectors of preferences for the employment offering. After developing a testable model of the components, antecedents, and consequences of employment brand knowledge, we review the existing employment brand and organizational attraction literature and identify multiple opportunities for additional research.*

# INTRODUCTION

Scholars have traditionally outlined a series of stages by which organizations hire new employees including: determining job vacancies, advertising open positions, applicants evaluating and responding to vacancy announcements, screening of applicants, extending job offers, and accepting or declining the job offers (Phillips & Gully, 2009). There are several other, common paths by which organizations match talent to job opportunities. First, two very different streams of research suggest that anywhere from 20% to 80% of all people that move from one job to another with no intervening spell of unemployment do so after receiving an unsolicited offer to interview (Fallick & Fleischman, 2001; Lee, Gerhart, Weller, & Trevor, 2008). In other words, organizations frequently reach through the bureaucracy to make unsolicited offers to currently employed individuals not seeking employment. Second, workers apply for employment independent of advertised vacancies. Modern estimates are difficult to come by but data collected from a large bank showed that 19% of the employees hired from 1961 to 1964 were "walk in" and applied without having been encouraged to do so by "help wanted" advertising (Gannon, 1971). With nearly all mid- to large-sized firms in the United States having on-line application capabilities, there is no reason to think this rate is lower today. Finally, data from the National Organizations Study shows that 37% of employers frequently bypass the five stage process described earlier and recruit active and passive job seekers via employee referrals (Kalleberg, Knoke, Marsden, & Spaeth, 1996, p. 138).

Although the traditional I/O psychology lens offers important insights as to how individuals seek employment and respond to recruiting efforts, the earlier trends suggest there are alternative ways individuals make decisions about where to apply that are not captured by this framework. The purpose of this chapter is to offer an alternative view to the traditional job search and choice literature grounded in consumer psychology. Specifically we will be reviewing the employment brand literature that has emerged over the past 15–20 years (Barrow & Mosley, 2005). There are a number of stellar reviews of the pure I/O psychology and hybrid I/O psychology-consumer psychology based recruiting and job choice literature (see Barber, 1998; Cable & Turban, 2001; Schwab, Rynes & Aldag, 1987, respectively). Although we acknowledge and occasionally draw upon this previous work, we ground our review in the frameworks of consumer psychology, specifically employment branding. As Cable and Turban's (2001) review covered the literature published before 2001, our review generally covers the literature published from 2001 to the present.

This chapter is organized into five sections. In the section on product brands, we introduce the concept of brands from the consumer psychology literature. In the section on worker-based employment brand equity, we translate brands from the perspective of the consumer to the worker actively or passively considering employment options. Next, we review the attributes of the employment offering; again translating the consumer psychology conception of product and service attributes to the employment context. In the section on activities used to develop workers' employment brand knowledge, we examine how employers seek to create employment brand knowledge in the minds of prospective workers. Finally, we conclude the chapter with a review of organizational attraction. Although this is a construct developed and frequently used by I/O psychologists, we felt it too important not to mention in a review of the employment brand literature.

Throughout this chapter, we use the term "worker" as an all-encompassing term to denote individuals who currently sell or may sell their labor to an individual or organization for economic reward (Kelloway, Gallagher, & Barling, 2004, p. 110). Labor is broadly defined to include physical, emotional, and mental energies (Kaufman, 2004). Thus worker encompasses blue and white collar workers, professional and technical workers, knowledge workers, supervisors, middle managers, and nonowner executives. The term excludes individuals who are employers, what the Marxist might call capitalists: someone who owns the means of production, purchases the labor powers of others, and does not sell their own labor power (Wright & Perrone, 1977).

We considered using the word "employee" instead of worker but this implies individuals who are currently employed. When we discuss the employment brand we may be referring to the employment knowledge structures of the current employees of a focal firm and/or individuals not affiliated with the focal firm. These outside individuals might include those employed but actively seeking alternative employment or fully engaged workers that might be potential lateral hiring targets (Gardner, Stansbury, & Hart, 2010). Others with employment brand knowledge include the unemployed, including both those looking for work and those fully engaged in nonwork endeavors. Outside individuals might also include future workers. For instance, large employers such as Texas Instruments, IBM, Boeing, and others sponsor science career themed summer camps for middle and high school students both to increase the number of students who pursue science as a career but also as a way to create employment brand knowledge in future workers (Shellenbarger, 2006).

## PRODUCT BRANDS

The American Marketing Association defines a brand as a "name, term, sign, symbol, or design or a combination of them intended to identify the goods and services of one seller or group of sellers and to differentiate them from those of competitors" (Keller, 1993, p. 2). Although the concept has an interesting modern history (Blackett, 2009), brands have very ancient roots. Archeologists have discovered in the remains of the Indus Valley civilization (~2600 BC), what is today India, small square seals that were sold to manufacturers and merchants to mark, distinguish, and transmit information about the quality of goods sold (Moore & Reid, 2008).

"Brands," of course, are components of but distinct from the goods or services they represent. A product is anything that is offered on the market for consumption, attention, acquisition, or use that may satisfy consumer needs or wants. Numerous generic products might satisfy specific consumer wants and needs. Some products and services have attributes and benefits that make them different and sometimes better than competitors' offerings including packaging, delivery, financing, product design, or features. Brands transmit to consumers both generic and distinguishing product utility but also unrealized and unarticulated intangible benefits of ownership and consumption such as heritage, symbolic and emotional meaning, status, and prestige (Berthon, Hulbert, & Pitt, 1999; Keller, 2008). For example, even though they satisfy very similar wants and have similar features, the Apple Inc. branded portable media player iPod is positively distinguished in nearly all consumers' minds from the Sansa View produced by SanDisk on multiple tangible and intangible dimensions.

Brands "do" a great deal both for consumers and sellers. In developing and understanding the utility of brands, and by extension employment brands, it is important to understand the presumed choice environment in which consumers make purchasing decisions. The field of consumer psychology presumes consumers are making decisions much more complicated than the binary decisions of choosing between two similar products or choosing to purchase or not purchase a particular product. Given a vector of needs and/or wants to be satisfied, consumers face an enormous number of competing choices and products. Nearly all wants can be satisfied with solutions from multiple product categories. A consumer simply wanting to relieve itchiness on their back torso could choose among mechanical back scratchers, DVD-based programs on arm and back stretching to better reach the itch, over the counter or prescribed cream and pills, and for some conditions, intradermal injections of the botulinum toxin (Botox) in the affected area (Weinfeld, 2007). In addition, consumers usually face a number of choices within each product category. A consumer seeking to travel from Cincinnati, OH to Memphis, TN via rented automobile has several rental companies and automobile brands from which to choose. Consumers must also frequently decide whether to continue the use of known products or make an intra- or interproduct category switch. Complicating this highly complex choice environment, consumers face costs for the acquisition of product utility information, ambiguity about the risks and benefits of each competing choice, information-processing limitations, bounded rationality, and an imperfect understanding of their own needs and wants (Keller, 2008; Swait & Adamowicz, 2001).

Amid this backdrop of overwhelming choice and human limitation, brands simplify consumers' decision making and allow sellers to communicate the utility of their offerings and distinguish them from competitors both within and across product categories. At the simplest level, brands identify for consumers the source or producer of the product. Faced with a myriad of restaurant choices near an unfamiliar highway off-ramp, brands that identify the available restaurants helps consumers distinguish among the offerings thus simplifying choice. Information about the product or service associated with the brand reduces search costs, reduces the perceived risks of the purchase decision, and increases the confidence consumers place in their final decision. In short, brands allow consumers to confidently make perceived better decisions with significantly less thought (Broyles, Schumann, & Leingpibul, 2009; Keller, 2008).

Brands also provide utility to consumers during and after consumption. Brands serve as symbolic devices that allow consumers to communicate both to others and themselves the type of person they are or would like to be (Berthon et al., 1999; Keller, 2008). Shoppers purchasing groceries from one of the Whole Foods Market chain of stores communicate to themselves and others that they aspire to be socially responsible, health conscious, and are sufficiently wealthy to pay premium prices for organic and "natural" goods that are scientifically indistinguishable from their nonorganic cousins (Goodchild, 2009). Consumers are personally rewarded when their brand choice reinforces their aspirational identity and signals this identity to others (Berthon et al., 1999).

For sellers, brands allow them to help consumers identify and re-identify their goods and services. When promoting specific products, brands allow sellers to create an identity for what would ordinarily be a commodity thus reducing consumer search costs. The differentiation brands create for products in the minds of consumers allows the seller to charge a price premium above what can be charged for generic products or commodities. Finally, brands allow sellers to communicate consistent messages about products' intangible and tangible benefits thus facilitating customer segmentation (Berthon et al., 1999; Keller & Lehmann, 2006).

### Concept of Employment Brand

One may reasonably wonder whether the concept of product/service brand can be fruitfully mapped over to the concept of employment brand. As defined earlier, a *brand* is a symbolic representation of goods and services that allows sellers to distinguish, in the minds of consumers, their products from competitors'. In the marketing literature, the consumer is the actual or prospective purchaser of products while the seller is the party offering products for sale (AMA, 2010). In the employment domain, it is the employer that is the actual or prospective purchaser of a worker's labor while the worker sells their talents, energies, commitment, and willingness to submit to the employer's work processes (Budd & Bhave, 2009; Garner, 2004, p. 564; Garrow, 1994; Kaufman, 2004). If in employment transactions the worker is the seller and the employer is the consumer the brand concept might be inappropriate to apply to employers and employment but relevant for workers hoping to distinguish themselves in the minds of prospective employers. The job search section of any bookstore has a range of books advising job searchers how to create successful worker brands (e.g., Bence, 2009).

One of the primary contributions of this chapter is to suggest that greater progress can be made in the study of employment branding by shifting the theoretical foundation from OB and I/O psychology to consumer psychology. At first glance, positioning workers as consumers of employment offerings may seem nothing more than a minor shift. Although this repositioning is consistent with the classical perspective of labor markets, it is inconsistent with the labor system tradition and is a shift with previous reviews of the employment branding literature.

The classical perspective emphasizes a perfectly competitive labor market where many agents conduct labor transactions under conditions of full information and few barriers to movement (Arrow, 1973). Forces of market competition determine the supply of and demand for labor, which is bought and sold freely as a commodity. Workers and firms are assumed to have perfect information and can move freely in response to changes in supply and demand in different parts of the market. Hence, the market for labor resembles the exchange market for many goods and services. Human capital theory (Becker, 1964) emphasizes differences among people, rather than among jobs, as determinant of recruitment/employment opportunities in the general labor market (Spence, 1974). Individuals are assumed to survey the lifetime opportunities open to them and exchange their labor services for the optimal employment opportunity.

In the labor system tradition, labor markets are conceived as arenas in which workers exchange their labor power in return for a wage in order to live. Capitalists are the "buyers" in these transactions and control that labor within the labor process (Wright, 1980). Moreover, institutional theory posits that labor markets are "dual" or "stratified" (Piore, 1969). The labor market is understood as divided into various segments or strata, each of which can be identified by a characteristic set of wages, working conditions, opportunities for advancement, and level of turnover. Job opportunities vary along these strata and because of the existence of barriers; workers in one stratum are impeded to move to another more desirable one. Workers' do not choose or "purchase" employment opportunities but may participate in a limited set of labor strata whose opportunities are highly constrained by the employee choices made by employers.

We fully recognize legitimate components of both perspectives. The framework we propose for employment branding builds on assumptions consistent with the classical tradition. Although some employers in some industries treat labor and thus workers as commodities, from the U.S. Colonial era to the present time employers have competed with each other to hire and retain the best talent for jobs of all levels of complexity (Prude,

1983; Tam & Woo, 2011). Given this competition for talent (Chambers, Foulon, Handfield-Jones, Hankin, & Michaels, 1998), we view workers not as passive vessels of undifferentiated labor waiting to be "purchased" by employers but as cognitive and emotional beings (Wright, Dunford, & Snell, 2001) that vary in the components and quality of talents and with their own vectors of preferences for employment, location, pay, and perquisites. Given a sufficiently large number of applicants, and a low selection ratio, modern selection techniques allow nearly all firms to identify applicants with the highest level of desired skills. Acquiring these skills requires firms to attract a large number of autonomous applicants and for the best applicant to freely choose the organization's employment offering (Phillips & Gully, 2009).

Employment branding researchers have three broad theoretical frameworks from which to study this phenomenon. One option is the frameworks used to examine how people choose from among employment options (Schwab et al., 1987). This broad based research stream focuses on how *job seekers* search for, evaluate, and choose from among existing employment opportunities. After reviewing this literature, we concluded that the focus on active job seekers and existing job openings would not be the best fit as employment branding is concerned with how workers searching or not searching for employment process and respond to information about symbols that represent abstract employment offerings. The second option is to use a hybrid of the marketing and job search literatures. Cable and Turban (2001) used such a hybrid model in their review of the employer brand knowledge literature. This approach, which is used by many of the studies reviewed in this chapter, focuses on how job seekers store and use information about *organizations* to make application, interview, and job acceptance decisions. Employer attributes and associations, while important drivers of employment search and acceptance behavior are but a small component of individuals' total brand knowledge (Keller & Lehmann, 2006).

Consumer psychology is the study of "the dynamic interaction of affect and cognition, behavior, and environment by which human beings conduct the exchange aspects of their lives" (Peter & Olson, 2005, p. 5). By simply recognizing employment as an exchange between workers and employers, we concluded that grounding our employment branding framework in the existing theories of consumer psychology was superior to adapting job search and I/O recruitment theories to the employment exchange context.

Before offering our definition of employment brand we want to address the semantic issue of whether the term "*employer* brand" or "*employment* brand" is most appropriate. *Employer* brand is clearly the most commonly used term. A full-text search of EBSCOhost's "Business Source Premier" resulted in 1,258 articles using the terms "employer brand/ing" and only 429 using the terms "employment brand/ing." A commonly cited definition of employer brand is "the package of functional, economic, and psychological benefits provided by employment and identified with the employing company" (Ambler & Barrow, 1996, p. 187). A 2001 Conference Board report defined employer brand as "the identity of the firm as an employer" (Dell, Ainspan, Bodenbert, Troy, & Hickey, 2001, p. 10). Neither definition is consistent with the concept of "brand" as discussed in mainstream marketing literature the frameworks of which we are using to structure this chapter. For the reasons discussed later, we have chosen to use the term employment brand.

Brands are generally thought of as identifying and differentiating the *goods and services* of a seller (Keller, 1993, p. 2). In the employment context, "goods and services" would be employment – what the employer offers in exchange for workers' efforts and how their physical, mental, and emotional energies are deployed while working. Ambler and Barrow's (1996) and Dell et al.'s (2001) definitions focus on the employment-related information associated with the corporate brand (Keller, 2008). This is a legitimate and useful perspective when trying to create and manage a corporate identity in the minds of its many stakeholders (Brown & Dacin, 1997). Our interest is the identity or brand of the product – employment – in the minds of current and potential workers and how workers' knowledge structures associated with the employment brand affect their response to the marketing of the brand (Keller, 1993). Take for example employment as a programmer at Microsoft. We are not directly interested in Microsoft's identity and reputation as an employer; in other words, the employment information stakeholders associate with the Microsoft Corporation. We instead are interested in "Microsoft" as a symbol that provides identity to employment offerings and how information associated with "Microsoft" as an employment brand symbol affects workers' responses to the marketing of their programming job. Borrowing heavily from Keller (1993) we define employment brand as "names, terms, signs, symbols, or designs or a combination of them intended to identify the employment offering of one employer and to differentiate it from the offerings of competing employers."

Employment brands, like product brands help workers make perceived better decisions about beginning, ending, and continuing employment transactions with less thought. Several scholars have noted that consumers rely more on brands when making service purchase decisions than product purchase decisions due to the intangibility of and variance in quality of services (Berry, 2000; Keller, 2008). We suggest that for most individuals, employment brands are more important when making employment decisions than product brands are when making purchasing decisions due to the importance of work in human life, the intensive trading of "self" for employment offerings, and the intangibility and uncertain quality of the employment product before beginning employment.

Understanding individuals' feelings and knowledge of employment offerings is important because work is important to most people. In discussing the centrality of work to the human experience, Kelloway et al. (2004) noted that work is metaphorically presented as the purpose of humanity in one of the most influential accounts of the origin of the human species. Genesis 2:15 reads: "The LORD God took the man and put him in the Garden of Eden to work it and take care of it." Work, beyond the activity required to gain food and shelter, has been a fundamental component of the human condition since prehistoric times (Arendt, 1958; Donkin, 2001). People, Americans in particular, generally work even when they are not required to do so. Beyond providing the means for self and family survival and comfort, work provides status, personal identity, and opportunities for social interaction (Kelloway et al., 2004). Several studies show that 90% or more of American big prize lottery winners continue to work for another person or organization even when they have sufficient funds not to do so. Surveys of the U.S. population show the vast majority of Americans agree they would continue to work if lottery winnings made employment unnecessary (Arvey, Harpaz, & Liao, 2004; Highhouse, Zickar, & Yankelevich, 2010; Kaplan, 1985).

Worker transactions with employers require more than the exchange of discrete resources, they involve the constant presence and exchange of "self" (Goffman, 1959). Karl Marx's (1906) treatise Capital makes this exchange quite explicit. He states, a worker sets "in motion arms and legs, head and hands, the natural forces of his body ... " (p. 198) in order to create products and services of value. More than just passively thinking or providing physical labor, workers must constantly use the self to *will* the body and mind to act in accordance with the employer's needs. He writes, "Besides the exertion of the bodily organs, the [labor] process and that, during the whole operation, the workman's will be steadily in consonance with his purpose ... " (Marx, 1906, p. 198). Hochschild (1983) extended this insight by pointing out that workers' expenditure of mental energy also includes the self-control, suppression, and coordination of internal emotions and the public facial and bodily display of observable emotions. "This type of [emotional] labor calls for a coordination of mind and feeling, and it sometimes draws on a source of self that we honor as deep and integral to our individuality" (p. 7).

Before forming an employment relationship, workers generally have very limited knowledge of the tangible and intangible resources to be gained from the prospective employment exchange. For most workers in modern industrialized economies, the employment relationship is an open-ended transaction; details emerge only as time passes and relevant contingencies arise. When a worker accepts employment, the job duties six months or six years hence are not fully specified. Specifics about future salary, promotions. training, recognition, etc. are purposefully left vague (Baron & Kreps, 1999. p. 62). Intangibles such as equity, voice, dignity, purposeful activity, personal fulfillment, status, identity, and social relations, are insupposable (Budd & Bhave, 2009). Employment brands fill in these gaps and allow potential workers to efficiently make perceived better decisions and feel more confident in their decisions after making them.

**Proposition 1a.** Workers rely more on employment brands when making employment decisions than when making consumer product and service decisions.

**Proposition 1b.** The role of employment brands is more important in making employment decisions (i) the greater the importance work plays in a person's identity; (ii) the more the "self" in the form of physical, mental. and emotional labor is required as a medium of exchange in the employment relationship; and (iii) the greater the uncertainty of and variability in attributes of the employer's employment offering.

### Consumer-Based Brand Equity

As we have mentioned several times earlier, a brand is something that resides in the minds of individuals that identifies a good or service. The marketing literature grounds this thinking on standard models of human memory. These theoretical models posit that information is stored as bundles of information in the brain as 'nodes.' Nodes are connected to one another via links of varying strength. When a node is activated via the recall or encoding process, other nodes linked to the activated nodes are also activated and their information recalled depending on the strength of the connection between them. This information then becomes available for use. Thus, a node becomes a potential source of activation of other nodes either when new information is coded or retrieved from memory (Collins & Stevens, 2002, p. 1122; Keller, 1993).

Consider the example of a person contemplating purchasing donuts. A person may think of *Krispy Kreme* branded donuts because of their strong association with the donut product category (Doonar, 2004). The consumer's knowledge associated with the Krispy Kreme donut brand should also come to mind: the light and fluffy texture; sweetness; and the sensation of the donut melting in the mouth. The knowledge associated with the brand could come from personal experience, word of mouth, or advertising. Thus brand knowledge is conceptualized as the memory node containing brand identity information to which other nodes of information about the brand are linked (Keller, 1993; Shocker, Ben-Akiva, Coccara, & Nedungadi, 1991).

The broad set of knowledge associated with a brand is assumed to have two dimensions, brand familiarity and brand attitude. Brand familiarity is the strength of the brand identity node in consumers' memory. It is manifest as (1) recognition when the brand name is given and (2) the likelihood the brand name will come to the consumer's memory when considering a purchase from a specific product category (Brown & Wildt, 1992). If a consumer decided she needed to travel from Salt Lake City to Nashville, what is the likelihood Southwest Airlines would come to mind? Brand attitude, the second dimension of brand knowledge, is conceptualized as a summary of the totality of memory node associations, with meaning, held by consumers about the brand. These associations include direct and indirect benefits from the product or service. Each attribute and benefit can be described in terms of its favorability, strength, and uniqueness (Keller, 1993).

Consumers with brand familiarity and a positive brand attitude linked to the brand respond differently to marketing efforts than consumers lacking such mental structures. The differential response may be behavioral, increased attention and interest, deeper evaluation, pre- and post-consumption satisfaction, and ultimately greater purchase probability. Marketers call this attentional and behavioral bias "customer based brand equity." A brand has positive customer-based brand equity when consumers react more favorably to a product and the way it is marketed when identified with a brand than when it is not. Imagine two separate groups of individuals. One group is told they have won a *cruise* to Alaska; the other group is told they have won a *Royal Caribbean cruise* to Alaska. The group told the name of the branded cruise line will respond more vigorously to the announcement than the group told they have won a generic cruise (Faircloth, Capella, & Alford, 2001). Keller (2008, p. 50) recounts a beer taste testing with two different subject groups. Both groups tasted six different beers, one of which was Guinness, a strong tasting, dark beer. One group was told the names of the beers they tasted; the other group was not. The group that knew the names of the beers detected significant differences in taste among the beers across multiple dimensions. The group not told the names identified Guinness as very different from the other five but identified virtually no differences among the five remaining beers. The perceived taste distinctions made by the individuals given the names of the beers were a manifestation of brand equity, a function of the brand familiarity and the brand attitudes linked to the beer brands.

## WORKER-BASED EMPLOYMENT BRAND EQUITY

The focus of this chapter, of course, is worker-based employment brand equity (WBEBE). Workers have in their memories a variety of distinct employment brands identifying and distinguishing various employment offerings. Associated with these employment brands are two dimensions of employment brand knowledge: (1) employment brand familiarity – the strength of the employment brand node in the worker's memory. Brand knowledge is also manifest as (2) employment brand attitude – the attitude directed toward the brand summarizing individuals' understanding of the attributes of the employment offering and the perceived utility of these attributes. Fig. 1 summarizes the WBEBE model and serves as an outline for the remainder of this chapter.

Employment brand knowledge, composed of employment brand familiarity and employment brand attitude is best understood as a formative rather than reflective variable. Classical test theory assumes that items of a variable are intercorrelated, imperfect *reflections* of an underlying latent construct and thus considered a reflective measure. Measures sometimes do not represent reflections of latent constructs but instead combine to *form* the latent construct. Such formative measures are viewed as "causing" the latent construct; the items are not assumed to covary (MacKenzie, Podsakoff, & Jarvis, 2005). Employment brand knowledge is not the empirical representation of an underlying latent construct but instead, employment brand attitude and employment brand familiarity combine to create the construct (Keller, 1993).

Employment brand knowledge results in WBEBE, defined as the manifestation of the differential effects that employment brand knowledge has on workers' responses to the marketing of that employment brand.

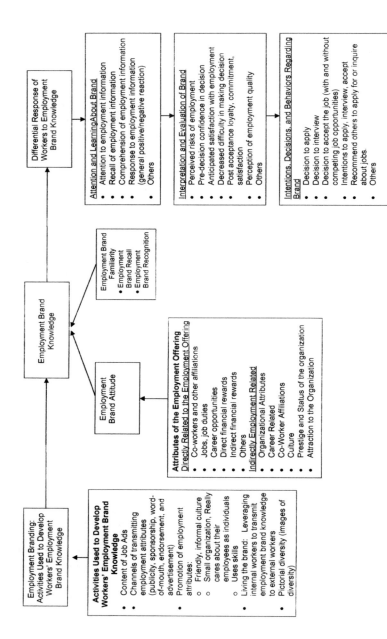

*Fig. 1.* Model of the Antecedents, Components, and Consequences of Employment Brand Knowledge.

Positive WBEBE is the manifestation of favorable worker responses to an employment offering and the way it is marketed when the offering is identified with a brand than when it is not (Keller, 1993, p. 2). When a recruiter approaches a happily engaged employee at another firm, a job opportunity identified with a brand with positive employment brand knowledge will be more carefully considered and more actively pursued than a generic job opportunity or a job opportunity without positive brand knowledge. When a star employee is slighted by the regional vice president and decides to seek alternative employment, he is more likely, without prompting, to think of unadvertised employment opportunities associated with robust employment brand knowledge structures in his memory than brands without such knowledge structures. Finally, when the star MBA finance graduate is choosing among multiple job offers, she is likely to accept the position with the most positive employment brand knowledge in her memory nodes.

## Employment Brand Knowledge

The two dimensions of employment brand knowledge discussed earlire are employment brand familiarity and employment brand attitude. Brand knowledge resides in workers' associative memory structures and is a direct function of their stored experiences with the brand. These experiences can be in the form of direct and indirect contact with the employment brand. For instance, many companies maintain databases of high performing former employees for future recruiting and hiring (Hirschman, 2000). These former employees' employment brand knowledge is based on their direct experiences as an employee. Word of mouth from current or former employees is an indirect source of employment brand knowledge. In the past, indirect sources would have been a limited set of information drawn from workers' family and social networks. With today's social media, blogs, and other sources of first-hand information from employees, word of mouth information is a critical source of brand knowledge (Dutta & Fraser, 2009). Firms' marketing efforts to communicate employment brand information is another source of workers' information. This can be in the form of explicit communications of open positions or employment branding efforts by the firm to create knowledge structures in potential workers for future recruiting (Brandt & Shook, 2005; Faircloth et al., 2001). The Crete Carrier trucking company has an advertisement on the back end of their semi-trailer trucks that reads "SATISFIED DRIVER SIXTY-THREE FEET AHEAD." This advertisement is designed to create the image of a satisfied driver and associate it with Crete Carrier as an employment brand. Finally, as will be discussed in more depth later, employment brand knowledge is derived from workers' experiences with firms' corporate and product brands (Collins, 2007). For instance, workers with robust product and corporate brand knowledge of the Union Pacific rail company will have a level of employment brand familiarity and attitude linked to Union Pacific as an employment brand as well. In the following sections, we will review the components, consequences, and the antecedents of employment brand knowledge placing special emphasis on what firms do to manage this knowledge.

*Employment Brand Knowledge: Brand Familiarity and Brand Attitudes*

### Brand Familiarity

Workers making employment search, pursuit, and acceptance decisions behave like consumers making purchase decisions. In one decision path there is a recognized need for employment. This might be a proactive need on the part of a currently employed person for new employment or the need of an unemployed person to find work. The person searches their memory as well as published company listings for firms to which they might submit unsolicited applications. They also use a variety of sources of job postings to find and submit applications to advertised openings. In the second decision path, the person, employed or unemployed, is approached directly and encouraged to apply for an open position by a representative for the employer. As aforementioned, 20–80% of all workers who move from one job to another do so after receiving an unsolicited offer to interview (Fallick & Fleischman, 2001; Lee et al., 2008). We will use the two employment paths to better explain the concept of employment brand familiarity.

Individuals seeking an employment opportunity can only theoretically consider the *available set* of employment brands – brands that exist and for which there might be actual employment opportunities. From the available set of employment brands, the *awareness set* includes the set of brands which the worker is aware. The worker then examines and processes information about a subset of the awareness set resulting in the *processed set* and the *unprocessed set* of employment brands. Employment brands in the processed set are categorized as acceptable alternatives, rejected alternatives, or those put on hold – not further considered for employment opportunities. The employment brands considered acceptable alternatives, called the *consideration set*, are more fully analyzed and the person makes the decision to apply and interview, and if offered a position, accept (Brisoux & Cheron, 1990; Brown & Wildt, 1992; Posavac, Sanbonmatsu, Cronley, & Kardes, 2001). For the decision to apply for openings, the worker is only constrained by their time and energy available to submit applications. For interview and job choice decisions workers, like consumers, are limited to considering brands for which they have the sufficient personal resources to exchange for the employment opportunity.

Consistent with the marketing literature, we propose that employment brand familiarity is composed of two empirical manifestations: (1) *employment brand recognition*, manifest as workers' ability to confirm exposure to the employment brand when the brand name is given as a cue. A sample question partially representing this construct might be "I have seen or heard information" regarding jobs at [insert employment brand name]. And (2) *employment brand recall*, manifest as workers' ability to recall the brand from memory when given different employment contexts as a cue. For instance, a student might be asked, "List the brands identifying jobs filled by students from this college in your major." A worker might be asked "Name as many employment brands for jobs that you would qualify for that located in the tri-county area" (Keller, 1993, 2008).

Keller (1993) argued that brand recognition is most important when consumers make choices with available brand identification; for example when a consumer must choose between soda brands in the grocery store aisle. Greater familiarity with the brand, even independent of brand attitude, leads to affinity for the brand, which leads to brand choice (Shocker et al., 1991). Keller argued that brand recall is most important for memory-based choices; making a decision in the absence of brand stimuli. For example, thinking of a restaurant at which to eat after pulling the car out of the driveway (Posavac et al., 2001). We argue that both components of familiarity are important for employment brands. Obviously, brand recognition plays an important role in workers' decisions to apply to employment advertisements (Collins, 2007; Knox & Freeman, 2006). Brand recognition also likely plays a critically important role in workers' decisions to pursue opportunities presented via unsolicited offers to interview. Owing to the proliferation of corporate web pages and the associated capability of submitting applications and resumes on-line, unsolicited applications represent a growing and important proportion of companies' applicant pools (Heneman & Judge, 2009, chapter 5). Self-referred employees perform better and have longer tenures than employees prompted to apply by employment adverts (Zottoli & Wanous, 2000). We are not aware of research on the thought process by which such workers submit unsolicited applications but it seems likely this behavior represents more of a memory-based rather than stimulus-based choice making employment brand recall an important precursor of this behavior (Posavac et al., 2001).

**Proposition 2a.** Employment brand familiarity is positively associated with workers' decisions to apply for advertised employment opportunities.

**Proposition 2b.** Employment brand familiarity is positively associated with workers' decisions to pursue unsolicited offers to interview.

**Proposition 2c.** Employment brand familiarity is positively associated with workers' decision to submit unsolicited applications for employment.

*Brand Attitude*

Consumers maintain information about brands in their memory. The informational nodes linked to the brand are called brand associations. These include attributes, benefits, images, feelings, sensory impressions, etc. In short, all of the signals emitted by the brand and retained in consumer memory (Faircloth et al., 2001). Owing to human information processing and memory limitations, consumers cannot retrieve, process, and utilize all the factual and affective brand associations at any one time and thus rely on attitudes to facilitate the storage and retrieval information associated with brands (Faircloth et al., 2001). Attitudes, defined by Fishbein and Ajzen (1975, p. 6) as "a learned predisposition to respond in a consistently favorable or unfavorable manner with respect to a given object," function as information simplifying heuristics for the information stored about each brand. The result is that the constellation of information and feelings associated with each brand is manifest as a brand attitude summarizing the information stored about the brand in memory. Spears and Singh (2004) define a brand attitude as the "attitude toward the brand that is a relatively enduring, unidimensional summary evaluation of the brand that presumably energizes behavior" (p. 55). The authors are clear to specify brand attitude as a "summary evaluation" to distinguish it from the evaluative expression of attitudes in the form of beliefs, feelings, and behaviors (p. 55). Dozens of studies suggest that brand attitude leads to brand intentions which lead to brand choice (Spears & Singh, 2004).

Borrowing heavily from Spears and Singh (2004, p. 55) we define employment brand attitude as an "attitude toward the employment brand that is a relatively enduring, unidimensional summary evaluation of the brand that presumably energizes job search, pursuit, and acceptance behavior." Employment brand attitude summarizes the information stored in memory that is associated with the brand. Reviewing and integrating two decades of research Spears and Singh (2004) developed and validated a new measure of brand attitude that could easily be adapted to employment brand. Using a semantic differential scale, consumers rate the brand as appealing/unappealing, bad/good, unpleasant/pleasant, unfavorable/favorable, and unlikeable/likeable. We suggest one of the most fruitful avenues of future research in employment branding is the creation and validation of a measure of employment brand attitude.

> **Proposition 3.** Employment brand attitude is constructively associated with workers' differential responses to employment brand information. This includes (a) attention and learning about an employment brand; (b) interpretation and evaluation of an employment brand; and (c) intentions, decisions, and behaviors toward the brand.

# CONSEQUENCES OF EMPLOYMENT BRAND KNOWLEDGE DIFFERENTIAL RESPONSE TO MARKETING EFFORTS

Hoeffler and Keller (2003) distinguish between three types of attentional and behavioral biases consumer exhibit in response to positive brand knowledge. These are (1) attention and learning about the brand; (2) interpretation and evaluation of the brand; and (3) behaviors and decisions regarding the brand. Below, we will briefly explain each and propose analogues for the employment brand context. Throughout this chapter we will be using the term "strong brand;" by this we mean brands with well-developed brand knowledge structures in the minds of potential and actual consumers: high brand familiarity and strong, positive, and unique associations with the brand. For instance, we would suggest that the IKEA brand is a strong brand in that furniture consumers are familiar with it and have generally positive associations (In IKEA we trust, 2009).

### Attention and Learning about the Employment Brand

As discussed earlier, the mechanism by which strong brands produce the differential consumer responses to marketing efforts is rooted in theories of associative memory. Building on this framework, marketers suggest that strong brands have two advantages when it comes to the attention paid to the brand and the information retained. First, consumers are more likely to involuntarily notice and process information about brands with which they are familiar. Second, strong brands have memory-encoding advantages over weak brands. Consumers already have the knowledge structures in place to add new information and information about the brand is more likely to be noticed from the informational clutter. Building on what we know about consumers, we should expect that workers will more readily pay attention to and learn more about existing, robust employment brands relative to the attention paid to and learning about employment brands with less developed knowledge structures (Hoeffler & Keller, 2003, pp. 423–424).

Barber (1998) began to address these issues in her review of the job choice literature. She looked at the limited, mostly practitioner literature on how to attract the attention and motivate application behavior of job seekers (pp. 38–45). Recent research continues to examine what stimuli grab the attention of and motivates this population (Walker, Feild, Giles, & Bernerth, 2008). The employment branding perspective used in this chapter broadens the population from job seekers to all workers, employed or not, seeking for employment alternatives or not. This perspective broadens the information domain from job advertisements to all employment information.

Consistent with the consumer branding literature, employment brands with positive employment brand knowledge should result in increased attention to employment information provided by the employer or received from indirect sources such as former employees, social media, and the popular press; better comprehension of employment information, whatever the source; more positive reactions to employment information; better remembering of employment information; and greater willingness among passive and active job seekers to listen to recruiters' information provided about job opportunities (Alba & Hutchinson, 1987; Johnson & Russo, 1984; Kent & Allen, 1994; Lehmann & Pan, 1994; Simonson, Huber, & Payne, 1988).

**Proposition 4.** Greater employment brand knowledge, manifest as positive employment brand attitude associated with the brand and greater employment brand familiarity will result in greater attention and learning about the employment brand. This includes greater attention to, recall of, and comprehension employment information as well as favorable reaction to employment information.

## Interpretation and Evaluation of the Employment Brand

Following the learning and coding of brand information, brand knowledge is associated with more positive interpretations and evaluation of brand information (Hoeffler & Keller, 2003). It appears there are two processes that drive these outcomes, direct and indirect effects. As a direct effect, positive brand attitude leads to more positive evaluations of the brand (Brown & Stayman, 1992). Similarly, more developed brand knowledge structures increase confidence in the brand leading to more positive interpretations and evaluations (Dacin & Smith, 1994). As an indirect effect, greater brand knowledge increases consumers' confidence in the legitimacy of the product or service thus increasing positive evaluations (Erdem, 1998).

We should expect to see a positive association between employment brand knowledge and the positive interpretation and evaluation of a brand. Translating some of the marketing outcomes into employment outcomes we might expect to see employment brand knowledge to be constructively associated with perceptions of employment quality (Wernerfelt, 1988), perceived risks of the employment decision (Ailawadi, Lehmann, & Nelson, 2003; Broyles et al., 2009), pre- and post-choice confidence in the decision (Dacin & Smith, 1994; Laroche, Kim, & Zhou, 1996), decreased decision difficulty (Mushukrishnan, 1995), and increased post-acceptance loyalty, satisfaction, and commitment to the employment offering (Agrawal, 1996; Berry, 2000; Broyles et al., 2009).

**Proposition 5.** Greater employment brand knowledge, manifest as positive employment brand attitude associated with the brand and greater employment brand familiarity will result in more positive interpretations and evaluations of employment brand information. This includes lower perceived risks with the employment decision, pre- and post-decision confidence, decreased decision difficulty, and increased post-choice loyalty, commitment, and satisfaction.

## Intentions, Decisions, and Behaviors Regarding the Employment Brand

The broad message of the employment brand equity model outlined in Fig. 1, suggests that employment brand knowledge ultimately leads to workers' intentions, decisions, and behaviors toward the brand and that this process is mediated by consumers' attention and learning about the employment brand and their interpretation and evaluation of the employment brand. In short, employment brand knowledge leads to increased learning, positive evalua-tions, increased brand intentions, and finally brand choice.

The vast majority of the research classified as focusing on employment brand focuses on modeling the antecedents of job pursuit and job choice of active job seekers (Barber, 1998; Chapman, Uggerslev, Carroll, Piasentin, & Jones, 2005). Thus, the intentional and behavioral dependent variables from this literature correspond nicely to the consumer branding variables (Broyles et al., 2009). Relevant outcomes include intention to apply (Herriot & Rothwell, 1981), intention to interview (Barber, 1998), intention to accept (Powell & Goulet, 1996), decision to apply and interview (Barber & Roehling, 1993), and decision to accept (Cable & Judge, 1996). Considering the importance of word-of-mouth information about a brand plays in consumer and worker behavior (Van Hoye & Lievens, 2009), willingness to recommend an employment brand to others would seem to be an important behavioral consequence of employment brand knowledge (Libai, Muller, & Peres, 2009).

> **Proposition 6.** Greater employment brand knowledge, manifest as positive employment brand attitude associated with the brand and greater employment brand familiarity will be positively associated with intentions, decisions, and behaviors regarding the brand. This includes intentions to apply, interview, and accept; decisions to apply, interview, and accept; and willingness to recommend an employment brand.

# ATTRIBUTES OF THE EMPLOYMENT OFFERING

As discussed earlier, nearly all of the scholarly work on employment branding is "inspired" by marketing and consumer psychology-based research but is fully grounded and structured by the field I/O psychology. The research on attributes of the employment offering reviewed below is no exception. We do our best to frame this research in the marketing and consumer psychology model of employment brand outlined in Fig. 1 but due to the nature of the research must resort to interpreting what has been done using the endogenous I/O psychology framework.

The extant employment branding literature has identified various components of employment attributes related with pay, opportunities for advancement, location, career programs, and organizational structure (Lievens, Hoye, & Schreurs, 2005; Backhaus, Stone, & Heiner, 2002; Knox & Freeman, 2006). However, most studies in the employment branding

(EB) field tend to mix various attributes without necessarily making theoretical distinctions. In order to offer a more parsimonious framework and clarity, we differentiate between directly and indirectly related employment attributes. Directly related descriptive features involves the actual work attributes such as pay, opportunities for advancement and job security, whereas research on indirectly related employment attributes that are still part of the employment but not specific to the work itself. This includes the culture, coworker affiliations, structure of the organization, etc. Table 1 summarizes various directly and indirectly related employment attributes we identify in the extant employment branding literature below.

Although the notion of employment branding is influenced by the marketing discipline, research on employer attributes has its roots in the I/O

***Table 1.*** Summary of Employment Branding Attributes Noted in the Literature.

| | |
|---|---|
| *Directly related employment attributes* | Career related |
| • Pay | • Advancements |
| • Opportunities for advancement | • Training |
| • job security | • Career programs |
| • social/team activities, physical activities | • Opportunity to move around in the company and work in different roles |
| • task diversity | • Long-term career progression |
| • travel opportunities | • Educational opportunities |
| • Offers high starting salary | • Apprentice program |
| • Offers scope for creativity in your work | |
| • Opportunities for international travel | Co-worker affiliations |
| • Opportunities to work and live abroad | • Employs people with whom you feel you have things in common |
| • Offers variety in your daily work | • Competence of workforce |
| • Requires you to work standard hours only | • Has an international diverse mix of colleagues |
| • Working with customers | • High-quality incumbent workforce |
| *Indirect employment attributes* | • Caring for their employees |
| Organizational attributes | • Regarded as prestigious employer |
| • Location | • Has a dynamic, forward-looking approach to their business |
| • Organizational structure | |
| • Organizational culture | |
| • Age of the organization | |
| • Size of the organization | |
| • Performance indicators (sales and profit) | |
| • Empowering employees | |
| • Work councils (union representation) | |
| • Meritocracy | |
| • Innovativeness | |
| • Flexible benefits | |
| • Benefits | |

psychology discipline in the context of worker satisfaction. This research has mapped out core employment attributes such as training, task variety, independence, and control that are broadly related to job satisfaction across a number of samples and populations (Barling, Kelloway, & Iverson, 2003). There is also research suggesting that satisfaction varies depending on the employment attributes. For example, workers may be satisfied with their jobs and the work itself (directly), and with their coworkers and supervisors (indirectly) but not satisfied with their employers' opportunity for promotions (Robbins & Judge, 2009). Although research on satisfaction and employment attributes is useful for the EB research domain, it has generally focused on current employees and how directly related attributes impact current worker satisfaction. Largely ignored are potential workers outside the organization and what directly and indirectly related attributes may shape their employment brand knowledge.

Given the patterns in the satisfaction research, a natural starting point is compensation as a form of employment attribute. The satisfaction research suggests that pay correlates with job satisfaction but it is moderated by level of pay. That is, pay among workers living below poverty line is strongly linked with job satisfaction. However, once a worker reaches pay levels above $40,000 per year, this relationship seems to disappear (Judge, Piccolo, Podsakoff, Shaw, & Rich, 2010).

Drawing on the satisfaction literature (e.g., Dreher, Ash, & Bretz, 1988), researchers have offered additional insights as to the link between compensation and the employment brand knowledge of potential workers outside of the organization. For example, research has shown that both pay level and flexible benefits as forms of employment attributes may trigger different worker responses. Williams and Dreher (1992) explored the hiring process of bank tellers in 352 US banks. Their findings indicated that pay level was related to job acceptance rates but surprisingly unrelated to the number of teller applicants. In contrast to their predictions, higher pay did not result in more people applying for the job. This is consistent with the aforementioned finding that pay level is correlated with job satisfaction only at the lower pay levels. Moreover, in contrast to their predictions, pay level was positively related with length of time it took to fill a position. In other words, the more money offered for a job the longer the length of time to fill this vacancy. They speculated that this could be the result of banks having to increase salaries in order to attract external workers. Only flexible employment benefits tailored to the individual's needs were related to job acceptance rate. The authors suggested that this could be the result of young women applying for these bank teller jobs that already have employed spouses but that benefits and flexible work arrangements better suited their current life situation at home.

Recent EB research has also found that pay may not be as important of an employment attribute for job acceptance among applicants. For example, Lievens and Highhouse (2003) explored five directly and indirectly related employment attributes among final year college students and bank employees. Findings indicated that of the five attributes, pay (directly related) was the least statistically significant as an attribute for organizational attractiveness. Other indirectly related attributes linked with organizational attractiveness were innovativeness ($r = .43$), working with customers ($r = .41$), advancements ($r = .40$), and competence ($r = .38$). Moreover, Lievens et al. (2005), studied both directly and indirectly employment attributes among potential job applicants for the armed forces (directly related: pay and benefits, task diversity, social/team activities, physical activities, travel opportunities; indirectly related: structure of the organization, opportunity for advancements, job security, and educational opportunities). However, results suggested that only task diversity and opportunity to work in team-based jobs impacted organizational attractiveness among a total of 576 high-school seniors. In other words, the findings seem to suggest that work-related attributes is more important than attributes related to the overall organization to influence worker response.

One reason as to why the other employment attributes was not significant may be due to the fact that the study only rated one organization at a time and did not considered the strength, favorability, and uniqueness of these attributes in relation with other organizations. That is, it seems likely that we would find differential responses among workers if we placed various compensation attributes in relation to other employer's compensation and benefit packages. For example, if given a choice between two employers with different compensation and benefits, one might find that some workers may opt for flexible benefits rather than higher pay without such benefits (similar to Williams and Dreher's (1992) logic above). Moreover, a job applicant may compare two companies' retirement plan and accept a job offer based on the company's 401-K retirement plan with 6% matching contribution. One company may offer a generous college tuition reimbursement plan for a worker's children, not offered by the other company. The point here is that the uniqueness of compensation attributes as a form of employment brand knowledge may play an important role in determining worker response. Moreover, Although Williams and Dreher (1992) did explore different competitive levels of compensation (low, mid, or high pay), scant research exist on how variable pay versus fixed pay, salary versus hourly rate wages, stock option plans, profit sharing plans operate as employer brand knowledge. Hence, we posit that:

**Proposition 7.** Employment attributes with respect to strength, favorability, and uniqueness of the overall compensation package impacts differential worker response.

## International Employment Branding Attribute Research

There is also an existing literature focusing on employment attributes and organizational attractiveness in an international context, that is, outside the United States. The majority of these studies have focused largely on internal branding (e.g., Gapp & Merrilees, 2006; Hwang & Chi, 2005; Papasolomou & Vrontis, 2006; Wallstrom, Karlsson, & Salehi-Sangari, 2008). A handful of international studies have explored external branding (e.g., Han & Han, 2009; Lievens, 2007). Interestingly, studies focusing on external workers have almost exclusively involved indirectly related employment attributes (an exception is Lievens et al., 2005). For example, Hannon (1996) explored employment attributes in Japan using a large sample size of senior students (11,000) from engineering and liberal arts programs. Students were asked to evaluate 150 firms and their attraction based on age, size, and two performance indicators (sales and profit). Workforce size was related to organizational attractiveness for all cohorts. The logic was that size would indicate stability and opportunities for advancement through the corporate ladder, which seemed consistent with the Japanese culture. Surprisingly, the age of the company, symbolizing tradition and standing, and believed to be praiseworthy and desirable, especially in Japan, was not associated with applicant attraction. Apparently, the propensity to survive is not by itself an attractive organizational attribute. Moreover, sales and profits had a differential impact on engineering and liberal arts cohorts. Sales were more attractive for engineering and science students whereas profit was more attractive for liberal art students, yet little rationale for this differential result was provided. A study in Germany by Backes-Gellner and Tuor (2010) explored nonobservable workplace attributes of employment offering among 204 companies. Their findings suggested that work councils (a common form of union representation in German firms), apprentice programs, and high-quality incumbent workforce operated as signals of an appealing workplace and resulted in positive worker employment brand knowledge. Placing these studies in a broader context suggests that job applicants may pay close attention to organizational characteristics at a superficial level and operate as self-selection screening mechanisms, even without more specific information about the nature compensation.

Missing in the international EB research stream are studies exploring different workers response to employment attributes and how they vary across cultures. Given the ongoing globalization and proliferation of communication information technology (Gibson & Gibbs, 2006), opportunities to work across national borders seems likely to impact potential worker responses. That is, some applicants might purposefully seek employment that allows for travel abroad. Although Lievens et al. (2005) offered some insights as to the relationship between organizational attractiveness and opportunity for international travel in a military context; he did not find any significant results. This result is limited to a military context and cohort that may not be applicable across different industries and generalizable among different age groups. More research is clearly needed.

As a conceptual starting point, scholars interested in employment branding in an international context, may turn to the international strategic human resource management (ISHRM) domain. This field has explored various success factors such as personality, language skills, prior international experience, self-selection that may impact expatriates success during an international assignment (for an extensive review see Caligiuri, Tarique, & Jacobs, 2009). The emphasis has been on selecting internal workers for international opportunities abroad (e.g., Tarique & Schuler, 2008; Caligiuri & Colakoglu, 2007). However, largely ignored is the importance of international assignments as an employment attribute to generate desired worker response from external workers (i.e., intentions to seek employment)? Many external workers seeking employment may find it appealing with opportunities to work for the company in a different country.

Drawing on the ISHRM literature, focusing on the individual, language skills, international experience, and open to experience would logically drive people to seeking job opportunities in companies that offer international work employment (Tarique & Schuler, 2008). In terms of employment attributes, directly related attributes about the nature of the job – specific type of occupations that could be transferable to an international context (e.g., software development) or international career opportunities may both drive positive worker response. Indirectly related employment attributes such as the organizational global structure and location of its subsidiaries might further drive worker response. Knowledge about the specific country (e.g., culture, history, and geography) in which the company is conducting business may further impact the likelihood of positive workers response. For example, for some workers, a company with a subsidiary in Melbourne, Australia may be more appealing than a company with a subsidiary in Tallin, Estonia depending on workers interests. Hence

**Proposition 8.** Worker characteristics such as being bilingual, holding international travel experience, and personality dimensions will drive positive worker response toward companies with international related employment attributes.

## Employment Imagery

The idea of working at a company that has international work opportunities can also be tied to one's feelings one may experience, or imagery, associated with the visualization of working in a particular place. Consider this: you have just received a phone call from the University of Alaska. They have heard about your research and are offering a job. Apart from the directly related attributes such as pay and tenure requirements, we assume that one would visualize what it would be like to live and work in Alaska, an indirectly related employment attribute. That is, workers have images of what it would be like to work in a specific geographic location which contributes to forming employment brand knowledge.

Given the Alaska example earlier, a few scholars have included location as part of employment attributes but generally conceptualized it as the relative distance between work and worker's home (e.g., Highhouse, Hoffman, Greve, & Collins, 2002; Lievens & Highhouse, 2003). Although it is possible that one may visualize a potential commute between the home and the workplace, a more theoretically interesting issue is the worker's self-generated imagery of working at a different company which may or may not involve moving to a different location. However scant research exists that would fall in the category of employment imagery. One exception is Lievens et al.'s (2005) work on trait inferences. Drawing on Aaker's (1997) work on person-descriptive traits, Lievens and colleagues explored worker knowledge among applicants for the armed forces. They identified three relevant attributes associated with our notion of imagery: excitement (daring, exciting, and thrilling), cheerfulness (cheerful, friendly, and original) about the organization, and ruggedness (tough, rugged, and masculine). All three attributes seem to touch on the imagery of employment. With regard to excitement, it may relate to directly related attributes of work: do I expect the work to be exciting? How about my coworkers, will they create excitement for my work and at the workplace? In terms of cheerfulness, is the workplace cheerful? Are people happy at work and would I feel the same way? As for ruggedness, the imagery could involve workers' imagery of handling weapons, driving military equipment, spending time in nature, much of which can be seen in military branding recruitment commercials. Lievens and colleagues' work suggest that both excitement and cheerfulness are important imaginary employment attributes that explains workers' attraction to military organizations.

We believe the notion of employment imagery is a promising one for future EB research. Worker imagery seems to play an important role while entertaining employment opportunities. Relating employment imagery to employment attributes, scholars may further map out both directly and indirectly related imagery. For example, drawing on Lievens and colleagues' work, employment imagery as a directly related employment attribute can be related to the work itself (e.g., what would it be like to work with this boss?) or the indirectly, (e.g., would I be happy working in this company?). It is conceivable that various forms of employment imagery can have significant impact on building employment brand knowledge. However, as highlighted in the Alaska example earlier, employment imagery may extend outside the workplace itself and include location attributes. For example, I may visualize living in Alaska and imageries that may come to mind could be scenic views, cross-country skiing and impressive white water rivers. It may also trigger visualizations of brutally cold and dark days, endless snow shoveling, and dead car batteries. However, this line of research is, to our knowledge, a wide open field for future scholarly inquiries. Researchers may find it fruitful to explore the differential impact regarding various forms of worker imagery as outlined earlier. Worker imagery as it relates to both directly and indirectly employment attributes and nonemployment attributes, is a key component for building employment brand knowledge and impacting worker employment response. Hence

**Proposition 9.** Worker self-generated employment imagery will be positively associated with employment brand knowledge and workers' responses to employment brand information.

### Organization Culture

Organizational culture, defined as a system of shared values and beliefs (Schein, 1985), can in many ways be seen as part of an employment brand (Bergstrom, Blumenthal, & Crothers, 2002). A number of studies have focused on the importance of organization culture from an internal brand-building lens (Wallstrom et al., 2008). Organizational culture can shape worker values and commitment to the organization, and scholars have embraced the role of the human resource management function as a supporting mechanism to further drive culture-related initiatives (Burmann & Zeplin, 2005; Miles & Mangold, 2004; Sheridan, 1992). Others have placed culture in the corporate branding context. For example, similar to Turban and Keon (1993), Wheeler, Richey, Tokkman, and Sablynski (2006) explored the relationship between corporate brand identity and worker personality traits (need for achievement and self-esteem), organizational culture and worker turnover. Findings suggest that the need for achievement moderated the relationship between corporate brand identity and worker intent to remain employed with the organization. That is, the more an organization's brand stresses value-goal or cultural congruence, the more likely workers will embrace corporate culture post hire.

Organizational culture, as part of building employment brand knowledge among external workers, has been given much less attention. Similar to the internal branding research suggesting that organizational culture can operate as a retention mechanism, research on external workers indicates that culture can also function as an attraction mechanism. For example, Collins and Stevens (2002) found that conveying various directly and indirectly related employment attributes impacted the success of early recruitment efforts. Within this research domain, researchers have suggested that an organizational brand can influence workers' perception and ideas of the organization's culture, which may trigger favorable worker responses. Along similar lines, Kowalczk and Pawlish (2002) explored six well-known Silicon Valley firms and found that the strategic resource of an employer brand (corporate brand measured by reputation) could partially reflect external perception of culture. The organization's culture could in effect operate as mechanism for driving employment brand knowledge. Given the role of organizational culture in the context of employment branding, some organizations are actively attempting to alter their culture toward a market-driven culture tailored to appeal to its customer based, which would also include potential future employees (Ogbonna & Harris, 2002).

Although the extant EB research points out the potential strength of organization culture as an indirect employment attribute to attract workers, much more research is needed in this area. For example, as much as culture can be a source of strength, researchers may want to explore the downside of having a strong culture and how it manifests itself in worker's mind and links with their attention and learning, interpretation and evaluation, and decisions and behaviors. As a conceptual starting point, there is a large research domain on staffing focusing on worker-job and worker-organization fit issues for successful recruitment, maximizing worker performance, and improve retention (Winfred, Bell, Villado, & Doverspike, 2006; Yaniv & Farkas, 2005). In the context of organizational culture, we can translate the notion of worker/job/organization fit, to overall culture fit and subculture fit. Organizations generally have different subcultures linked with specific jobs within different departments – job-related subcultures. For example, the engineering department may hold a unique subculture, in part driven by worker's training and expertise, which may differ with the subculture in the sales department. To what extent these job-related subcultures may clash and interfere with the overall organizational culture resulting in differential worker response remains an empirical question. The answer may be the nature of the overall culture. On the one hand, we could postulate that strong overall cultures (a culture that is easily identifiable, widely shared, and perceived positive) may in fact override job-related subcultures triggering differential worker responses. That is, an engineer may accept a job offer based on the overall knowledge of the company's culture (e.g., it is perceived to be a social responsible culture). On the other hand, job-related subcultures may play a more important role for workers seeking employment in a context of a weak overall organizational culture. For example, the engineer may accept the job offer based on the subculture she experienced while visiting the engineering team she would work for (with little concerns about the company being social responsible). Thus, both worker/culture fit and worker/subculture fit may impact worker response:

**Proposition 10.** The employment attributes of overall organizational culture and job-related subcultures play important roles in worker responses to employment brand knowledge.

## ACTIVITIES USED TO DEVELOP WORKERS' EMPLOYMENT BRAND KNOWLEDGE

Scholars have given ample attention to the tactics organizations use to develop potential workers' employment brand knowledge. For the past 30 years or so, the focus of this research has been the impact of advertising and recruiting contact on applicants' employment behaviors. These are still robust streams, but the current trend is to use an employment brand model to consider several different means to impact employment brand knowledge and worker responses to employment opportunities.

### Advertisement Job Ads for Building Employment Brand Knowledge

A number of papers have examined external workers' early exposure to the organization through various forms of marketing advertisements. The focus on advertisement in the EB research stream is, in part, a result of a change from a manufacturing economy toward a knowledge-based one, which creates a need for organizations to differentiate themselves in the minds of workers with multiple employment options. Ewing, Pitt, Bussy, and Berthon (2002, p. 3) argues that "more and more firms may turn to advertisement to create 'employment brands' and thereby offer an enticing vocational proposition that is compelling and differentiated."

Within this research stream, studies have suggested that the amount of information included in job ads coupled with the perceived company image trigger worker attitudes and differential worker responses. For example, Belt and Paolillo (1982), in their experimental study involving 218 graduate and undergraduate students, asked participants to rate restaurants on a 20 point image scale. The results suggested that the image of the organization impacted whether participants would read the recruitment ad and their intentions to follow through with a job application. However, no difference was found when they tested different students with different majors in their response to job ads. In addition to the image serving as an attention mechanism, Feldman, Dearden, and Hardesty (2006) found an association between the amount of information provided in recruitment ads and organizational attractiveness and the intent to follow through with a job application; the more information provided about the organization, the greater the attraction. They also found that participants who received more detailed information about the organization, job, and work context reported more positive attitudes toward both the advertisement and the organization.

Both Belt and Paolillo (1982) and later Feldman et al. (2006) studied how content and image of the company impacted worker attitudes. In contrast to Feldman and colleagues testing the attitudinal reactions to hypothetical ads, Belt and Paolillo (1982) concluded that workers are generally familiar with a large variety of organizations. A central, yet unexplored question in this research stream is how workers' pre-existing employment brand attitudes interact with the content of recruitment ads to shape employment brand knowledge and subsequent worker responses. It is likely that organizational and job ads might trigger different worker responses contingent upon their existing employment brand attitudes. One worker might hold strong negative employment brand attitudes toward an organization's attributes operating in the tobacco industry or their reputation for having strong antiunion management, or overall treatment of employees and working conditions. From an organizational interest, even if an organization can do little in the short run in terms of pre-existing worker attitudes, more practically, the concern turns to how organizations can alter and change negative worker attitudes about their organization into positive ones in order to attract talent. Hence

**Proposition 11.** Pre-existing worker attitudes moderate the relationship between content in job ads and employment attraction.

Important to note here, and relevant for the entire chapter, most studies linking employment brand antecedents with various worker responses, have been designed using convenience samples. Although we can clearly learn a lot from students considering entering the job market, we do not know how work experience influences reactions and attitudes toward job ads. Within this research limitation, qualitative research may add additional insights, especially on factors involving worker attitudes. Scholars may want to interview workers and unpack the dimensions of worker attitudes as they may impact employment brand knowledge and trigger differential worker responses. For example, having years of experience reading and applying to job ads may alter one's expectation as to what should be presented in the job ad, which may influence attitudinal reactions and subsequently worker response. Moreover, different types of jobs with different salaries may further interact with content and worker attitudes. Some job ads may necessarily be more comprehensive given the nature of the job. We perceive a lot more exciting research can be conducted involving job ads based on different methodologies.

### Recruitment and Building Employer Brand Knowledge

There is also established theoretical and empirical work in the larger recruitment domain (which includes job advertisement) focusing on the importance of conveying employment brand knowledge to attract potential job applicants (Behrend, Baker, & Thompson, 2009; Breaugh, 2008; Collins, 2007). Ferris, Berkson, and Harris (2002) in their review of the person-organization fit literature, outlined a prescriptive model which emphasizes organizations' strategic efforts to maximize the acquisition of talent through interviewer persuasion. They highlighted the importance of nonwork-related issues, persuasive speech, total compensation, and interviewer character-istics. Moreover, they argued that an active promotion of organizational reputation rather than focusing on actual job attributes is a stronger recruitment tool. Part of the logic may be that workers do not stay in one position as they are promoted but work in the same organization during this career progression.

Empirical research supports the notion that organizations can take actions building employment brand knowledge in the recruitment process. Gatewood, Gowan, and Lautenschlager (1993) explored three different worker images (general corporate image, recruitment image, and correlates of images) and found support for the notion that these images are related to the information available about them. Interestingly, they noted that participants in their study had little agreement about the corporate (image of the name of an organization) and recruitment image (image associated with its recruitment message). Moreover, both corporate and recruitment images of the organiza-tion were strong predictors of initial decision to pursue contact with organizations (i.e., worker response). The practical implication of these findings is that organizations can build positive employment brand attitudes (via images) by simply communicating organizational and work-related attributes through ads, web pages, and other media.

Similar to research on job ads, important work has been done investigating the role of workers' attitudes and actions taken by organiza-tions in recruitment to build employment brand knowledge. Using a sample of 1955 engineering students, Collins and Stevens (2002) explored how workers' employer brand image moderated positive exposure to four early recruitment-related activities (publicity, sponsorship, word-of-mouth endor-sement, and advertisement) and applicant decisions to apply. In contrast to our conceptualization used in this chapter, they defined employer brand image as potential applicants' attitudes and perceived attributes about the job or organization (implicitly making a directly and indirectly related employment attribute distinction). In line with previous marketing research, results suggested that early recruitment-related activities were indirectly related with intensions to apply. Similar to advertisement-related research outlined earlier, workers' favorable impressions of the company (attitudes) and job attributes (salary, location, advancement opportunity, etc.) had a strong impact on workers' decision to apply when receiving information about the company through word-of-mouth endorsement. This suggests that the channel through which employment attributes are transmitted is critical for impacting workers' attitudes.

Adding to research on employment brand channels, Allen, Otondo, and Mahto (2007) focused specifically on the recruitment websites used to attract worker interest in the early recruitment stages. They reported that workers' attitudes toward the website (e.g., using this website is a satisfying experience) drove their attitudes toward organizations (e.g., in your opinion, how does this organization compare with other organizations of the same type and size?). Moreover, workers' attitudes toward organizations had a central role in moderating a series antecedents and outcomes; it mediated workers' perception of organizational familiarity (have you ever heard of this organization), organization image (rated by social responsibility), job information (e.g., how much employment or job opportunity-related information did the website provide compared with what you expected to find?), and organization information (how much information about the organization did the website provide compared with what you expected to find?) with the outcome of employment intention (what are the chances that you will pursue employment with this organization within the next 12 months?).

Although both Collins and Stevens' (2002) and Allen et al.'s (2007) studies highlight the importance of the channel through which workers acquire employment brand knowledge, we believe taking a closer look by making a distinction between directly and indirectly related employment attributes might add insights to this line of research. We know that the amount of information about employment attributes and word-of-mouth play key roles in impacting worker attitudes and possibly intentions to apply to a job. Extending this logic, it is conceivable that word-of-mouth as a channel would have an even stronger impact on *indirectly* related employment attributes and subsequent worker attitudes and worker response. Unless the word-of-mouth originates from the person being replaced, this person is more likely to have first-hand knowledge about the culture, work relations, leadership styles for instance, rather than the actual content of the job. Hence

**Proposition 12.** The effect of the channel used to transmit employment brand knowledge to workers is moderated by indirectly related employment attributes.

*Internal Workers Building Employment Brand Knowledge*

Organizations have also realized the power of leveraging their internal workforce as a mechanism to build employment brand knowledge among external workers (e.g., Bergstrom et al., 2002; Gapp & Merrilees, 2006; Harris, 2007; Miles & Mangold, 2004; Punjarsi & Wilson, 2007). A general trend in this line of research suggests a discrepancy between internal and external workers' employment brand knowledge of the organization (de Chernatony, Cottman, & Segal-Horn, 2006). For example, Knox and Freeman (2006) explored the impact of the employer brand image in the recruitment market (among potential recruits and their recruiters during the recruitment process). They offered a long list of employment attributes (e.g., freedom to work, friendly, informal culture, small organization really cares about their employees as individuals, uses your degree skills). Their study suggests that employment brand knowledge does positively correlate with graduate recruitment intentions, which is consistent with the general employment brand and employment ad research. More importantly here, their findings also suggested that there are significant perceptual differences between recruiters and job applicants with respect to employment brand knowledge. This is perhaps not surprising given the importance of word-of-mouth channels to build employment brand knowledge.

Recruiters, viewed as the internal workforce representatives, indicated an inflated view of employment attributes compared to external workers. From a pure marketing strategy, the misalignment between internal and external workers can have negative consequences. In the same way inflating product quality may have negative impacts on customer satisfaction and reduce chances for repeat and returning buyers, positively exaggerating employment attributes to external workers can result in perceived lower company reputation. If hired, a worker may experience disappointment, negative attitudes, lower commitment, and decide to leave the organization. Thus, it seems necessary to consider the source and intentions with leveraging internal workers to transmit employment brand knowledge. For example, a recruiter would seem to have different reasons for sharing information about employment attributes for example to assure a job acceptance from a talented applicant. An internal worker offering information about the company to an outside friend has different intentions for sharing insights about the employers and may give the "real picture." Based on the different sources and intentions of the sender, the credibility and trust in the content of the employment brand knowledge might be affected and generate different worker response. Thus

**Proposition 13.** The credibility and trust in the employment brand knowledge is impacted by the source of the sender.

In order to further bridge the employment brand knowledge gap between current and external workers, some organizations leverage their current employees by acting as brand ambassadors to "live the brand" and communicate employment brand knowledge to external stakeholders who in turn might become workers themselves (Girod, 2005; de Chernatony et al., 2006). Front line workers may interact with potential recruits as they respond to their customer needs which organizations try to leverage (Burmann & Zeplin, 2005). A case in point is LL Bean that markets their employment attributes through their current employees that, by living the brand, may attract more customers and potential workers. Many of their current workers were customers that applied and were hired for open sales positions. One benefit they offer to their employees, is the option to buy returned but fully functional sporting goods such as kayaks and tents at a significantly reduce price. Accordingly, the LL Beans workers live the brand through their products and transmit employment attributes in a holistic fashion to external stakeholders. Returning to the directly and indirectly related employment attributes distinction, Ferris et al. (2002) argued that organizational attributes are more important factors to build employment brand knowledge and subsequent positive worker response. It would seem, both from a practical angle as observed at LL Beans, and from a theoretical one offered by Ferris and his colleagues, that transmitting organizational indirectly related employment attributes would reduce the knowledge gap and build employment brand knowledge among external workers. Hence

**Proposition 14.** Workers living the brand through its product and services will transmit indirectly related employment attributes.

## Building Diversity Employment Brand Knowledge

Both marketing practitioners and scholars have realized the importance of tailoring to a diverse customer base in order to reflect the US demographics as can be noted in diversity representation in various commercials, news anchors, movie casts, and sitcoms. Research in the broader diversity domain suggests that workplace diversity may provide different perspectives and insights necessary to solve complex problems and can add a competitive edge for teams and organizations (Erhardt, 2011; Erhardt, Werbel, & Shrader, 2003; Jackson, Joshi, & Erhardt, 2003; Joshi & Roh, 2009). The challenge for many organizations is to cast a wider net to attract talent that would generate an "added value in diversity."

In the employment branding context, some scholars have suggested that women and minorities are specially targeted through "pictorial" diversity tactics to drive organizational attraction (Avery & McKay, 2006). Minorities are assumed to react positively to diversity in job ads based on their perceived compatibility with the company determined by their existing employment brand knowledge. Organizations have become more astute with making sure ethnic and gender diversity is portrayed in recruitment advertisements (Avery & McKay, 2006; Backhaus et al., 2002; Thomas, 1993). For example, Perkins, Thomas, and Taylor (2000) explored advertisement and recruitment of minorities by showing racial composition of employees portrayed in ads. Their findings suggest that these ads may assist in recruiting minority job seekers. Interestingly however, the same pictures do not seem to have the same effect on nonminorities. That is, pictorial diversity does not appear to work as an effective recruitment tool for white male workers. One implication is that organizations must leverage the pictorial diversity in their advertisements using images of current work with discretion to attract talent from the entire labor pool. If not, organizations run the risk of alienating nonminorities in the process and undermine the process of reaching talent across gender and ethnic lines.

**Proposition 15.** Employment brand knowledge may be developed in the minds of minority workers by communicating pictorial diversity. Nonminorities are less likely to notice, retain, or be affected by such images.

Research has also indicated that, apart from the pictorial effect of diversity in ads, job applicants also respond differently to the characteristics of the recruiters themselves. Using data from 93 MBA candidates, Thomas and Wise (1999) explored organizational attractiveness factors among MBAs. Factors included types of jobs, organizational attributes, diversity, and recruiter characteristics. In line with Perkins et al. (2000), minorities placed greater emphasis on diversity factors, but also on the recruiters' characteristics (race, gender, and personality) than did nonminority candidates. Interestingly, job and organizational factors indicated little differences in responses between minority and nonminority participants. That is, minorities did not seem to have different preferences with respect to directly employment attributes. However, when examining differences in indirectly related employment attributes, Smith, Wokutch, Harrington, and Dennis (2004) found evidence suggesting that potential workers reported more favorable attraction to organizations offering affirmative action programs than diversity management programs. They speculated that management driven diversity initiatives could inadvertently lead to rising resentment; attending diversity workshops may create uncomfortable situations for women and minorities.

In short, research on diversity issues related with employment branding research suggests that women and minorities respond differently to images of employment brand diversity representation and that specific workplace actions with respect to diversity initiatives may have differential impacts on worker response. However, more research is clearly needed in this area. Perkins et al. (2000) noted that minorities did not show more interest in directly related employment attributes compared with nonminorities. Yet, this might change if we consider directly related employment attributes such as the composition of the team. Beyond the "pictorial" diversity factor, sharing specific demographic data of teams in which the applicant might work may drive positive worker attitudes and subsequent positive worker response; the demographics of coworkers could play a deciding factor in whether a worker accepts a job offer. For indirectly related employment attributes such as the diversity composition of executive boards (Erhardt et al., 2003), mentorship geared toward women and minorities (Ibarra, 1993), and overall familiarity of the employment brand with respect to discriminatory lawsuits (Robinson & Dechant, 1997) may impact worker response as well. We believe this line of research is promising as the workplace continues to diversify and organizations are attempting to attract and retain a diverse workforce.

**Proposition 16.** Both directly and indirectly related diversity employment attributes impacts organizations' ability to recruit and attract a diverse talent pool.

# ORGANIZATIONAL ATTRACTION

Much of the I/O psychology influenced employment brand research is grounded on a foundation of organizational attraction as opposed to the consumer psychology framework of employment brand knowledge (brand attitudes and brand familiarity) used to structure this review. To complete the review of the existing EB literature, we provide a brief overview of this construct and its use in the EB-related research stream.

Organizational attractiveness research addresses the questions of why individuals are attracted to organizations and which factors and elements of the construct affect the quantity and quality of organizations' applicant pools (Barber, 1998). Attraction is defined as the generation of applicants by means of getting potential candidates to view the organization as a desirable place to work (Rynes, 1991). Underlying the concept of attraction is the idea that the greater the number of qualified applicants an organization attracts, the larger the pool of applicants from which to choose will be, resulting in greater utility for the organization's selection system (Boudreau & Rynes, 1985; Cable & Turban, 2001).

Assuming the job choice process begins with the individual decision to pursue advertised employment with an organization, extensive efforts have been devoted in understanding which factors influence individuals' pursuit decisions (Barber, 1998; Gatewood et al., 1993). The single most important factor is the degree of person-organization fit in terms of the compatibility between the applicants' values and needs and those of the organization (Kristof, 1996). For example, Cable and Judge (1996) found that person-organization fit perceptions (i.e., congruence between applicants' values and their perceptions of the recruiting organizations' values) were important in job-choice decisions, even after controlling for the attractiveness of job attributes.

Scholars have found that organization image, subsequent information search, and organization familiarity are also related to pursuit intentions. Application decisions are thought to be influenced by potential applicants' impressions of an organization's attractiveness as an employer identified as the applicant's perception of the organization's image (Cable & Graham, 2000; Gatewood et al., 1993; Lievens & Highhouse, 2003), and its overall familiarity (or brand awareness), which determine subsequent applicants' information search and intention to pursue employment (Barber, 1998; Cable & Turban, 2001; Highhouse, Zickar, Thorsteinson, Stierwalt, & Slaughter, 1999; Rynes, 1991). Factors such as job characteristics, position scarcity, salary & benefits, location, industry, human resource systems, social consciousness, and value statements have been found to influence organizational attractiveness (Barber & Roehling, 1993; Breaugh, 2008; Bretz & Judge, 1994; Highhouse & Hoffman, 2001; Highhouse et al., 2002). Although previous research often looked at each of these elements individually, most recruitment studies have begun increasingly to examine the effects of multiple information sources on organizational attractiveness (Collins & Han, 2004; Ployhart, 2006; Van Hoye & Lievens, 2005).

Recent literature on attraction has also focused on the functional benefits or value derived from the components of the employment offering. Instrumental attributes tend to represent objective job and organizational attributes (e.g., pay and location), whereas symbolic attributes such as organizational personality or reputation represent the subjective meanings and inferences that people ascribe to the job and the organization. Less research has been devoted to examining the experiential and symbolic benefits of the employment offering, which are related to the "feelings" associated with the employment experience. Some authors have analyzed attraction from the marketing perspective to introduce symbolic aspects such as the instrumental-symbolic framework (Lievens & Highhouse, 2003), organizational personality (Slaughter, Zickar, Highhouse, & Mohr, 2004) or the organization's reputation as a source of pride in being a member (Cable & Turban, 2003). These studies found that symbolic attributes provided an incremental explanation of organizational attractiveness beyond that provided by instrumental attributes.

Depending on the measure used, the organizational attraction construct typically includes a number of components ranging from affective attitude toward an organization, viewing it as a desirable entity, exerting effort to work for it, wanting to interview with the organization, choosing to interview with the organization, choosing to interview; job pursuit intentions, intentions of accepting a job offer, and accepting a job offer (Aiman-Smith, Bauer, & Cable, 2001; Barber, 1998). Studies use organizational attraction as a dependent variable (i.e., applicant attraction outcomes) in research on job-pursuit intentions, job/organization attraction, and acceptance intentions or job choice; and as an independent variable when studying job and organizational attributes, recruiter characteristics, perceptions of recruitment process, perceived fit, perceived alternatives, and hiring expectancies (Chapman et al., 2005).

As can be seen, organizational attraction measures typically combine attitudinal (i.e., affect toward an organization) and intentional (i.e., job-pursuit intentions), and behavioral (job acceptance) measures. Proponents of this construct contend that attitudes precede behaviors in line with Fishbein and Ajzen's (1975) theory of reasoned action. Although this may optimize the predictive power of the construct it makes it less useful in a more formal employment brand framework that distinguishes between brand associations, brand attitudes & familiarity, and behavioral responses to employment brand knowledge.

In the WBEBE model, organizational attraction appears as an indirect attribute of the employment offering (see Fig. 1). Organization attraction is an attitude toward a large variety of organizational information associated with the corporation offering the employment. Ultimately, this attitude is combined with several other information sources about the job (direct and indirect attributes) that ultimately lead to employment brand attitude.

## Future Research

Given the relevance of the organizational attraction construct in the literature, we offer several potential avenues for future research efforts. In general, we advocate the need to reconceptualize the construct of attraction in the light of the WBEBE model, which would have significant implications for the development of research into employment branding. Specifically, a shift is needed toward a definition of attraction in line with the marketing perspective on how brands work, which would move the prevailing paradigm away for understanding job attraction as a combination of attitudes, intentions, and behaviors and focus exclusively on the affective feelings of attraction to the organization.

Two other more specific areas of research deserve further attention: temporal dimension and the target of research. First, as Ehrhart and Ziegert (2005, p. 913) contend research on attraction typically considers attraction to an organization at a single point of time based on a "snapshot" of information available about the organization. However, according to our WBEBE model, there is a temporal element in individuals' branding knowledge. Rather than basing themselves solely on recruitment sources, individuals gather, interpret and evaluate information about organizations over a period of time. Although Ehrhart and Ziegert (2005) noted the need for research regarding the influence of time on applicant attraction, little research exists on this issue. To shed further light on the importance of these factors there is a need for longitudinal attraction research to assess the elements of the WBEBE model herein proposed.

Finally, another area of future research concerns the target of research in traditional attraction research. With few exceptions (e.g., the work of Highhouse et al., 1999), existing studies have focused almost exclusively on early recruitment stages, targeting potential applicants who are either currently searching for a job or planning to participate in the recruitment process soon (Barber, 1998). Oftentimes, these studies rely on samples of undergraduates or graduate students, which seem a limitation in the broader EB research domain. Building from the employment brand model, job seekers are one important group of individuals among others with employment brand knowledge. However, current employees of a focal organization and other individuals not affiliated with the focal organization, including fully engaged workers, unemployed individuals or future employees, also possess employment brand knowledge. Accordingly, we propose to extend research attention beyond academic settings in an attempt to generalize findings to larger, more diverse samples. In that sense, we consider the attraction literature would benefit from drawing their samples from a population broader than that of students or potential applicants in the early stages of recruitment.

# CONCLUDING REMARKS

This chapter has presented a framework for reinterpreting the recruiting, organizational attraction, and job choice literature within the domain of marketing, specifically consumer psychology. We have attempted to accomplish three goals. First, we have provided the established and budding employment brand researcher an overview of the product/service branding literature. Using theoretical frameworks from the marketing literature, we have provided a means for translating the employment offering into a good that can be branded and managed in the minds of potential workers. This is a dramatic shift from the perspective of developing the "*employer* brand;" that is, developing associations with the corporate brand developing its identity as an employer. Second, we have provided a comprehensive review with an associated bibliography of nearly all the employment branding work that has been published over the past 15 years. Researchers considering making a contribution to this stream will be well serviced with this inventory and summary of previous work. Finally, we provided 16 propositions that identify important gaps in the employment brand literature.

A major focus of this chapter has been untangling constructs to clear the way for more theory-based research. We would discourage the use of measures of organizational attraction that include affect, intentions, and behaviors. As Fig. 1 makes clear, facts and feelings about brands that identify employment offerings are summarized by the holistic brand attitude. Attraction to the organization is but one of many associations that combine to form this brand attitude. Combined with brand familiarity, brand attitude then affects the attention workers pay to the brand, their intentions toward the brand, and ultimately their behavior. Organization attraction combines all of these processes into one construct and does not provide managers with a useful framework for influencing worker behaviors. Simply using affective organizational attraction as a primary independent variable is not much different than examining the impact of workers' perceptions of coworker relations on job choice. Future researchers need to focus on understanding how the constellation of brand associations lead to employment brand attitude and how brand attitude leads to attention, intentions, and behavior.

Lastly, we would emphasize that there is a great opportunity for future research in the employment brand space. Although these are mapped out in our propositions, we would point out that a typology of brand associations is undeveloped. Very little work has been done on employment brand familiarity. Although there is a growing literature on how organizations influence job choice, grounding future work in the employment brand knowledge model broadens the scope of possible research and provides a roadmap for strong theoretical contribution.

## REFERENCES

Aaker, J. (1997). Dimensions of brand personality. *Journal of Marketing Research, 34*(3), 347–356.

Agrawal, D. (1996). Effects of brand loyalty on advertising and trade promotions: A game theoretic analysis with empirical evidence. *Marketing Science, 15*, 86–108.

Ailawadi, K. L., Lehmann, D. R., & Nelson, S. A. (2003). Revenue premium as an outcome measure of brand equity. *Journal of Marketing, 67*, 1–17.

Aiman-Smith, L., Bauer, T. N., & Cable, D. M. (2001). Are you attracted? Do you intend to pursue? A recruiting policy capturing study. *Journal of Business and Psychology, 16*, 219–237.

Alba, J. W., & Hutchinson, J. W. (1987). Dimensions of consumer expertise. *Journal of Consumer Research, 13*, 411–454.

Allen, D., Otondo, R., & Mahto, R. (2007). Web-based recruitment: Effects of information, organizational brand, and attitudes toward a web site on applicant attraction. *Journal of Applied Psychology, 92*(6), 1696–1708.

Ambler, T., & Barrow, S. (1996). The employer brand. *Journal of Brand Management, 4*, 185–206.

American Marketing Association. (2010). *Resource Library: Dictionary*. Available at http://www.marketingpower.com/_layouts/Dictionary.aspx?dLetter = C. Retrieved on July 7, 2010.

Arendt, H. (1958). *The human condition*. Chicago: University of Chicago Press.

Arrow, K. (1973). Higher education as a filter. *Journal of Public Economy, 2*, 193–216.

Avery, D. R., & McKay, P. F. (2006). Target practice: An organizational impression management approach to attracting minority and female job applicants. *Personnel Psychology, 59*, 157–187.

Arvey, R. D., Harpaz, I., & Liao, H. (2004). Work centrality and post-award work behavior of lottery winners. *Journal of Psychology, 138*, 404–420.

Backes-Gellner, U., & Tuor, S. N. (2010). Avoiding labor shortages by employer signaling: On the importance of good work climate and labor relations. *Industrial and Labor Relations Review, 63*, 271–286.

Backhaus, K., Stone, B., & Heiner, K. (2002). Exploring the relationship between corporate social performance and employer attractiveness. *Business & Society, 41*, 292–318.

Barber, A. E. (1998). *Recruiting employees: Individual and organizational perspectives*. Thousand Oaks, CA: Sage Publications, Inc.

Barber, A. E., & Roehling, M. V. (1993). Job postings and the decision to interview: A verbal protocol analysis. *Journal of Applied Psychology, 78*, 845–856.

Barling, J., Kelloway, E., & Iverson, R. (2003). High-quality work, job satisfaction, and occupational injuries. *Journal of Applied Psychology, 88*, 276–283.

Baron, J. N., & Kreps, D. M. (1999). *Strategic human resources: Frameworks for general managers*. New York: Wiley.

Barrow, S., & Mosley, R. (2005). *The employer brand: Bringing the best of brand management to people at work*. West Sussex, UK: Wiley.

Becker, G. S. (1964). *Human capital*. New York: National Bureau for Economic Research.

Behrend, T., Baker, B., & Thompson, L. (2009). Effects of pro-environmental recruiting messages: The role of organizational reputation. *Journal of Business Psychology, 24*, 341–350.

Belt, J., & Paolillo, J. (1982). The influence of corporate image and specificity of candidate qualifications on response to recruitment advertisement. *Journal of Management, 8*(1), 105–112.

Bence, B. (2009). *How YOU are like shampoo for job seekers: The proven personal branding system to help you succeed in any interview and secure the job of your dreams*. Las Vegas: Global Insight Communications.

Bergstrom, A., Blumenthal, D., & Crothers, S. (2002). Why internal branding matters: The case of Saab. *Corporate Reputation Review, 5*, 133–142.

Berry, L. L. (2000). Cultivating service brand equity. *Journal of the Academy of Marketing Science, 28*, 128–137.

Berthon, P., Hulbert, J. M., & Pitt, L. F. (1999). Brand management prognostications. *Sloan Management Review, 40*(Winter), 2.

Blackett, T. (2009). What is a brand. In: R. Clifton & J. Simmons (Eds), *Brands and branding* (pp. 13–26). Princeton, NJ: Bloomberg Press.

Boudreau, J. W., & Rynes, S. L. (1985). Role of recruitment in staffing utility analysis. *Journal of Applied Psychology, 70*, 354–366.

Brandt, J. P., & Shook, S. R. (2005). Attribute elicitation: Implication in the research context. *Wood and Fiber Science, 37*, 127–146.

Breaugh, J. A. (2008). Employee recruitment: Current knowledge and important areas for future research. *Human Resource Management Review, 18*, 103–118.

Bretz, R. D., & Judge, T. A. (1994). The role of human resource systems in job applicant decision processes. *Journal of Management, 20*, 531–551.

Brisoux, J. E., & Cheron, E. J. (1990). Brand categorization and product involvement. In: M. E. Goldberg, G. Gorn & R. W. Pollay (Eds), *Advances in consumer research* (Vol. 17, pp. 101–109). Provo, UT: Association for Consumer Research.

Brown, J. J., & Wildt, A. R. (1992). Consideration set measurement. *Journal of the Academy of Marketing Sciences, 20*, 235–243.

Brown, S. P., & Stayman, D. M. (1992). Antecedents and consequences of attitude toward the ad: A meta-analysis. *Journal of Consumer Research, 19*, 34–51.

Brown, T. J., & Dacin, P. (1997). The company and the product: Corporate associations and consumer product responses. *Journal of Marketing, 61*, 68–84.

Broyles, S. A., Schumann, D. W., & Leingpibul, T. (2009). Examining brand equity antecedent/consequence relationships. *Journal of Marketing Theory and Practice, 17*, 145–161.

Budd, J. W., & Bhave, D. (2009). The employment relationship. In: A. J. Wilkinson, N.A. Bacon, T. Redman & S. Snell (Eds), *The SAGE Handbook of human resource management* (pp. 51–70). Thousand Oaks, CA: Sage.

Burmann, C., & Zeplin, S. (2005). Building brand commitment: A behavioral approach to internal brand management. *Journal of Brand Management, 12*(4), 279–300.

Cable, D. M., & Graham, M. E. (2000). The determinants of job seekers' reputation perceptions. *Journal of Organizational Behavior, 21*, 929–947.

Cable, D. M., & Judge, T. A. (1996). Person-organization fit, job choice decisions, and organizational entry. *Organizational Behavior and Human Decision Processes, 67*, 294–311.

Cable, D. M., & Turban, D. B. (2001). Establishing the dimensions, sources, and value of job seekers' employer knowledge during recruitment. In: G. R. Ferris (Ed.), *Research in personnel and human resources management* (Vol. 20, pp. 115–163). Oxford, UK: JAI Press/Elsevier Science.

Cable, D. M., & Turban, D. B. (2003). Firm reputation and applicant pool characteristics. *Journal of Organizational Behavior, 24*, 733–751.

Caligiuri, P., & Colakoglu, S. (2007). A strategic contingency approach to expatriate assignment management. *Human Resource Management Journal, 17*, 393–410.

Caligiuri, P., Tarique, I., & Jacobs, R. (2009). Selection for international assignments. *Human Resource Management, 19*, 251–262.

Chambers, E. G., Foulon, M., Handfield-Jones, H., Hankin, S. M., & Michaels, E. G. (1998). The war for talent. *The McKinsey Quarterly,* 44–57, Number 3.

Chapman, D. S., Uggerslev, K. L., Carroll, S. A., Piasentin, K. A., & Jones, D. A. (2005). Applicant attraction to organizations and job choice: A meta-analytic review of the correlates of recruiting outcomes. *Journal of Applied Psychology, 90*, 928–944.

Collins, C. (2007). The interactive effects of recruitment practices and product awareness on job seekers' employer knowledge and application behavior. *Journal of Applied Psychology, 92*(10), 180–190.

Collins, C., & Stevens, C. (2002). The relationship between early recruitment-related activities and the application decisions of new labor-market entrants: A brand equity approach to recruitment. *Journal of Applied Psychology, 87*(6), 1121–1133.

Collins, C. J., & Han, J. (2004). Exploring applicant pool quantity and quality: The effects of early recruitment practices, corporate advertising, and firm reputation. *Personnel Psychology, 57*, 685–717.

Dacin, P. A., & Smith, D. C. (1994). The effect of brand portfolio characteristics on consumer evaluations of brand extensions. *Journal of Marketing Research, 31*, 229–242.

de Chernatony, L., Cottman, S., & Segal-Horn, S. (2006). Communicating services brands' values internally and externally. *Service Industries Journal, 26*(8), 819–836.

Dell, D., Ainspan, N., Bodenbert, T., Troy, K., & Hickey, J. (2001). *Engaging employees through your brand* (The Conference Board No. R-1288-01-RR). New York: The Conference Board.

Donkin, R. (2001). *Blood, sweat, and tears: The evolution of work.* New York: TEXURE.

Doonar, J. (2004). Krispy Kreme doughnuts. *Brand Strategy, 185,* 10–11.

Dreher, G., Ash, R., & Bretz, R. (1988). Benefit coverage and employee cost: Critical factors in explaining compensation satisfaction. *Personnel Psychology, 41,* 237–254.

Dutta, S., & Fraser, M. (2009). When job seekers invade Facebook. *McKinsey Quarterly, 3,* 16–17.

Ehrhart, K. H., & Ziegert, J. Z. (2005). Why are individuals attracted to organizations?. *Journal of Management, 31,* 901–919.

Erdem, T. (1998). Brand equity as a signaling phenomenon. *Journal of Consumer Psychology, 57,* 131–157.

Erhardt, N, L. (2011). Is it all about teamwork? Understanding processes in team-based knowledge work. *Management Learning, 41*(1), 87–112.

Erhardt, N., Werbel, J., & Shrader, C. (2003). Board of director diversity and firm financial performance. *Corporate Governance: An International Review, 11,* 102–111.

Ewing, M. T., Pitt, L. F., Bussy, N. M., & Berthon, P. (2002). Employment branding the knowledge economy. *International Journal of Advertising, 21,* 3–22.

Faircloth, J. B., Capella, L. M., & Alford, B. L. (2001). The effect of brand attitude and brand image on brand equity. *Journal of Marketing Theory and Practice, 9,* 61–76.

Fallick, B. C., & Fleischman, C. A. (2001, April). *The importance of employer-to-employer flows in the U.S. labor market.* Washington, DC: Federal Reserve Board.

Feldman, D., Dearden, W., & Hardesty, D. (2006). Varying the content of job advertisements: The effects of message specificity. *Journal of Advertising, 35*(1), 123–141.

Ferris, G. R., Berkson, H. M., & Harris, M. M. (2002). The recruitment interview process: Persuasion and organization reputation promotion in competitive labor markets. *Human Resource Management Review, 12,* 359–375.

Fishbein, M., & Ajzen, I. (1975). *Belief, attitude, intention, and behavior: An introduction to theory and research.* Reading, MA: Addison-Wesley.

Gannon, M. J. (1971). Sources of referral and employee turnover. *Journal of Applied Psychology, 55,* 226–228.

Gapp, R., & Merrilees, B. (2006). Important factors to consider when using internal branding as a management strategy: A healthcare case study. *Journal of Brand Management, 14,* 162–176.

Gardner, T. M., Stansbury, J., & Hart, D. (2010). The ethics of lateral hiring. *Business Ethics Quarterly, 20,* 341–369.

Garner, B. A. (2004). *Black's law dictionary.* St. Paul, MN: West.

Garrow, T. S. (1994). *The employee as consumer.* Unpublished doctoral dissertation. The University of Southern California.

Gatewood, R. D., Gowan, M. A., & Lautenschlager, D. J. (1993). Corporate image, recruitment image, and initial job choice decisions. *Academy of Management Journal, 36,* 414–427.

Gibson, C., & Gibbs, J. (2006). Unpacking the concept of virtuality: The effects of geographic dispersion, electronic dependence, dynamic structure, and national diversity of team innovation. *Administrative Science Quarterly, 51,* 451–495.

Girod, S. (2005). The human resource management practice of retail branding: An ethnography within Oxfam trading division. *International Journal of Retail & Division Management, 33*(7), 514–530.

Goffman, E. (1959). *The presentation of self in everyday life.* New York, Ny: Doubleday Anchor.

Goodchild, S. (2009, 29 July). *Organic food 'no healthier' blow*. London Evening Standard. Available at http://www.thisislondon.co.uk/standard/article-23725592-organic-food-no-healthier-blow.do. Retrieved on July 9, 2010.

Han, J., & Han, J. (2009). Network-based recruiting and applicant attraction in China: Insights from both organizational and individual perspectives. *International Journal of Human Resource Management, 20*(11), 2228–2249.

Hannon, J. (1996). Organizational attractiveness in Japan: A screening perspective. *International Journal of Human Resource Management, 7*(2), 489–509.

Harris, P. (2007). We the people: The importance of employees in the process of building customer experience. *Journal of Brand Management, 15*(2), 102–114.

Heneman, H. G., & Judge, T. A. (2009). *Staffing organizations*. New York, Ny: McGraw-Hill Irwin.

Herriot, P., & Rothwell, C. (1981). Organizational choice and decision theory: Effects of employers' literature and selection interviews. *Journal of Organizational Psychology, 54*, 17–31.

Highhouse, S., & Hoffman, J. R. (2001). Organizational attraction and job choice. In: C. L. Cooper & I. T. Robertson (Eds), *International review of industrial and organizational psychology* (pp. 37–64). Chichester, UK: Wiley.

Highhouse, S., Hoffman, J. R., Greve, E. M., & Collins, A. E. (2002). Persuasive impact of organizational value statements in a recruitment context. *Journal of Applied Social Psychology, 32*, 1737–1755.

Highhouse, S., Zickar, M. J., Thorsteinson, T. J., Stierwalt, S. L., & Slaughter, J. E. (1999). Assessing company employment image: An example in the fast food industry. *Personnel Psychology, 52*, 151–172.

Highhouse, S., Zickar, M. J., & Yankelevich, M. (2010). Would you work if you won the lottery? Tracking changes in the American work ethic. *Journal of Applied Psychology, 95*, 349–357.

Hirschman, C. (2000). Reserve space for rehires. *HR Magazine, 45*(1), 58–64.

Hochschild, A. R. (1983). *The managed heart*. Berkeley, CA: University of California Press.

Hoeffler, S., & Keller, K. L. (2003). The marketing advantages of strong brands. *Journal of Brand Management, 10*, 421–445.

Hwang, I., & Chi, D. (2005). Relationships among internal marketing, employee job satisfaction and international hotel performance: An empirical study. *International Journal of Management, 22*(2), 285–293.

Ibarra, H. (1993). Personal networks of women and minorities in management: A conceptual framework. *Academy of Management Review, 18*, 156–187.

In IKEA we trust. (2009). *Cabinet Maker, 5367*, 7, 15 May.

Jackson, S., Joshi, A., & Erhardt, N. (2003). Recent research on team and organizational diversity: SWOT analysis and implications. *Journal of Management, 29*, 801–830.

Johnson, E. J., & Russo, J. E. (1984). Product familiarity and learning new information. *Journal of Consumer Research, 11*, 542–550.

Joshi, A., & Roh, H. (2009). The role of context in work team diversity research: A meta-analytic review. *Academy of Management Journal, 52*, 599–628.

Judge, T., Piccolo, R., Podsakoff, N., Shaw, J., & Rich, B. (2010). The relationship between pay and job satisfaction: A meta-analysis of the literature. *Journal of Vocational Behavior, 77*, 157–167.

Kalleberg, A. L., Knoke, D., Marsden, P. V., & Spaeth, J. L. (1996). *Organizations in America: Analyzing their structures and human resource practices*. Thousand Oaks, CA: Sage Publications.

Kaplan, H. R. (1985). Lottery winners and work commitment: A behavioral test of the American work ethic. *Journal of the Institute for Socioeconomic Studies*, *10*, 82–94.

Kaufman, B. E. (Ed.). (2004). Employment relations and the employment relations system: A guide to theorizing. *Theoretical perspectives on work and the employment relationship* (pp. 41–75). Champaign, IL: Industrial Relations Research Association.

Keller, K. L. (1993). Conceptualizing, measuring, and managing customer-based brand equity. *Journal of Marketing*, *57*, 1–22.

Keller, K. L. (2008). *Strategic brand management.* Upper Saddle River, NJ: Pearson Education Inc.

Keller, K. L., & Lehmann, D. R. (2006). Brands and branding: Research findings and future priorities. *Marketing Science*, *25*, 740–759.

Kelloway, E. K., Gallagher, D. G., & Barling, J. (2004). Work, employment, and the individual. In: B. E. Kaufman (Ed.), *Theoretical perspectives on work and the employment relationship* (pp. 105–131). Champaign, IL: Industrial Relations Research Association.

Kent, R. J., & Allen, C. T. (1994). Competitive interference effects in consumer memory for advertising: The role of brand familiarity. *Journal of Marketing*, *58*, 97–105.

Knox, S., & Freeman, C. (2006). Measuring and managing employer brand image in the service industry. *Journal of Marketing Management*, *22*, 695–716.

Kowalczk, S., & Pawlish, M. (2002). Corporate branding through external perception of organizational culture. *Corporate Reputation Review*, *5*, 159–174.

Kristof, A. L. (1996). Person-organization fit: An integrative review of its conceptualizations, measurement, and implications. *Personnel Psychology*, *49*, 1–49.

Laroche, M., Kim, C., & Zhou, L. (1996). Brand familiarity and confidence as determinants of purchase intentions: An empirical test in a multiple brand context. *Journal of Business Research*, *37*, 115–120.

Lee, T. H., Gerhart, B., Weller, I., & Trevor. (2008). Understanding voluntary turnover: Path-specific job satisfaction effects and the importance of unsolicited job offers. *Academy of Management Journal*, *51*, 651–671.

Lehmann, D. R., & Pan, Y. (1994). Context effects, new brand entry, and consideration sets. *Journal of Marketing Research*, *31*, 364–374.

Libai, B., Muller, E., & Peres, R. (2009). The role of within-brand and cross-brand communications in competitive growth. *Journal of Marketing*, *73*, 19–34.

Lievens, F. (2007). Employer branding in the Belgian Army: The importance of instrumental and symbolic beliefs for potential applicants, actual applicants, and military employees. *Human Resource Management*, *46*(1), 51–69.

Lievens, F., & Highhouse, S. (2003). The relation of instrumental and symbolic attributes to a company's attractiveness as an employer. *Personnel Psychology*, *56*, 75–102.

Lievens, F., Hoye, G., & Schreurs, B. (2005). Examining the relationship between employer knowledge dimensions and organizational attractiveness: An application in a military context. *Journal of Occupational and Organizational Psychology*, *78*, 553–572.

MacKenzie, S. B., Podsakoff, P. M., & Jarvis, C. B. (2005). The problem of measurement model misspecification in behavioral and organizational research and some recommended solutions. *Journal of Applied Psychology*, *90*, 710–730.

Marx, K. (1906). *Capital: A critique of political economy* (F. Engles, Ed.) (S. Moore & E. Aveling, Trans.). New York: The Modern Library.

Miles, S., & Mangold, G. (2004). A conceptualization of the employee branding process. *Journal of Relationship Marketing*, *3*(2), 65–87.

Moore, K., & Reid, S. (2008). The birth of brand: 4000 years of branding. *Business History, 50,* 419–432.

Mushukrishnan, A. V. (1995). Decision ambiguity and incumbent brand advantage. *Journal of Consumer Research, 22,* 98–109.

Ogbonna, E., & Harris, L. (2002). Managing organizational culture: Insights from the hospitality industry. *Human Resource Management Journal, 12,* 22–53.

Papasolomou, I., & Vrontis, D. (2006). Using internal marketing to ignite the corporate brand: The case of the UK retail bank industry. *Journal of Brand Management, 14*(1/2), 177–195.

Perkins, L., Thomas, K., & Taylor, G. (2000). Advertising and recruitment: Marketing to minorities. *Psychology & Marketing, 17*(3), 235–255.

Peter, J. P., & Olson, J. C. (2005). *Consumer behavior and marketing strategy.* New York: McGraw-Hill Irwin.

Phillips, J. M., & Gully, S. M. (2009). *Strategic staffing.* Upper Saddle River, NJ: Pearson/ Prentice Hall.

Piore, M. J. (1969). On-the-job training in the dual labor market. In: A. R. Weber, F. Cassell & W. L. Ginsberg (Eds), *Public-private manpower policies* (pp. 101–132). Madison, WI: University of Wisconsin.

Ployhart, R. E. (2006). Staffing in the 21st century: New challenges and strategic opportunities. *Journal of Management, 32,* 868–897.

Posavac, S. S., Sanbonmatsu, D. M., Cronley, M. L., & Kardes, F. R. (2001). The effects of strengthening category-brand associations on consideration set composition and purchase intent in memory-based choice. *Advances in Consumer Research, 28,* 186–189.

Powell, G. N., & Goulet, L. R. (1996). Recruiters' and applicants' reactions to campus interviews and employment decisions. *Academy of Management Journal, 39,* 1619–1640.

Prude, J. (1983). *The coming of industrial order: Town and factory life in rural Massachusetts, 1810–1860.* Cambridge, UK: Cambridge University Press.

Punjarsi, K., & Wilson, A. (2007). The role of internal branding in the delivery of employee brand promise. *Journal of Brand Management, 15*(1), 57–70.

Robbins, S., & Judge, T. (2009). *Organizational behavior,* 13/E. Saddle River, NJ: Prentice Hall.

Robinson, G., & Dechant, K. (1997). Building a business case for diversity. *Academy of Management Executive, 11,* 21–31.

Rynes, S. L. (1991). Recruitment, job choice, and post-hire consequences: A call for new research directions. In: M. D. Dunnette & L. M. Hough (Eds), *Handbook of industrial and organizational psychology* (Vol. 2, pp. 399–444). Palo Alto: Consulting Psychologists Press.

Schein, E. H. (1985). *Organizational culture and leadership.* San Francisco: Jossey-Bass.

Schwab, D. P., Rynes, S. L., & Aldag, R. J. (1987). Theories and research on job search and choice. In: K. M. Rowland & G. R. Ferris (Eds), *Research in personnel and human resources management* (pp. 129–166). Greenwich, CT: JAI Press.

Shellenbarger, S. (2006). In their search for skilled workers, big employers go to summer camp. *The Wall Street Journal,* p. D1, 23 February.

Sheridan, J. (1992). Organizational culture and employee retention. *Academy of Management Journal, 35*(5), 1036–1056.

Shocker, A. D., Ben-Akiva, M., Coccara, B., & Nedungadi, P. (1991). Consideration set influences on customer decision-making and choice: Issues, models, and suggestions. *Marketing Letters, 2,* 181–197.

Simonson, I., Huber, J., & Payne, J. (1988). The relationship between prior brand knowledge and information acquisition order. *Journal of Consumer Research, 14,* 566–578.

Slaughter, J. E., Zickar, M. J., Highhouse, S., & Mohr, D. C. (2004). Personality trait inferences about organizations: Development of a measure and assessment of construct validity. *Journal of Applied Psychology, 89,* 85–103.

Smith, W. J., Wokutch, R. E., Harrington, K. V., & Dennis, B. S. (2004). Organizational attractiveness and corporate social orientation: Do our values influence our preference for affirmative action and managing diversity? *Business & Society, 43,* 69–96.

Spears, N., & Singh, S. N. (2004). Measuring attitudes toward the brand and purchase intentions. *Journal of Current Issues and Research in Advertising, 26,* 53–66.

Spence, A. M. (1974). *Market signalling: Information transfer in hiring and related processes.* Cambridge MA: Harvard University Press.

Swait, J., & Adamowicz, W. (2001). Choice environment, market complexity, and consumer behavior: A theoretical and empirical approach for incorporating decision complexity into models of consumer choice. *Organizational Behavior and Human Decision Process, 86,* 141–167.

Tam, P., & Woo, S. (2011). Talent war crunches start-ups. *The Wall Street Journal,* February 28, B1.

Tarique, I., & Schuler, R. (2008). Emerging issues and challenges in global staffing: A North American perspective. *International Journal of Human Resource Management, 19,* 1397–1415.

Thomas, D. (1993). Racial dynamics of crossrace developmental relationships. *Administrative Science Quarterly, 38,* 169–194.

Thomas, K., & Wise, G. (1999). Organizational attractiveness and individual differences: Are diverse application attracted by different factors?. *Journal of Business and Psychology, 13*(3), 375–390.

Turban, D. B., & Keon, T. L. (1993). Organizational attractiveness: An interactionist perspective. *Journal of Applied Psychology, 78,* 184–193.

Van Hoye, G., & Lievens, F. (2005). Recruitment-related information sources and organizational attractiveness: Can something be done about negative publicity? *International Journal of Selection and Assessment, 13,* 179–187.

Van Hoye, G. V., & Lievens, F. (2009). Tapping the grapevine: A closer look at word-of-mouth as a recruitment source. *Journal of Applied Psychology, 94,* 341–352.

Walker, H. J., Feild, H. S., Giles, W., & Bernerth, J. B. (2008). The interactive effects of job advertisement characteristics and applicant experience on reactions to recruitment messages. *Journal of Occupational and Organizational Psychology, 81,* 619–638.

Wallstrom, A., Karlsson, T., & Salehi-Sangari, E. (2008). Building a corporate brand: The internal brand building process in Swedish service firms. *Journal of Brand Management, 16*(1/2), 40–50.

Weinfeld, P. K. (2007). Successful treatment of notalgia paresthetica with botulinum toxin type A. *Archives of Dermatology, 143,* 980–982.

Wernerfelt, B. (1988). Umbrella branding as a signal of new product quality: An example of signality by posting a bond. *Rand Journal of Economics, 19,* 458–466.

Wheeler, A., Richey, R., Tokkman, M., & Sablynski, C. (2006). Retaining employees for service competency: The role of corporate brand identity. *Journal of Brand Management, 14*(1/2), 96–113.

Williams, M., & Dreher, G. (1992). Compensation system attributes and applicant pool characteristics. *Academy of Management Journal, 35*(3), 571–595.

Winfred, A., Bell, S., Villado, A., & Doverspike, D. (2006). The use of person-organization fit in employment decision making: An assessment of its criterion-related validity. *Journal of Applied Psychology, 91*, 786–801.

Wright, E. O. (1980). Class and occupation. *Theory and Society, 9*, 177–214.

Wright, E. O., & Perrone, L. (1977). Marxist class categories and income inequality. *American Sociological Review, 42*, 32–55.

Wright, P., Dunford, B., & Snell, S. (2001). Human resources and the resource based view of the firm. *Journal of Management, 27*, 701–721.

Yaniv, E., & Farkas, E. (2005). The impact of person-organization fit on the corporate brand perception of employees and of customers. *Journal of Change Management, 5*, 447–461.

Zottoli, M. A., & Wanous, J. P. (2000). Recruitment source research: Current status and future directions. *Human Resource Management Review, 10*, 353–382.

# ABOUT THE AUTHORS

**Matt Bloom**, Ph.D., is an associate professor in the Management Department at the Mendoza College of Business, University of Notre Dame. He received his Ph.D. from Cornell University. Before receiving his doctorate he worked as paramedic, psychiatric technician, and then as a consultant for Arthur Young & Company and American Express. Matt's current research interests center on well-being at work and include exploring topics such as what work is like when people experience it as a calling and what conditions help people to be at their cognitive and emotional best at work. He is currently undertaking a program of research to study well-being among people in the caring professions.

**Joyce E. Bono** is a professor of management at University of Florida (she was at University of Minnesota when this chapter was written). She received her Ph.D. from the University of Iowa in Organizational Behavior. The central focus of Dr. Bono's research is employees' quality of work life, with research addressing topics ranging from leadership, affect, motivation, job satisfaction, and gender to positive personality traits. She has authored scholarly articles in the *Academy of Management Journal*, *Journal of Applied Psychology*, *Personnel Psychology*, *Psychological Bulletin*, *Journal of Personality and Social Psychology*, and *Leadership Quarterly*. Manuscripts she co-authored have been awarded the 2002 Academy of Management, Human Resource division Scholarly Achievement Award and the 2007 Center for Creative Leadership–Leadership Quarterly Award. In 2007, Bono was awarded the Society for Industrial and Organizational Society's (SIOP) Early Career Award. She has served on the editorial boards of *Journal of Applied Psychology*, *Journal of Management*, *Personnel Psychology*, and *Leadership*, and as an associate editor for *Academy of Management Journal*.

**Prithviraj Chattopadhyay** is a professor of management at the Hong Kong University of Science and Technology. He received his Ph.D. in management from the University of Texas at Austin. His research interests include relational demography and diversity, managerial cognition and affect, and employment externalization. His research has been published in journals such as *Academy of Management Review*, *Academy of Management Journal*,

*Administrative Science Quarterly, Journal of Applied Psychology, Organization Science*, and *Strategic Management Journal*. He is a member of the editorial board of the *Academy of Management Review, Academy of Management Journal, Journal of Applied Psychology*, and *Organizational Psychology Review*. He and Drs Elizabeth George, Sim Sitkin, and Jeff Barden won the 2007 *Academy of Management Review* best paper award.

**Amy E. Colbert** is an associate professor of Management & Organizations in the Henry B. Tippie College of Business at the University of Iowa. She received her Ph.D. from the University of Iowa in organizational behavior and human resource management. A primary goal of Dr. Colbert's research is to investigate the ways in which leaders influence individual work experiences and team and organizational outcomes. She is especially interested in the ways in which leadership influences the connections that employees form with their work, their coworkers, and their organizations. She has also examined the role of individual differences in leadership processes, with a focus on how leader individual differences influence leadership effectiveness and on how follower individual differences influence their responses to leadership. Dr. Colbert has published scholarly articles in the *Academy of Management Journal*, the *Journal of Applied Psychology*, and *Personnel Psychology*. She currently serves on the editorial boards of the *Academy of Management Journal, Personnel Psychology, Journal of Organizational Behavior*, and *Leadership Quarterly*.

**Cristina Cruz** is an associate professor of Entrepreneurial Management and Family Business at IE Business School, Madrid, Spain. She also holds the Bancaja Chair of Young Entrepreneurship at IE University. Her research focuses on corporate governance, family firms' management, and entrepreneurship in the context of family-controlled firms. Her work has been published in journals such as *Academy of Management Journal, Administrative Science Quarterly*, and *Journal of Business Venturing*. She holds a Ph.D. in economics and management from Universidad Carlos III de Madrid, having also completed an executive development program in family business management at IE Business School.

**Michelle K. Duffy** is the BOARD of OVERSEERS of Human Resources and Organizational Behavior in the Carlson School of Management at the University of Minnesota. She received her M.A. in psychology from Xavier University and her Ph.D. from the University of Arkansas. Professor Duffy's research investigates the antecedents and consequences of antisocial behavior at work, the role of employee mood and emotions such as envy in organizational life, and the facilitators of employee well-being. Her work has been published in outlets such as the *Journal of Applied Psychology, Academy of Management Journal, Organizational Behavior and Human Decision Processes*, and *Journal of Occupational Management*. She is the recipient of three grants from the *Society for Human Resource Management*. She currently serves on the editorial boards of the *Journal of Applied Psychology, and Organizational Behavior and Human Decision Processes* and is an incoming associate editor for the *Journal of Management*.

**Niclas L. Erhardt** received his Ph.D. from the School of Management and Labor Relations at Rutgers University. He holds a B.S. degree from the School of Industrial and Labor Relations at Cornell University. He also holds two M.S. degrees in Industrial Relations from Iowa State University and Rutgers University. Professor Erhardt has a wide research interest including team-based knowledge work, workplace diversity, employment branding, and Strategic Human Resource Management. His work has been published in journals including *Journal of Management, Human Resource Management Review, Management Learning*, and *Corporate Governance: An International Review*. He teaches courses in Human Resource Management, Organizational Behavior and Industrial Relations.

**Shainaz Firfiray** is a doctoral candidate in Management at IE Business School in Madrid, Spain. Her research interests include workplace identities, diversity, leadership, and work-life balance.

**Timothy M. Gardner** is an associate professor of management at the Owen Graduate School of Management at Vanderbilt University (Nashville, TN). He earned his Ph.D. at the School of Industrial and Labor Relations at Cornell University. His current research interests include labor market competition, lateral hiring, and employment branding.

**Elizabeth George** is a professor of management at the Hong Kong University of Science and Technology. She received her Ph.D. in management from the University of Texas at Austin. Her research interests include employment externalization, relational demography, diversity, and institutional theory. Her research has been published in journals such as *Academy of Management Review, Academy of Management Journal, Administrative Science Quarterly, Journal of Applied Psychology*, and *Organization Science*. She, along with Prithviraj Chattopadhyay, Sim Sitkin, and Jeff Barden, won the 2007 *Academy of Management Review* best paper award. She is a senior editor for *Organisation Studies*, and is a member of the editorial board of the *Academy of Management Journal* and *Journal of Organizational Behavior*.

**Theresa M. Glomb** is the McFarland Professor of Organizational Behavior in the Carlson School of Management at the University of Minnesota. She received her Ph.D. and M.A. in social, organizational, and individual differences psychology from the University of Illinois in 1998 and her B.A. in psychology from DePaul University in 1993. Professor Glomb has conducted research and published in the areas of emotions and mood in organizations, job attitudes and behaviors, emotional labor, and workplace victimization including incivility, aggression, and sexual harassment. She has published in outlets such as *Journal of Applied Psychology, Organizational Behavior and Human Decision Processes, Academy of Management Journal*, and *Journal of Occupational Health Psychology*. She currently serves on the editorial boards of the *Academy of Management Journal, Journal of Applied Psychology*, and *Organizational Behavior and Human Decision Processes*. Professor Glomb teaches in the masters, doctoral, and executive programs at the University of Minnesota in the areas of organizational behavior and human resources. In 2003 Professor Glomb received the Carlson School of Management Award for Excellence in Teaching and in 2006 she received the Carlson School of Management Award for Excellence in Service.

**Professor Luis R. Gomez-Mejia** holds the Benton Cocanougher Chair in Business at the Mays Business School, Texas A&M University. Before that he was a Council of 100 Distinguished Scholar at WP Carey Business School, Arizona State University (ASU), where he also held the Horace Steel Chair. He was a Regent's professor at ASU and has recently received the Outstanding Alumni Award from University of Minnesota and awarded the title of Doctor Honoris Causa at Carlos III University (Spain). He is a fellow of the Academy of Management and member of the "Hall of Fame" of the Academy of Management (which includes 33 members of approximately 20,000 members in the Academy of Management). He has published more than 200 articles and 12 books in the management field, receiving numerous awards for his research. His research has been cited close to 8,000 times (Harzing's Publish or Perish), with 25 individual publications that have received over 100 citations. During the past 10 years much of Gomez-Mejia's research has focused on family firms, with several articles on this topic published in *Academy of Management Journal,*

*Administrative Science Quarterly, Strategic Management Journal, Journal of Management Studies,* and *Entrepreneurship Theory and Practice.*

**Luis L. Martins** is an associate professor of management at the McCombs School of Business at the University of Texas at Austin. He received his Ph.D. in management and organizational behavior from the Leonard N. Stern School of Business at New York University. His research focuses on the dynamics of diversity, particularly in the context of virtual teams and global virtual work. He also studies the role of managerial cognition in organizational change and innovation.

**Carlos Martin-Rios** is assistant professor of management and co-director of the Master in Human Resource Management at the Carlos III University of Madrid (Spain). He received his Ph.D. from Rutgers, The State University of New Jersey (New Brunswick) in Industrial Relations and Human Resource Management. His current research interests are concerned with organization studies in aspects of organizational control systems evolution, competitiveness, and innovation. Specifically, the organizational and behavioral aspects of work design and control solutions with an emphasis on people management in knowledge-intensive work settings. In addition, he is also currently working on interfirm knowledge transfer from the social network theory perspective. His recent work has been published in *Human Resource Management* and *European Journal of International Management.*

**Carmen Kaman Ng** is a Ph.D. candidate in management at the Hong Kong University of Science and Technology. She received her BBA from the Hong Kong University of Science and Technology. Her research interests include relational demography, escalation of commitment, and stakeholder reactions to corporate social responsibility programs.

**Marieke C. Schilpzand** received her Ph.D. in Organizational Behavior from the Georgia Institute of Technology. Her current research focuses on team dynamics, particularly in terms of team diversity, team cognition, and global virtual work.

**Tao Yang** is currently a Ph.D. student in Human Resources and Industrial Relations in the Carlson School of Management at the University of Minnesota. He received his M.A. and B.A. in human resource management from the Renmin University of China in 2009 and 2007. His research interests include emotions and mood at work, emotional labor, abusive supervision, and employee well-being.